Practical Guide to Veterinary Hospital Design

Practical Guide to Veterinary Hospital Design

FROM RENOVATIONS TO NEW BUILDS

Vicki J. Pollard, AIA, CVT
Ashley M. Shoults, AIA

AAHA Press

© 2018 by Vicki J. Pollard and Ashley M. Shoults

All rights reserved. No part of this publication may be reproduced or transmitted in any form or by any means, electronic or mechanical, including photocopying, recording, or in an information storage and retrieval system, without permission in writing from the publisher.

Disclaimer: This information is intended to help you make good management decisions, but it is not a replacement for appropriate financial, legal, or other advice. AAHA does not assume responsibility for and makes no representation about the suitability or accuracy of the information contained in this work for any purpose, and makes no warranties, either expressed or implied, including the warranties of merchantability and fitness for a particular purpose. AAHA shall not be held liable for adverse reactions to or damage resulting from the application of this information or any misstatement or error contained in this work. AAHA shall be held harmless from any and all claims that may arise as a result of any reliance on the information provided.

AAHA press

American Animal Hospital Association Press
12575 West Bayaud Avenue
Lakewood, Colorado 80228
800-252-2242 or 303-986-2800
press.aaha.org

ISBN-13 978-1-58326-057-9

Library of Congress Cataloging-in-Publication Data
Names: Pollard, Vicki J., 1975– author.
Title: Practical guide to veterinary hospital design : from renovations to
    new builds / Vicki J. Pollard, AIA, CVT, Ashley M. Shoults, AIA.
Description: Lakewood, Colorado : American Animal Hospital Association Press,
    [2018] | Includes bibliographical references and index.
Identifiers: LCCN 2018032907 | ISBN 9781583260579
Subjects: LCSH: Veterinary hospitals—Designs and plans.
Classification: LCC SF604.7 .P65 2018 | DDC 725/.592—dc23
LC record available at lccn.loc.gov/2018032907

Senior Manager, Publishing: Laura Esterman
Managing Editor: Karie Simpson
Acquisitions Editor: Constance Hardesty
Cover Designer: Robin Taylor
Compositor: Jane Raese
Developmental Editor: Katherine H. Streckfus
Proofreader: Ashley Moore
Indexer: Kate Bowman

Cover images: Foto Imagery / Tim Murphy. Courtesy of VCA PetCare Veterinary Hospital, Santa Rosa, California VCA, Inc. (front cover). David Dietrich Photography. Courtesy of Upstate Veterinary Specialists and Emergency Clinic, Greenville, South Carolina (back cover, top left). Foto Imagery / Tim Murphy. Courtesy of Woodhaven Veterinary Clinic, Edmonds, Washington (back cover, top right). Courtesy of Four Seasons Veterinary Specialists, Loveland, Colorado (back cover, bottom right).

Printed in the United States of America

We dedicate this book to all the wonderful clients
we have had the privilege of working with
through the years. This book could not
have happened without you.

COMPANION WEBSITE

Access more photos, tie-ins to the *AAHA Standards of Accreditation*, Fear Free design tips, and more on the companion website!

Visit aaha.org/VHD and unlock the bonus content with passcode VHDE1.

CONTENTS

Acknowledgments *ix*

Introduction *1*

SECTION ONE: PROJECT PLANNING

1. The Evolution of Veterinary Hospital Design *5*
2. The Dream Hospital *9*
3. Defining the Scope of the Project *11*
4. Project Budgeting *15*
5. Leasehold Practices: Choosing the Right Space *19*
6. Adaptive Reuse Projects *27*
7. Freestanding Buildings: Choosing the Right Land *31*
8. Strategies for Remodels and Additions *38*
9. Project Timeline *43*

SECTION TWO: AN OVERVIEW OF HOSPITAL DESIGN

10. The Fear Free℠ Design Movement *51*
11. Four Features of Good Hospital Design *56*
12. Biological Risk Management *62*
13. AAHA Accreditation Standards *68*
14. Branding and Curb Appeal *74*
15. Transparency in the Hospital *80*
16. Generational Dynamics in the Workplace *84*
17. Planning for Growth and Future Expansion *88*
18. Sustainable Design *93*
19. Basic Rules of Floor Plan Design—Small Hospitals *99*
20. Basic Rules of Floor Plan Design—Large Hospitals *104*
21. Specialty/Referral Hospitals *109*
22. Emergency Hospitals *115*
23. Feline Hospitals *120*
24. Equine and Large Animal Hospitals *125*
25. Mixed Animal Hospitals *132*

SECTION THREE: THE DESIGN OF VETERINARY SPACES

26. Reception Areas *137*
27. Exam Rooms *143*
28. Laboratory, Pharmacy, and Charting *148*
29. Treatment Areas *155*
30. Intensive Care Unit *161*

- **31** Dental Services *166*
- **32** Diagnostic Imaging *171*
- **33** Specialty Imaging *176*
- **34** Oncology *188*
- **35** Additional Specialty Services *195*
- **36** The Surgery Zone *199*
- **37** Physical Rehabilitation *206*
- **38** Animal Housing *212*
- **39** General Wards *220*
- **40** Isolation Wards *223*
- **41** Ancillary Services *226*
- **42** Hospital Support Spaces *232*

SECTION FOUR:
BUILDING SYSTEMS AND FINISHES

- **43** HVAC Design *241*
- **44** Plumbing Design *251*
- **45** Medical Gas Design *257*
- **46** Noise Control *260*
- **47** Lighting Design *267*
- **48** Flooring *275*
- **49** Walls and Ceilings *285*
- **50** Doors and Windows *291*
- **51** Color Palettes *296*
- **52** Furnishings *302*
- **53** Equipment Coordination *310*

SECTION FIVE:
CONSTRUCTION AND OCCUPANCY

- **54** Regulatory Requirements *319*
- **55** Project Delivery Methods *325*
- **56** Estimating Versus Bidding *331*
- **57** The Construction Process *335*
- **58** The Jobsite *339*
- **59** Project Closeout *344*
- **60** Post Move in—Warranties and Maintenance *347*
- **61** The Dos and Don'ts and Tales from the Trenches *351*

Conclusion: The Future of Veterinary Care *356*

Bibliography *359*

Index *361*

About the Authors *371*

ACKNOWLEDGMENTS

We would like to thank our amazing business partners, Heather Lewis, Tony Cochrane, Sean McMurray, and Sarah Boman, for their inspiration and endless support.

We would also like to thank Jerry Oglesbee, Jeff Mullikin, and Basel Abu-Dayyeh, as well as Chris Fravil and the rest of the team at Animal Arts, for all their time and energy in helping to make this book a reality.

We thank Deanne Bonner, RVT, CVPM; Daniel D. Chapel, AIA, NCARB; and Andrea Frederick for their thorough reviews.

Finally, we would like to express our gratitude to AAHA for giving us the opportunity to share what we have learned with the veterinary community.

ABOVE ALL, I would like to thank my husband, Justin, who supports and encourages me every day... I was waiting for you. —Vicki

TO CHADWICK, for being my rock and my best friend. And to Braxton and Harrison for being the motivation that gets me out of bed each day. You three complete me. —Ashley

INTRODUCTION

One of the joys of a career in veterinary medicine is the diversity of paths open to every practitioner, from the practice type you choose, to the patients you care for, to the level of specialization you attain.

Included within these paths is the opportunity to become the owner of your own practice. Ownership empowers individual veterinarians to develop their own methods and style of practice and to find fulfillment in the care of their clients and patients.

An important part of practice ownership is building your own physical space in which to house your business.

In the early days of veterinary medicine, the veterinary entrepreneur could build a hospital with reasonable financial risk and with more guarantee of reward. Today, the complexities of the modern world require a more sophisticated approach. Market pressures, competition, the rise of corporate groups, the cost of everything, and the level of sophistication of veterinary consumers come together to require those who build practices to be knowledgeable, to plan carefully, and to minimize mistakes.

This book was written for veterinarians, practice managers, and those who support the opportunities that still abound in veterinary medicine. The people on your team are your greatest resource, but as the builder, the doer, and the changer, the physical spaces you create will be your most important asset. These spaces should be well organized, well thought out, and useful. They should allow you to provide the sophisticated and compassionate care that clients expect, patients deserve, and you have dedicated your career to providing.

Whether you are planning to build out a small leasehold for a general practice or to construct a freestanding building for a large specialty practice, it is important to understand how the design of all of the spaces that compose your new hospital can help you make the most of the business you build. This book provides a broad understanding of all aspects of planning, designing, and building a successful hospital. The chapters are succinct and organized into topics that follow a chronological order, from the initial dream of your hospital to move-in. As you read, listen for your own truth and find your own inspiration.

SECTION **ONE**

Project Planning

CHAPTER 1

THE EVOLUTION OF VETERINARY HOSPITAL DESIGN

The contemporary veterinary hospital of today is a relatively new concept; in fact, the treatment of small or companion animals dates back only to the early twentieth century. Prior to this, veterinary medicine focused on the care and treatment of large animals—almost exclusively horses. Thus, the typical veterinary hospital often simply resembled a barn. Horses were then, and remain today, very valuable animals; they not only served as a status symbol for the elite but were invaluable as a means of general transportation and as a tool for agriculture.

Prior to the mid-1800s, the United States economy was primarily agrarian, land based, and rural. The family farm stood as the foundation of this system, and while a network of extended family members made up the work force, horses provided the actual power that made the farm economically viable. Farm animals were not pets, but instead the fundamental resource upon which the farm was founded. The cats and dogs living on the farm existed to support the enterprise. They fulfilled particular duties, such as catching mice or guarding livestock, and their wellbeing was marginalized.

With the Industrial Revolution in the late 1800s, people began migrating to the urban commercial hubs, and the need for rural horsepower waned. Horses were still useful: they moved the materials, goods, and people of urban America from place to place. But for the average working family, there was still no room, economically or literally, to own pets.

As the population of cities grew, so too did the population of horses. In places like New York City, the amount of manure produced by these vast herds of horses actually posed a public health hazard. Life was not easy for these animals, and the practice of overworking and even abusing horses was widespread. As a result, organizations focused on the prevention of cruelty to animals were founded, and while these initial societies were formed with the intention of protecting horses specifically, they represented a new awareness and an inclination and commitment to value animals.

When World War I began, horses were called upon to play an integral role in the war effort, supporting and moving the military. But the need for horses declined dramatically as automobiles, trolley cars, and other means of transportation, pushed by the innovations developed during the war, came to the fore in the 1920s and 1930s. As the mobile middle class grew, and the US economy transitioned from farming to manufacturing to service-oriented businesses, the stage was set for the veterinary profession to shift.

Families began moving to the suburbs, and for the first time in history they had the space and disposable income to own pets. As a result of these social changes, veterinary medicine shifted from equine care to companion animals, forever altering the landscape of the veterinary industry and the facilities that serve it.

The earliest true progenitor of the modern veterinary facility was the freestanding small animal clinic situated in these early suburbs. These facilities were relatively modest in size and generally paralleled the human medical offices of the time, which were built to resemble residential homes. In many early layouts, there was a reception area that looked like a formal living room, an adjoining office, and one or two large examination rooms. Later, with the emerging importance of diagnostic lab work, facilities would often include a laboratory.

Radiology technology was still in its infancy, and anesthetics were still primitive and dangerous. Viruses had only recently been identified, antibiotics had yet to be invented, and the veterinary facilities of the time reflected those limitations. These early companion animal clinics were built simply to enable veterinarians to see animals more efficiently than they could by operating as mobile businesses providing house calls.

The Great Depression would unfortunately delay any further growth of the companion animal profession until after World War II, and the design of facilities in this time period would remain fairly stagnant. The eventual Allied victory over the Axis powers ushered in a new "modern" era and marked the beginning of a period of great enthusiasm and confidence in emerging technologies and medicine. In this postwar period, the commercial landscape was rapidly changing, and savvy veterinarians soon began building practices to suit America's newfound modern spirit. As early as the late 1940s, new facilities were being designed to look dramatically different from their earlier "house-like" predecessors, often in the International Style, which is characterized by its lack of ornamentation and use of glass, steel, and reinforced concrete to create "light"-looking structures. The interior configurations had not yet evolved significantly, however, and the patient capacities of these practices were still very limited, as they were generally still one-doctor practices. Indeed, multiple-doctor practices were very rare up to this point, and even multiple exam rooms were only beginning to be commonplace.

The areas for medical procedures during this time were still minimal, but animal holding space was generous. The common practice of the time was to hold animals at the facility until they fully recovered, instead of releasing them to be cared for by their owners at home. Doctors often examined and medicated animals in the runs or wards where they were housed, reserving the treatment areas, if they existed at all, for surgery and more invasive procedures.

With the 1950s and 1960s came the rise of the nuclear family. The economy boomed and companion animal ownership skyrocketed. This era saw the single largest increase in the development of companion animal facilities in American history. It was driven by excitement about the new technologies in veterinary medicine and the unrivaled economic opportunity and affluence of the middle class.

Administrative spaces in veterinary hospitals now began to develop with the addition of business offices and separate reception counters in the waiting area. Prior to these changes, doctors commonly conducted business for the facility either at a freestanding desk located in the reception room or in an adjacent doctor's office. A shared laboratory and pharmacy, accessible to the receptionist, became common, and separate treatment and surgery rooms began to be included. Surprisingly, up to this point the surgery room was not viewed as an aseptic environment, and it was common to clean and prepare instruments and even scrub inside the surgery room. The X-ray machine was also located in surgery.

Most facilities designed in the mid-1960s were simple and compact, but the majority included two or even three exam rooms. The treatment and surgery areas were still minimal, but the beginnings of the "outpatient" unit started to emerge: the reception area, an exam room, a laboratory, and a pharmacy. Still missing from these facilities, however, was a cohesive medical treatment area—and the understanding that the medical areas could and should be separated from animal holding.

The medical and surgical areas of a typical veterinary hospital became more developed in the 1970s. The reception area now commonly included a centralized counter, and cat waiting areas were starting to be separated from dog waiting areas. By the end of the decade, the contemporary veterinary facility as we know it had arrived. These facilities were clearly divided into three separate functional zones: outpatient, medical procedure, and animal holding. The treatment area acted as a centralized hub for the entire facility, and surgery was now an isolated aseptic room. The X-ray machine was now housed separately in its own area. Large shared doctors' offices were becoming more common, and amenities such as lounges and break rooms for employees were also being included.

Ancillary services, such as boarding, grooming, and retail, would come next, during the upwardly mobile 1980s. This era of rapid growth in the technology sector marked the beginning of the information age—which affected veterinary medicine, not only because of new medical equipment but because of the new computers and software becoming available. By the 1990s, the profession was seeing a tremendous upsurge in facilities that included expanded services, and the contemporary "full-service" veterinary facility that we now know was born. The veterinary hospital now included retail displays, grooming salons, and animal boarding, all underscored by an emphasis on both client convenience and medical technology.

The 2000s continued to bring vast improvements in computing power and digital information storage. Hospitals grew, both in size and capabilities, in order to accommodate the new advanced equipment and to facilitate the complex and diverse medical procedures that were now possible. Sophisticated laboratory equipment continued to decrease in size, and diagnostic imaging, such as computed tomography (CT) and magnetic resonance imaging (MRI), became more affordable and more accessible. Specialty departments, such as oncology, ophthalmology, physical rehabilitation, and internal medicine, continued to develop, while business-management areas expanded in an effort to further improve customer service and advance marketing strategies.

The Great Recession of the late 2000s and early 2010s slowed the physical development of new veterinary facilities, but perceptions of the value of animals remained strong and unwavering in American society. Companion pet ownership gave way to companion pet stewardship, and animal control transitioned into animal advocacy, demonstrating the society's continued commitment to animal rights. For many people, pets moved beyond being simple surrogate family members to become companions in life and fur babies.

Today, the modern animal lover is on the move, chasing job opportunities and career advancement all across the country. In many cases, this nomadic and remote lifestyle means we can no longer depend so heavily on family ties, and consequently we turn to our pets to provide comfort and companionship. There exists no typical American household anymore, yet the majority of people in our society's modern family units choose pet companionship in one form or another, and the contemporary veterinary facility needs to be able to meet the varied needs of an increasingly diverse clientele. The evolution of the companion animal facility has been over a century in the making, moving from a small cottage industry, built around the solo practitioner, to an advanced, full-service medical and pet service center offering sophisticated diagnostic technology and specialty medicine and treatment.

As diverse as the modern family has become, the modern veterinary facility has kept pace. And although medical technologies—and quality of care—have become ever more advanced, veterinary hospitals themselves in many ways are still designed to suit the philosophy of their owners and the communities they serve. This is why, as you travel far and wide, you will still find small one-doctor practices as well as vast specialty centers with 25 doctors or more. There are tiny facilities in major city centers, hospitals that still look like family homes in towns, hospitals in strip malls in suburban communities, and hospitals that look like modern masterpieces.

▼ ▼ ▼

WHILE THE LOOK, location, and style of the hospital you will build is entirely your choice, the advances made through the evolution of veterinary hospital design will help you to create a facility that will be the basis for the quality of care that you will provide to your patients for many years to come. This book will help you refine your vision and take the steps needed to make that vision a reality.

CHAPTER 2

THE DREAM HOSPITAL

Over the years, veterinary industry consultants have promoted the concept of the dream hospital. Chasing the dream hospital has always been an important driver of innovation in veterinary medicine, and it still is today. Although your project must be based in financial reality, it is equally important to build something that is worth the investment.

New veterinarians generally have larger debts out of school than their mentors and predecessors. Hospitals are also more expensive to build than ever before. Therefore, today's entrepreneurial veterinarians may need to take a different approach to building their first project, such as pooling collateral with other owners or building a modest space, such as a leasehold buildout.

Even a small step into practice ownership can pay off in a short period of time if the practice owner is both business-minded and passionate. For example, one veterinarian who built out a small leasehold in an urban district dreamed of being a strong and vital part of the neighborhood. To demonstrate this vision, the front lobby contained a lending library, a coffee bar, and a large retail section. The practice also contributed to neighborhood causes. Within two years of opening, the hospital was not only very profitable but had also become a hub of social activity in the neighborhood, just as the veterinarian had envisioned.

First projects can be stepping stones to second and third projects as a practice matures and grows. Established veterinary practices have a much easier time building new projects. Practices can generally borrow 70%–100% of what they gross annually, minus debts. So a financially healthy, high-grossing practice is most able to afford a substantial building. Many of the award-winning hospitals featured in veterinary media outlets are built by mature practices. At this scale, it is even more critical to build the dream that you, your team, and your clients care about.

As an example of the power of a visionary idea, consider the Fear Free℠ initiative, founded by veterinarian Dr. Marty Becker. Fear Free provides the tools to veterinary professionals to allow them to attend to the emotional wellbeing of their patients as much as to their physical wellbeing, taking care to use strategies to reduce their fear, stress, and anxiety. (The Fear Free concept, and why it matters for veterinary practice building design, is covered thoroughly in Chapter 10, with additional information in other chapters where applicable.) The profession is just beginning to learn how this movement will change the face of the veterinary practice. It is one vision, but it will change the physical environments of every veterinary hospital that embraces Fear Free operations, from the smallest lease space to the largest freestanding building.

Other veterinarians have created hospitals around other approaches to practice. For example, the "pets are family" concept has helped guide the creation of compassionate and caring spaces, and numerous projects have crafted their unique solutions based on this approach.

Before you begin to plan your building design, you may already know what your dream is, or you may need to draw on other sources through brainstorming, reading, thinking, and learning with the goal of developing your own vision. The key is to find what you are looking for and to have a firm conviction about what you want to do before you put your life savings on the line to do it.

Regardless of the size of the hospital or the scope of your budget, every great project is built on a dream.

CHAPTER 3

DEFINING THE SCOPE OF THE PROJECT

Getting started with defining the scope of a project can be a chicken-and-egg problem. It's difficult to know what you can do unless you know how much you can afford. But it is just as difficult to define your budget until you know what you want to achieve! To make matters more complicated, architects do not traditionally include programming—the art of transforming a wish list into a defined scope of work—in their services, so many veterinarians find that they are trying to make early project decisions on their own.

Because a veterinary hospital is a complicated project by nature, it is not advisable to try to navigate these waters without some professional help. But because programming is not a standardized process, it is helpful for you to know what steps most veterinarians need to take so you can streamline your earliest project decisions.

Before you begin your project planning, you should first undertake any other major things you want to accomplish with the practice that are outside the scope of the building project. For example, if you plan to use the opportunity of building a new facility as a springboard to rebrand your practice, you should embark on this process beforehand.

When you are ready to commit to the construction of your new facility, begin by defining the scope of your project. For determining the size of freestanding hospital projects, there are some broad general rules that may help.

- The average doctor seeing patients needs two to three exam rooms in order to be efficient. The average exam room translates to between

900 and just over 1,200 square feet of building area. As an example, if your practice has two doctors seeing patients, then five to six exam rooms will be required, and the new building will likely be between 4,500 and 7,200 square feet.

- In traditional practices, the number of medical workspaces should roughly match the number of exam rooms. In other words, if you have four to six exam rooms, you will likely need a minimum of two to three treatment stations, a surgery room, and a special procedures room (such as dental) to support the caseload the exam rooms generate. Note that this ratio is changing slightly in heavily wellness-based practices, which may need more exam rooms than treatment and medical stations.

- If you incorporate two-door exam rooms, your building will be larger. If you instead utilize single-door exam rooms, your building will be smaller.

- If your practice is something other than a standard general practice, such as a feline practice, or if your practice offers other ancillary services, such as boarding, your ratios and square footages will be different from these average rules of thumb.

You can test your ideas about the size of your hospital against an average cost per square foot, plus 35% for soft costs (that is, costs that are not related to the construction itself, such as architectural and engineering fees, permit fees, and legal expenses), to get a general idea for whether your intended project can be accomplished within a realistic budget. If it cannot, this should be communicated to your professionals, i.e., practice management consultant, accountant, architect, right away so that they can help you think about the project budget in a more carefully considered manner.

Assuming your ballpark guesstimates are close to your expectations, it's time to develop a detailed, room-by-room "program of spaces." The first step is to develop your own wish list. Depending on the situation, this may be a very private or a very inclusive process. For those who have projects that can be planned in the open, and who already have a staff on hand at their current practice, it is a good idea to include staff members so that their input can be heard. You might consider a survey or another similar method for staff members to express their thoughts and ideas anonymously.

Many architects begin with client wish lists and requirements and develop a simple spreadsheet tool to predict the size of a project. The spreadsheet typically calculates the size of each room in the hospital and then multiplies by a grossing factor, which accounts for wall thickness and circulation square footage (that is, the spaces needed for moving between rooms, such as corridors). For a typical veterinary hospital, the room size totals should be multiplied by a factor of 1.35 to obtain an accurate prediction of the overall square footage. This is a greater factor than is needed in many other building types because veterinary hospitals require a lot of circulation, and the circulation paths must be wide enough to accommodate animals of all sizes.

As an example, the space requirements for three 10 × 10-foot exam rooms are equal to 100 square feet each, or 300 square feet in total. With the grossing factor, you will need approximately 405 square feet to accommodate these rooms.

Veterinary Center
Small Animal Facility

Functional Areas			Quantity	Size	Net S.F.	Load	Gross S.F.
Total Floor Area		2,948 S.F.					
Public							
Waiting							
Waiting Area		coffee bar, sm. retail area	1	12 x 16	192	130%	250
Janitor's Closet		for mop storage up front	1	4 x 6	24	130%	31
Reception	check in/out	3 stations (inline)	1	12 x 10	120	130%	156
		third for client education area					
Food Storage Room			1	7 x 9	63	130%	82
Exam Rooms		ok w/1 door would prefer 2 door	3	8 x 10	240	130%	312
Special Procedures Room		also to be used as 4th exam	1	12 x 12	144	130%	187
		and sm. meeting room					
		chemo admin (no fume hood req'd)					
		storage for ultrasound machine					
Public Restroom			1	7 x 9	63	130%	82
Medical							
Pharmacy		in hallway, 1-2 workstations	1	7 x 12	84	130%	109
Laboratory		as part of tx or in hall between	1	7 x 8	56	130%	73
Treatment							
3 Stations		2 tub tables, 1 dry	3	10 x 12	360	130%	468
		1 of these stations will be used as dental station					
		2 computer stations					
		scrub sink and sterilizer					
Ward Viewed from Treatment		12' cage bank, 9' cage bank 1 run	2	8 x 12	192	130%	250
Radiology		plan for digital in future	1	9 x 12	108	130%	140
		rad storage					
Surgery		1-2 tables	1	12 x 14	168	130%	218
Isolation		doubles as ward	1	7 x 9	63	130%	82
Support							
Employee Restroom			1	7 x 9	63	130%	82
Drs' Area / Fish Bowl		open to treatment	1	10 x 10	100	130%	130
Laundry, Food Prep, Storage		washer and dryer	1	9 x 12	108	130%	140
Kitchen / Break Room		table for 2	1	10 x 12	120	130%	156
Total Proposed Small Animal Hospital					2,268		2,948 s.f.
Available Square Footage							2,950
Net Difference							2

An example of a programming spreadsheet.

One of the reasons architects can be useful in developing this initial program is that they know the building code requirements for room sizes, the number of bathrooms the code requires, how much space stairs and elevators will take up, and so on. So although you can come up with a rough estimate with these methods, your architect should be able to provide a more accurate estimate even before the actual design of the building begins.

The room-by-room program spreadsheet can then be developed and checked against an average cost per square foot. If this cost still exceeds your budget, you may need to decrease

DEFINING THE SCOPE OF THE PROJECT

the scope of the project. Or perhaps you can find another creative solution, such as utilizing an existing building shell, to reduce some of the costs.

Assuming that you and your professionals can come to a reasonable balance between your wish list and the budget, the next step typically is to delve into a simple conceptual design process, often referred to as a "test fit." This is a bubble diagram of sorts that puts the program of spaces on paper so you can see how the project physically fits on the site and how the major building elements relate to each other. At this stage it is not necessary for all the rooms to fit exactly right or for much detail to be included. The goal is to see if the project can work and whether it will be doable.

In working on your test fit and on your earliest design solutions, be aware of "scope creep," which is the process of adding just a little bit more to the project here and there. Just a little scope creep can easily add 5% to the project cost.

If you need to reduce the size of the project at this point, the per-square-foot construction cost will tend to rise as efforts are made to condense and compact more program into smaller and smaller spaces. In other words, jamming more things into a smaller space does not save money.

Moreover, shrinking beyond a certain point will require compromising on functional areas such as exam rooms and treatment, since restrooms, hallways, and other essential spaces have a fixed lower limit.

▼ ▼ ▼

BEFORE JUMPING INTO any formal decision on building new or renovating, take the time to properly assess what you want and what you truly need. The often-complicated process of building a veterinary hospital can be made simpler with a solid set of goals.

CHAPTER 4

PROJECT BUDGETING

Veterinary hospitals are expensive buildings to construct, which makes project budgeting all the more critical for success. The first step for a practice considering an investment as large as a construction project is to create a business plan. This is a plan for revenue generation to support business expenses. Veterinarians should have a business plan in place before they begin to develop plans for a hospital. In order for a practice to put together a plan, it needs to have a reasonable idea of the expenses that will be incurred in designing and building a new facility. This chapter will cover the basics for determining project costs.

In order to estimate approximately how much building your money will buy, it is helpful to understand how a construction budget is assembled. Hard costs are construction costs as well as land costs. Soft costs, as mentioned earlier, are the non-building-related costs that are required to complete a project, such as permitting and design fees.

Construction costs are typically quoted in dollars per square foot of building area. The national average hard cost for construction of a veterinary hospital in the peak market economy of 2017, for example, was approximately $275 to $375 per square foot for new, freestanding buildings and $140 to $200 per square foot for leasehold buildouts. These costs vary according to location and other factors, such as the complexity of the project. Consult construction index reference sources such as RSMeans for the most up-to-date figures and for information on how your location might compare to the national average. In general, construction costs in the US are higher on the coasts, in urban areas, and in northern climates than in other areas of the country. For example, costs in Arkansas might be substantially lower than costs in New Jersey to construct comparable facilities. Canadian pricing is more consistent from coast to coast, but the average project in Canada tracks with some of the highest costs in the US.

Construction costs in the US tend to be subject to an inflation rate of about 3.5% per year. That means that, all other things being equal, it would cost about 35% more to construct a project today than to construct the same project 10 years ago. Market highs can further inflate costs, as can skilled labor shortages.

Construction cost budgets are broken out generally into the following categories or divisions. These divisions are part of the MasterFormat of specifications produced by the Construction Specifications Institute and Construction Specifications Canada (there are additional categories that do not apply):

Division 01: General Requirements (project overhead costs)
Division 03: Concrete
Division 04: Masonry
Division 05: Metals (includes structural and decorative metal)
Division 06: Wood (includes cabinetry)
Division 07: Thermal and Moisture Protection (includes insulation, roofing, and sealants)
Division 08: Openings (e.g., doors and windows)
Division 09: Finishes
Division 10: Specialties (includes things like toilet accessories, etc.)
Division 11: Equipment
Division 12: Furnishings
Division 21: Fire Suppression
Division 22: Plumbing
Division 23: Heating, Ventilation, and Air Conditioning (HVAC)
Division 26: Electrical
Division 31: Earthwork (includes fencing, grading, utilities, etc.)
Division 32: Exterior Improvements
Division 33: Utilities

Your contractor or cost estimator will usually present these costs according to this industry standard format. These divisions also correspond to the architect's specifications. By breaking out costs into a standard format, it is easier to compare your project to other projects and track changes in the budget as the design progresses.

In addition to the hard costs, your project will also have soft costs, which typically amount to 30%–35% of the construction costs. Below is a breakdown of this percentage:

- 12%–15%: furnishings and equipment.
- 8%–10%: architecture and engineering fees.
- 5%–10%: inflation and contingencies.
- 3%: miscellaneous.

A pro forma can be a useful tool to illustrate how your costs will relate to the amount of income you will need to generate. A pro forma is a financial statement estimating future revenues and costs and should be done according to generally accepted accounting principles (GAAP). It is an essential part of your business plan and goes hand in hand with estimating construction costs. If you need assistance in developing a pro forma, enlist a skilled accountant or practice management consultant.

A sample pro forma is illustrated on the opposite page.

Most accountants recommend an ideal rent-to-income ratio of 7%. Rent refers to all the

Sample Pro Forma for 6,000 S.F. Veterinary Hospital

Category		Notes
Hard Costs		
Land Cost	$750,000	Enter land purchase cost
Building Cost ($275 / s.f.)	$1,650,000	Probable cost per s.f. including escalation contingency
Total Hard Costs	**$2,400,000**	
Soft Costs		
Professional Fees (architecture and engineering)	$181,500	11% typically covers range of professional fees
Contingency (5% of building cost)	$82,500	
Regulatory & Utility	$24,750	Typically between 1% and 2% of cost of building
Miscellaneous (legal, etc.)	$16,500	1%
Financing Costs		
Appraisals	$5,000	
Construction Loan		
Points (1%)	$16,500	
Interest (8.25%)	$56,719	
Permanent Loan Commitment (1.5%)	$24,750	
Closing Costs	$47,710	Typically 2%–3% of the loan amount
Total Soft Costs	**$455,929**	
Total Project Costs	**$2,855,929**	
Financing		
Equity (20%)	$571,186	
Permanent Loan	$2,284,743	
Loan Payment per Year (20yr 7.5%)	$147,655	
Return on Equity per Year (5%)	$28,559	
Total Annual Financing Costs	**$176,214**	
Operating Expenses per Year		
Real Estate Taxes (1%)	$16,500	
Insurance (0.5%)	$8,250	
Utilities ($2 / s.f.)	$12,000	
Maintenance	$4,500	
Total Annual Operating Expenses	**$41,250**	
Required Cash Flow or "Rent"		
Annual Cash Flow	$217,464	
Monthly Cash Flow/Rent	$18,122	

costs you need to pay monthly to rent or own and maintain your building. Young practices may have slightly more rent/income and older practices may have slightly less. However, your accountant and financial adviser should review the amount of money you want to borrow to ensure it is reasonable.

After developing an initial pro forma, some new practices will discover that their budget will prohibit them from building their dream hospital. This is normal. Most practices cannot afford everything on their wish list. The key is to align the budget and the scope of the project, which may require a few attempts. In some cases, it might be a matter of reducing the size or complexity of the project. In other cases, practices may choose to go an alternate route, such as pursuing the reuse of an existing building or developing a lease space. (Some of these options are considered in Chapters 5, 6, and 8.)

▼ ▼ ▼

THE KEY TO FINANCIAL SUCCESS with your project is to recognize the importance of thorough and accurate budgeting. You will need to enlist help from your accountant, your architect, a financial planning professional, and others to get off on the right foot with a budget that is both comprehensive and realistic.

CHAPTER 5

LEASEHOLD PRACTICES: CHOOSING THE RIGHT SPACE

Location, location, location. The old adage holds true for veterinary hospitals as much as anything else. Choosing to start your veterinary business in a leasehold space is a good way to get off the ground and give yourself the means to grow. But before you jump into signing a lease, you need to understand the viability of the market for a veterinary hospital in the area where you hope to set up your practice. The neighborhood you choose will have an effect on the size of the hospital and its potential for success.

MARKET VIABILITY

It is important to start your research by looking into the existing and potential market around a desired location. The following are a few of the most important things to know about the local neighborhood:

- The number of households.
- Household sizes.
- The makeup of housing (single family, apartments, etc.).
- Average disposable income.
- Geographical limits to your market, as determined by existing neighborhoods, natural barriers, freeways, and circulation patterns.
- Competition, such as other veterinarians, specialty/referral centers, and mass providers.

A leasehold property built out into a veterinary specialty hospital. (Foto Imagery / Tim Murphy. Courtesy of Upstate Veterinary Specialists and Emergency Clinic, Asheville, North Carolina.)

There are various consultants with expertise in demographics and site analysis who can help you gather and assess this information. You can also do it yourself using various sources, including the following:

- The American Veterinary Medical Association (AVMA) publishes the *Veterinary Service Market for Companion Animals* every five years. Its intent is to expand veterinary knowledge about the American companion animal population regarding demographic characteristics and the use of veterinary medical services.

- The Bureau of Labor Statistics (part of the US Department of Labor) has some general data for the veterinary profession in each state.

- Some private companies provide predictive modeling of demographic areas. These companies provide map data and link it to US Census Bureau data and other data for accurate and up-to-date information.

- It can also be helpful to walk the neighborhood and speak with other businesses and service providers.

ZONING AND NEIGHBORS

After you have selected a general area or neighborhood, what are the next steps in finding the right lease space?

The first things to consider are zoning restrictions and permitted uses. Every jurisdiction has its own zoning code. First, determine the zoning of the potential property. You can do this through a web search or by contacting the local jurisdiction. Once you know how the property is zoned, review the permitted uses within that zone. If "animal clinic" or "veterinary clinic" is on the list of permitted uses, it is safe to proceed to the next step.

Be aware, however, that many jurisdictions are particularly concerned about whether animals are staying overnight inside the facility and whether there are going to be outside dog runs. Those two criteria can push a hospital out of the simple "veterinary clinic" category and can quite often make a practice an unpermitted use. It is important to understand these potential limitations before settling on a space.

It can be quite time consuming and expensive to pursue a space only to find out that a veterinary hospital is not a permitted use in the area. Do not assume the landlord or the realtor is going to know about zoning restrictions for the property. It is amazing how many times a practice has moved forward only to find out later, when the plans are submitted to the building department, that the proposed hospital is not a permitted use. (For more information on zoning, as well as state regulations affecting veterinary facilities, see Chapter 54.)

Along with the zoning, many commercial developments have restrictions that were put in place when the development was built. Even if a veterinary hospital is a permitted use according to the zoning, if the particular development has a restriction against veterinary hospitals, then a hospital cannot go into any of the spaces. Do all the due diligence at the outset to ensure your project will be allowed in the space.

Many jurisdictions also have restrictions on signage that can affect how the image of the business is projected. One of the AAHA standards for accreditation (under "Facility: Housekeeping and Maintenance") is for signage that is in good repair and promotes a professional image (AAHA, 35). If you are looking at a leasehold, review the condition of the existing signage of the development and speak with the landlord about options for new signage.

It's important that the neighbors are accepting of a veterinary hospital within the area. Some people have a negative perception of veterinary hospitals. They assume they will be loud, smelly, and disruptive to their own businesses.

A proactive and friendly approach with potential neighbors can go a long way toward dispelling these fears.

EXISTING CONDITIONS

When the research has been completed and it is understood that a veterinary hospital can go into any potential leasehold spaces under consideration, it is time to carefully consider the physical attributes of those potential locations. There are exterior, interior, and utility demands to take into account.

Exterior

"It's a leasehold project, so all the exterior improvements are the landlord's responsibility." Don't make this assumption. When checking with the planning and zoning department about zoning for the site, ask whether exterior items are required to be brought up to code when the plans are submitted for a building permit. If the answer is yes, then it will be necessary to negotiate with the landlord over responsibility and costs for these improvements.

Specific exterior items to be aware of include the following:

- Parking: Are there enough parking spaces, and is there an adequate number of handicap-accessible spaces? Where are they in proximity to the unit? Are the curb cuts up to code, and is the path to your front door accessible?
- Sidewalks: Are the sidewalks around the building in good condition?
- Surrounding area: Is there a nearby area where clients and staff can walk dogs?

Other items of importance are adequate site lighting and a safe path to the facility. AAHA gives accreditation points under "Facility: Housekeeping and Maintenance" for exterior lighting that provides adequate illumination for the safety of clients and practice team members (AAHA, 35). In most leasehold spaces, parking is in one location, but in some situations client parking may be in front of the building and employee parking in the rear. Inspect all the parking and access points and check that both staff and clients will have a safe area to park and walk to the facility.

Condition of the Exterior Façade: How Much Will the Landlord Let You Change?

Entry Doors and Storefront

Depending on the age of the building, the condition of the existing façade could be in question. If it is in disrepair, is this something the landlord is willing to upgrade? Will you be able to paint or refinish the existing storefront? Many developments require all the storefronts in the complex to have the same look.

Is the existing storefront insulated? Many older buildings do not meet current energy codes, and this can affect the code compliance of the tenant space.

Trash Enclosures

Check the location, availability, and condition of the onsite trash enclosure. Some jurisdictions have strict requirements for trash enclosures, and if one doesn't currently exist, you may be required to provide one.

Roofing

The condition of the existing roof can have implications for the interior of the space. Existing roofs may not have sufficient roof insulation, which may affect heating and cooling design. If the roof is in poor condition, this can be an item to negotiate with the landlord before signing a lease. As will be discussed later in the chapter, rooftop heating, ventilation, and air conditioning (HVAC) units often need to be replaced. If rooftop units are being added or replaced, it may be a good opportunity to make needed improvements to the roof. If roofing repairs are required, you may have to use the landlord's approved roofer.

Interior

Interior Dimensions and Encumbrances

Some interior conditions may restrict the layout of the space. Existing columns can be buried in walls, but their placement can still affect room layouts and sizes and where you can place major pieces of equipment. It is very inconvenient for a column to land in the middle of the X-ray machine, for example. If there is a choice between a space with columns or without, the space with-

The location of existing columns in a lease space can place restrictions on your floor plan.

out is going to provide much more flexibility in the new layout.

As you examine the space, determine whether there are any other existing interior features that are unmovable. For example, a former bank space may have a large concrete vault that would be expensive to remove. In any existing space, there could be mechanical, plumbing, or electrical equipment serving the whole building that is therefore not removable.

Look at the condition of the floor slab. Veterinary practices require waterproof finishes in certain areas, and many of these finishes have strict requirements for slab water content and condition. Examine the existing floor slab to see if there are any red flags, such as cracking or unlevel areas that may indicate a bigger problem.

Change in Grade

Depending on the topography of the area, there may be a change of grade either within the individual unit or between units. There may be a step within the suite that poses restrictions on the layout of the new space, or there may be a step from one suite to the next. This could play a part in the viability of future expansion.

Other Items

There are a number of other issues to check for in evaluating an existing building. You may in fact wish to hire an inspector to conduct a thorough evaluation. Some of the areas to be aware of are the following:

- Drywall and ceilings: Are there any signs of potential moisture or leaks that could affect the use of the space or the renovation?

- Separation between the suites: The building department will care about fire separation between spaces, so an awareness of what is already in place and what might need to be added later can save time and money down the road. Along with separation of the spaces, take note of the presence of existing fire alarm and sprinkler systems.

- Vertical dimensions of the space: If the roof or floor deck above is low, it limits the types of systems that can be used, increasing overall design and construction costs.

- Dimensions of the space: Generally, square spaces make better veterinary facilities than long, narrow spaces.

Size of the Leasehold Space

The size of the space you are looking for depends primarily on the number of doctors and staff and the expected volume of patients. As a general rule, a practice with two to three exam rooms could fit within 1,800 to 2,400 square feet. A practice with four or five exam rooms requires about 3,600 square feet at minimum, and often more. If your practice also offers ancillary services, such as grooming, this will add to the overall square-footage requirements.

Leasehold spaces come in many shapes and sizes. It may seem like strip malls are a row of rectangular boxes, but it's amazing how often that is not the case. The ideal configuration is a minimum width of 35 to 40 feet to a maximum width of 60 feet, and a minimum depth of 70 feet to a maximum depth of 90 feet. The absolute minimum width for the smallest leasehold practice is 23 feet. Anything narrower than this will be difficult to work with.

Nine-foot ceilings are needed for effective medical spaces—with at least an additional 30 to 36 inches above these 9-foot ceilings. This means that the clear height to the bottom of the structure elements, such as joists and beams, in a lease space should be no less than 12 feet above the finished floor.

When you review spaces for their overall size and dimensions, consider the possibility of future growth within the complex. Might there be a possibility of acquiring the neighboring spaces in the future? If neighboring spaces might become available, it's a good idea to look at those spaces, too, if possible, to determine their viability.

Utility Requirements

Finally, there are the nitty-gritty utility items that should be verified before selecting a leasehold space. Veterinary hospitals have large needs for mechanical and plumbing as well as electrical infrastructure. These demands are much higher than they are for a typical retail or business function. Below are some typical demands for a veterinary hospital with four to five exam rooms.

Plumbing

Domestic water usage for a hospital of this size averages approximately 32 gallons per minute, requiring, ideally, a 1.5-inch connection to the water meter. Increasing the size of a water connection may result in large fees from the utility company, so it's better to ensure the building has the required utilities before proceeding. A minimum 4-inch tenant sanitary sewer connection is also ideal.

Electrical

Electrical demand in a veterinary hospital can be very large. Specialty equipment, including X-ray machines, exam and surgery lights, autoclaves, warming blankets, and anything with a

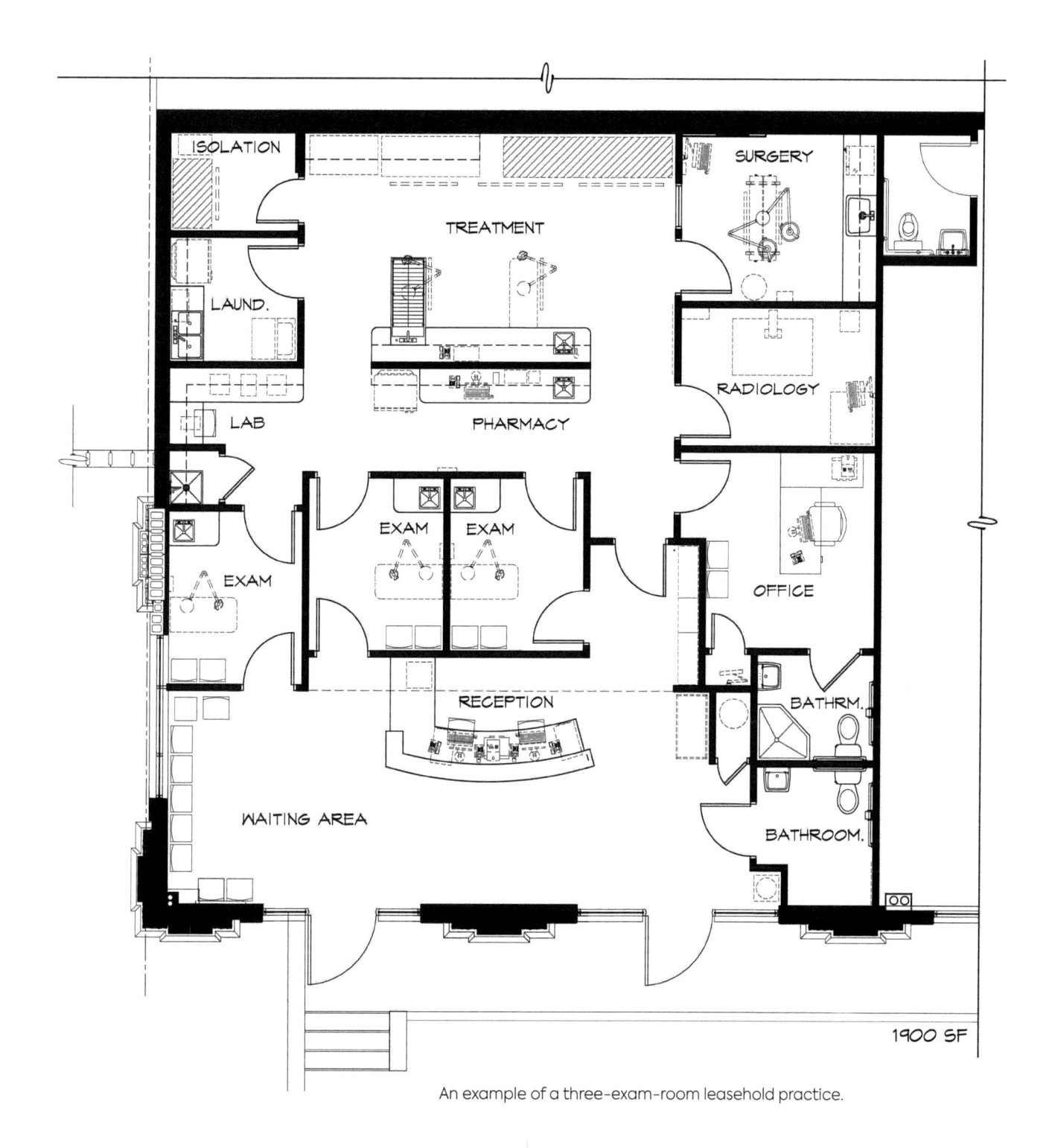

An example of a three-exam-room leasehold practice.

heating element, raises the electrical demands over those of a standard business use. Some of this equipment may require dedicated outlets. It is best if the lease space is supplied with a 208-volt (V), 3-phase (PH) service. A hospital of up to 4,500 square feet will require 400 amps (A) of service. Up to 6,000 square feet will require 600 A of service. As with water service, these can be changed and increased if there are other factors that make the location perfect—anything is possible with enough money.

LEASEHOLD PRACTICES: CHOOSING THE RIGHT SPACE

Mechanical

Veterinary hospitals require more air exchanges and larger mechanical units than a typical retail business. Are the existing units sufficient for the needs of the practice? How old are they? Typically, units over 15 years old should be considered for replacement. You need to consider what the landlord is willing to provide and what will fall into the construction budget when negotiating a lease.

Heating, ventilation, and air conditioning usage is measured in tons. A mechanical unit provides a certain tonnage of heating and cooling. Ideally, the ratio would be 200 square feet per nominal ton in hot, humid climates, or up to 275 to 300 square feet per nominal ton in cool, temperate, and dry climates. Inspect any existing mechanical units and determine how many tons are available.

The best, most comfortable configuration for a hospital is four zones, or rooftop units. Having this level of supply provides the best thermal management and odor control. Three zones, however, can be adequate, and, if absolutely required by the landlord, the space, or structural limitations, two zones can work, though there will be additional exhaust requirements that can be accommodated with supplemental exhaust fans.

The bottom line is that, before signing on the dotted line for any lease space, carefully inspect and research the property to ensure it will be the best home for your practice.

CHECKLIST

BEFORE YOU SIGN YOUR LEASE

- ☑ Review contract with your lawyer.
- ☐ Confirm maximum tenant finish allowance.
- ☐ Determine when your lease starts.
- ☐ Try to include a noncompete clause so the shopping center will note be able to lease to a pet store with veterinary services.
- ☐ Include language that allows you to remove veterinary-specific equipment like surgery lights, anesthetic waste gas, runs, etc. upon leaving/vacating the space. Typically, anything attached stays with the building when you leave.
- ☐ Include language in the lease to give you the option of "first right of refusal" for adjacent spaces as they become available.
- ☐ Design space to allow for easy expansion into adjacent space.

NOTE: THE DRAWBACK TO LEASING IS THAT MONEY INVESTED IN THE IMPROVEMENTS STAYS WITH THE SPACE WHEN YOU MOVE OUT.

Things to consider before you sign on the dotted line.

CHAPTER 6

ADAPTIVE REUSE PROJECTS

An adaptive reuse project is a project that gives new life to an existing building. These projects became quite common during and after the Great Recession as veterinary practices looked for ways to complete their projects more efficiently. In fact, choosing a viable existing building can be an excellent way to save money and reuse existing infrastructure. Like a hermit crab finding a great shell, you may find that the right existing building can be a great asset for your veterinary practice.

If you decide to consider an adaptive reuse project, go about it just as you would for other projects by performing the proper market analysis. Choose a building in the right location for your practice, with good visibility and access, and away from the competition. Don't forget to check the zoning regulations to ensure the buildings you have under consideration are zoned appropriately for veterinary use.

Some buildings are better fits for renovating into a veterinary space than others. The most useful buildings are open-shell commercial structures. Veterinarians purchasing and adapting the right building can typically save up to 15% compared to the cost of constructing a new freestanding building. Less debt equates to less risk and more value for the dollars spent. If this approach sounds interesting to you, you will need to engage a design or construction professional early in the process to help you evaluate existing buildings. It is important to get the right space, as the wrong one could cost you more money than you would have saved.

The following types of buildings are good candidates for remodeling into a new hospital:

- Small grocery stores.
- Pharmacies.
- Electronics stores, such as a Best Buy.
- Some office buildings with commercial-grade construction.
- Other commercially constructed buildings with open shells.

Many of the buildings that would make good veterinary hospitals already have features that make them desirable. For example, defunct Blockbuster video stores made excellent buildings for veterinary conversion because they were about the right size for a hospital of four or five exam rooms. In addition, they were often in prominent and visible locations, and they typically had plenty of parking, as well as flat roofs on which to locate mechanical units.

While there are exceptions, the following types of buildings typically are inappropriate for conversion into veterinary hospitals:

- Residences.
- Old restaurants.
- Funeral parlors (which tend to be very "residential" in construction type).
- Wood-framed buildings.
- Old automotive facilities or warehouses.
- Metal prefabricated buildings (for example, Butler buildings).

Some people may wonder why warehouses and metal buildings are on the inappropriate list, as they are also open shells, often with clear structure heights. There are several reasons:

- These buildings are typically categorized as "warehouses" under the building code. Once they are converted to business occupancies, they need to be brought up to code compliance, often at considerable expense.
- They are built with lightweight construction and often cannot support additional roof loads, including the loads imposed by new mechanical equipment, but sometimes also from much more minor loads. For example, it is not uncommon for older warehouse buildings to be unable to support the load of new lights, ceilings, and fire sprinkler piping.
- Warehouse buildings tend to have flimsy exterior construction assemblies with poorly insulated walls and roofs.
- Such buildings are not always in prominent locations in town, and they may not have the visibility, access, site improvements, and utilities that are needed to adequately support veterinary hospital construction.

Once you have chosen a building that is a good candidate for conversion, review it for the following requirements:

- Triple-check the zoning to ensure it is zoned correctly and get it in writing from the zoning department. (See Chapters 7 and 54 for additional zoning and regulatory issues.)

The Adobe Animal Hospital building was formerly a human pharmacy. (Posh Pooch Portraits. Courtesy of Adobe Animal Hospital, Los Altos, California.)

- Review the clear height on the interior. A minimum clearance of 12 feet is required from the floor slab to the bottom of the structure above in order to have at least 9-foot ceilings. Higher spaces will allow your architect to do more with the lobby and other public spaces.

- Verify the condition of the building, as described in the previous chapter for leasehold projects.

- Have your contractor or design professionals verify that adequate utilities are available at the building. If they are not, ascertain the viability and cost of bringing these utilities to the space.

- Visit with the building permitting authority to understand what you would need to do to the building to bring it into compliance with current codes. For example, in Florida and California, hurricane and seismic

ADAPTIVE REUSE PROJECTS 29

codes, respectively, may add additional structural requirements to your project.

▼ ▼ ▼

UNDER THE RIGHT conditions, an adaptive reuse project can be a highly advantageous means of building your new hospital with the potential for accessible, visible locations and open spaces of the right size and shape. But don't let the lure of an existing building shell, and the possible cost savings it could bring, lead you down the path of purchasing a building with costly and perhaps insurmountable hidden issues. As with any major investment, thoroughly research any potential sites before you commit.

CHAPTER 7

FREESTANDING BUILDINGS: CHOOSING THE RIGHT LAND

Finding the perfect site on which to locate your new veterinary hospital will take a lot of research, patience, and a bit of luck. The number and availability of suitable sites for any project can pose a challenge and significantly more so for veterinary facilities that have additional planning and zoning restrictions.

PHYSICAL SUITABILITY

After you've completed your market viability research and pinpointed the general area where you would like to locate, the most important considerations in selecting a site are visibility and access. Can your clients easily find and then access the site? Is it easy to see from the road? If the answer to these questions is not an unqualified yes, then seriously consider another site.

Ideally, people need to be able to safely access the site without fighting traffic, making a long detour, or waiting long periods for traffic to clear. The visibility of the site is imperative. Buildings hidden behind trees or large grade changes are not the best option. Can you easily and quickly describe to your clients how to get there? If not, it's probably not a great location.

Your best site options should be located central to the area that you serve. This keeps current and future clients from having to drive across town. It also makes sense to think about natural geographic boundaries. Physical obstacles like rivers, mountains, green belts, freeways, or specific

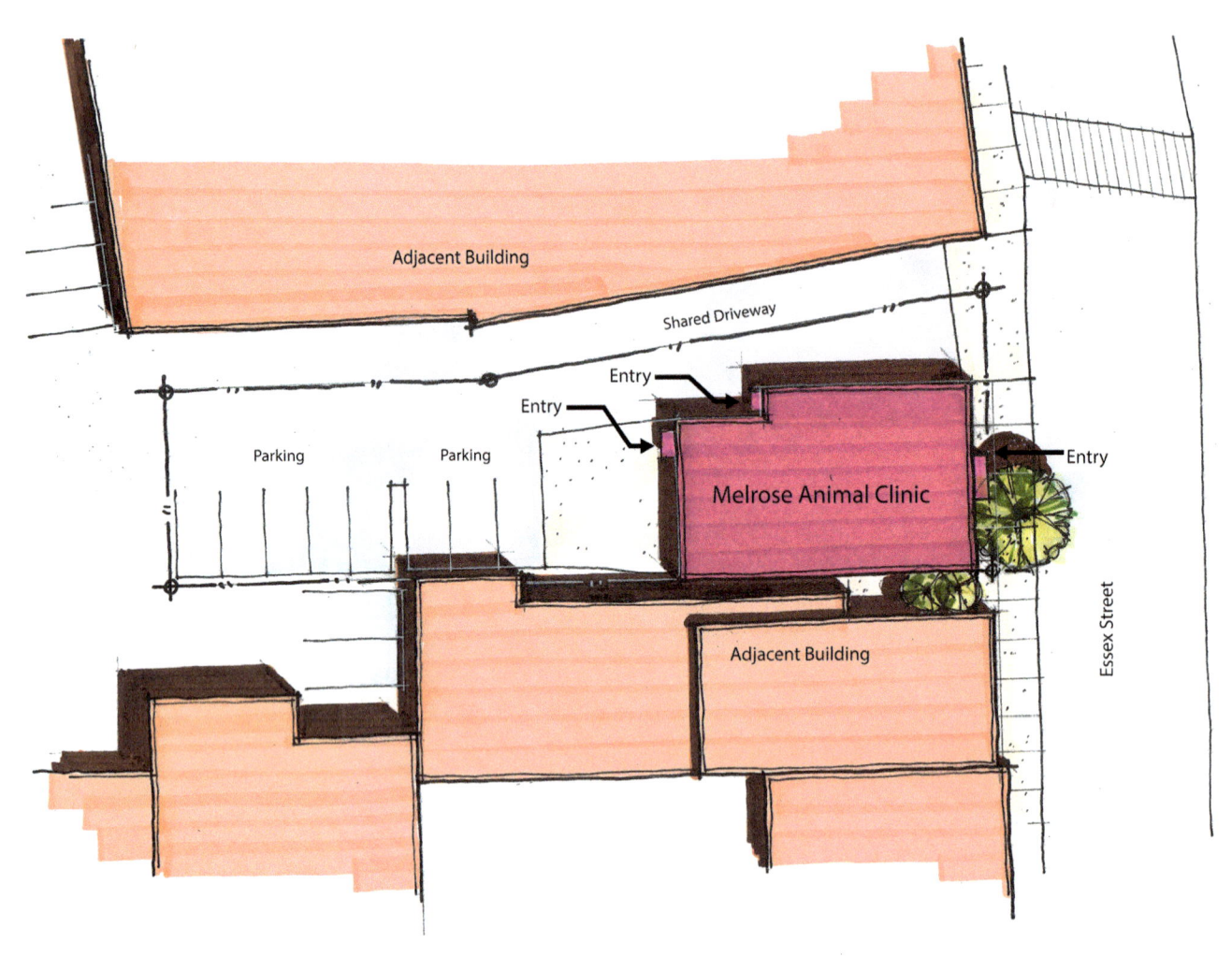

The site plan for a hospital in a busy downtown area. The hospital has good visibility from the street and off-street parking for client convenience. (Courtesy of Melrose Animal Clinic, Melrose, Massachusetts.)

neighborhoods can create real or imagined obstacles for people when they think about visiting your hospital.

You do not necessarily need the very best site in the area. Instead, look at sites that are not located on the best intersection in the area you plan to serve but are instead located close by. Another possibility is to locate at the edge of your existing community with an eye to where future growth may occur. In both of these cases, the cost of land will probably be more reasonable than in the very center of town or at the best intersection.

SITE CAPACITY

On the most basic level, you need to find out if your proposed building will fit on your selected site. A simple way to determine this is to calculate site coverage. As a general rule, your building will cover 20%–25% of the site. If your building is 6,000 square feet, your site should be approximately 24,000 to 30,000 square feet. (An acre is equal to 43,560 square feet.)

If your building covers only 20%–25% of the area, what happens with the rest of the site? The other 75%–80% will be taken up by zoning setbacks, easements, landscaping, parking, drive lanes, and maybe a little room for expansion. For example, many sites commonly include the following:

- Front, side, and rear setbacks and road right-of-ways.

- An additional portion of the site devoted exclusively to landscaping.

- Sight, sound, and distance buffers to adjacent properties, particularly if the zoning of adjacent parcels is residential.

- Stormwater retention/detention ponds (that is, water that soaks in or evaporates, or retention, and water that is held onsite and then released at a controlled rate, or detention).

- Parking at a ratio of one parking space per 250 square feet of building area. Consider also how much space you will need for parking based on your client and staff needs. Include drive aisles, maneuvering, and turnaround space for delivery vehicles, trash trucks, and fire apparatus.

- Space on the site unoccupied by parking or the initial building (equal to about one-third of the building size for future expansion).

- A significant outdoor space set aside for training or animal exercise.

If some of these elements can be reduced or eliminated, you can reduce the size of the site. If the site is an odd shape, has a lot of slope, or has some limits on development because of wetlands, then you will need a bigger site.

The following are some additional ideas to consider as you look for a site to purchase:

- Choose a site that is in the best location you can afford for the market area you are serving. Remember that your clients will form impressions about your practice based on the neighborhood and the surrounding environment.

- Choose a site that is square to moderately rectangular in shape. A site that is too long and thin, or oddly shaped, may not be amenable to a good site design or floor plan.

- Consider the location of drainage features, such as stormwater detention areas, which should be downhill from the building. This may seem obvious, but the location of these features may restrict your development of the site.

- In northern climates, consider issues related to snow removal and storage.

TOPOGRAPHY AND SOILS

The effect of topography and soils is often overlooked during the initial site selection process. A steep, sloping site can cause the driveways and sidewalks to be too steep for handicapped access, make it difficult to keep the site drainage away from the building, and increase the foundation costs.

Soil geology can also dramatically affect site development and building costs. For example, it can be very expensive to blast out bedrock,

The site plan for a more rural hospital in Lomira, Wisconsin. (Edmunds Studios, Inc. Courtesy of Veterinary Village, Lomira, Wisconsin.)

remove expansive clay, or build expensive foundations. If the site contains a lot of fill dirt, you will probably need to remove and replace the fill before you can build. Other site-specific geologic issues include high water tables or an excess of organic material.

Avoid these traps by commissioning a topographic survey and a soils report before you finalize the purchase of a site.

PLANNING AND ZONING

To protect the value and quality of their cities and neighborhoods, local government agencies impose planning and zoning regulations on building sites. Each year brings more—and sometimes onerous—regulations, and each year it takes more time, money, and effort to satisfy these requirements. In addition to normal constraints, such as setbacks and allowable uses, these regulations can dictate landscaping, site access, availability of utilities, facility appearance, and even funding of offsite street or utility improvements.

Almost every significant town, county, or city in the US has planning or zoning laws and ordinances. These ordinances control the following:

- What a site can be used for.

The completed hospital. (Edmunds Studios, Inc. Courtesy of Veterinary Village, Lomira, Wisconsin.)

- How far back from the property lines the building must sit.
- How many parking spaces are required.
- In some instances, what the building looks like.
- How much building can be located on the site.
- Building height and massing (the perception of the general shape and form of the building).

The time and expense involved in making a zoning or planning application and waiting for the municipality to review it have increased dramatically. Because time equals money, the cost to your business has also increased. That is why it is important to research the regulations that may apply to your site before you make any purchase.

Planning and zoning regulations also dictate how a site is titled and platted. For this reason, it is critically important for the owner to know before buying a site what the planning and zoning requirements are for that particular parcel. Although it is possible to apply for and receive a variance for specific zoning requirements, the primary goal in purchasing a piece of ground is to acquire a parcel where a veterinary hospital is a "use by right" and where your building will conform to the setback, parking, height, and area requirements. In most city locations where veterinary hospitals are allowed, the municipality also requires some level of site and design review or a conditional use permit. Applying for a conditional use permit, a variance, or even a zoning change can be a time-consuming and costly process, with no guarantees of success.

In addition to the normal zoning issues mentioned above, many urban areas have "overlay zones," that is, another layer of zoning that will also affect how a site can be developed and what can be built on it. Often overlay zoning deals with aesthetic or quality-of-life issues. These zones may include historic districts, view corridors, entrances to urban areas, urban redevelopment, and landscape districts. The requirements of an overlay zone can be very stringent, and the review process can be both time consuming and subjective in nature.

ENCUMBERANCES AND EASEMENTS

As land becomes scarcer, and as governmental regulations increase, finding land that is not encumbered by onerous easements, encroachments, deed restrictions, covenants, or a clouded title is becoming more difficult. Prior to purchasing any ground, be sure you know what you are buying. Never depend solely on the word of the listing real estate agent or the existing owner.

In addition, contact the utility company about the availability of electricity, gas, water, and sewer. Find out if there are any utility easements encumbering the property. Finally, have a title company do a title search prior to purchasing the ground to determine if there are untold legal encumbrances of any kind on the property.

ENVIRONMENTAL ASSESSMENT

The area with the greatest potential for liabilities and costs is the matter of hazardous waste pollution and disposal. Most people are familiar with asbestos, but there is also the potential for hydrocarbons, heavy metals, and industrial wastes to affect the buildability of selected sites. In locations with a history of dense urban development and heavy industry, a high number of sites are contaminated by hazardous wastes generated onsite or passing through from nearby sites.

It is important to make sure the site you select does not have any hidden environmental challenges. The best way to do this is to commission a basic environmental assessment for any site you are considering. The ramifications of purchasing a site that contains even threshold levels of environmental pollutants can be dramatic. In most cases, a Phase 1 Environmental Assessment can identify environmental conditions that may adversely affect the development of your site.

OTHER CONSTRAINTS

Wetlands, historic districts, coastal commissions, protected watersheds, and urban renewal areas also have regulatory requirements that affect sites. From tideland Virginia to coastal California, local and federal governmental agencies have earmarked certain areas for special consideration and additional regulation. Therefore, it is wise to thoroughly investigate any site you are considering to identify potential regulatory constraints. These can include the following:

- Protection of wetlands.
- Control of storm drainage runoff and protection of watersheds, waterways, and aquifers.
- Protection of historic or natural vegetation, including heritage trees.
- Protection of wildlife.
- Wildfire mitigation.
- Slope stabilization.
- Seashore protection.
- Archaeological site preservation.

▼ ▼ ▼

IT IS WORTH noting that when you select a site, the potential hidden costs are as important as the listed cost of the site. Be sure to fully investigate all of the potential risks before making a purchase.

CHAPTER 8

STRATEGIES FOR REMODELS AND ADDITIONS

There are many reasons a veterinarian might choose to remodel or build an addition onto an existing facility: to accommodate hospital growth, to offer new medical or ancillary services to clients, to rejuvenate an outdated facility, to attract or retain staff, or to transition to new practice owners when the existing owners are planning to retire.

What are the signs to look for that indicate it is time to remodel? These key factors can prompt a hospital renovation:

- More floor space is required to accommodate growth, whether this is due to providing new services or increased staffing needs.

- There is a perceived need to stay competitive. Sometimes the opening of a new practice nearby triggers thoughts of renovating.

- The decor is outdated and does not reflect the quality of medicine that is currently being practiced.

- There is a desire to increase productivity by enhancing the traffic flow of the hospital.

- The hospital is now part of a corporation, and the company has set aside funds to remodel or renovate the practice, either to match the corporate model or for any of the above-mentioned reasons.

- There is a plan to either sell the practice or bring on a new associate and renovation will make the hospital more desirable.

A RENOVATION MAY NOT BE THE ANSWER

Sometimes it is less expensive to start fresh than it is to renovate. If an existing facility is so outdated that the expense to renovate outweighs what it would cost to build new, it might be better to consider the alternatives. Things to consider when approaching this decision include the following:

- Services need to grow in several areas at once. If most of the floor plan is affected, then it may be more cost effective to build new than to renovate.

- The renovation would require moving existing structural walls or features, such as support posts, that would be very costly to relocate or modify.

- Either the site is not zoned correctly under up-to-date zoning codes or other arduous zoning restrictions apply.

- The building systems, such as HVAC, are so outdated that they would require full replacement.

Code upgrade requirements are often triggered by renovations. An existing facility does not have to meet new building or energy code requirements, but as soon as renovations begin, any area being upgraded needs to be brought up to current code. In some cases, the entire facility will need to come up to current standards. Energy codes are getting more stringent, and it can be costly to bring old buildings up to the new standards.

WHEN RENOVATIONS MAKE SENSE

There are times when it is clear that a renovation is the best choice for the practice. Below are examples of typical scenarios:

- The practice only needs a facelift. If the renovation is generally limited to upgrades of colors and materials, it can be cost effective.

- The practice does not have a choice about its location. If you're in a very land-constrained area, a renovation may be the best way to improve services, as it may not be possible to choose new land.

- The area to be renovated is very distinct. If, for example, the practice needs to add an ancillary service or piece of specialty equipment, such as a CT scanner, it makes a lot of sense to work around this one new element.

- A portion of the practice is underutilized. For example, if the practice once offered large animal services and does not now offer them, the leftover large animal spaces may easily convert to additional square footage for the small animal practice.

WHERE TO START

If it has been decided that renovation is the direction to go, what happens now? The next step would be to develop some very early plans to help define the scope of the renovation and apply some early budget numbers. In budgeting at this stage, be very conservative, as renovations are notoriously difficult to estimate due to unknown conditions that may exist. The tendency is for the scope of the project to creep up and for cost estimates to increase.

This is sometimes called "while we're at it" syndrome. For example, you decide to repaint your lobby and you realize how shabby it makes your exam rooms look, so you repaint the exam rooms, but then your treatment area looks dingy, so you need to repaint there, too, and on and on until you've repainted the entire hospital. Thus, apply generous contingency factors of up to 20%–25% on initial budget estimates to protect yourself from unknowns and scope creep.

Once you have an idea of the desired scope of the project and a reasonable estimate of the expected costs, it is important to put together a business plan or update your existing one. Having a business plan will help you obtain preliminary financing commitments. There are numerous accountants and practice consultants who are experts in the veterinary industry who can assist you. Generally speaking, at the maximum, your total debt load should equal 70%–100% of your gross billing per year.

Finally, begin to assemble a team. A major renovation or construction project is not for the faint of heart, and selecting the right people to work with throughout the process is critical. In some jurisdictions, the process of going through the building department and receiving a building permit can be difficult. The right team, including the architect, engineers, and contractor, can make the process easier.

TYPES OF PRACTICE RENOVATIONS

As mentioned previously, a renovation can range from a simple update of your finishes to adding a whole wing to the hospital. Here is a breakdown of some of the options with different types of renovations.

The 3-D conceptual design for the reception/entry area of a large specialty practice. (Courtesy of VCA West Los Angeles Animal Hospital, Los Angeles, California [VCA, Inc.].)

For a small interior facelift, consider the following:

- Enhancing lighting: This can be achieved either by increasing the amount of daylighting through new skylights or exterior windows or by installing new electrical lighting to improve poorly lit areas of the hospital. Installing dimmer switches on new lighting fixtures in animal areas can provide for gradual lighting transitions and make the animals more comfortable. Adding dimmer switches also helps to reduce overall power usage.

- Using or adding color: The best place to add color is on the walls, where it can easily be changed again in the future. It's better to choose subtle or neutral colors for more permanent items, such as cabinetry. When repainting, use a coordinated color scheme throughout the hospital to create a cohesive image that represents the core mission of the practice. A cheerful reception area can set the tone for the practice and provide current and potential clients with the right first impression.

- Increasing transparency: Opening up the interior spaces with windows or glass partitions makes the hospital feel larger, lets in daylight, and sends a message of openness to clients. Possible approaches include using glass or partial-glass doors wherever possible and, where views need to be controlled, replacing solid partitions with frosted glass or glass block.

Interior design and architecture firms with experience in color palette selection can be very helpful in selecting an appropriate look and color scheme. Three-dimensional rendering tools can help illustrate how the space will look when it is complete. These images will help you to visualize the space and can also be used as marketing tools for staff and clients.

Taking on a large-scale remodel is a greater endeavor. It can involve rearranging or repurposing rooms or building an addition. As well as the code compliance issues mentioned above, if the renovation includes an addition or site expansion, site limitations—such as easements, proximity to neighboring properties, and parking capacities—also need to be studied.

HOW TO MINIMIZE THE EFFECTS OF A RENOVATION

One of the keys to making the renovation process as smooth as possible is communication. Select a few key people to make the remodeling decisions for the hospital, or for specific portions of the hospital, during the renovation. Fewer decision makers and more people running the hospital will keep the process focused.

Enlist one person to be the owner's representative to order and coordinate the delivery of new equipment and communicate on a regular basis with the design and construction team. Depending on the size of the project and the practice, it is not always in the best interest of the practice to select the hospital manager for this job.

Have a clear plan for the renovation process, including timelines for construction, phasing, parking adjustments, and desired outcome, and keep staff and clients informed of the plan and the progress throughout. Post updates on current and projected events so everyone involved can be prepared to make any necessary accommodations. Work with the construction team regarding construction phasing and expected downtimes. Being prepared for occurrences such as power turn-offs to the building will help decrease any stress or anxiety that may occur.

It is important to communicate with both your architect and your contractor about your need to keep the practice operational during the renovation. This may not be a simple matter, and it may require one or more of these strategies:

- A phasing plan showing how different operational areas will be shifted around as needed.

- Temporary facilities for all or some of the operations.

- Specific plans for power shutdowns.

- Evening and weekend construction work to minimize negative effects on operations.

▼ ▼ ▼

PROPER PLANNING WILL help make the renovation as successful as possible. As you plan your renovation or renovations over the years, keep the scope simple and true to your vision for the practice. Do your research with your design team in the planning stages, and budget with a conservative approach to protect the project from cost overruns. Well-planned renovations can help your practice grow significantly in revenue and help you stay relevant in future years.

CHAPTER 9

PROJECT TIMELINE

Laying out a project timeline is always a complicated process. A simple remodel can take several months, and the design and construction of a new freestanding hospital can take 18 months or more. It's important to have an understanding of the design and construction process so that you can make decisions about your budget and schedule before committing to what can be a long and expensive, but rewarding, process.

All of the types of construction we have discussed so far—the remodel or renovation of an existing hospital, the buildout of a lease space, an adaptive reuse project, or a new, freestanding hospital—require three distinct phases of work: predesign, design, and construction. Each phase can be broken down into various subcategories. If you become familiar with the basic phases, you will be better able to understand the time it takes to get from the dream for your hospital to the reality.

THE PREDESIGN PHASE

The predesign phase lays the groundwork for the project. It is the most overlooked phase, but it is also the most important, because everything done later will be built upon this initial stage. The predesign phase can take as little as a month or as long as several years. There are four elements to the predesign phase:

- Research time: This includes the time you spend working with your accountant and lender to establish project financing, and with your architect or management consultant to develop market and feasibility studies to establish the project scope and site capacity. This is the time to begin making decisions about your options—building new, building out a lease space, remodeling, and so on—and, if necessary, to decide on site options.

- Decision time: It is important to factor in an appropriate amount of time for you to make good, solid decisions. Many owners underestimate the time it will take for them to assemble a team, fully review design and other consultant proposals, and make final decisions.

- Predesign reports time: In order to move forward, you will likely need some reports. If this is an existing building, you may need a hazardous materials survey as well as "as-built" drawings that accurately describe the existing building layout. If this is a new building, you will need a site survey, a Phase 1 Environmental Report, and a geotechnical (soils) report. This information prepares the way for the design phase and often turns up concerns that may affect your decision to purchase the property or go ahead with the project.

- Action time: You will usually find that when it's time to act on a decision, such as purchasing a piece of property, it will take time to draw up contracts, have your attorney review the language, and then obtain sign-off from all parties. Figure that it will take a minimum of a few weeks for any significant contract to be reviewed and signed by all of the concerned parties.

Begin design/programming meetings with your architect to establish the scope and parameters of your project, justify the economics, and develop the image you want your facility to have.

THE DESIGN PHASE

Once you have approved the building program, the next step is the design phase. Depending on the size and complexity of your project and the design firm you have hired, the design phase is commonly separated into two processes: schematic drawings and construction drawings. The schematic drawings are the initial drawings prepared by the architect based on the approved building program. They incorporate the owners' input, wish list, and requirements and help the owners visualize the elements of the project. The schematic drawings are then developed into the construction drawings. The construction drawings are the technical drawings that the contractor will use to construct the facility. The two types of drawings have specific goals, as described below.

Schematic Drawings

Schematic drawings lay out the basic configuration and image of the building. Often they are used to obtain preliminary pricing or to secure governmental approval or financial commitments. For the architect, they are the basic drawings that are, with refinement, later developed into the construction drawings. The actual time it takes your architect to develop schematic drawings is dependent on a realistic and well-thought-out program, the architect's ability to understand and translate your ideas onto paper, and the degree of familiarity the architect has with veterinary facility design. If you are building a freestanding hospital, it should take one to two months for you and your architect to work through the schematic design and get to the point where the drawings are acceptable to you. The architect can then begin on the construction drawings.

Construction Drawings

During the construction drawing phase, the architect will create the drawings from which the contractor will bid and build your project. These drawings are the basis for your legal contract with a contractor. For a freestanding hospital, it takes approximately three to six months to complete the construction drawings (including architectural, structural, mechanical/plumbing, and electrical drawings and specifications).

This timeline will vary based on the complexity of the project and on the specifics of any required planning and zoning reviews, which can lengthen the process in some jurisdictions.

THE CONSTRUCTION PHASE

The construction phase is the most exciting part of the project. After months of work, your ideas and research finally become reality. But before you can actually build your project, you must apply for a building permit. The length of time it takes to obtain the building permit will depend on your local governmental agency. Applying for and pulling a permit can vary from two weeks in a small town or rural county to several months or more in a large metropolitan area. A few jurisdictions may require up to a year to issue a building permit. In large cities, an expediter is often required to interface with city officials and move the documents around to the right person. Investigate how long a building permit takes to acquire in your town, county, or city so that this timeline may be built into your overall schedule.

Whether you have preselected your contractor and arranged a negotiated contract or plan to have several contractors competitively bid your project, this is also the time for them to develop their "hard bid." It typically takes three weeks for contractors to bid a project. It also takes time to evaluate the bid or bids and then enter into a contract. A realistic time frame for the bidding phase, including contractor selection and finalization of a contract, would be about six weeks. Be aware that many final bids come in higher than expected, and that often a value engineering (VE) process must be undertaken to bring the final cost of construction in line with your budget. It can take time to identify what is absolutely necessary and what is expendable on your project.

Once approvals have been obtained, financing is in order, contracts are signed, and bids agreed to, it is time to break ground.

The contractor starts from the ground up: foundations of concrete are poured, then the walls go up, the exterior is completed, and the roof is added. Finally, the interior rooms are framed and finished. Depending on the size and complexity of the project and the time of year, the amount of time needed to build a hospital will vary. The construction of a storefront build-out usually takes 3 to 4 months. A freestanding veterinary hospital can take as long as 10 to 12 months. If you are located in the far north, building through the winter months can add still more time to this phase.

Congratulations! If you've gotten this far, you've lived through the predesign, design, and construction phases. Now, it's time to move in. One point to remember that may seem obvious: allow yourself some time to get moved in and set up. For twenty-four-hour facilities, careful coordination related to equipment transfer and existing hospital downtime must be considered and incorporated into the schedule.

This is also the time to celebrate a job well done. Once you've moved in, it's a perfect time to ramp up your marketing plan, have an open house, welcome new clients, and show off your new facility.

OTHER CONSIDERATIONS

Here are some other details that are important for you to know:

- Project schedule: In the construction and design world, there is a saying that goes as follows: "You can't have fast, inexpensive, and high quality. You can pick two, but you can't have all three." Be realistic with your timeline. Asking your design and construction team to meet unreasonable timelines can lead to more costs and potential problems than having to wait a bit longer to open the doors to your new facility.

- Government agencies: With each passing year, the time it takes to obtain even simple approvals from local government agencies increases. Unfortunately, the only thing you can do is be prepared. The services of a civil engineer and architect are commonly required to prepare the right planning drawings and documents, help submit this information, and attend city and planning board presentations. As a general rule, expect to spend at least three to six months on the planning department review process, and longer if rezoning is required.

Typical project timelines for leasehold and freestanding veterinary facilities.

- Architects: Trying to save time or money by selecting an architect with little or no relevant experience could mean you end up spending a significant amount of your time educating them.

- Contractors: Consider negotiating with a general contractor early in the process. A good contractor who is involved in the process can provide reliable preliminary pricing and early input on optimum construction methods. This may require that you sign up for preconstruction services from the contractor, usually for a stipulated fee. Frequently, that fee will be rolled into the contractor's bid if they are selected to build the project. When things are busy, it is also beneficial to get onto the contractor's schedule early. There are now times when it can be extremely difficult to find enough contractors willing to spend their time to competitively bid for projects.

▼ ▼ ▼

TAKE YOUR TIME at the beginning of any project to ensure that your goals are realistic—that is, aligned with what is possible both financially and in terms of time frame. Be sure to hire an experienced team, and be sure to communicate with them effectively from day one to ensure that your goals become their goals, and your dream a reality.

SECTION **TWO**

An Overview of Hospital Design

CHAPTER 10

THE FEAR FREE^{SM} DESIGN MOVEMENT

The ancient Greek physician Hippocrates is credited with saying, "Cure sometimes. Treat often. Comfort always." While it is true that Hippocrates was referring to the care of humans when he made this statement, there can be no doubt that it applies equally well to modern veterinary practice. As our knowledge has progressed, we've become ever more aware of the link between physical and psychological wellness for animals.

The goal of the Fear Free^{SM} initiative is to create a whole health model by integrating that link between the physical, psychological, and emotional into everyday veterinary practice. Fear Free hospitals break the cycle of fear and the damaging effects of stress by providing approaches to care that create positive, anxiety-free, stress-free relationships between veterinarians, veterinary technicians, and pets.

A well-designed hospital can support Fear Free operational approaches, but beyond that, it can help to transform the way pets experience veterinary care. Fear Free facility standards consider every one of a pet's senses to create a calm and soothing experience.

Fear Free facility standards for hospital accreditation are separated into these categories:

- General Fear Free Design.
- Fear Free Cleaning and Housekeeping.
- Fear Free Design for Dogs and Cats.

- Fear Free Housing.
- Fear Free Lighting and Sound Engineering.
- Fear Free Mechanical Engineering.

The following paragraphs will provide general suggestions to assist you with implementing Fear Free design in your hospital. Whether your goal is to achieve Fear Free practice accreditation or simply to create a stress-free environment for the animals in your care, these ideas will get you started.

GENERAL FEAR FREE DESIGN

This category encompasses a variety of concepts related to the layout and design of the physical spaces within a hospital.

One of the most stress-inducing aspects of any veterinary visit is the time spent waiting in the hospital for the appointment to begin. Fear Free facility standards begin with solutions that help to reduce stressful initial experiences and reduce or eliminate client wait times.

One solution is to create separate lobbies for dogs and cats, or to include view blocking in single lobbies. Preventing dogs and cats from interacting or even seeing each other can go a long way toward reducing anxiety, regardless of the brevity of wait times.

We can take this concept even further by eliminating the waiting room altogether. In this model, patients and their owners are escorted directly to an exam room, either through the front entry of the hospital or through an exterior door directly into an exam room.

In existing hospitals, it is possible to reduce indoor wait times with operational methods that do not involve changing the space. For example, the client can wait in the car and be alerted to exam room availability via text. Some hospitals use restaurant-style silent pagers and provide clients with a comfortable outdoor waiting area to use in nice weather.

Another general component of Fear Free design is to separate species as much as feasible throughout the hospital, including in ward spaces and treatment areas. To prevent the inefficiency created by separating spaces, veterinarians using this approach can connect separated treatment rooms by shared spaces, such as doctors' stations, and can connect any spaces with interior glass windows to keep an open and connected feel for hospital staff and doctors.

FEAR FREE CLEANING AND HOUSEKEEPING

Dogs and cats use their sense of smell in a far more sophisticated way than we do as humans. They process many more odors and use olfactory clues to understand their surroundings. Therefore, it is important to consider the relationship between hospital housekeeping and the way a pet experiences the space.

Fear Free hospitals employ pheromone dispensers to mask odors and send natural, calming olfactory signals to pets. However, a well-managed hospital should also consider its cleaning products. The best cleaning products eliminate odors and sanitize spaces without leaving offensive odors of their own. Specific cleaning products are not mentioned in this chapter because cleaning products are always evolving, but be sure to use products that are made specifically for animal care and leave few odors and residues behind.

FEAR FREE DESIGN FOR DOGS

Most dogs communicate their stress through visible behaviors such as barking, panting, yawning, hypersalivating, whimpering, and shaking, as well as through invisible signs, such as those expressed via pheromones that warn other dogs of danger. Some dogs will shut down behaviorally and may appear to be calm and resting while in fact they are frozen with fear.

When designing veterinary spaces for dogs, the key is to minimize all types of fear reactions by preventing the stressors that cause dogs to behave in these ways. The best approach for achieving this is to provide choices—choices for the practice to examine, treat, and house the dog, and choices for the dog to control his position, his body, and some aspects of the hospital environment.

One simple method is to provide enough space within an exam room to examine dogs on the floor. This method is particularly helpful for large dogs. Again, this concept can be carried further into the hospital by providing floor space in treatment to perform procedures on the floor when appropriate.

Another way to prevent stress, and even aggressive behavior, in dogs is to prevent them from facing each other in ward spaces. This can be achieved by designing single-sided ward spaces or by staggering the traditional dog runs so that dogs do not have to face each other across the aisle.

FEAR FREE DESIGN FOR CATS

Cats and veterinary visits are synonymous with stress. Almost everything that can occur during a visit to the veterinary hospital is a known stress trigger for cats, including unfamiliar smells, unfamiliar human contact, and a lack of control over their environment.

Unlike stress in dogs, stress in cats tends to be more difficult to see. But as with dogs, with cats it is possible to minimize the factors that create stress and fear.

One way to do this is to create feline-only exam rooms. If possible, feline exam rooms should have views to the outside, both for more pleasant sights and to provide natural light. These rooms should also be free of stress-inducing dog smells. They can include a climbing structure to allow cats a choice of vantage points, as well as cat toys to give them the opportunity to relax through play and hiding.

Cats have a higher thermal neutral zone than dogs and humans—that is, a higher range of ambient temperatures to maintain optimal metabolic activity. Therefore, to help reduce stress in cats, ensure that ward spaces are not drafty or too cold. If possible, cat exam and ward spaces should have their own temperature controls to keep these areas warmer than the rest of the hospital, ideally 75 to 80 degrees.

Another way to reduce stress in cats—and in dogs as well—is to utilize a Fear Free color palette. When choosing colors for the walls and materials in the hospital, follow these principles:

- Avoid manmade materials that appear to fluoresce to dogs and cats, including some bright white plastics and some clear plastics. A Wood lamp can be used to determine whether the material will appear to fluoresce to animals.

- Choose colors in the visible spectrum that cats and dogs can see best: blues, greens, and purples.

The Fear Free color palette plays to our pets' visual range.

- Choose light colors that allow cats to leverage their superior night vision to comprehend their built environment in low-light situations.

FEAR FREE HOUSING

There are several critical concepts to know for housing animals in ward spaces. First is the continued separation of species. It is important that cats cannot hear, smell, or see dogs.

Another critical concept is providing views outside the wards. This can be either pleasant outdoor views or views to neutral indoor spaces where staff are performing routine tasks. These views should not include other animal ward spaces or stations where animals are being treated.

It is also very important provide animal caging of the right size. Both dogs and cats should be able to move freely, express normal behaviors, and assume normal postures within their enclosures. Feline housing must meet the following criteria:

- Cages are designed so that cats are not set at floor level.

- Cages are tall and wide enough to allow the cat to move without touching the sides of the enclosure.

- Cage units should be no more than two cages tall so that staff can easily see cats and remove them from cages without reaching over their heads.

Due to dogs' varying sizes, caging criteria for dogs is less defined. But dog runs in medical wards should be wide and shallow rather than deep and narrow. Wide, shallow runs encourage natural behaviors, provide dogs with more room to maneuver, and are better designed for the sizes and shapes of dogs. Individual cages should be tall enough to allow dogs room for normal posture. (See Chapter 38 for more information on animal housing.)

FEAR FREE LIGHTING AND SOUND ENGINEERING

The benefits of daylighting have been thoroughly studied in human healthcare and have been shown to reduce patient recovery time. As dogs and cats are psychologically similar to humans, daylighting provides the same healing benefits. Further studies have also shown that daylighting improves staff productivity.

In addition to locating windows in animal wards and exam rooms, utilize full spectrum LED lighting in animal-occupied areas of your hospital. Modern LED lighting produces superior spectral distribution and a higher quality of light for indoor environments. It is also advisable to use bulbs with a cooler color temperature (3,500 K or higher on the Kelvin scale). These bulbs are more like natural daylight than bulbs in the lower ranges.

Noise control has been a topic of concern in the animal care industry for a very long time. Traditionally, the approach has been to mitigate noise that has already occurred. The Fear Free approach considers prevention to be the first line of defense, including preventing barking; preventing noise outside the range of human hearing that can still be heard by animals, such as noise produced by mechanical equipment; and preventing unnecessary noises, including the sound of slamming cage doors and audible paging systems.

With as much noise as possible prevented, it becomes easier to mitigate the remaining noise through the more traditional strategies of reduction, isolation, dissipation, and masking.

When considering noise prevention and mitigation methods, it is always important to remember that dogs and cats not only hear sounds inaudible to humans but also hear them better. These factors make noise reduction a critical goal for designing healing spaces for animals.

FEAR FREE MECHANICAL ENGINEERING

It is a well-known fact that indoor air quality affects the wellbeing of people and animals. Veterinary hospitals are especially prone to poor indoor air quality due to odors, humidity, pet hair and dander, chemicals, and heavy cleaning. In order to provide the best in Fear Free care, it is necessary to ventilate a hospital with forethought and expertise.

Although it is not a requirement of Fear Free, consider designing the air system so that air from canine spaces is not recycled into feline spaces. Use pressure relationships to move air from fresher and cleaner low-odor spaces, such as exam room and lobby areas, to "dirtier" areas, such as laundry and bathing spaces. This will prevent offensive odors from permeating the hospital.

▼ ▼ ▼

THE BEST TIME to consider creating a Fear Free hospital building is in the early stages of designing a new facility. That said, there are many Fear Free concepts that can readily be incorporated into an existing facility that will provide patients with a better and more stress-free experience.

CHAPTER 11

FOUR FEATURES OF GOOD HOSPITAL DESIGN

Veterinary hospitals have evolved to become both more sophisticated and less "clinical." As this evolution continues, it is important to recognize some lasting concepts that have persisted. These are basic core concepts, and they should be incorporated into any hospital design.

In this chapter, we'll discuss four of these core concepts:

- Design for context.
- Functional procedural spaces.
- Sanitation.
- Noise mitigation.

DESIGN FOR CONTEXT

While every hospital needs to be useful and efficient, the best hospitals are inspired by their communities, their clients, and the physical environment. This is one of the best things about veterinary hospitals compared to other businesses—many veterinary hospitals are still tied strongly to their communities and to a sense of place. Thinking about the context of your building can give it character, make it stand out from your colleagues' practices, and make it uniquely yours. As you begin the design process, you may wish to consider the following:

- The type and style of local buildings.
- Building traditions in the community.
- A connection to the best parts of the building site.

Here are a few ideas from some successful hospitals:

- Locate your hospital in an area of town where it can become memorable: For example, if your building can't be at the street corner, can it be at the bend in the road, or in the brand-new shopping center? Consider how people will approach your hospital and how they will view it from the outside. These 30,000-foot views are extremely important to your project over time, as before long your community will know where you are and how to find you.

- Design around an idea: For example, one hospital designed the entire facility around a break room where the doctors' and staff

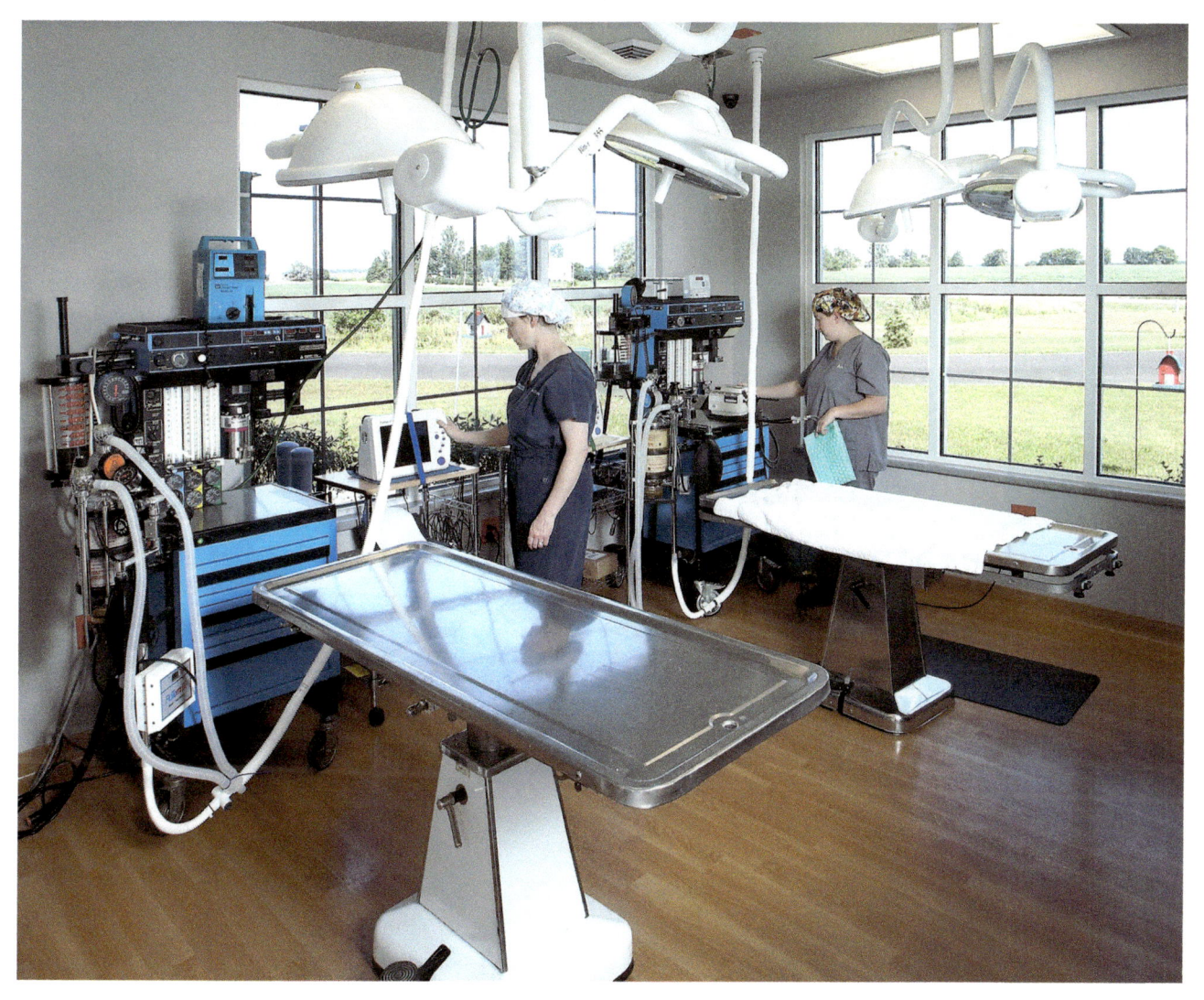

These large windows bring daylight and the out-of-doors into this surgery room, taking advantage of this hospital's rural setting. (Edmunds Studios, Inc. Courtesy of Veterinary Village, Lomira, Wisconsin.)

FOUR FEATURES OF GOOD HOSPITAL DESIGN

This hospital blends in with its landscape by utilizing wood-shingled siding and expansive windows. (Foto Imagery / Tim Murphy. Courtesy of Woodhaven Veterinary Clinic, Edmonds, Washington.)

members' children could gather and "hang out" after school. This design reinforced a life-work balance that was very important to the practice. Identify the life and work ideals that are most important to you and your business and communicate them to your architect so that he or she can prioritize design decisions in the same way that you do.

- Design around a site feature or an excellent view: If you have a natural feature to enjoy, be sure that the hospital takes advantage of this, in terms of both harmonizing with nature and inviting views into the building interior. This approach to design will make the place that you work every day that much more enjoyable.

- Use local materials and trades: In this way, you can take advantage of local craftsmanship and feel connected—and important—to your community.

FUNCTIONAL PROCEDURAL SPACES

Procedural spaces should be designed with attention to detail. These environments have a direct effect on the quality of your work and on your efficiency. Think of the evolution of kitchen design. Your home kitchen is an ergonomic environment that is designed to suit your needs, store your tools, and allow you to work quickly. Your procedure area is a similar type of space and should prioritize workflow, efficiency, and safety for staff and patients.

- Start with the layout of the space.
  - Identify work areas and circulation areas to optimize flow and minimize steps.
  - Understand how you will work at each station. Focus on the area at the end of the workstation where most people stand. Make sure it is not too close to other workstations or to circulation spaces.
  - Some good rules of thumb are that layout stations should be about 3 to 4 feet away from treatment tables if this space is not to be used for circulation, whereas the space at the sides and outboard end of the table, where people stand, should be 5 feet from the nearest obstruction.

- Consider details that make a difference.
  - Frame views into other spaces, such as adjacent workspaces and patient wards. This will promote easy communication, allow for easy monitoring of patients, and create an environment that feels open.
  - Design the ceiling as well as the floor. For example, consider exactly how lighting fixtures are placed relative to your veterinary work areas. Design places to hang all of your ceiling-mounted equipment so that nothing has to be supported from a flimsy ceiling tile.

- Coordinate the space effectively with equipment.
  - Understand where equipment is placed and why.
  - Consider clearances, power, and plumbing requirements. Power outlets should be located to prevent the need for any extension cords. Simply designing the clearance for each piece of equipment can be a lengthy exercise but is very worthwhile.

- Design equipment to be within reach and safely out of the traffic flow. Don't cover every inch of the wall with counters: provide some nooks for stashing carts and equipment so the main floor space can remain clear. Another specific example here is the dental unit—with a little careful planning, a slightly higher counter can be designed so that the unit can be parked underneath.

The nicest treatment areas and procedural spaces are the ones that are efficient without feeling cluttered. One trick of the trade is to keep as many items as possible off the floor. Lighting, power, oxygen, scavenger, and IV tracks can be placed overhead at treatment tables to make for a cleaner floor area.

Storage cubbies can be placed over animal caging to provide convenient spaces for plugging in pumps and storing equipment, which also helps to keep the floor clear. It's important to include the types of storage that you and your

Exam lights and IV tracks are mounted above each treatment table. (Foto Imagery / Tim Murphy. Courtesy of VCA West Los Angeles Animal Hospital, Los Angeles, California, [VCA, Inc.].)

staff members are most likely to use, such as drawers and upper cabinets, and exclude lower base cabinets that require staff to bend over in order to remove or replace supplies.

SANITATION

Designing easy-to-sanitize spaces is an important part of creating a safe and healthy veterinary medical setting. Although it is exciting to see a trend toward less clinical-looking veterinary environments, do not forget that the spaces must always be durable and easy to clean and sanitize. What follows are some general principles:

- Understand your biological risk management protocols (see Chapter 12 for more on this subject).

- Pay special attention to areas that need to be sanitary, such as the surgery zone. The most critical area is the transition between the floor and the walls.

- Align the cleaning protocols with the finishes. This means being sure that finishes can hold up to the type of cleaning they will receive.

- Ensure that all surfaces can be sanitized. There are a few exceptions to this rule. For example, chairs in the waiting area will be more comfortable if they are fabric covered, but even in these cases it's a good idea to ensure that the fabric can be heavily cleaned if needed. Another example is carpet used in a conference space. Just to ensure the carpet can be cleaned thoroughly on a regular basis, use a vinyl-backed carpet, even if animals will not be in the space.

NOISE MITIGATION

A quiet hospital is a good place to work. It is good for patients, and it is good for clients. Although the details of noise control are covered in more detail in Chapter 46, it is critical to remember to design the hospital with noise control in mind from day one. Here are some important guidelines:

- Reduce stress for animals so they're less likely to vocalize.

- Always provide two doors between dog wards and client spaces. Although you don't want noise leaking into treatment, it is even more critical that it doesn't leak into exam rooms, the lobby, and other public spaces. Many modern hospitals, in an attempt to become more open, forget about this double layer of defense and end up with a louder space than they would prefer.

- For ease of cleaning and maintenance, most surfaces in hospitals are hard and shiny. These surfaces are also the ones that create the most noise, and there is little that can be done to change that. Therefore, ceilings are the primary surface for noise control.

- Reduce unnecessary noise. Today there is the option of using quiet casters for equipment, quiet latches on caging, and nonaudible paging systems. The more noise that can be removed from the hospital setting, the more pleasant it will be for everyone.

▼ ▼ ▼

DESIGNING A HOSPITAL is a process that is loaded with details and decision-making points. It can be easy to lose sight of the basic requirements that make hospitals successful and long lasting, as well as functional and comfortable places to work. Keep these basics in mind and refer to them often throughout your design process.

CHAPTER 12

BIOLOGICAL RISK MANAGEMENT

Lots of humans, lots of animals, and lots of veterinary medicine add up to the necessity for lots of cleaning. But even with frequent cleaning, it is impossible to keep a veterinary hospital truly clean unless it is designed with biological risk management in mind.

The first step in designing a veterinary hospital to minimize biological risk is to understand the primary modes of disease transmission in veterinary facilities. They are, in decreasing order of importance, as follows:

- Fomite transmission.
- Fecal/oral transmission.
- Direct contact.
- Aerosol transmission.

FOMITE TRANSMISSION

Despite the fact that many designers focus on aerosol transmission, the primary cause of disease transmission in veterinary hospitals is fomites—contaminated inanimate objects or materials, including food, drinks, instruments, and clothing. Methods to help prevent fomite transmission include the following:

- Develop a protocol for how staff handles animals and cleans caging.

- Provide convenient handwashing sinks, glove dispensers, and hand sanitizer stations. Use sanitizers that are specifically developed for use in animal care facilities, and remember that hand sanitizers do not kill nonenveloped viruses.

- Provide convenient ways to sterilize equipment, including sinks, sterilizing equipment, laundry machines, and dishwashers.

- Disallow the use of reusable mops and design your janitorial area to utilize today's cleaning systems.

- Provide gowning and decontamination areas for use when handling contagious animals.

- Install animal housing designed to prevent unnecessary animal handling.

FECAL/ORAL TRANSMISSION

There are three main areas to focus on in the prevention of fecal/oral transmission: facility layout, use of appropriate materials, and proper use of water and disinfectants.

Facility Layout

The key to proper facility design is to ensure the isolation of contagious disease. Here are examples of methods for achieving that goal:

- Provide outside access for isolation rooms.

- Treat contagious animals only in isolation rooms.

- Provide a prep area for gowning and decontamination within the isolation rooms or in a vestibule outside of them.

- Locate janitorial areas near the areas they are meant to serve.

- Design wards and cleaning protocols within rooms to clean the dirtiest areas first, followed by cleaner areas. For example, remove solid waste from dog runs, hose down runs, then clean aisleways in front of runs.

- Design the hospital and overall cleaning protocols to clean from rooms that are lowest risk to rooms that are highest risk. For example, healthy wards should be cleaned before isolation wards.

- Lay out laundry, utility, and pack/prep spaces to prevent contamination of clean items.

Use of Appropriate Materials

Before selecting the materials for your hospital, consider the methods you plan to use to clean the building. Materials should always be able to withstand your chosen cleaning method. Also remember that biofilms develop over time regardless of your daily cleaning methods and will require abrasive action to remove.

For hose-down rooms, including dog wards, your finishes will need to be extremely durable and should include seamless flooring with an integral base, waterproof wall materials, rot- and mold-resistant backing materials, galvanized doors and frames, appropriate ceiling materials—including washable, sag-resistant tiles and vapor-tight fixtures—and high-performance coatings for exposed metals.

Proper Use of Water and Disinfectants

Be careful about your use of water. Introducing water into spaces that are not designed for water cleaning can damage finishes and will only encourage the growth of contaminants and biofilms on surfaces. The best way to ensure the long-term life of your finishes is to accomplish proper cleaning and disinfection without hosing.

There are benefits and risks to cleaning with pressure systems. Benefits include reducing water usage and properly dispensing chemicals, but if you choose to utilize a pressure system in your hospital, follow these guidelines:

- Select a medium-pressure system.

- Select wall and floor finishes designed to withstand water at high pressure.

- Remove solids before spraying to minimize the risk of aerosolization of contaminants.

- Choose a pressure cleaning system that has a proven history of effectiveness in animal care facilities.

- Engage the manufacturer early in the design process to ensure that the system is designed correctly.

It has been proven that it is impossible to disinfect and degrease using hot water unless the water is at least 180°F. Water this hot is unsafe to use. While some disinfectants are more effective when used with warm water, there are equally effective protocols designed for cool-water cleaning. It is also important to ensure that the chemicals you are using are effective for the pathogens you are trying to eliminate. Always dilute chemicals according to the manufacturers' recommendations and rinse them thoroughly to prevent unnecessary corrosion of the materials' surfaces.

DIRECT CONTACT

In veterinary practices, a special area of concern with transmission of disease through direct contact is animal-to-animal contact. Fortunately, this is one transmission mode that is easy to prevent with good design in animal circulation and ward spaces.

Use glass-fronted runs to prevent nose-to-nose contact between dogs in wards. Design circulation areas to be wide enough to prevent accidental contact between animals, and keep infectious animals completely out of the traffic flow of other animals.

AEROSOL TRANSMISSION

While aerosol transmission comes in fourth for biological contamination, it is still very important to consider when designing a hospital. Proper HVAC design will be covered at length in Chapter 43, but here are some general concepts to bear in mind:

- Dogs are much more capable of spreading disease through the air than cats. Do not place dog runs across from each other in wards if infectious disease is a risk factor.

- Supply air in wards over the aisles and exhaust air over the runs.

Well-ventilated cages and runs deter the spread of disease and greatly improve the quality of animal environments.

- Remember to design your HVAC system to prevent contaminated air from returning to the supply air stream.

- Ventilate air through animal environments when possible to reduce the spread of disease, reduce the size of air handling requirements, and deliver fresh air directly to your patients.

- Reducing stress is the key to lowering the risk of cats in your care contracting upper respiratory disease. Always house cats in quiet environments away from dogs. For cats that you will be housing for a length of time, provide at least 9.5 square feet of area per cat, and remember to enrich the enclosures with towels, blankets, beds, and toys.

THE FUNDAMENTALS

Floor Design and Drains

Proper cleaning of any facility begins with the floor. In hose-down areas, the floor slab must be thoughtfully designed.

- Slope floor drains at a minimum of 0.25 inches per foot in runs and a maximum of 0.25 inches per foot in walking areas.

- Maintain a minimum thickness in the slab as required by your structural engineer. This may mean making slabs thicker in areas with drains.

Individual floor drains at the back of dog runs are generally preferable over trench drains. Trench drains tend to be more difficult to clean

BIOLOGICAL RISK MANAGEMENT

and are more likely to spread contaminants between runs. They also require more water at the top end of the drain to create enough volume to flush properly.

Most cat wards do not have floor drains. In the event that you require one, install a hinged drain to prevent litter from entering the line and clogging the drain.

Handling Solids

Removing solid waste prior to cleaning runs is essential to biological risk management for the following reasons:

- Leaving solids in runs sabotages the effectiveness of disinfectant chemicals.

- Aerosolized solids lead to environmental contamination.

- Drains designed to accept solids can easily trap other items, such as blankets and toys, leading to clogs.

One of the best methods for dealing with solid waste is to design a "poop closet" into your facility. This special janitor's closet houses a large flushing rim or clinical sink, an exhaust vent for odor control, and a hose and floor drain for cleanup.

Hose Bibs and Reels

One of the easiest ways to recontaminate cleaned surfaces is to drag a hose around on the floor. The type of hose system you choose depends on the size of the room you are cleaning with this method. For a large dog ward, choose a ceiling-mounted hose reel with a clutch to control the speed of the hose return in order to avoid damage to adjacent ceilings and walls. This system will keep the hose off the floor. For a medium-size hose-down room, use a small, manual-wind hose reel mounted on the wall, and for a small hose-down room, opt for a hose bib with the hose mounted on a bracket on the wall.

If you need to hose down cages in your hospital, the cages should be constructed of stainless steel. They should also be designed to be pulled out from the wall to prevent water from getting into spaces that cannot be properly cleaned or dried.

Sinks

Heavy-duty, stainless steel sinks in varying depths and sizes are the best choice for veterinary hospitals. Use small bar sinks in your exam rooms. If it complies with your practice philosophy, one sink located in the hallway near a group of exam rooms may be just as practical.

In laboratories and treatment areas, use shallow sinks that comply with Americans with Disabilities Act (ADA) guidelines. Lab sinks will often be equipped with a long apron to provide a surface on which to stain slides and handle fecal samples.

In spaces like pack/prep, where you will be disinfecting instruments, install deep sinks with integral drain boards.

Cleaning Dry Areas

It is important to install cleanable materials even in the dry areas of your facility. Seamless floor materials, such as sheet vinyl or epoxy/resin with an integral cove base, are good examples. The proper placement of janitorial closets also must be considered, along with the need to provide mop service basins in each closet for filling cleaning buckets. Be sure to make it as easy as possible to clean all hospital surfaces, including walls, high ledges, and deep corners. In addition, it is important to provide enough storage space throughout the hospital to prevent clutter.

▼ ▼ ▼

REMEMBER TO DISCUSS your biological risk management goals and protocols with your design team during your schematic design interview. Knowing what your goals are early in the process will enable your team to properly design the building spaces, the HVAC and other systems, and the materials and finishes in alignment with your needs.

CHAPTER 13

AAHA ACCREDITATION STANDARDS

If your goal is to become an AAHA-accredited practice, and you are thinking about renovating or building a new hospital, there are a variety of standards that apply directly to how your building should be designed and how it should function once it's operational. With forethought and a sound design, your facility can help you achieve accreditation.

The AAHA accreditation standards are a flexible, point-based system giving practices the opportunity to choose the standards that work for them. It should be noted that there are some mandatory items denoted with an MA classification number.

AAHA has taken the main document *AAHA Standards of Accreditation* and highlighted the items that relate to hospital design in a subdocument titled "Structural and Interior Design of the Building." The criteria included in this subdocument are divided into 12 categories ranging from Anesthesia Standards to Surgery Standards. The remainder of this chapter provides an overview of some of the key design-related items as of 2016.

MEETING THE STANDARDS THROUGH PROPER PROGRAMMING

Many of the standards can be achieved by including the correct rooms for the correct functions within your facility. Some of these spaces include exam rooms, treatment areas for anesthesia induction, isolation rooms, radiology suites, dental procedure areas, and surgical suites. Some of the specifics are listed here:

Anesthesia Standards

- AN01—The practice has a designated area for induction of general anesthesia (AAHA, 2).

- AN02—A designated recovery area outside of the surgical suite is utilized (AAHA, 2).

  The recovery area can double up for other animal housing needs, but it should be close to the surgery area and must provide adequate means for caring for patients during extubation.

Contagious Disease Standards

- CD08—The practice utilizes a single-purpose isolation room where activities are restricted to providing care to contagious patients (AAHA, 8).

  Locating this room as best you can so that key medical staff can keep a watchful eye on patients is essential. Generally, placing it directly adjacent to the main treatment area or ICU is optimal. Where this proximity is not possible, a video monitor with an alarm is viable. Although it's not part of the AAHA standards, outside access for admittance and discharge of patients can help minimize contamination risks. Planning where equipment and materials will be stored within the room will also assist you in meeting the recommended standards of care.

- Proper flooring that is easy to clean, floor drains, hose bibs, sanitary wall finishes, dedicated exam tables, and proper lighting will assist you in meeting the parameters in CD11-17. This room should have negative air pressure in relationship to the surrounding spaces (CD16) and should not recirculate air back into any other space (CD17) (AAHA, 5).

Surgery Standards

- MA37 and 38 state that surgical suites must be designed to be closed, that they must be single-purpose rooms, and that they must minimize the potential for contamination (AAHA, 14). (Again, "MA" means "mandatory.")

  This means that surgery rooms cannot be utilized for any other purpose. For example, you are not permitted to induce the patient in the room, nor are you allowed to scrub inside the surgical suite. Surgical suites are to serve one purpose only: surgery.

  Storage within surgical suites should be limited to closed, glass-fronted upper cabinetry. In fact, storing surgical packs in this type of cabinetry can help preserve their sterility.

  Impervious, stain-resistant countertops may also be installed in surgical suites. However, lower cabinets should not be included in any surgery design as they impede proper cleaning and disinfecting protocols.

  Other design elements that minimize the potential for contamination and the spread of disease are highlighted throughout the *AAHA Standards* and are meant to be considered in every space within a hospital.

- The Surgery Standard (Patient and Sterile Field Preparation) SX07a states that surgical preparation rooms must be separate

A properly equipped isolation room with tiled floor and walls for ease of cleaning. (Foto Imagery / Tim Murphy. Courtesy of VCA West Los Angeles Animal Hospital, Los Angeles, California [VCA, Inc.].)

from the surgical suite but may serve additional purposes if proper maintenance and cleaning protocols are utilized to safeguard against contamination. This means that you can use your treatment room as a surgery prep area, but you must maintain it properly (AAHA, 14).

MEETING THE STANDARDS THROUGH EQUIPMENT PLANNING

Many of the standards relating to building design involve equipment coordination and planning. Topics can range from power and lighting needs to radiation shielding. Here are a few standouts of which you should be aware.

Laboratory Standards

- Standards for laboratory spaces include adequate electrical circuits and outlets (LA13g) and permanent space for standard equipment as indicated by manufacturers' recommendations (LA13d) (AAHA, 40).

Your architect and electrical engineer will need to coordinate the locations of equipment and outlets to ensure these standards are met. It may also be necessary to change the height of upper cabinetry or the depth of countertops in order to accommodate specific equipment.

If space is an issue in the lab, you can install open, adjustable shelving on the walls with high electrical outlets to free up counter space.

Diagnostic Imaging
- MA14—Quality diagnostic images are generated on the premises (AAHA, 36).

    This requirement can be achieved with a traditional X-ray system utilizing a properly ventilated and equipped darkroom or through the use of a computed radiography or a digital radiography system.

Radiation Safety
- DG17—The protective barrier effect of the walls and doors is such that occupants of adjacent areas do not receive radiation above recommended levels (AAHA, 37).

    In order to properly carry out this recommendation and ensure the health and welfare of your staff and clients, you will need to engage a radiation shielding physicist who specializes in providing shielding reports for radiology rooms. A physicist can also complete the report for your CT, fluoroscopy, MRI, and I-131 rooms. A physicist's report is required in many jurisdictions, and it is valuable to engage a physicist during the design development phase of the project so your architect can incorporate the requirements into the design.

Equipment
- DG55—Adequate working space around three sides of the X-ray table is provided (AAHA, 38).

    Meeting standards such as this is one of the reasons it is important to decide on your large pieces of equipment early on in the design process. Your architect will need to know the dimensions of the table to ensure the room is sized correctly.

- DG 56/57—To gain these credits, two X-ray illuminators or high-resolution viewing stations are also required to be in the hospital, with one dedicated to surgery (AAHA, 38).

    A good and convenient location for the second viewing station, or computer station with a larger monitor, would be in a hallway or work area adjacent to the exam rooms.

Surgery Standards
Patient and Sterile Field Preparation
- SX09—Equipment and supplies in the surgical preparation room/area include, among other items, the following:
    > SX09f—A vacuum to remove loose hair and debris.
    > SX09g—A wet table (AAHA, 15).

    Often the two items above are not considered during the design process. The vacuum could be a simple, stand-alone, self-contained unit that fits neatly in a base cabinet in the surgical induction area. The wet table may get lost in the shuffle when discussing ease of traffic flow into the surgical suites, with a gurney station getting the spotlight. Wet tables are useful for cleaning animals prior to surgical procedures and should be in close proximity to the surgery area as per MA37.1 (AAHA, 14).

Surgical Suites
- SX37—Surgical suites should have the following:
    > SX37d—Viewing windows, reducing the need to open the door (AAHA, 16).

A simple window in the wall between the surgery room and adjacent surgical prep area, or a window between two adjacent surgical suites, can increase the efficiency of the staff by allowing for visual communication.

> SX37e.1—A ventilation system that is specially filtered to minimize aerosolized microorganisms (AAHA, 16).
> SX37f—A laminar (nonturbulent) flow ventilation system (AAHA, 16).
> SX37g—Positive-pressure airflow (AAHA, 16).

Depending upon the type of surgical procedures being performed and the overall standard of care, the mechanical system for the surgery area can be critical to positive patient outcomes. Positive pressure and strategic locations for air supply are a starting point, while laminar flow, high-efficiency particulate air (HEPA) filtration, and other advanced systems, such as ultraviolet germicidal irradiation, should be considered for more specialized surgical rooms.

CONSIDERING THE PATIENT FIRST

Patient Care
General
- PC13—The facility design and movement of clients and patients through the practice provides for appropriate separation of animals. This may include considerations such as allowing for species segregation within lobby areas (AAHA, 9). PC81 spells out separation of species whenever possible in patient housing as well (AAHA, 13).

As discussed in previous chapters, separation of species can be a critical element in preventing unnecessary stress.

- PC14—The practice minimizes the potential for dangerous interactions between pets and clients (AAHA, 9).

As a minimum standard, 5 feet should be used for the width of any area where two canines on leashes with their owners will pass by each other. This minimum distance should be maintained not only in the main medical corridors but also in the hallways directly outside the exam rooms where a close encounter between two unfamiliar animals may suddenly occur.

Surgery Standards
To gain a few more points toward accreditation, you can meet the requirement for SX08 by providing a means to suspend animal extremities to facilitate surgical preparation (AAHA, 15). The typical way to do this is by providing a ceiling-mounted track that can be used for suspension of fluids or, in this case, limbs. You can also attach a piece of angle iron to the ceiling and drill holes in it every few inches and suspend a metal rod. The patient's limb can then be suspended from this support.

BUILDING CODES COVER IT, TOO

Building codes automatically cover some of the standards on the AAHA list. Due to life safety concerns related to emergency lighting and standards for mechanical systems, the following AAHA standards should be easily addressed.

Housekeeping and Maintenance

- HM27—Exterior lighting provides adequate illumination for the safety of clients and practice team members (AAHA, 35).

- HM12—Surgical laundry is cleaned separately from regular laundry (AAHA, 34).

Safety Standards

General

- SA11—Adequate emergency lighting exists. Battery-operated lights or alternate power sources are maintained, tested, and inspected on a monthly basis (AAHA, 26).

Fire Safety

- SA27—An appropriate number and type of fire extinguishers are readily available and properly maintained (AAHA, 27).

▼ ▼ ▼

A WELL-PLANNED BUILDING can help you reach your goal of achieving AAHA accreditation. If you start with a well-defined program, make decisions early about the equipment that will be used in the hospital, and concentrate on creating a healthy environment for both your staff and the animals in your care, you can earn a significant number of credits.

CHAPTER 14

BRANDING AND CURB APPEAL

First impressions do count. Your hospital building, landscaping, and signage send a message to your community about the type of medical care and service you and your hospital provide. This first impression can dramatically shape clients' perceptions of your practice.

This general rule can work to your advantage. It means that you can use the design of your hospital's exterior, interior, landscaping, and signage to set the tone for how you want your practice to be viewed by your community and your potential clients.

DEFINE YOUR MESSAGE

Branding is the first step in relaying who you are to your community. This often involves creating a logo, a color scheme, and possibly a tag line or a mission statement as well. Regardless of what form your branding takes, the most important thing is to keep your materials and your message thoughtful, professional, and consistent.

In the veterinary world, logos are usually designed around some variation on the theme of companion animals. On the one hand, this often works well, as it can immediately communicate your purpose. On the other hand, it can be difficult to come up with a design that looks unique. You can differentiate your practice from other veterinarians more thoroughly through your color scheme and your tag line or mission statement. Your logo shows people what you are; your tag line can tell them who you are.

Melrose Animal Clinic before and after they rebranded and completed a renovation of their hospital. The bright, professional appearance reflects the practice's philosophy of care. (Foto Imagery / Tim Murphy. Courtesy of Melrose Animal Clinic, Melrose, Massachusetts.)

BRANDING AND CURB APPEAL

Once you have developed your brand, you can carry it through into the design of your hospital and the ground on which it sits. The first step in this process is often to develop a site plan for your property, which will define the orientation of your building and your parking lot and where they sit on your site. This is the time to define the message you wish to send through your building's physical presence.

If you are building a general practice in a small or historic setting, for example, you may wish to design your facility to take advantage of the aesthetics of the community to convey a homelike character and comfortable atmosphere. If you are building a specialty/referral practice, on the other hand, you may prefer to design your building with a more modern look to indicate that your practice provides state-of-the-art care with the most modern technology.

PRACTICAL CONSIDERATIONS

Some practical things to consider as you begin to plan the design of your site include the following:

- Develop your floor plan to allow for at least two exterior doors, one for your clients and one for staff and deliveries. This second door should be out of view for your clients. You should also ensure that your trash receptacle is screened from your clients' view.

- Design your building to make a statement and create features to enable you to place signage in a prominent location.

- Design your parking lot to allow for flow-through circulation, if possible, and consider the types of vehicles your clients generally use when deciding upon the sizes of parking spaces and drive aisles.

- Remember to locate drainage features, such as stormwater detention areas, downhill from your building, as their location may restrict where you can place buildings and parking on the site. Consider incorporating your drainage areas into your overall design scheme by turning them into green space and minimizing hardscape areas.

CONSISTENCY IS KEY

Once you've determined the basics, be creative with the details. The one rule is to be consistent from the curb to the front door.

Start with your signage. Make sure the size of your sign is appropriate for your site. Can it easily be read from the road by the occupants of passing cars? The image on your sign is important as well. Does it match your branding? Does it convey why your practice is special? Finally, bring your building to the curb by integrating some aspect of the building's design or its materials into the design of the sign.

Most jurisdictions require a separate sign permit. Your signage company will assist you with navigating the local codes and submitting the necessary drawings for permit.

Continue to communicate your desired image with your landscaping. Develop an approach that complements your location in the community and the personality of your practice. If you are concerned with conservation, for example, a xeriscaped garden can reflect this. A formal garden would convey a more traditional approach. If your practice includes

These sculptures add a playful element to this hospital's main entrance area. (Foto Imagery / Tim Murphy. Courtesy of VCA PetCare Veterinary Hospital, Santa Rosa, California [VCA, Inc.].)

alternative medicine, perhaps an oriental garden is right for you. If you are looking to try something more whimsical, a topiary garden might be just the thing.

Even the simplest landscaping can be enhanced with the inclusion of features and accents. Something as small as a fountain or a sculpture can make a dramatic statement.

Finally, consider your exterior architecture. People often choose to support businesses that are successful and professional because they want the best for themselves and their pets. A veterinary hospital that gives the appearance of professionalism and success from the street is more likely to attract clientele from this positive first impression.

What you place front and center on your building is a direct reflection of what you believe to be important. The owners of the specialty hospital in the image on the next page chose to place their linear accelerator room on the front of the building, clad in reflective metal. What better way to illustrate the high-tech approach of this practice?

The high-tech look of Upstate Veterinary Specialists and Emergency Clinic. (David Dietrich Photography. Courtesy of Upstate Veterinary Specialists and Emergency Clinic, Greenville, South Carolina.)

BRINGING YOUR BRANDING INSIDE

While the first impressions created by your property and the exterior of your building are very important, so is maintaining the consistency of your brand. If you designed the exterior of your building to suit the character of your neighborhood, or designed it to be sleek and modern, how do you carry that into your lobby and beyond? One option is to bring some of the materials and design aesthetics you used on your building's exterior into the interior. Large, glass exterior windows, for example, can be brought into the interior and used for exam rooms or treatment areas. Wood cladding on the building can be brought inside as trim or as an accent wall feature.

Another way to infuse your branding into your building is to add accent walls in your color scheme with paint or other materials. A design idea that has gained popularity recently is to create a logo wall. This can be as simple as mounting a version of your logo to a wall in your lobby or as dramatic as mounting the logo to a wall that has been surfaced with stone or tile.

REMEMBER YOUR PATIENTS

Whatever your choices may be, in the end your site design must support animal health and welfare. As you consider design and branding issues, don't overlook the following:

This tiled accent wall located behind the reception desk at the Adobe Animal Hospital incorporates stainless steel for the hospital's logo. (Posh Pooch Portraits. Courtesy of Adobe Animal Hospital, Los Altos, California.)

- Remember to select plants that are animal friendly and nonpoisonous. Plants with thorns should only be placed away from walkways and places where clients might walk their dogs. Only hardy and acid-tolerant plants should be placed where they are likely to be urinated on.

- Ensure that your grounds are secure from feline and canine escape artists. Provide security at outdoor exercise areas. If possible, provide two security enclosures between dog play yards and roads. Be certain any catios or cat porches are escape-proof as well.

- When choosing materials, remember to avoid things that can injure animals, such as metal landscape edging and large, jagged rocks.

- Include designated elimination areas that are easy to maintain, and have waste disposal bags and cans readily available.

▼ ▼ ▼

THE DESIGN OF your building begins the day you select your site. Use the design of the property as an opportunity to make the best possible first impression. It should reflect who you are and the type of medicine you practice.

BRANDING AND CURB APPEAL

CHAPTER 15

TRANSPARENCY IN THE HOSPITAL

A brief online search of the term "transparency in business" yields articles from industry leadership sources such as Forbes.com representing a wealth of opinions, case studies, and data. The consensus is that transparency is not only a good idea but also essential in today's world for a healthy business and productive employees. The influence of Generation Y—the generation of people born between the years 1981 and 2000—has a lot to do with why transparency is now recognized as a vital ingredient for business. These people are highly educated and have had access to limitless information. Thus, they expect transparency and open information in the workplace about the goals, processes, and infrastructure of their employer.

Transparency is especially important in a healthcare environment—including veterinary medicine. It must extend to clients: to instill trust, practices must allow clients to participate in the care of their furry family members. This can be as simple as engaging clients in the overall direction of their pets' healthcare, or it can be as complex as involving the client in the nitty gritty of what happens "behind closed doors" at the hospital.

Transparency is both a metaphor and a physical reality. Generally, a practice must *want* to feel open in order to create a physical space that is transparent. Physically transparent spaces allow for a better view of what is happening, better connection, better understanding, and better trust building. For example, one large veterinary practice reported that the hospital reduced—and practically eliminated—incidents of clients complaining about their bills for emergency procedures when policies were changed and clients were invited in to view these procedures. Clients could see what efforts were taken, could quickly participate in decision making, and reported that they appreciated the increased level of care. This is an extreme example, but it is indicative of the type of approach that can build mutual trust and understanding within a hospital setting.

Once you have decided to build a building incorporating a transparent approach, what does this mean for your hospital design? There are still some important considerations about privacy, safety, and basic decorum, but in general, veterinary doctors are quite free to dismiss the barrier between themselves and their clients. In fact, this has always been the norm in equine medical practices, where clients have typically been able to stay and watch procedures.

RECEPTION AND WAITING

How does transparency relate to improving customer service? That depends on how willing you are to allow your clients into the center of the action.

Many practices have already reduced the size of the front desk and turned the receptionist into a greeter. Why not take the next step by decentralizing the desk entirely? This concept has already been incorporated into some animal shelters, such as Peninsula Humane Society in San Francisco. The shelter has an open reception area where adoption counselors equipped with iPads meet potential adopters in several comfortable seating areas. This is the ultimate in transparency, as it removes all disconnecting infrastructure (see Chapter 26 for more information about reception area trends).

EXPANDING YOUR CLIENTS' VIEW

It seems straightforward to create open and transparent client areas. But what about the barrier between the client areas of your hospital and the medical spaces? Does it really need to be there, or can it be perforated? In equine medicine, as mentioned above, practitioners are accustomed to doing everything in front of their clients, including exams, procedures, specialty imaging, and even surgery. While this may not work in a small animal practice, there are many ways you can surprise your clients by welcoming them to participate.

One possibility is to perform specialized wellness procedures such as acupuncture in the room with the client. Clients do not have to help or assist, for their safety, but being present can be gratifying for them and can have a positive influence on the behavior of their pets. These benefits can last far longer than the procedure itself, both for the pet owner and for your practice. It's easier to build a following of loyal customers if they understand what you do and feel welcomed to be a part of it.

Another approach is to open up the exam room itself. In the example at the top of the next page, waterfall glass is used on the front of the exam room to partially obstruct the view and protect privacy while still allowing the space to feel open and transparent.

Some hospitals have a place where a client can visit with a critically ill pet. This isn't an easy thing to do, as it involves having your clients in the middle of things, but it can be

(Foto Imagery / Tim Murphy. Courtesy of Upstate Veterinary Specialists and Emergency Clinic, Asheville, North Carolina.)

worthwhile. Many clients will appreciate the opportunity to be with their sick pets.

VIEWS TO IMAGING AND SPECIALTY SERVICES

For hospitals that have expensive equipment such as CT, MRI, linear accelerator, or rehabilitation equipment, there is no reason why these have to be hidden in the rear of the hospital. It is common, for example, for hospitals offering rehabilitation services to place these areas up front. This gives clients convenient access to these ancillary services.

CONNECTION ACROSS THE MEDICAL WORKSPACE

Medical workspaces are a great place for open/transparent design approaches, not so much for the client but for the efficiency and connection of the staff. Glass-windowed "fish bowls" are a great place for doctors and techs to work while keeping an eye on the medical area.

Many practices find great success in placing glass between treatment and ICU, between surgery and induction, and between offices and treatment areas. Openness can and has in many case studies been shown to improve communication, to allow patients to be monitored more effectively, and to create a feeling of teamwork and collaboration.

OFFICE AREAS

Transparency is also a great metaphor for your office areas. Gone are the days when doctors holed up in isolated offices. While a moment of privacy is still required in anyone's productive workday, new offices are more visually connected and more flexible than offices in the past. For associates, technicians, and staff, open work areas may also be sufficient, provided that there is some acoustical control in the space.

▼ ▼ ▼

IN DESIGNING A transparent hospital, it is more about people than buildings. Think about what you can do to engage your clients and your staff and build a more trusting, open, and transparent business, along with a space to match.

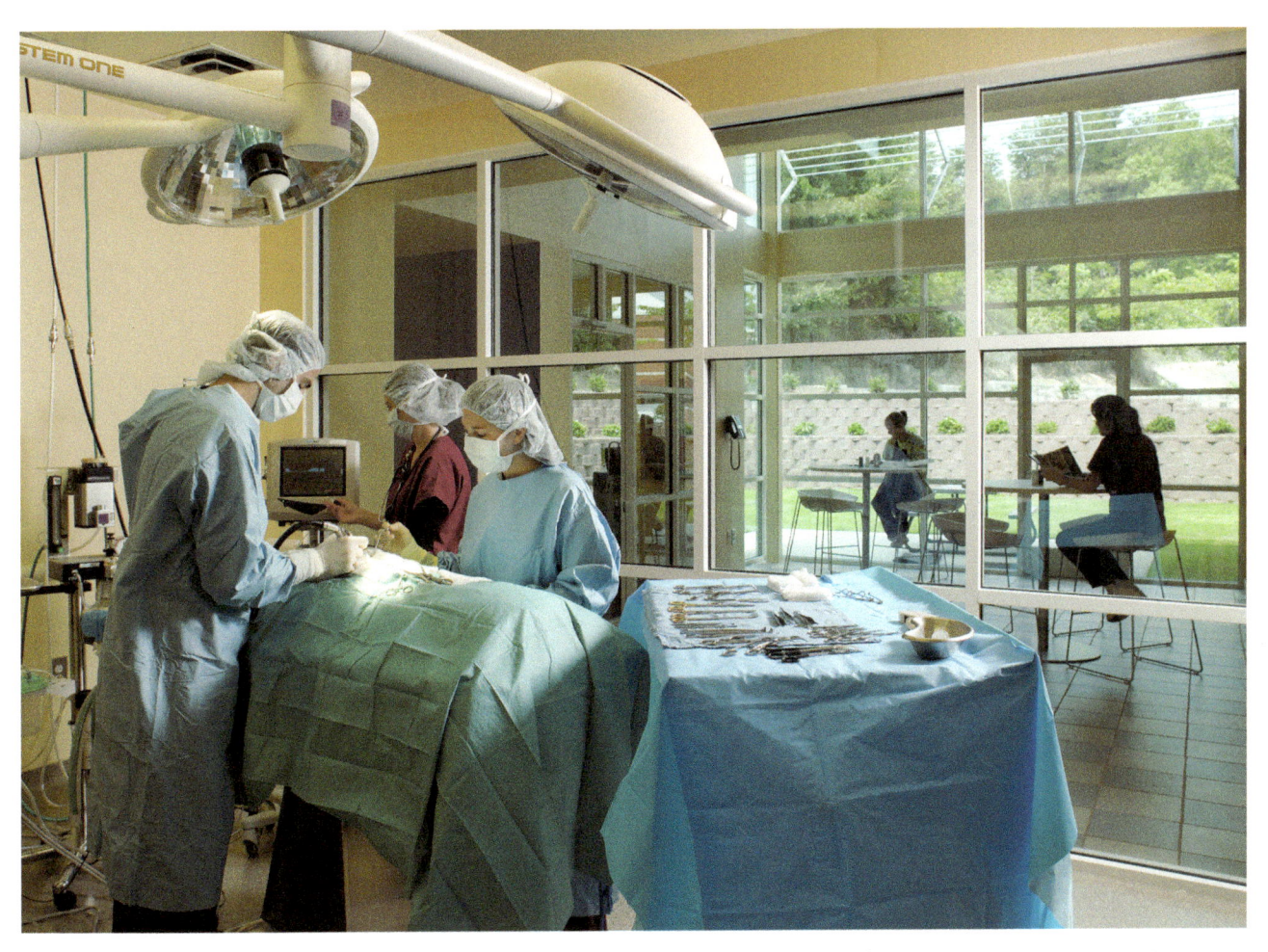

This surgery suite has a visual connection to the outdoors through the staff break room. (David Dietrich Photography. Courtesy of Upstate Veterinary Specialists and Emergency Clinic, Greenville, South Carolina.)

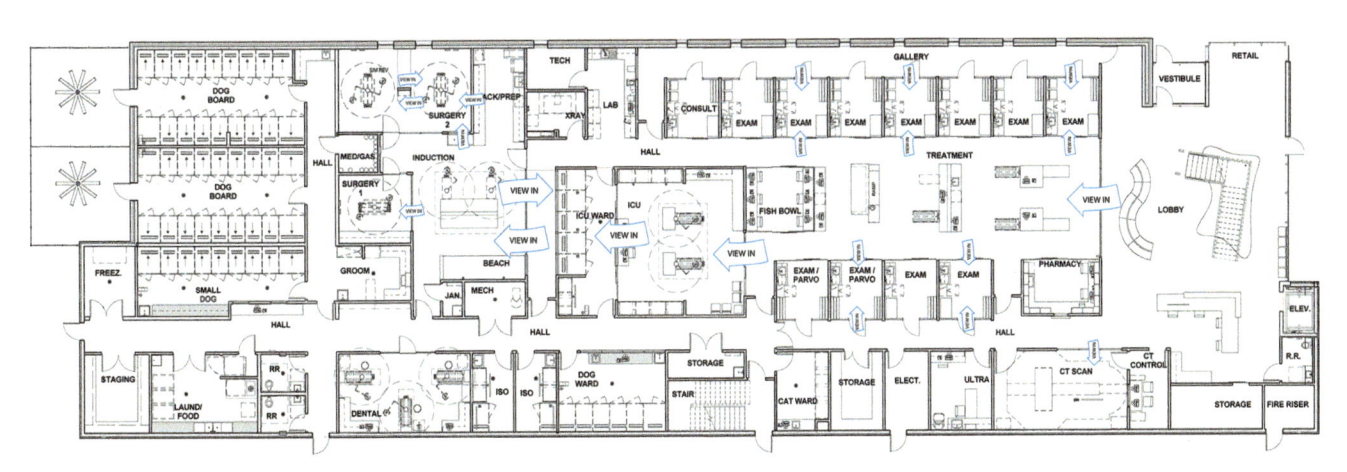

A floor plan for a transparent hospital with views directly from the lobby to treatment, as well as views into the ICU and surgery core. From the front lobby, clients can view the medical spaces, creating a one-of-a-kind accessible experience. (Courtesy of the PARC—People, Animals, Revolutionary Care, Fort Worth, Texas.)

TRANSPARENCY IN THE HOSPITAL

CHAPTER 16

GENERATIONAL DYNAMICS IN THE WORKPLACE

You can create powerful, effective workplace relationships by treating your colleagues and your clients the way they want to be treated.

So, how can this be accomplished? The simple answer is by understanding their expectations, their values and preferences, and how they see the world around them. Everyone is different, and to truly get to the heart of these differences involves taking the time to develop personal relationships. But you can get a head start by looking at the general drivers for each of the generations of people whom you work with and for, and understanding how your business structure and practice philosophy can accommodate them.

The people currently seen in the workforce, and as clientele, mostly come from the four following defined generations:

- The Silent Generation (born between 1928 and 1945): People from this generation tend to be disciplined. They believe in teamwork and in using creativity to "do more with less." They tend to respect authority, and they believe in order and in following directions.

- Baby Boomers (born between 1946 and 1964): This generation tends to be very adaptive to new situations in the workplace. They are goal oriented and work well in situations that call for teamwork. They also tend to have a high level of confidence and a positive attitude.

- Generation X (born between 1965 and 1980): Individuals from this generation tend to be more self-reliant and less impressed by authority figures. They value a greater work-life balance than older generations and they appreciate feedback and recognition. They are also very comfortable utilizing technology.

- Generation Y, also known as Millennials (born between 1981 and 2000): Millennials crave opportunities for self-expression. They are very adaptable, are exceptional multitaskers, and enjoy change and challenges. They are more interested in their lives outside of work, and will often not seek advancement in order to protect this dynamic. In 2015, Millennials edged out Generation X as the largest share of the labor force (Fry).

HOW THIS APPLIES TO YOUR STAFF

With all of this said, the ultimate goal of any business should be to move beyond labels and to build affinity between all members of the staff by treating everyone as individuals with knowledge and skills to share.

Take a collaborative approach and look for ways in which to engage the different members of your staff in tasks together. One method of realizing this collaborative approach is through reverse mentoring. For example, have your younger employees mentor your older staff on newer technologies and applications. If you are creating a Facebook page for your hospital, pair a tech-savvy younger employee with an older staff member who might better understand the type of content to share and the style in which it should be shared in light of the practice's philosophy and branding.

HOW THIS APPLIES TO YOUR CLIENTS

Availability of Information

In the age of Google, everyone has a wealth of information and options available to them quite literally at their fingertips. In a matter of moments, potential clients can locate every local animal hospital, see what services they provide, read about the veterinarians and staff, and see reviews of those hospitals.

Creating a website that is cohesive with your branding, easy to navigate, friendly, and informative is a vital part of showing clients and potential clients that you are ready and able to meet their needs.

Social Media

More and more of your clients are going to be social media savvy as time goes by. This includes not only your newer, younger clients but many of your older clients as well. This is an opportunity for your business. For little to no cost to you, and for a very small investment in time from your staff, you can utilize various social media outlets to communicate with your community about who you are, what services your practice provides, and what causes or ideals are important to you.

Options include Facebook, Instagram, and Twitter. These outlets offer you the ability to carry your branding to the next level. More importantly, they give clients and potential clients the chance to learn about your practice, your services, your team, your professionalism, and your commitment to caring for their animals before they even walk through your front door.

People expect to be treated well and for their pets to receive the best care possible. The web is your first opportunity to show people that *your* hospital is the place they can expect to find this.

Catering Your Services

It is probably safe to say that gone are the days when veterinary medicine consisted only of basic treatment for sick animals. Today, with the culture shift to viewing pets as members of the family and the emergence of myriad specialty medicine options, your clients will be looking to you for more and different services. Even for general practitioners, this could mean adding more diagnostics, rehabilitation services, or Eastern medicine, such as acupuncture. Where do you see the trends in your community going? How can you find a way to fill a niche that no other veterinarian in your vicinity is already filling?

Catering Your Customer Relations

In this age of technology, how can you provide your clients with new and better ways to communicate with you and to make utilizing your services easier and more convenient?

Here are several options:

- Online consultations.
- Online appointment scheduling.
- Online pharmacy refills.
- Automated billing.
- Text or email appointment reminders.
- Email and text communications for at-home care, etc.

HOW THIS APPLIES TO THE DESIGN OF YOUR HOSPITAL

Your hospital is an investment that should last for years to come. In order to ensure a healthy future for your practice, design and build your hospital with an eye to what the future of veterinary care will bring. Know who your clientele is now and who they will become over the next couple of decades. You want the building you are investing in today to remain authentic and relevant in a world where consumers have more and more choices and access to information. A few options to help you achieve these goals are explored below.

The Medical Spa

Find ways to make your veterinary hospital less clinical and more visually and physically appealing as a place of healing and wellness. Use natural materials, incorporate lots of natural light, and create an affirming environment. The spa analogy is especially relevant because it incorporates the idea of choice of services and treatment protocols.

The Concierge

Replace your reception desk and staff with concierge services. The concierge acts as the liaison between the client and the doctor. He or she will communicate through digital media, texts, email, and so on, coordinate online consultation, answer client questions, do follow-ups, coordinate future services, and assist clients with options for the care of their pets. Since your clients will have an established communication-intensive relationship with your concierge staff, a small check-in station can replace a full reception desk.

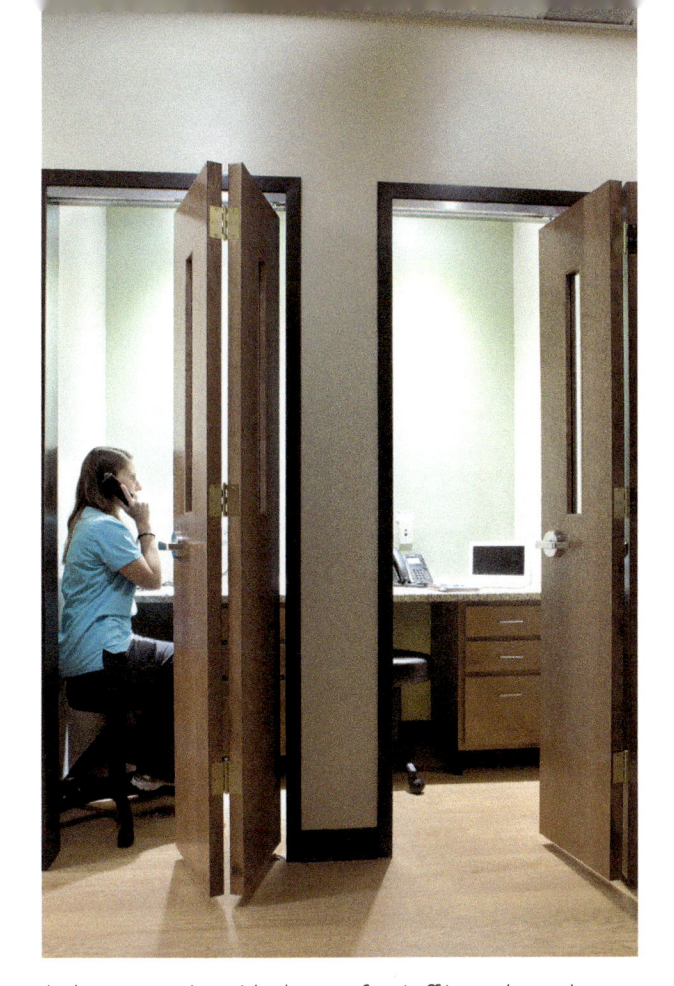

A phone room is an ideal space for staff to make and receive calls away from waiting clients. (Foto Imagery / Tim Murphy. Courtesy of Loyal Companions Animal Hospital, Saint Charles, Illinois.)

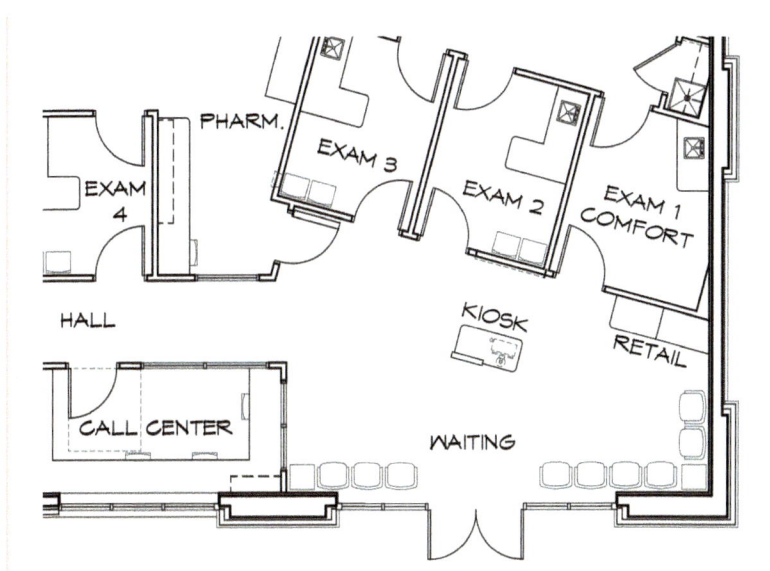

This concierge kiosk fosters a personal experience for clients and their pets. (Courtesy of Thrive Veterinary Care, Southglenn, Colorado.)

Moving in this direction can also help you shift to a paperless practice. Your concierge staff can work with portable laptops or tablets that can access patient records, be used to take credit card payments, and fully communicate with your clients. This will allow you to eliminate the need for dedicated file storage and create a more open work environment where staff can be more mobile and can communicate more effectively. (See Chapter 26 for more information on this concept.)

The Wellness Room

Include one or more spaces within your hospital that will serve as multifunctional examination, wellness, and minor treatment rooms where clients can be with their pets while they receive care. As diagnostic imaging becomes more portable, these rooms may also incorporate imaging. Use technology such as digital display monitors in these rooms to engage and educate your clients. Your general treatment area in this scenario will be much smaller and the medical spaces in your hospital will be weighted toward special procedures, surgery prep, and surgery.

▼ ▼ ▼

KNOWING WHO YOUR clients and staff are, and what drives and motivates them, will help you to create a practice that is welcoming and communicative and that provides the care and services that will help you become a fixture in your community.

CHAPTER 17

PLANNING FOR GROWTH AND FUTURE EXPANSION

Successful veterinary practices grow over time. The problem is that accommodating this growth can be an expensive and time-consuming endeavor. This is why many hospitals become overcrowded before they take on a relocation or expansion project.

Planning for a future expansion should start from day one. This chapter will review several reasonable expansion strategies for veterinary projects. Not every strategy is applicable to every project, so they have been organized by building type.

LEASEHOLD PRACTICES

People occupy leaseholds for a variety of reasons. Most commonly, it is because this is the most affordable strategy for getting into a physical space. By definition, leasehold practices are young or new. Many will expand over time and will become overcrowded in their spaces. Below are some ways to plan for expansion of leasehold practices:

- Plan to move: It sounds like a nonstrategy, but knowing that leasing space is a temporary endeavor should affect your planning. In this case, the leasehold should be fit out as affordably as possible. Don't spend money on fancy finishes or high-end infrastructure. Invest in the practice instead, and in building your clientele. From an accounting perspective, it is more cost effective to choose a standard piece of equipment than to have one custom built. For example, choose prefabricated exam tables in lieu of custom-built ones. These items are depreciable assets, which is beneficial from an accounting perspective. Under most lease agreement terms, you are also allowed to take equipment items with you when you move, which means that you can reuse them in your next space.

- Don't box yourself in: If you plan on expanding in place, don't lease a space next to the third-generation family business that is never going to leave. Instead, look for a space next to shorter-lived businesses. If one of these businesses vacates sometime in the future, jump on the opportunity to run some numbers to see if this is the right time to lease additional space and expand the hospital.

- Plan more than one location: Some veterinarians find that developing a series of leasehold veterinary hospitals can be a great way to expand, make some money, and be their own competition. Veterinary practices that employ this strategy tend to be very business-minded. They also tend to have a strong brand so that any location can appear to be interchangeable in terms of quality and service.

OLDER FREESTANDING BUILDINGS

Many baby boomer veterinarians have sold, or are in the process of selling, their practices (and hence their buildings) to younger veterinarians. Other practices have the same ownership and have survived in one location for several decades. Regardless of how you arrived at owning an older building, this can be a tricky situation to evaluate. Some older buildings are beyond their useful life. Others can be sensibly remodeled. You will need to have your building evaluated by an experienced design professional to decide how much of an investment might make sense. The following strategies are often employed by veterinarians who are expanding in older buildings:

- Build new on the same property and tear the old building down: This is a great approach if you have both the money and the land to do this and if your old hospital is too dilapidated to remodel. The pros of this approach are that you can stay in the same, familiar location, save money on a land purchase, and maintain your current business completely intact throughout the construction of the new facility. The con is the cost of building a new building.

- Build a new addition and remodel the older hospital: This approach works very well if the expansion has a specific purpose—for example, an equine practice might expand on the same site and add a small animal practice. Another example would be building an addition to house specialized equipment, such as a CT machine.

- Rearrange the workflow of your old hospital to gain additional capacity: This approach is very common, and yet it is very painful for the practice while it is in progress. If you plan to rearrange services within the same four walls in order to reuse space in a more efficient way, keep in mind that you will need to keep your business running during the remodel. Either the remodel will need to be phased, meaning that select areas are remodeled and completely finished, followed by other areas, or you may need to find a temporary location for your business during the remodel. Pictured on the opposite page are examples of before and after floor plans of a practice that renovated its interior square footage for vastly improved capacity. This practice chose to occupy a temporary location during the remodel.

NEW FREESTANDING BUILDINGS

Practices that have the opportunity to build a new freestanding building have the prospect of a blank slate for planning future expansions. In fact, there is no reason *not* to plan for future expansion if you believe your practice will grow over time. Here are some considerations:

- Purchase a little more land than is needed so you have the option of expanding your current building in the future. If you're developing this idea, leave room along one side of the current hospital to allow for all portions of the hospital (client, medical, and patient/support) to later be expanded.

- Consider "shelling" a portion of the building. In other words, build an area of the building that has no interior finish. This way you can expand into this area in the future without changing the building footprint. This strategy can also work if you're purchasing an existing building: you can purchase a building that is larger than you need, with the idea that you will fill it eventually.

In addition to these larger-scale strategies, there are many smaller-scale ideas that will help your future expansion take place in the most efficient way possible:

- Oversize the utilities, including gas, water, sewer, and electric, to accommodate future expansion.

- Place plumbing lines deeper so they can be expanded outward in the future.

- Invest in ways to keep infrastructure neat and tidy so it's easier to expand. An example is keeping your data cables in bundles or trays above the ceiling, and always using conduit in walls so that lines can be located and rerouted as required.

- Design enough space above the ceiling to easily access and reroute mechanical ductwork as needed in the future. For example, it is best to have at least 30 inches between the bottom of the roof joists and beams and the ceilings, in order to allow for easy access to ductwork.

- Do not place major infrastructure items in the way of future expansion. For example, it is very expensive to relocate main electrical switchgear, generators, main sewer lines, etc.

- Think ahead about how you will expand exam rooms. This is always the biggest headache. Perhaps the exam rooms can be located on the side of the building that is closest to the building expansion so they can be expanded in the future while maintaining good traffic flow.

EXISTING FLOOR PLAN
1,817 SQUARE FEET - MAIN FLOOR

0   4 FT   8 FT   16 FT

FLOOR PLAN
1,817 SQUARE FEET - MAIN FLOOR

0   4 FT   8 FT   16 FT

The original plan for this 1,817-square-foot hospital (left). The renovation (right) doubled the exam and treatment capacity without adding square footage. (Courtesy of Melrose Animal Hospital, Melrose, Massachusetts.)

PLANNING FOR GROWTH AND FUTURE EXPANSION

▼ ▼ ▼

IN SUMMARY, PRACTICES should plan ahead for growth, which comes inevitably with success. Practices that plan ahead for expansion will be more profitable in the long run.

CHAPTER 18

SUSTAINABLE DESIGN

In broad terms, sustainable or "green" architecture considers both the exterior and interior environments as well as the preservation of natural resources. It is based on design and technologies that are renewable and sustainable. Designs that consider lower energy expenditure and less water usage can save money on utility bills while also making for a more enjoyable, comfortable, and productive workspace.

"Sustainability," as used in design and construction, has many interpretations. This chapter will explain sustainability in the context of design strategies, systems, and material choices that are appropriate for veterinary hospitals. It will follow the framework of the Leadership in Energy and Environmental Design (LEED) checklist, which is still the most commonly accepted benchmark for evaluating sustainable strategies for commercial buildings such as veterinary hospitals.

SUSTAINABLE SITE STRATEGIES

Ideas about how, where, and why to place a building on a piece of land have changed throughout history based on economics and local restrictions. Almost all buildings are governed by a large array of site codes and energy guidelines. These can be very helpful in deciding how the project will address the site, but many tried-and-true vernacular strategies, e.g., local forms based on historical knowledge about the climate, can and should be used in addition to these to ensure that the project will be as energy efficient and environmentally friendly as possible.

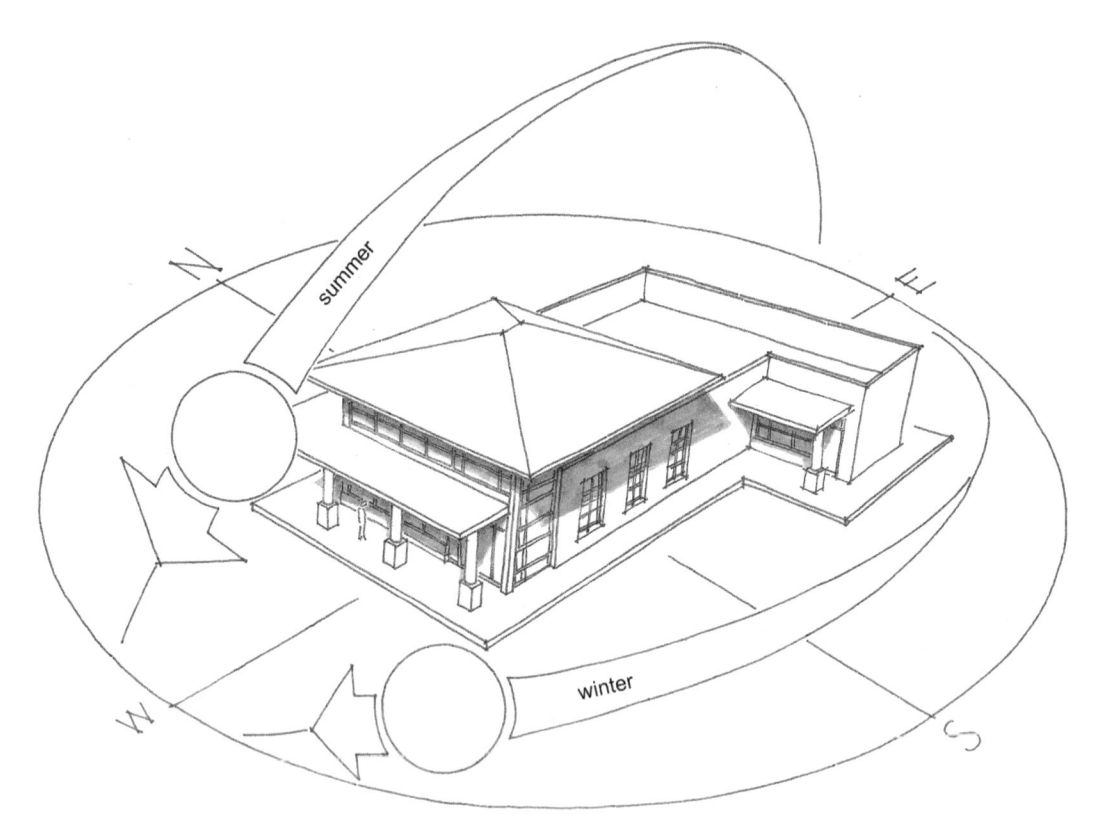

A solar orientation diagram showing how this building is protected from the hotter summer sun while still allowing light and warmth to reach the south-side windows in the winter months.

The first big issue is building with solar orientation in mind. This means considering your building's solar exposure. Does it receive direct sunlight for a good portion of the day? How far north or south is your property? Buildings located near the equator will receive a lot of solar radiation and sunlight year round, while the farther north or south you go, the less sun the building will receive in the winter months.

Buildings farther from the equator need to employ sun-gathering strategies in the winter months to cut down on heating costs. Buildings in warm climates need sun-shading strategies to cut down on cooling costs. In most temperate climates, buildings should be placed on east/west exposures to maximize the north and south faces. However, in far northern climates, a building that is oriented on a north/south axis will gather more warmth from the sun all winter long.

The other important aspect of building orientation is the proper placement of windows. Even though you may be somewhat limited by the layout of your building, consider the effect of exterior openings on the energy usage of your building. The worst exposure for solar gain is the west side of a building, due to the extremes of afternoon sun in most areas of the continental United States. The best exposure is the south side, because it is possible to use overhangs that block the summer sun when it is high in the sky but allow solar gain in the winter when the sun is low in the sky. Your mechanical engineer can take the placement of your windows into account when sizing your mechanical system. If a building is properly oriented and has properly placed windows, the size of the mechanical system can be reduced.

Unfortunately, not all projects are new buildings located on a large site where sunlight can be harvested. In urban settings, for example, finding ways to get sunlight into a building can be challenging, but it is still worth doing whenever possible to create happier and healthier employees.

The sustainable site section of LEED encourages designers to reduce the "heat island effect" of their buildings—that is, the high air and structure temperatures created by the absorbed solar energy of hardscaped urban areas. The following are some very good and simple principles that do not add dramatically to construction costs:

- Use a white or light-colored roof in hot and temperate climates. These roofs are ubiquitous in the design and construction industries, so it is possible to find good, affordable products. Light-colored roofs dramatically reduce solar heat gain, which is good for both the building and the site.

- Use deciduous plantings to shade parking areas during the summer. In the winter, when their leaves are gone, they allow for greater solar gain.

- Reduce dark, impervious paving. Concrete is a better paving choice than asphalt because it is much more reflective. Check with your local construction market to see if concrete is an affordable choice for your area.

- Green paving may be an option. These are concrete lattice pavers that allow green growth up through them. These work well in wetter areas of the country, where runoff is an issue and plants grow easily.

SUSTAINABLE MATERIAL STRATEGIES

The materials used to construct a building can affect the budget and the longevity of the project. Veterinary facilities are very hard on both exterior and interior finishes. A good strategy is to use materials that will weather well and are common in your area.

- Choose the most durable building structural system that your budget will allow.

- Choose long-lasting exterior materials that fit your local climate and will look good after many years of sun and rain exposure.

- Choose roofing materials that are cooling and long wearing.

- Choose locally sourced materials when possible to reduce costs and improve your odds of getting a good installation.

All of the issues that apply to exterior material choices are amplified on the interior of a veterinary facility. This is due to the intense amount of cleaning and wear the interiors of these facilities endure.

WATER-USE REDUCTION STATEGIES

One of the best strategies in the category of water conservation is to reduce or eliminate the need to use potable water for landscape

SUSTAINABLE DESIGN

irrigation. Xeriscaping and other forms of drought-tolerant landscaping, for example, can reduce irrigation needs by up to 50%.

You can reduce water usage in the building by installing low-flow toilets and urinals in bathrooms as well as low-flow faucets in bathroom and staff break room sinks. The same goes for showers if the building has them. Low-pressure water flow to medical and grooming areas, however, is usually not ideal. One way to reduce water use in these areas is to install automatic sensors on sinks. This is a great strategy because it also improves biological risk management for the hospital.

ENERGY AND ATMOSPHERE STRATEGIES

Reducing energy usage in an animal hospital is of the utmost importance. It is the best strategy for your budget, and an even better strategy for the environment. Veterinary hospitals use huge amounts of energy in moving air. In fact, the design of mechanical equipment is generally driven by "ventilation loads" rather than "envelope loads" (the effect of the outside envelope of the building) for this building type. Fortunately, it is possible to reduce energy usage by at least 25% over the industry-accepted baseline.

The energy consumption of HVAC systems can be reduced by installing units with energy recovery ventilators. Because veterinary facilities typically exhaust large quantities of air, energy recovery ventilators precondition the supply air with air that is exhausted by using a thermal exchange process.

Evaporative cooling systems can be effective in consistently arid climates because they use a lot less energy than traditional air conditioning. Of the technologies currently on the market, the best systems for hospitals use "indirect" evaporative cooling, which directs moisture into the exhaust air stream rather than introducing it into the building. Even in arid climates, most evaporative cooling systems need to be supplemented with a traditional air conditioning component that can assist with cooling during the humid days that still occur each year.

Be as creative as possible in different areas of a building. For example, if you are including boarding, and therefore have large areas for animal housing, consider allowing this area to float between a range of temperatures throughout the day. In this case, it's possible to maintain ventilation rates but use the mechanical units like whole house fans to reduce the cooling and heating of the moving air stream.

Some of the good design choices discussed in the "Sustainable Site Strategies" section of this chapter also reduce the size of the mechanical systems. Assuming the building is properly oriented and the windows are well placed, design the building configuration, envelope, windows, doors, and insulation to meet or exceed local energy codes. Install energy-efficient windows with double-pane, low-emissivity (low-e) glass. Add shades or awnings in high-sun locations. Plant deciduous shade trees on the south and west sides of the building to shade the summer sun, and coniferous trees on the north side to protect against winter weather conditions. In addition, use appropriate insulation in walls, roofs, and floors.

Sophisticated mechanical systems are only as good as their setup and installation. Be sure the building mechanical systems are installed and operating as designed. You should be able to receive hands-on training for your HVAC systems from your installer, and a knowledgeable HVAC maintenance company should be able to keep your mechanical systems operating at optimum performance. Engage this company by contract to inspect the equipment on a regular basis.

Commercial buildings expend tremendous energy in electrical lighting. Therefore, a good strategy for your overall energy costs is to reduce the consumption of electrical power. Design your hospital to optimize daylighting opportunities. Provide ways to control light levels by installing high windows, skylights, light tubes, windows with blinds and shades, and windows with awnings or eaves. In designing the electrical lighting, use high-efficiency lighting fixtures, which will primarily be LED fixtures. You will be required to install lighting control systems per code, which will automatically shut lights off when they are not in use.

RENEWABLE ENERGY

Many people are interested in supporting renewable energy technologies. Some renewable energy systems, such as wind power, are still very expensive. However, solar water heating is almost always a good payoff for a veterinary hospital. For some projects, photovoltaic technologies can be affordable if there are good local incentives. A building can also be designed with the proper conduits and roof design to be "PV ready," allowing you to add these systems in the future.

Geothermal systems can also reduce energy needs. The issue with geothermal systems is not how well they work, because they work very well. It's the initial up-front cost, which depends on the location of the project and whether that cost will be recouped over the life of the business. If you are considering a geothermal system, test the viability of this option by pricing it early in the project design stage.

INDOOR ENVIRONMENTAL QUALITY

Because everyone spends so much time indoors, building a facility to promote optimal air quality is important. Isolating activities that have a negative effect on air quality, providing adequate exhaust, and providing a fresh air supply can all result in greater comfort and more personal control over the indoor environment.

In a veterinary hospital, it is even more important than for other types of buildings to design spaces with good air quality, because of the presence of biological and chemical odors, dust, dander, and bacteria. However, if you follow the guidelines for veterinary hospital mechanical systems described in Chapter 43, you will well exceed basic code requirements for airflow and will be creating a healthy indoor environment.

THE FUTURE OF SUSTAINABLE DESIGN

As the green building industry has matured, many sustainable design strategies have become required by building codes. For this reason, it may seem less appealing to pursue a green approach to a project because the benchmark is set higher every year for achieving extraordinary performance.

However, there are some new trends that are moving us well beyond a checklist-based approach to creating green buildings. One that is both exciting and relevant to all healthcare projects is *biophilic design*. This design approach is based on the known fact that people connect best with spaces that feel natural. Spaces that feel natural can reduce stress, enhance creativity, and improve wellbeing.

Biophilic design can be employed in all locations, even urban environments. Inviting the sky into the space, having a green terrace or courtyard to look out to, using natural materials, and intentionally exposing the senses to a variety of input from outside the building can all help improve a workplace. Human hospitals have been pushing ideas of biophilic design because it helps business and patient outcomes, and the same should be done with veterinary care.

▼ ▼ ▼

ULTIMATELY, THE MOVEMENT to design environmentally responsible buildings still brings tremendous benefit to building owners, from lower operational expenses to more comfortable environments. Whether your project takes a checklist-based approach or simply uses sustainable design strategies to frame good project decisions, take advantage of all the knowledge you can tap into to create a building that does more with less.

CHAPTER 19

BASIC RULES OF FLOOR PLAN DESIGN—SMALL HOSPITALS

A small hospital needs to have an efficient floor plan, one that begins with a clear organizational structure that provides a framework for the entire design. The two basic concepts for organizing a small hospital are the traditional plan and the triangulated plan. The traditional plan has a front, middle, and back configuration. The triangulated plan pulls the "middle" to the side to produce a triangular traffic pattern. Although well-designed hospitals have many similar functional relationships, the specific layouts vary. The layout of your hospital should be based on what you wish to accomplish and the shape of the footprint of your building.

PLAN LAYOUTS

The Traditional Plan

In small freestanding facilities and storefront hospitals of approximately 2,500 square feet or less, the traditional "front, middle, back" configuration is generally the most efficient approach. The three zones reflect the three functional areas of the typical veterinary hospital. The front is the client area, including waiting, reception, and exam rooms. The middle is the medical procedure area, made up of the laboratory, pharmacy, treatment, radiology, and surgery. The back contains the patient wards and the utility support spaces.

These three zones are not divided equally: the middle medical zone will likely take up the largest amount of space, with some flexibility in

The traditional plan illustrated (top). The traditional plan with zones highlighted (bottom).

the client and animal housing areas depending on the choices you make on the layout of these spaces. Flow-through traffic, passing through spaces, minimizes travel distances between the functional areas of the hospital.

The Triangulated Plan

For any facility to operate smoothly, it must have a clear circulation pattern. With small facilities, circulation from one area to another often passes through one room, such as the treatment area. This can be the most efficient way of accommodating circulation requirements, but it also means that you have traffic through your workspace. The shortfall of the traditional plan is that all traffic from back to front has to go right through the treatment room. While this can cause conflict and confusion in larger facilities, it is less of an issue in a small hospital, but should still be taken into consideration and weighed against the potential benefit of having the treatment area act as the hospital's main hub, with easy access to all of the support functions.

A variation of the traditional plan is the triangulated plan. By pulling the middle to one side, the hospital forms a triangle instead of a corridor. This kind of plan eliminates traffic through the medical area and can significantly shorten the distance between what was once the front and back of the plan. In this scenario it's possible to create a hub out of the doctors' station by

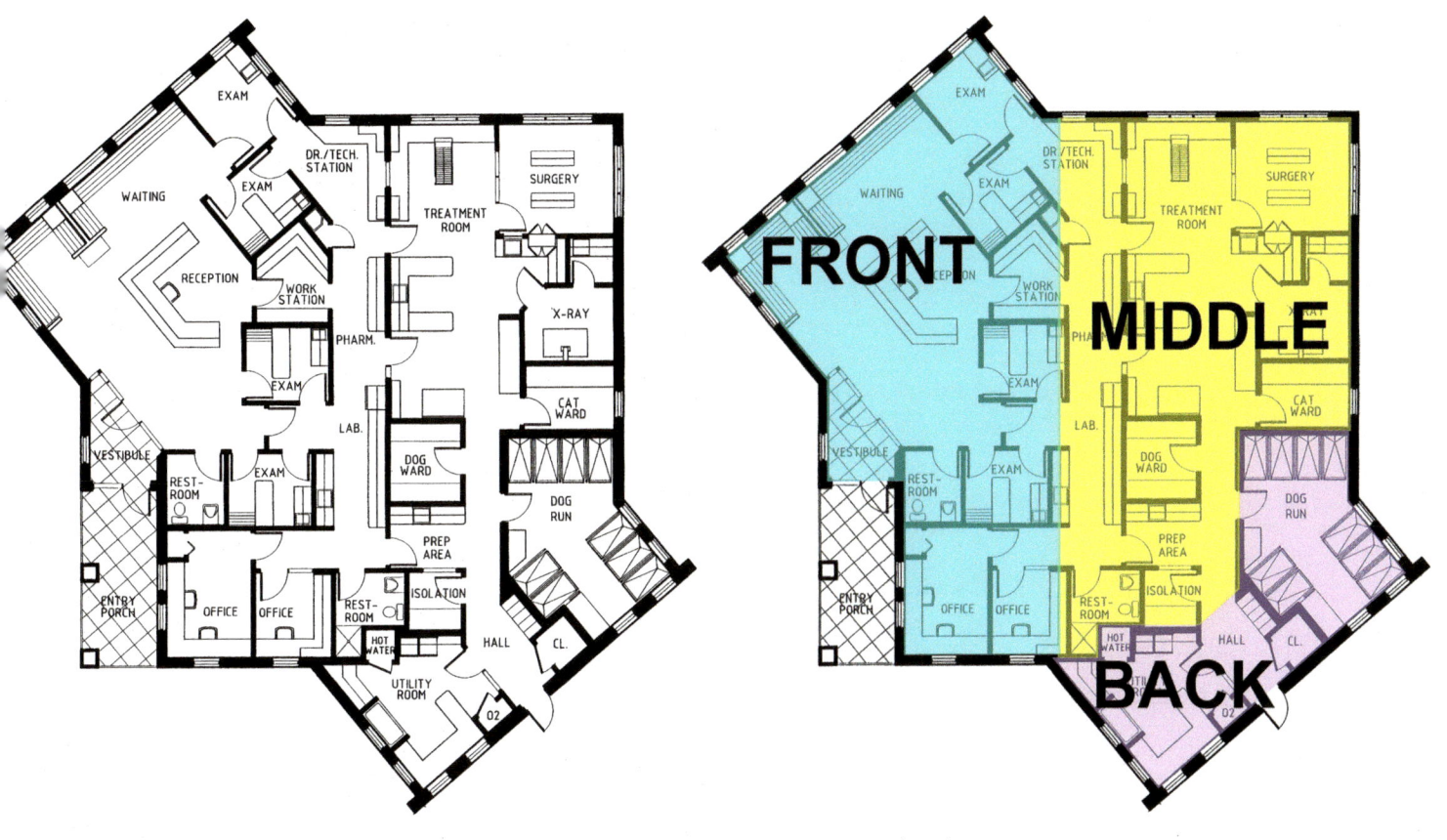

The triangulated plan illustrated (left). The triangulated plan with zones highlighted (right).

placing it at the center of the triangle, establishing a control point for the whole hospital.

In either layout, grouping similar functions together will cut down on odor and noise issues. Animal areas can be located together and should be separated from the area of the hospital that contains offices and other nonanimal areas.

ADDITIONAL ORGANIZATIONAL CONCEPTS

Many of the secondary decisions that are made as your floor plan develops can complement your overall organizational concept.

Laboratory/Pharmacy Buffer

In many facilities, the laboratory and pharmacy form a buffer between the exam rooms and the treatment area, becoming a de facto place where doctors and staff gather and most of the charting and impromptu discussion takes place. As a buffer, the laboratory and pharmacy area cuts down on the noise and visual clutter that could move from the treatment area to the exam rooms. However, if you don't feel that you need the buffer, you can design a more efficient and fast-moving plan by eliminating it. In this case, the laboratory is often part of treatment and the pharmacy may be a self-contained room or space. If veterinarians and staff can move directly from the exam rooms into the treatment area, it speeds up flow-

BASIC RULES OF FLOOR PLAN DESIGN—SMALL HOSPITALS

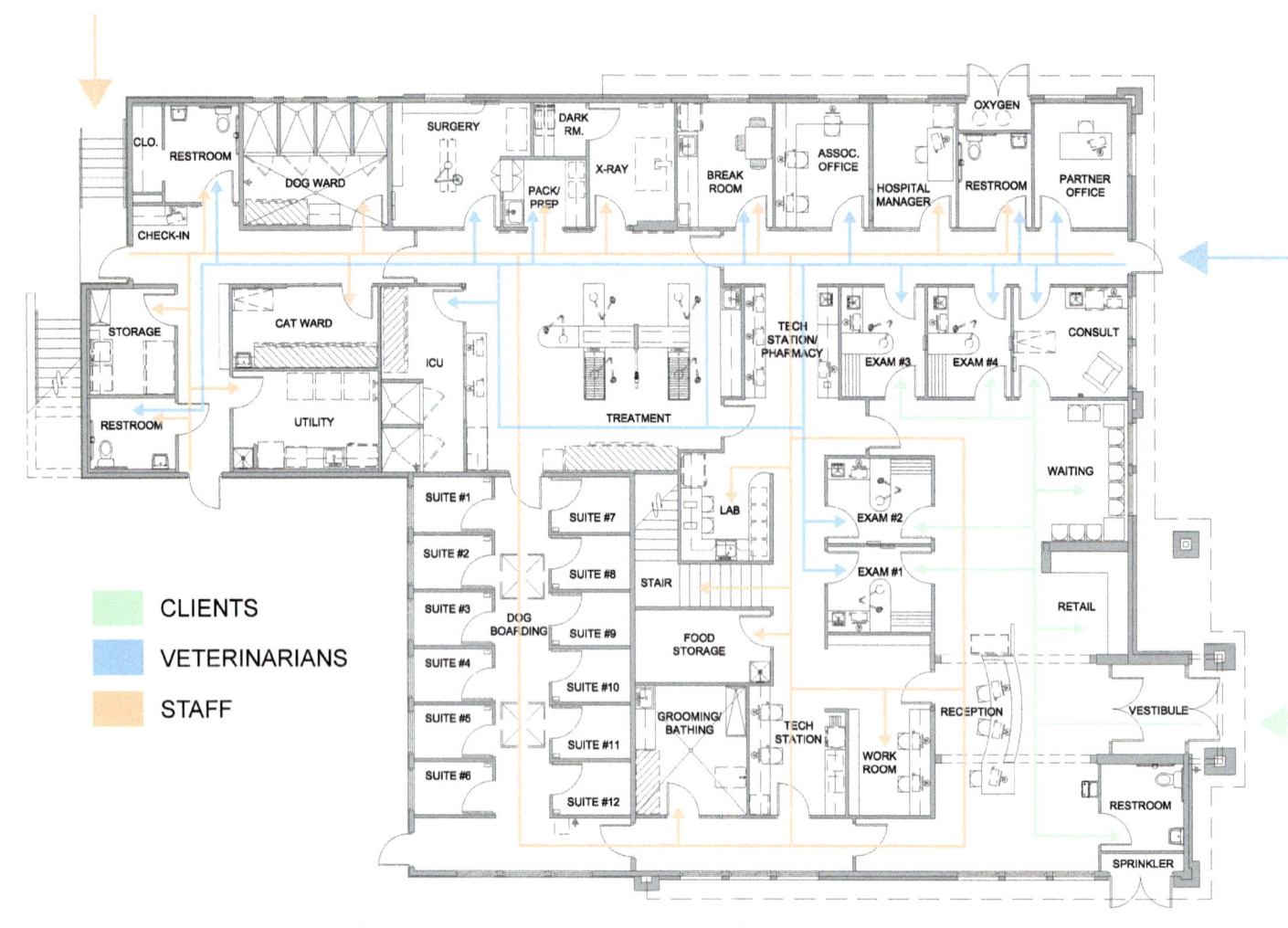

A plan that illustrates the traffic flow of clients, veterinarians, and staff. (Courtesy of Wellington Veterinary Hospital, Wellington, Colorado.)

through traffic. But it also means that whatever happens in the treatment area will probably be seen and heard in the exam rooms.

Maximizing Exam Room Capacity

Having an appropriate exam room layout is the single most important decision you face in the design of your facility. In small facilities (two to four exam rooms), you can position exam rooms in a straight line, side by side. This layout can use one of two basic configurations: one door or two door. One-door exam rooms are lined up along either the exterior wall of a freestanding building or the dividing wall in a storefront space, and each exam room has one door off the lobby or a hallway. The key to one-door exam rooms is laying them out so that the doctor can get into and out of the exam rooms without getting caught up in the traffic of the lobby or being approached by a client.

A slight variation on the one-door exam room approach is having exam rooms with direct access to the exterior or a nearby hallway, which allows for easy access for anxious patients. This plan also provides for a direct exit for services such as euthanasia. It simply requires saving some exterior wall space to lay out the exam rooms.

In two-door exam rooms, there is one door off the lobby/reception area and a second door going into the medical area. This layout offers a "back of house" entrance for the doctors into the exam rooms, without making them go through the lobby, and offers direct access to treatment if a patient needs to be transferred there quickly and efficiently. Plans with two-door exam rooms are significantly less space efficient than plans with one-door exam rooms.

Treatment as Hub

In most small floor plans, the treatment area is the hub around which radiology, pack/prep, wards, special procedures, and the doctors' station are grouped. The treatment area is used as a circulation space, but all of these rooms are so interactive that this is a necessity, not a detriment.

Surgery in a Corner

In contrast to the treatment area, the surgery room traditionally occupies a corner of the medical portion of the facility, preventing circulation through the surgery zone. The pack/prep area should be located immediately adjacent to surgery.

General Tips and Strategies

Below are some simple concepts to help you organize an efficient floor plan.

- Hospitals want to be square: Long, thin spaces make for challenging floor plans because they lengthen circulation paths.

- Start with the exam rooms: You will find when working on your veterinary floor plans that the arrangement of the exam rooms is the most relevant issue in whether the plan will work or not. Take your time with your team to get this room arrangement just right.

- Put big things on the perimeter: Just as putting the surgery room in a corner seems to really help a plan, other large spaces work well at the perimeter, where circulation can come up to these areas without going through them. Examples include break rooms and lobbies.

- Don't make treatment spaces too big: Most people who are new to veterinary hospital design create oversize treatment areas. In an effective treatment room, everything should be ergonomically arranged and within reach. Place generous circulation paths behind the ends of tables where people stand so that the space doesn't feel congested, but also create accessible side layout spaces adjacent and near the tables to store tools and supplies within reach.

▼ ▼ ▼

A GREAT VETERINARY hospital is not only a tool to help you practice more efficiently, it is an opportunity to do what you do best. To take your floor plan from good to excellent, decide on one element to be your focal point. Discuss this focal point with your architect and make it the centerpiece of your design. Your focal point may be a terrific surgery room or a fabulous client service area. This element should make a statement and should help to organize your plan and make your hospital unique.

CHAPTER 20

BASIC RULES OF FLOOR PLAN DESIGN—LARGE HOSPITALS

The previous chapter discussed the major organizing concepts as they relate to smaller hospitals with the traditional and triangulated plan approaches. But when it comes to larger hospitals (more than 10,000 square feet), it is necessary to rethink the organization in order to ensure proper flow and efficiency within facilities that provide more services and have greater numbers of staff, patients, and clients moving through them daily.

GROUPING FUNCTIONAL AREAS

To minimize conflict, confusion, and unnecessary circulation in large hospitals, it makes sense to divide the hospital into distinct areas. In order to create groupings that work, it is often easier to think in terms of general room attributes, such as support spaces versus work areas like treatment. Other considerations might include public versus private (waiting area versus animal wards), clean versus dirty (surgery versus isolation), noisy versus quiet (animal wards versus offices). A good way to test a grouping of rooms is to take your plan and do a number of overlays, shading different groups of rooms different colors and seeing how they best lay out in order to provide an efficient and functional workspace.

Parameters for what services need to have more of a connection to each other should be established during the programming process. Your design team will need a clear understanding of the services you will offer before putting pen to paper.

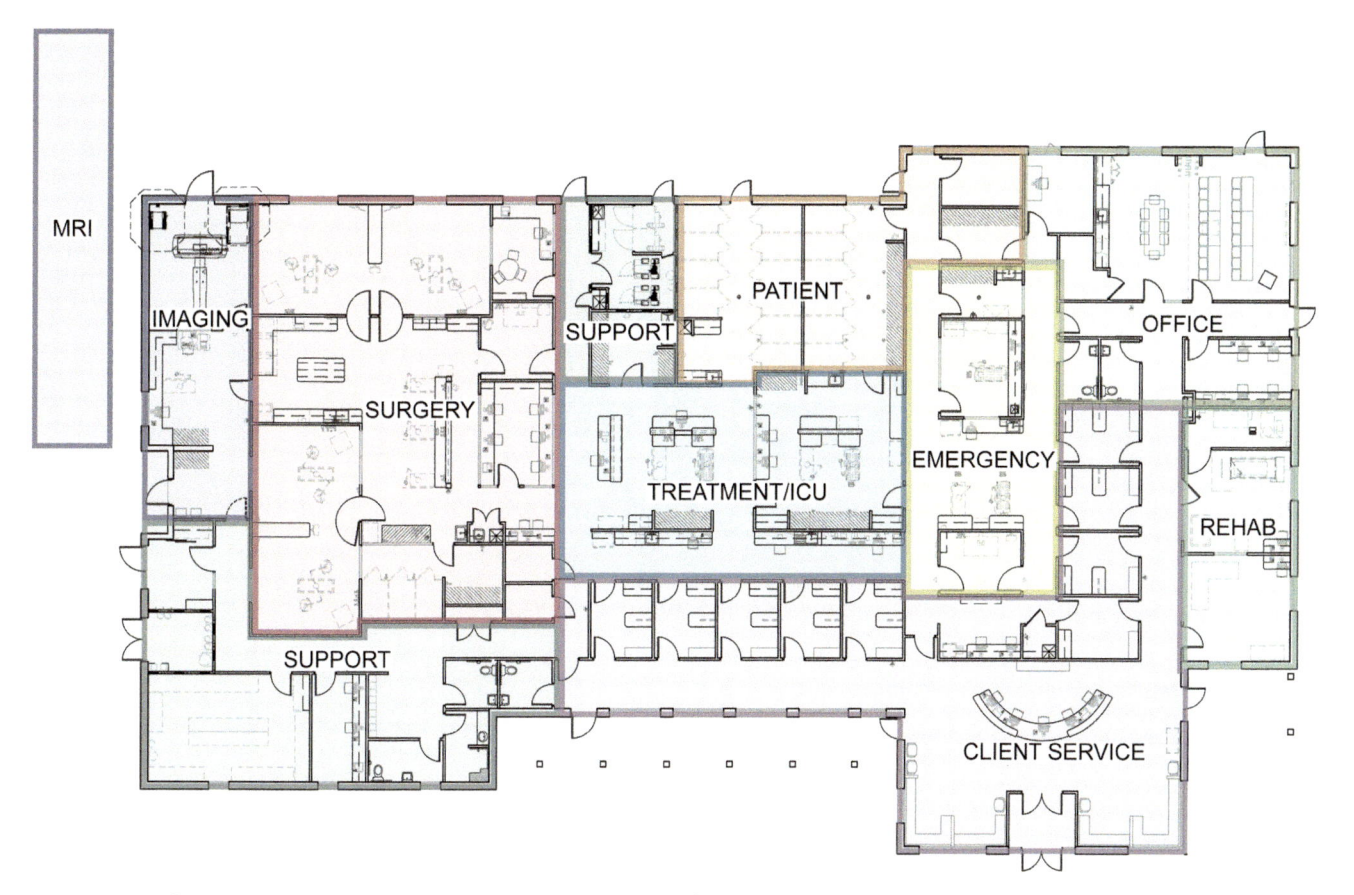

An example of how departments are grouped in a large hospital. (Courtesy of Veterinary Surgical Referral Practice, Cary, North Carolina.)

CIRCULATION PATHWAYS

In small facilities, circulation can pass through one room to get to another. Even though it means having traffic move right through a workspace, this is often the most efficient way to accommodate circulation requirements within smaller square footages. In larger facilities, however, it is preferable to create hallways with rooms off of them to accommodate greater circulation requirements. These circulation paths must be clear, clean, and readily apparent.

A simple way to test the circulation pathways as you are planning your hospital is to trace the routes that people take as they go about their daily duties. Trace the steps of veterinarians, technicians, receptionists, and kennel staff as well as paths taken for moving animals and for receiving materials, such as dog food. These paths should be as short and direct as possible. Staff circulation should be separated from client circulation whenever possible.

MAXIMIZING EXAM ROOM CAPACITY

Having enough exam rooms is one of the most important decisions facing you in the design of your facility. In smaller facilities, two to four exam rooms can be set up in a straight line, side by side. In larger facilities, however, a different approach is required. It is usually helpful

BASIC RULES OF FLOOR PLAN DESIGN—LARGE HOSPITALS 105

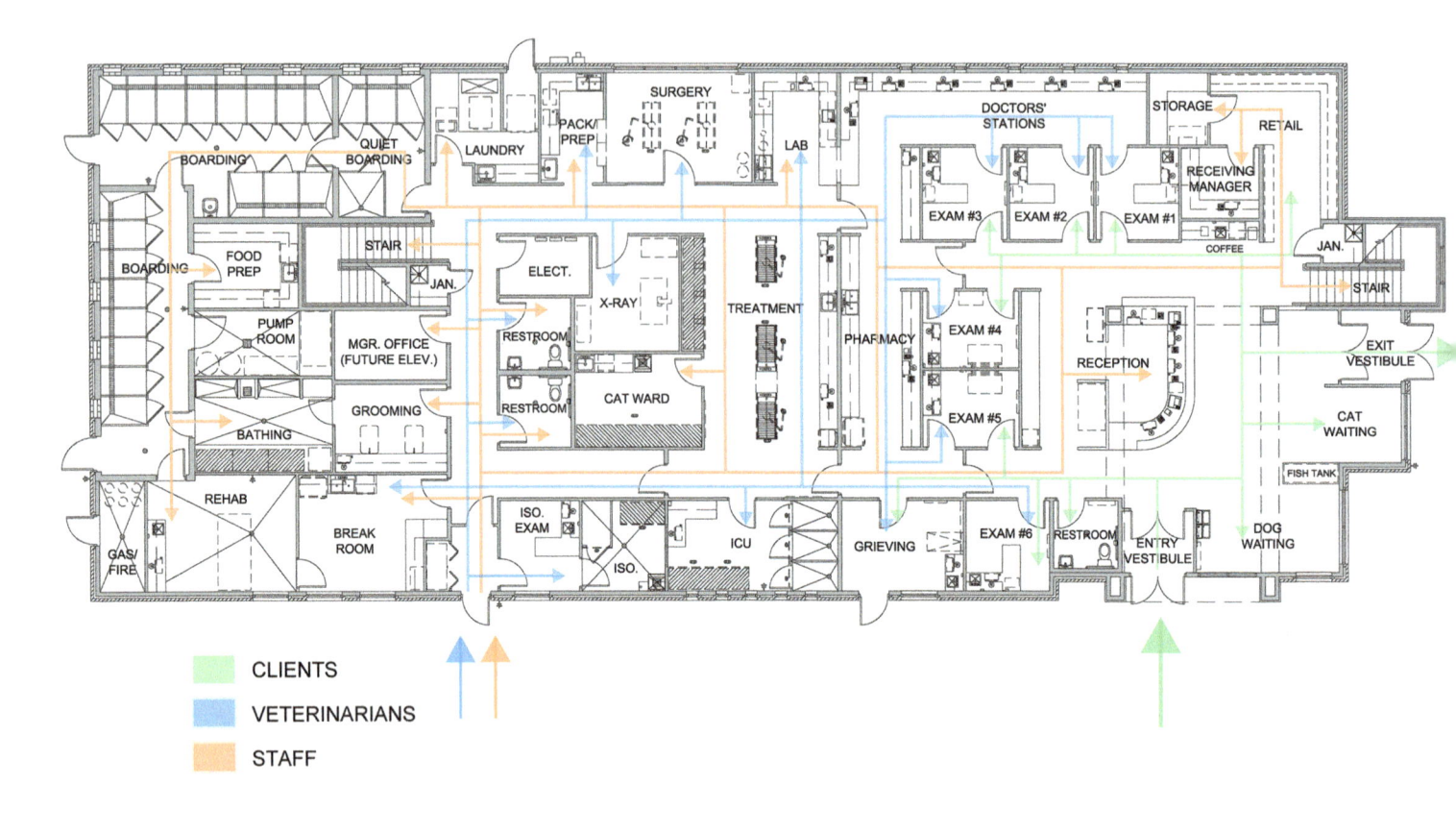

FLOOR PLAN - TRAFFIC FLOW
MAIN FLOOR

The traffic flow in this hospital was designed to minimize steps in this large space. Note the separation of client circulation. (Courtesy of VCA All Pets Animal Hospital, Boulder, Colorado [VCA, Inc.].)

to group exam rooms in twos or threes, because this is the typical number of exam rooms a single veterinarian can work. It is also important to group exam rooms—and specifically the entries to the exam rooms—so that the doors are visible from the reception desk, but this becomes more challenging as the number of exam rooms increases. Instead of single exam rooms, there will most likely be several groupings of exam rooms, or pods. To develop the most efficient plan in a multiple-doctor practice, visibility from the reception desk may have to be compromised.

Flex Exam Rooms

In both small and large hospitals, it may be beneficial to build in some flexible exam rooms that can act as additional treatment spaces (such as a dental station or ultrasound room) during the day. This will give you the ability to do more with the available space, maximizing the exam room and treatment area potential and possibly your ability to bring in revenue.

Reception Desk Layout

It is also important for large hospitals to consider the reception space and how it flows in order to help eliminate congestion within the waiting area. The typical reception desk is an in-line desk: the client walks through the front door, checks in with the receptionist, and sits in the waiting area before being called into the exam room; once the exam is complete, the client returns to the reception desk and is cashed out. This arrangement is space effective and logical for small hospitals; however, it can lead to congestion and crowding at the desk in larger hospitals.

With larger hospitals, it usually becomes necessary to consider more of an island-style reception approach with separate check-in and check-out areas. This approach helps to eliminate many of the conflicts at the desk by organizing the circulation into a one-way flow. In this model, your client leaves the exam room, moves to a checkout counter, and then exits through a different door or through the main door, but from a different direction. While this model is more effective at organizing traffic, it requires more square footage.

OTHER CONSIDERATIONS

Beyond the key items discussed above, other typical hospital concerns, such as noise reduction, may be exacerbated in larger hospitals. Below is a list of typical concerns to keep in mind when developing a large hospital plan:

- Provide a sound barrier created by a buffer, such as a hallway or sound-insulated walls, between client and staff areas. This should include a barrier between the exam rooms and treatment areas.

- Design the hospital traffic flow to discourage circulation through treatment areas. Circulation on the perimeters of these spaces is ideal.

- Recover animals from anesthesia in enclosed and separate quiet wards when possible.

- Create dedicated treatment areas inside critical patient wards. For example, create a dedicated ICU ward with its own treatment and recovery space.

- Locate wards close to exterior doors and provide convenient and sanitary exterior dog-walking areas to encourage staff to take the dogs out frequently. It's best to locate wards near exterior doors to prevent the need for dogs to be walked through the hospital to get outside.

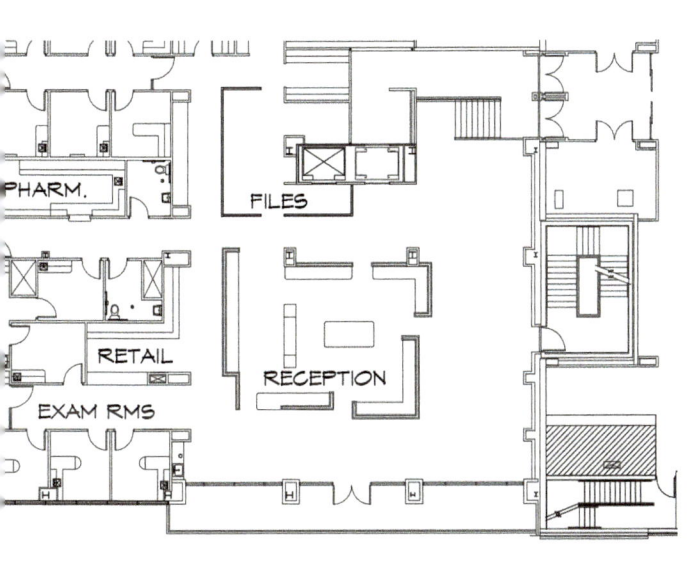

This square reception desk allows the hospital to separate clients by function as they come and go from the hospital. (Courtesy of VCA West Los Angeles Animal Hospital, Los Angeles, California [VCA, Inc.].)

BASIC RULES OF FLOOR PLAN DESIGN—LARGE HOSPITALS

- If possible, try to maintain a one-story hospital that is spread out horizontally. This is the optimal approach for function and efficiency.

- If you must build a multistory hospital due to space or site constraints, consider how the spaces need to relate to each other vertically. In order to solve all of the complex circulation patterns and to keep staff and public areas separated, it is usually necessary to develop a service stairway and elevator that are separate from the public stairway and elevator.

- Rather than having reception staff talking with clients on the phone at the front desk, consider building in a phone room where they can make and take client calls in a quiet location free from distraction.

▼ ▼ ▼

SUCCESSFULLY LAYING OUT an efficient plan for a large hospital can be challenging. Let your program and the relationships between departments guide you. Thinking about how to make circulation pathways work for you rather than against you will get you moving in the right direction.

CHAPTER 21

SPECIALTY/REFERRAL HOSPITALS

Fifteen years ago, specialty veterinary hospitals were relatively new, and trend discussions focused on the rise of specialization. Today, specialty/referral hospitals are common. While they take a significant up-front investment, they can be highly profitable because they typically combine the highest money-making services in a single facility.

Designing for this type of use should always begin with gathering information on the specialties to be offered to clients, how each area of the hospital will be used, and the specific requirements necessary to provide those services. There are two keys to achieving a good layout for this hospital type:

- Efficiency in flow and relationships to services: Functions that interact should be located near each other, for example, surgery and imaging.

- Separation of businesses or entities, if required: For example, a service such as rehabilitation may be offered through a separate business, and this may affect layout and traffic flow.

In the initial design stages, the architect and owners engage in a detailed interview process to gather all of the requirements for each service and the relationships between the services. It is also important to identify key equipment elements, as specialty hospitals are often designed around specific pieces of medical equipment.

Each of the following specialty hospital types will have its own unique design criteria:

- Specialty/referral.
- Specialty/emergency within a general practice.
- Surgery center only.
- Imaging center only.
- Cancer center only.

LAYING OUT THE SPACES

Room layouts in specialty hospitals depend on the equipment and people who will occupy the space and the circulation space needed around each piece of equipment. It is best to begin with a comprehensive list of requirements for each room. For example, if a hydrotherapy treadmill is planned in a physical rehabilitation suite, then the space needs to be sized appropriately. Not only is it a large piece of equipment, but you will also need a pump room, enough space around the treadmill for staff members who are working with the patient, and a storage area.

How the services relate to each other in a specialty hospital will help to inform where they are situated within the hospital. The more efficiently these groupings can be laid out, the faster doctors, staff, and patients can move from one area to another. Below are some examples of typical adjacencies in a specialty/referral hospital.

- Radiology should be adjacent to surgery, so that patients can be easily wheeled out to have any necessary X-rays taken before, during, or after a surgical procedure.

- This same reasoning applies to locating ultrasound next to cardiology.

- Outpatient services should be located toward the front of the hospital. To help create the best traffic-flow patterns within the hospital, place the patients that will be in the facility for the shortest time periods at the front of the hospital, and the patients expected to stay for longer amounts of time deeper into the building.

- Ancillary services such as rehabilitation can be separated from the other areas of the hospital and may have entirely distinct circulation, including their own entrance and exit.

MEETING UNIQUE NEEDS

Most specialty facilities tend to require more square footage than general veterinary practices due to the volume of services they provide and the equipment necessary to provide them. This can range from 14,000 square feet to 45,000 square feet or more. Although it is certainly ideal to have all of your services on one floor, this is not always achievable with buildings of this size.

High property costs or limited inventory in the real estate market may contribute to the need to utilize more than one level. When you turn down this path, you will also need to add in vertical circulation (stairs and elevators) as well as duplicate client areas, such as reception and waiting, and program elements such as additional radiology rooms, lab spaces, and animal holding areas, depending on how the program divisions occur. The three typical scenarios for these divisions are as follows:

- All medical spaces on the ground floor, with the staff and storage spaces on a different level, whether this is a second floor or a basement.

- Emergency and intensive care services on the main level, with specialty services, including surgery rooms, on a different floor.

- Exam rooms, outpatient treatment, and radiological services, such as linear accelerator, MRI, and CT, on the main level, with inpatient and staff areas on a different floor.

When deciding where to place these divisions, it is important to carefully consider, with your architect and engineers, the costs associated with designing and building spaces with special requirements on multiple floors.

It is also worth noting that the inclusion of major medical equipment, such as a linear accelerator or MRI, may drive the design decisions in a multifloor structure. For example, it is not practical to put a linear accelerator vault on a raised level because of its mass.

Another concern to keep in mind when deciding which spaces can be on which floor is the need to minimize the movement of animals. This could be due to a patient being under anesthesia or because they are critically ill or less mobile.

Separating Departments

Beyond general area groupings that are discussed in Chapter 20, specialty hospitals present additional complexities because of

An example of departmental layout in a large specialty hospital. (Courtesy of Veterinary Referral Associates, Gaithersburg, Maryland.)

SPECIALTY/REFERRAL HOSPITALS 111

departmental groupings. Depending on the business model of the hospital, it may be necessary to physically separate specific services so that they can stand alone as separate business entities. For example, an emergency and critical care business is often part of a larger entity. This emergency care department may operate like a mini clinic within the larger hospital, with its own entrance, exam rooms, triage, and surgery spaces. When separating departments, it is critical to develop a list of what can be shared and what must remain separate. In most instances, a staff break room may be shared, but sharing surgery rooms may not be feasible.

Traffic Flow and Visibility

Due to the higher number of exam rooms typically associated with a specialty/referral practice, visibility to the reception area from the exam rooms can be difficult to achieve. Typically, with larger numbers of exam rooms, pod layouts are the most useful approach. Each individual pod can relate to a specific service or back into a doctors' work area or a small treatment space. This can help with the organization and efficiency of the hospital's operations. If the entrances to the exam rooms are not visible to the reception area, it is still a good idea to have at least one common path that leads back to the reception area.

Just as with any large hospital, traffic flow linking these departments becomes especially critical. The largest hospitals may have oversize circulation spines or racetrack circulation patterns to keep all traffic flowing efficiently.

Accommodating Changing Technologies and Adding New Services

Whenever feasible, all hospitals should be built with some amount of flexibility for future expansion. This concept is especially true for specialty/referral hospitals. Think about how you can attract and retain future specialists. What technologies are they going to want to see or require when they join your practice? The following are a few ideas to keep in mind to meet changing technology needs and help provide some flexibility in your plan.

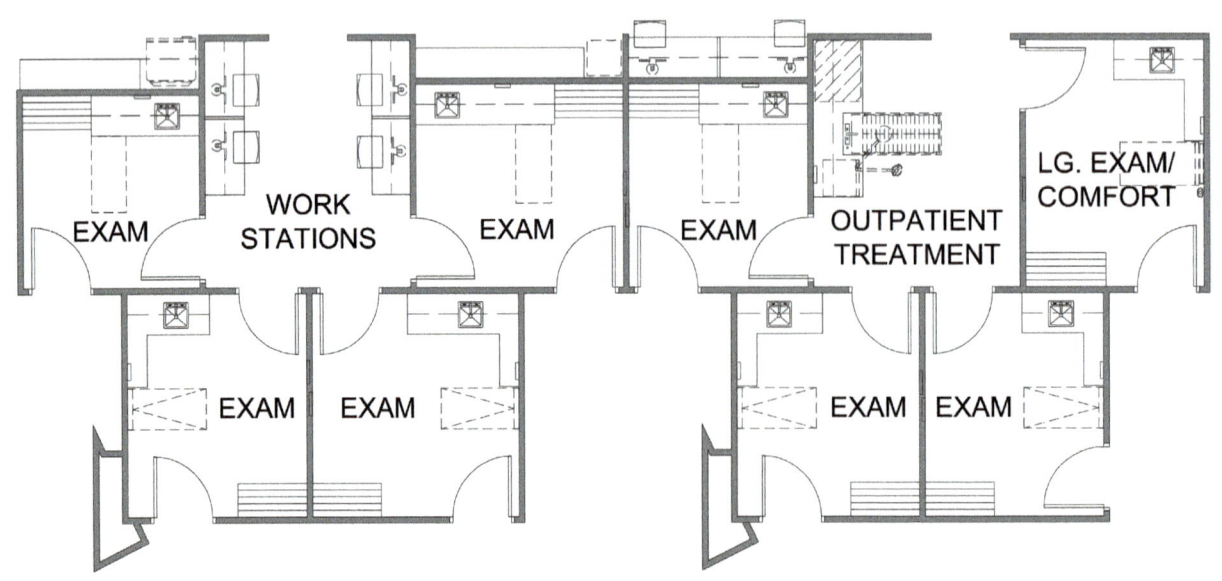

An excerpt of a plan from a hospital that incorporates both work stations and outpatient treatment within the pods' centers. (Courtesy of Coral Springs Animal Hospital, Coral Springs, Florida.)

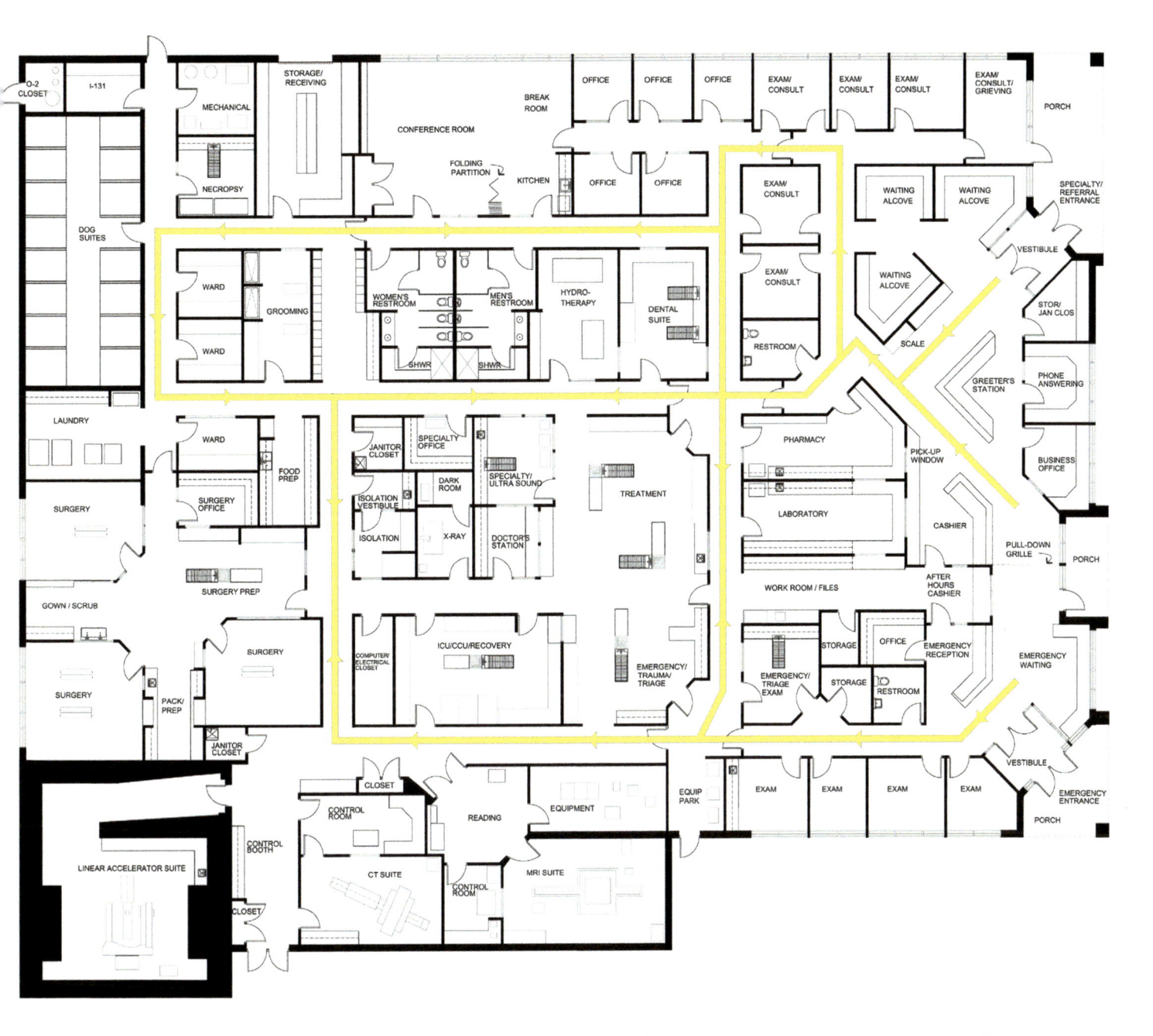

An example of a large specialty hospital with the racetrack traffic pattern. (Courtesy of VCA Mississauga Animal Hospital, Mississauga, Ontario [VCA Canada].)

- With all imaging areas, make an educated guess about "the next" machine you will need and then have your team design for this possibility. If the future machine will require more shielding, more power, more cooling, or more space, plan for it now.

› Don't forget to have your design professionals look at the path of travel for both current and future equipment into the building. If you can't fit it through the door, you cannot have it in your facility.

SPECIALTY/REFERRAL HOSPITALS

- If you aren't installing it now, but think you might in the future, plan for the power and space requirements for the following:
    › An emergency generator. Note that this is required for any building that has an MRI machine, as the machine cannot go down.
    › Automated inventory systems.

- Try to locate a few flex rooms near your exam room core to use in the future as exam rooms or as additional special procedure rooms.

- If you don't know exactly what specialty services you will provide in the future, build in a few procedure rooms that can be combination rooms for services such as cardiology and ultrasound.

- Design your hospital to expand so that entire departments can be added in the future.

▼ ▼ ▼

SPECIALIZATION IS LIKELY to remain a viable model for the foreseeable future, as it fosters an environment for providing the best specialized care from board-certified professionals. Specialty/referral hospitals are both dynamic and profitable. Planning them takes expertise, as they must be both specific to the services that are provided today and flexible for future growth.

CHAPTER 22

EMERGENCY HOSPITALS

Emergency hospital design starts at the street, because every extra second counts! Designing your site to expedite the journey to your front door is the first step to good emergency facility design. It is important to seek help from your design team to get this right. You will want to consider the following questions:

- Is the site and exterior building signage clear and concise, and does it inform the clients quickly that this is where they need to be and direct them to the entrance?

- Are the parking areas, curbs, ramps, and sidewalks laid out in such a way as to improve ease of access to the practice?

- Can the front desk staff easily see clients when they pull up or come through the front door with the patient?

- Are there oversize doors, double doors, or automatic doors to assist in getting sick or injured animals safely into the building?

- Is the exterior of the building well lit at night?

The approach you take to create an efficient and safe experience for your clients and patients as they find and enter the building should continue through the check-in process and be maintained throughout the patient's stay at your facility.

PROVIDING AN EFFICIENT AND CARING CLIENT SERVICE EXPERIENCE

As is true with any veterinary hospital, in an emergency hospital the entrance and reception areas are important for setting the tone for the service you're providing. A welcoming experience is especially important in an emergency hospital due to the higher stress levels involved.

The reception desk should be positioned close to the front door to allow for immediate communication with the client to assist in the triage process. This reinforces the patient-first philosophy and allows the staff to be readily available. The reception area also needs to have a clear sight line to the access door, the back medical spaces, and the exam rooms and waiting areas. The ability of front desk staff to step out quickly to assist clients should also be a design factor. As the last area your clients will experience, it is also important to consider separate client checkout stations or client care rooms to allow for private and potentially emotional conversations to occur. Locating these rooms out of the main traffic and triage flow will provide for a calmer, more client-focused experience.

The waiting experience can be especially difficult in an emergency setting. The first step is to try to eliminate, or vastly reduce, waiting time by providing more exam rooms and by moving clients into these rooms as quickly as possible. In human medical emergency departments, the speed of the first contact with the doctor and medical staff can dramatically affect patient outcomes. As the same is true in veterinary care, moving clients quickly to an area where their pets can be seen should be a top priority.

Waiting areas in emergency hospitals are more centered on long-term waiting for clients while their pets are being cared for in treatment. Provide options for short- and long-term waiting in the lobby, as well as some comfortable seating for clients who stay for long periods of time.

Consideration should be given to color, sound, and window locations when laying out the design of the waiting area. Ask the design team to prioritize creating a calming experience to ease the anxiety of the emergency department setting.

As the intermediate spaces that they are, exam rooms are the center of client care in an emergency hospital. They should be well equipped to enable staff to carry out their jobs, while at the same time they should help to calm both the client and the patient. Consider the following methods of meeting these objectives in emergency exam room design:

- Install lighting that can be bright for quick and efficient examinations but dimmable for when the client or the patient needs a calmer environment.

- Choose highly cleanable and durable finishes, keeping in mind that managing biological risk is most important in emergency situations.

- Include flexible seating to accommodate families.

- Incorporate monitors so that you can review imaging with clients.

- Incorporate flexible exam tables (such as fold-up tables) so large dogs can be examined on the floor when necessary.

Oversize exam rooms can be designed to be multifunctional for examinations, triage, and

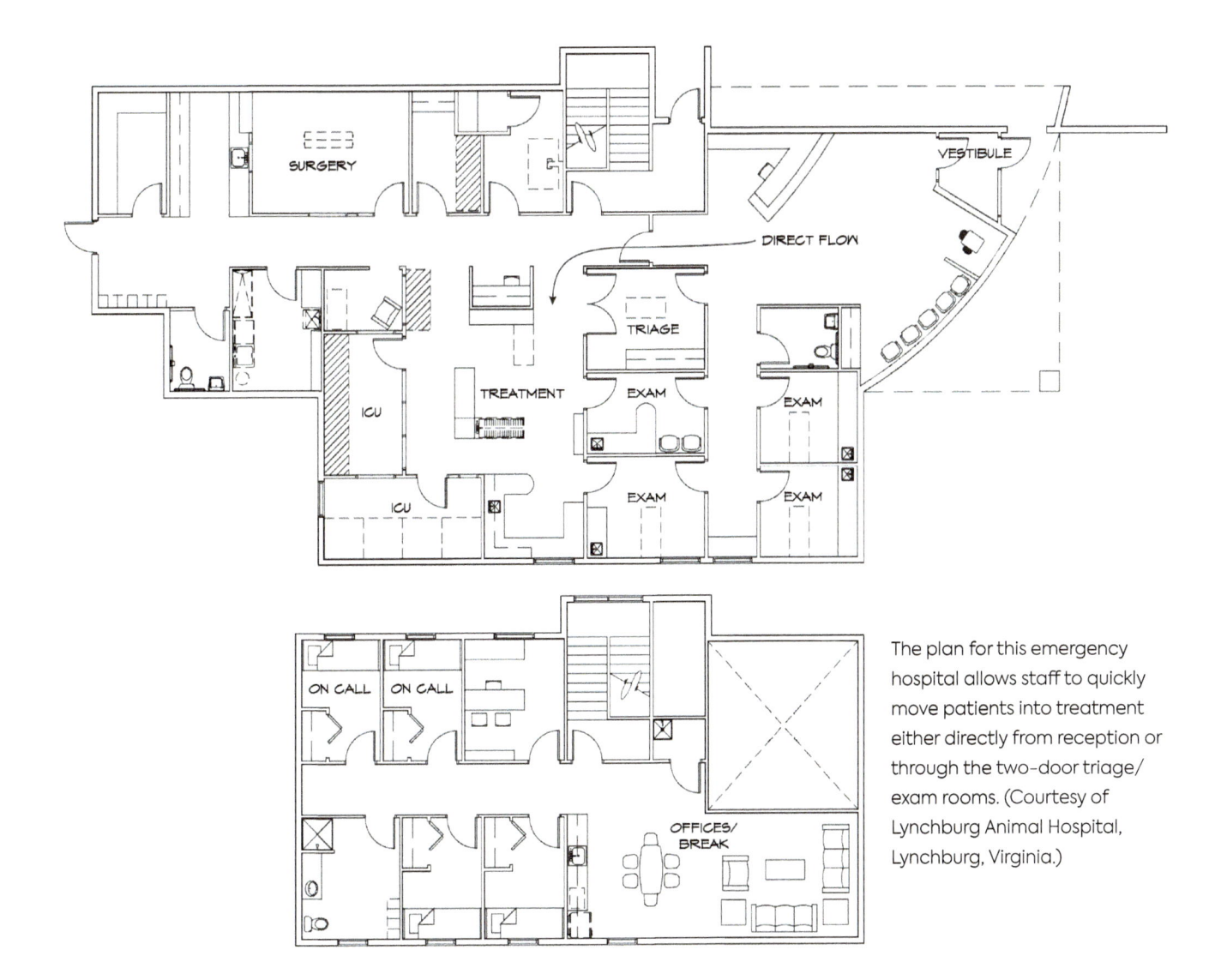

The plan for this emergency hospital allows staff to quickly move patients into treatment either directly from reception or through the two-door triage/exam rooms. (Courtesy of Lynchburg Animal Hospital, Lynchburg, Virginia.)

euthanasia. All exam rooms either should have a separate door to allow for quick access to the medical areas or should be located in such a way that one door allows for universal access within the hospital.

AVOIDING COMPARTMENTALIZATION

Compartmentalization leads to less flexibility and less opportunity for staff to assist each other. The more open the front areas are in an emergency hospital setting, the faster care can be given. The same is true throughout all client and medical spaces. Openness and transparency are important in the medical areas to enable better patient visualization and collaboration between staff. The exam rooms should open to the staff charting/work area. This space in turn should open to the main triage or treatment room, which should then open to the ICU space. This is the idea of an open core design.

It can sometimes be challenging to create an open core. On top of the staff work areas, the treatment space, and the ICU, there are also some critical components to the core that are not to be missed. The pharmacy, laboratory, radiology, and operatory spaces are integral to the successful treatment of a critical patient. The best way to envision these spaces is as spokes on a wheel. Each of these spaces should be located just outside this core but with quick access to it. Due to the higher volume of lab work and the need for fast results, the laboratory must be designed for efficiency. Central pharmacies, with access to both the front, for clients, and the back, for the medical staff, also need to be very efficient in emergency hospital settings.

The shift away from compartmentalization should continue with the storage of materials and patient housing. Patients, and materials to serve the needs of these patients, should be spread throughout the hospital, divided between levels of care.

There are still a few spaces that need separation—for example, to help with biological risk management, provide isolation rooms with separate entrances/exits in close proximity to the ICU.

PROVIDING A SAFE EXPERIENCE

Emotions and pain often run high in an emergency setting. Emergencies can occur any time, day or night. And most twenty-four-hour emergency facilities have the unique challenge of operating with just a skeleton crew through the overnight hours. This means staff and patient safety should be at the forefront of emergency hospital facility design.

A transparent entry vestibule with a secured interior door will enable your clients and their pets to get out of the weather while also providing overnight staff with the opportunity to look

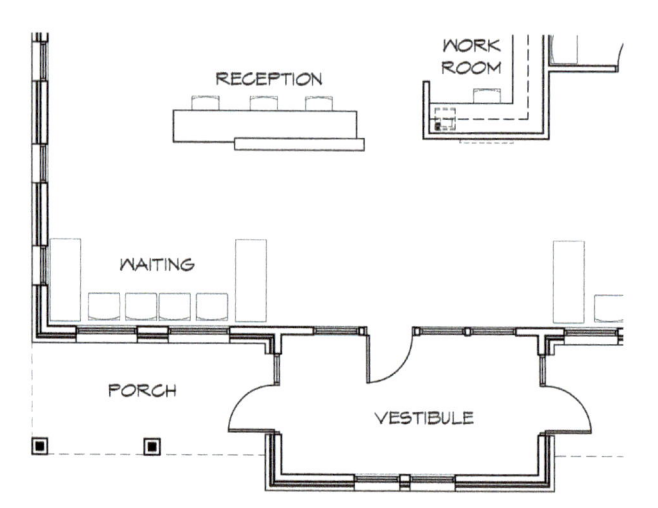

A vestibule, as illustrated in the plan segment in the above image, can protect clients and staff and help prevent accidental animal escapes. (Courtesy of Callbeck Animal Hospital, Whitby, Ontario.)

out from the reception desk or view a security monitor prior to buzzing them into the facility.

Locating a security monitor in the ICU area that allows staff to view not only the entry vestibule but also the parking lot and dog walking areas at night is important for safety. Equipping the reception area, as well as the ICU staff, with panic buttons with direct access to the authorities is also a good idea.

Two-door exam rooms, while convenient for traffic flow, have the added benefit of offering an emergency exit for those rare instances when a client may exhibit threatening behavior. Card access points can add another layer of security, controlling access to clinical and ward areas.

Finally, be sure to include on-call rooms for staff so they have a place to rest in a safe and secure area when they are working overnight.

SOME TRENDS TO CONSIDER

- Observation unit: Sometimes referred to as a "step-down" ward, an observation unit can provide an area for patients to continue the recovery process when they no longer need to remain in the ICU. This area can generally provide a quieter and less expensive option for your clients when the patient no longer requires fluids or critical care measures.

- Results waiting room: A separate space for stable patients awaiting diagnostic results can decrease the amount of time patients spend in an exam room, allowing for more patients to be seen. It can also help medical staff easily locate those clients waiting for test results.

- Client waiting areas in triage: A few practices have experimented with providing client observation and waiting areas in triage. Although many practices are not at all comfortable with this option—for good reasons, such as separating clients from chaos and emotional trauma—those who have tried this model have reported fewer complaints about services and billing. Under this model of emergency care, the client can readily see the work that is being done to save their pet's life. If clients are going to be in the triage space, it's best to provide a dedicated and demarcated area in which they can stand as well as the option of sitting or exiting the space if the situation is too much for them to handle.

▼ ▼ ▼

IN SUMMARY, THERE are three main things to keep in mind when designing an emergency hospital. First, the hospital should be laid out to provide an efficient and caring experience for the client and patient. The clients' first and last impressions are what will stay with them. Look for opportunities to create comfortable spaces for clients and patients in order to decrease their stress. Emergency medical care should be delivered as efficiently and calmly as possible. Second, the more visually and functionally open the core is, the more effectively the medical staff will be able to assist the patient and the client. Once the open core is achieved, be sure to locate the "spokes" to best assist the core. Finally, the security of the facility should be a primary consideration, particularly at night. Transparency does not have to mean a less secure facility. Use technology to help maintain a safe environment—for your staff, for your clients, and for the patients in your care.

CHAPTER 23

FELINE HOSPITALS

Veterinary practices that exclusively treat our feline friends are a growing specialty within the larger field of veterinary medicine. This is in part a response to the curious inversion of dog and cat statistics when it comes to medical care. Cats exceed dogs in numbers of household pets in the US, but veterinarians see more dog patients than cats. Can a cat-only practice benefit from this untapped market opportunity? Can a feline practitioner also attract from general veterinary hospitals the clients who want the best care for their cats?

Cat owners are constantly searching for veterinarians who understand cats better than they understand dogs. These clients are eager for creative and intelligent providers who can handle their pets with gentleness and care, give exceptional advice for the maintenance of good health, quickly reach the correct diagnosis when symptoms arise, and propose highly effective solutions for treatment. Passionate and smart feline practitioners are therefore the backbone of a successful cat-only practice.

What supports that backbone and enables the functioning of the practice? A cat-friendly facility. The following are features of a well-designed cat hospital:

- A safe and quiet waiting area.
- Abundant natural light.
- Exam rooms designed just for cats.
- Protections against escapees.
- Cat-appropriate caging for overnight stays.
- Biological risk management.

SMALLER PATIENTS = CHEAPER BUILDING . . . RIGHT?

One of the biggest misconceptions among veterinarians is that a cat hospital will cost much less to build than other facilities because the patients are smaller. Unfortunately, it's not that simple.

The reality is that space-saving opportunities are more limited than one might think. You can reduce the size of the waiting area and the exam rooms, and the treatment area can shrink a bit. However, you still need to have more or less the same equipment, and humans still need the same amount of space to maneuver around the equipment and cabinetry. Building codes likewise dictate a number of requirements that cannot be ignored. Therefore, even the most aggressive approach to minimizing the size of the spaces will typically result in a hospital that is still 80%–90% of what a general practice facility would be.

Next comes the assumption that the cost per square foot should be lower. However, the opposite is actually true. The reality shows very little reduction in the quantity of the costly components needed for the practice, such as cabinetry, equipment, doors, windows, bathrooms, lighting fixtures, and HVAC equipment. The reductions primarily occur in the amount of open area within spaces, and it is the open area that carries the lowest cost per square foot within a building.

You might expect your cat hospital to be slightly less expensive than other facilities, but be sure to align your expectations with real cost estimates before embarking on a project to ensure your budget will build a facility that will meet your needs and the needs of your staff and feline patients.

WHO ARE YOUR PATIENTS?

In most cases, veterinary practices focus on cats who come primarily for preventive care, less often for an illness or injury, and possibly one last time for a humane end-of-life appointment. Before beginning the design process, veterinarians need to determine how many exam rooms they will need, how euthanasia appointments will be handled, and how to handle isolation needs for infectious cats. Boarding goals, as well as any specialty services, should also be identified.

If a veterinary practice anticipates teaming up with rescue groups and shelters via partnerships or discounts, or providing space for community spay/neuter clinics, an additional set of design criteria will come into play. For instance, rescue cats typically carry a much higher rate of infectious disease, including numerous viruses, ringworm, parasites, and bacterial infections. Some of these felines may require housing, and heavy use of isolation areas should be anticipated.

ROOM-BY-ROOM CONSIDERATIONS

Vestibule

A vestibule serves two very important purposes: it makes it quite difficult for a loose cat to fully escape the building, and it provides a thermal barrier between the outside and inside environments, making the waiting room more comfortable.

Waiting Area

Waiting areas in cat hospitals can be much smaller than in general veterinary practices. The veterinarian should identify the maximum anticipated number of clients (including families) at any given time and provide adequate seating. Multiple surfaces, such as end tables, should be provided on which clients can place cat carriers, so that the cats are not on the floor. Keeping a cat elevated is a critical component for a stress-free environment. A sound system for white noise or for soft classical music may also help to minimize distractions and reduce stress. Studies show that species-specific music may be particularly effective.

Adoption Center

Adoption centers within veterinary hospitals have grown in popularity in recent years. They provide a needed resource to rescue groups and shelters while also attracting new clients and referrals to the practice. Adoption centers are typically adjacent to the waiting area and include a reasonable amount of glass and natural light, with ample space to allow for play structures, sleeping areas, and distance between eating and elimination areas. These spaces should include materials that are easy to clean and sanitize, and adequate storage and preparation areas should be nearby for food and cleaning equipment.

Exam Rooms

Exam rooms for cats require an exam table, which can either be a stationary counter (with cabinetry beneath) or a fold-down table attached to a wall. Furniture for client seating should likewise be considered, and all surfaces should be easily cleanable.

Exam rooms should also include a few cabinets for supply storage, space for a cat scale, and a work surface for charting. Some practitioners prefer to have sinks in exam rooms, while others do not.

These rooms can also be supplied with cat perches, views to the out-of-doors, and cleanable toys to help cats adjust to the environment.

Comfort Room

The room used for euthanasia should be larger than the standard exam room, as it will often involve the presence of the entire client family. It should be comfortable and should preferably be near a secondary exit so that clients can leave in a private manner. In addition, the path from this room to the freezer should not overlap client traffic flow.

Isolation

A separate exam room for infectious patients should be strongly considered: locating it adjacent to a secondary building exit is advisable, so that the patient can be escorted directly to the room without traversing the waiting area. An isolation room for hospitalized patients should likewise be provided. This room should be visible from the treatment area so that infectious patients can be easily monitored.

Treatment Area

The treatment area is the heart of the hospital, and it should be as close as possible to the exam rooms, surgery area, diagnostic equipment, charting stations, and holding areas for hospitalized cats. Adequate maneuvering space should be provided, and it must be very well lit. Cat hospital treatment rooms can be a fraction smaller than treatment areas in general veterinary facilities. You can create a truly cat-centric treatment area by including strategically placed hiding spaces—that are also easily accessible to your staff—as refuges that will attract stressed escapee cats.

Surgery

Since the patients in a feline hospital are relatively small, surgery rooms can likewise be smaller than surgery rooms designed to accommodate large dogs. Adequate maneuvering space must be maintained around the surgery table, as well as space for the anesthesia equipment, scavenging units, and other tools and equipment. As with any surgery suite, it must be designed as an aseptic environment with materials that allow for proper cleaning. The HVAC system should provide positive pressure in this room, and a scrub-in area should be located immediately outside the room. Pack/prep should be adjacent to surgery and may include pass-through windows or cabinetry.

Spaces for Diagnostic Equipment

Some diagnostic equipment carries shielding requirements, and for this equipment a radiation shielding physicist's report is required to determine the extent of shielding needed. Except for dental X-ray equipment, these items generally require their own enclosed rooms, depending on state regulations. As technology advances, and smaller equipment arrives on the market for cats and other small animal patients, this may further reduce the amount of floor area required. Shielding requirements may also become less intensive as technology advances.

Iodine-131

If you plan to incorporate an I-131 program into your hospital, you will need to first verify with your local planning jurisdiction that it is allowable at the proposed project site. I-131 services typically do not require a large amount of space, but you will need to have an adequate boarding area for patients, as well as all required accommodations based upon the radioactive levels of the patients and their eliminations. These requirements are more thoroughly discussed in Chapter 34.

Boarding

Many veterinarians, including cat-only practitioners, find that having a boarding program is a revenue incentive. Of course, cat owners are less likely than dog owners to utilize such a service, as in-home pet sitting is much less stressful for cats.

If you do plan to incorporate this service, you will want to provide cat-friendly housing. Ideally, it should allow for 9.5 square feet of area per cat. Tiered systems, such as cat towers, or systems with shelves or perches, are creative ways to provide more horizontal area without eating up too much floor space in your building. Divider panels can also provide flexibility, depending on the quantity of cats in your care. Unlike medical cat housing, where you might want to limit the mobility of the patients, healthy cats with longer stays should enjoy stress-free housing solutions, with plenty of space for the cats to walk, stretch, jump, and play, and with the litter box as far away as possible from food and water. Ventilation should ideally pull the air from the room through the cages and out of the building.

The Resident Cat

There are pros and cons to planning for a resident cat to live at the hospital. It often provides an otherwise homeless animal a second chance at life. It can also be a fun element for some of your clients, and the hospital waiting area can be designed to incorporate creative catwalks and play structures. The drawbacks include biological risk management and the effects that a loose cat can have on patients, who may be stressed around other cats. If you do plan to include a resident cat, plan ahead to provide places for the cat to play, eat, sleep, and use the litter box, and include a vestibule at every public exit from your hospital to prevent an accidental escape.

▼ ▼ ▼

THE NICHE MARKET of feline-only veterinary care can provide a unique business opportunity for veterinarians who wish to specialize in the care of cats. While the design of hospitals for cat-only care is very similar to the design of a typical general practice, there are some unique elements that should be recognized and accommodated by your design team.

CHAPTER 24

EQUINE AND LARGE ANIMAL HOSPITALS

All the creatures great and small include not only Great Danes and guinea pigs but also Thoroughbreds and Texas Longhorns. Designing hospitals for large animals presents some very unique challenges. This chapter will provide a broad overview of the most important requirements for practices that focus specifically on caring for larger animals, from practical planning to the importance of designing from the perspective of these patients.

CHOOSING LAND

Most large animal practitioners who build a physical facility, whether it be a small haul-in clinic or a larger referral hospital, need to be located in a more rural setting because of their client base or because of the need to find a parcel of ground large enough and zoned properly for large animal use. A rural location can offer many opportunities, such as easier regulatory processes, but it also poses some challenges. One of the biggest of these challenges concerns the utilities and infrastructure of the site. Ask these questions before purchasing land:

- If the buildings will be utilizing well water, what is the cost of digging a well that can provide a reliable water source to the property? What is the expected well water flow rate, and is this adequate for a veterinary practice?

- Will the well water need treatment, and if so, what will be the cost of that treatment?

- If the property needs a septic field, where would this need to be located to provide adequate distance from the well and any wells on adjoining properties? Typically, wells and septic systems must be separated by at least 100 feet.

- What is the cost of the septic system? Many animal facilities that are on septic need a separate holding tank for disinfectants to lose their effectiveness before entering into the main tank and field. This adds to the cost of the system.

- What is the cost of running electric to the site in the amperage necessary to run the hospital plus provide for future expansion? This question is especially important if the hospital has special equipment, such as imaging machines.

- If gas lines are not available, what is the cost for providing propane storage? What is the relative cost of propane versus electric in operating equipment?

You may also face the question of fire sprinkler system requirements on rural sites. While agricultural structures, including barns, are generally exempt from requirements for sprinkler systems, hospitals are subject to typical commercial building code requirements. What this means is that if it is not practical to have a fire sprinkler system, it will be necessary to work within the code-required limits for the type of hospital construction and building size limitations.

Before choosing a project site, have a design professional and contractor help you itemize the site utility costs, as they may help you test the viability of developing a particular site.

SITE PLANNING

In addition to planning for utilities, there are a number of other basic site design requirements for large animal hospitals that differ from those for small animal hospitals. These differences start with site planning and the ratio between the size of the site and the size of the hospital. For small animal hospitals, the general rule is that the site should be five times larger than the building. This ratio is not adequate for most large animal hospitals, as they have greater exterior space requirements. A better rule is that the site should be ten times larger than the structures in order to accommodate additional exterior space for parking trailers, small turn-out areas, unloading areas, and so on. If you are planning pastures or large turnouts, even more land will be required.

As with any site, it will be important to verify that it is usable and not steeply sloped or constrained by wetlands, utility easements, etc. Areas that are not usable cannot be counted toward the required ratio of land to building.

BUDGETING FOR A LARGE ANIMAL OR EQUINE FACILITY

Budgeting for large animal facilities can be complicated because project costs can vary widely. A simple barn or open structure may cost $75 to $100 per square foot, whereas a hospital facility for horses may cost as much as a small animal hospital. The rooms may be simpler, but they are bigger, and their durability needs are significant. They require tall ceilings, good flooring, a lot of plumbing for sanitation, and so on. For example, equine surgery rooms are typically hose cleaned, so they require even higher-performing finishes than small animal surgery rooms.

The best way to develop a sense of project costs is to define the basic building requirements and seek assistance from professionals who have designed or built this type of building before to help you balance your needs with the probable project costs. At this early stage, you should carry 20% in addition to the probable cost of the project for unknowns, and 35% for project soft costs. In other words, it is advisable to be able to cover at least one and a half times the earliest estimated cost of construction in order to feel secure that the project is likely to remain within your budget as it moves forward.

As with any practice, it is important to take on only as much debt as you can afford, and then to build the revenue to afford future growth. A veterinary practice financial adviser can help define this for you. The best plan may be to start with a relatively simple facility and plan for growth. Even a simple facility may dramatically improve the quality of life for a large animal or equine practitioner who has otherwise been providing only ambulatory service. A roof overhead can be a great stepping stone to future success, as a building can allow for diversification of services.

ORGANIZATIONAL BASICS

The best way to look at a large animal or equine project is as an indoor/outdoor space. Beginning with this viewpoint allows for an understanding that the outside spaces need to be planned as well as the inside spaces in order to create efficient and safe traffic flow for the whole hospital.

Start from the site plan and create clear circulation paths for vehicles, animals, and staff. Pay special attention to the location of the equine unloading zone, as this area can be very chaotic if not planned properly.

Cattle are a special case for circulation because of the equipment required to unload the cattle and move them via alleys and into chutes. Veterinarians who work with cattle tend to have specific ideas for how they should be moved, so it is best to design the facility around the veterinarian's preferred method.

Once inside, the plan should be segregated into very clear zones for staff and animals. A plan that is poorly organized creates inefficiencies, such as having to cross through animal zones to get to people zones (see below for an example of a clearly organized equine hospital floor plan). Note that in this plan, equine areas have a close connection to the out-of-doors, while support areas and human zones are located in the interior of the building.

LARGE ANIMALS ARE LARGE

The physical size of large animals guides much of the sizing of rooms in a hospital. Spaces need to be sized appropriately for the animals as well as for the large equipment required for their treatment. Appropriately sized spaces help to ensure everyone's safety. When planning a room with stocks, for example, be sure to design it with enough space on all sides of the stocks for animals to be moved safely.

On the following pages are some typical sizes for spaces in equine hospitals.

FLOOR PLAN
9,733 SQUARE FEET - MAIN FLOOR

(Courtesy of Tryon Equine Hospital, Columbus, South Carolina.)

- An exam alcove should be no smaller than 16 × 16 feet clear. This will feel very small if it is an enclosed room, but it is acceptable for an alcove in a larger room.

- An enclosed exam/treatment room without stocks should be 18 × 24 feet in dimension. For a room with stocks, enlarge this to provide 12 feet of clear space on three sides of the stocks.

- Surgery rooms should be 20 × 25 feet, and larger for specialty surgery spaces.

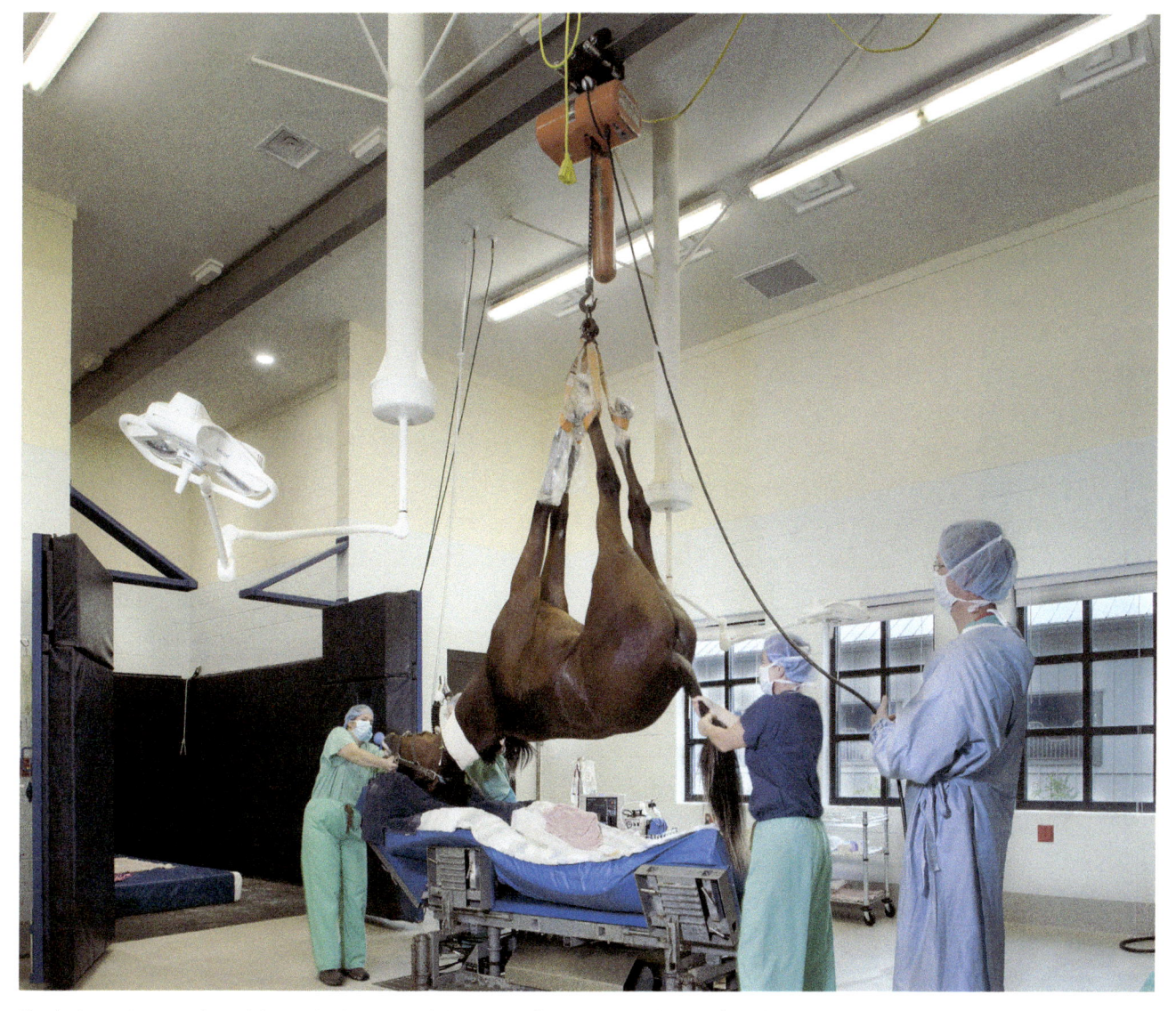

The hoist system and track keep the horse well above the floor level and away from lighting and other equipment in the surgery suite. (Foto Imagery / Tim Murphy. Courtesy of Tryon Equine Hospital, Columbus, South Carolina.)

- Barn aisles should be 14 feet wide to prevent horses in stalls from having contact with horses walking through.

- Typical stalls should be a minimum of 12 × 12 feet.

- Stalls for draft horses should be a minimum of 12 × 14 feet or 14 × 14 feet.

- Foaling stalls should be a minimum of 12 × 16 feet.

Rooms need to be tall as well. Twelve feet is the lowest practical ceiling height for working with large animals safely. For equine surgery and recovery areas, the veterinarian will have a specific preference on the height of the hoist beam, but 14 feet to the bottom of the beam is required to keep horses' heads from grazing the floor.

MATERIALS AND FINISHES

Large animal and equine spaces get used very hard. They need to be both durable and cleanable. In areas where animals may have contact with walls, design the wall materials to resist the forces exerted by large animals. The extreme example of this is surgery induction and recovery rooms for horses, which are typically designed with reinforced and fully grouted concrete block masonry walls. Concrete block masonry is a good choice for most large animal spaces.

Floor finishes can be difficult to choose. Exposed and sealed concrete floors are practical, but they are generally too slippery. Rubber mats can be used in areas where animals stand, but they must either be cleaned rigorously and dried thoroughly or sealed to the substrate below to prevent the growth of bacteria. This is a well-known potential danger in university settings, where unsealed mats have contributed to dangerous salmonella outbreaks.

Below are the possible options for covering large treatment rooms:

- Sealed rubber mats, seamed together.
- Poured rubber flooring.
- Poured urethane flooring.

Because poured products are very expensive (typically more than $20 per square foot), it is critical to use a product that has been developed specifically for this market and to do everything right, including reference checks, involving the manufacturer in creating the specifications for the flooring, and involving the installer in reviewing and testing the slabs for moisture content before installation proceeds. Ask your colleagues what floor products they have used and how successful they have been.

WORKING WITH THE PSYCHOLOGY OF LARGE ANIMALS

When considering all of the practical requirements of this building type, it is important to consider the viewpoint of the patients themselves. A hospital that is designed from the viewpoint of the patient is going to be one that works better. Because large animals are prey animals, it's best to create spaces that reduce fear. Put yourself in their hooves!

Dr. Temple Grandin's publications are a great source of information about designing effective spaces for cattle based on the way they think. Even if your facility is simple, her research can be very helpful for creating spaces that work effectively. For example, cattle resist being pushed forward, and they are inclined to try to go back to where they came from. Thus, gently curving paths work better for moving cattle than straight lines or tight curves.

People who regularly work with horses typically have a good understanding of what horses are going to fear and, by extension, what to avoid in equine hospital design. From a more positive viewpoint, the following general rules can be used to design spaces that reduce equine fear:

- Connect indoor and outdoor spaces. This way the indoor spaces do not feel as foreign.

- Provide views into pleasant spaces, such as outdoor turnout areas, rather than chaotic areas such as unloading zones and vehicular paths.

- Provide clear views across spaces. Blind corners can create opportunities for horses to fear what they may know is there but cannot see.

- Light spaces evenly to prevent shadows.

- Both horses and cattle will resist walking across drains, as they can appear frightening. Set drains out of the way of direct walking paths.

- Horses and cattle both fear social isolation. It is best to house horses in areas where they can see other horses unless there is a specific reason to have them separated, such as in the case of an isolation patient.

- Provide wide enough spaces that the horses are not afraid of walking through an area. Small, narrow, enclosed spaces can be threatening.

- Be sure the footing is sound and safe. Slippery floors can be both frightening and dangerous.

▼ ▼ ▼

EQUINE AND LARGE animal hospitals have their own design requirements. Sites require more planning and infrastructure. Spaces need to be larger and more durable. Handling large animals requires finesse that should be reflected in the design. What works best about large animal hospitals is their connection to the out-of-doors. For those taking on the design of a large animal facility, whether it will be a simple roof overhead or a referral hospital, try to capture this indoor/outdoor connection as much as possible to create spaces that are inherently in tune with nature. If you can achieve this goal, the facility will be enjoyable to work in for many years.

CHAPTER 25

MIXED ANIMAL HOSPITALS

Mixed animal hospitals that care for both small and large animals have always existed in veterinary medicine, and they are a viable business model, especially in certain markets. For example, mixed animal practices are common in Canada, perhaps in part because of the smaller population base in many areas. Another recent trend is to incorporate small animal practices adjacent to or under the same ownership as an existing equine or large animal practice. This arrangement can create a more diverse and economically sustainable business model for the large animal or equine practice. In any case, practices that treat multiple species must be able to offer the same quality of care for all their patients, and meeting this goal depends in part on a good and efficient hospital design.

SHARING RESOURCES

A good design in a mixed animal hospital can create the opportunity to share resources, equipment, and space without forming complex traffic patterns between the two sides of the practice. Below are three different approaches to designing an efficient practice of this type:

- Approach 1: Shared public space, shared support space, separate treatment space. In some practices, equine and small animal clients come in through the same front door. This is a great plan for practices that have a light small animal client load.

- Approach 2: Separate public space, shared support space, separate treatment space. In most mixed animal practices, and especially busy ones, it is more common to split clients at the lobby. Large animal clients come in one door and small animal clients come in through a second. If the two lobbies are adjacent to each other, it may be possible to share staff between the two sides of the business. In other cases, where staff is not shared, the two sides can be designed to be physically distinct, with separate front doors, parking areas, and welcome porches.

- Approach 3: No lobby on the large animal side. If the large animal haul-in side of the business represents a very small amount of space, clients may check in in the lobby but otherwise hang around in the large animal or equine treatment space, which is generally where they want to be anyway. This doesn't work when there is a lot going on in the treatment room, but it may be workable for one or two clients at a time.

Once a practice has decided how client traffic flow should be organized, it's time to consider the staff and support areas of the hospital. As a rule, it is most efficient to share as many spaces as possible in order to reduce capital expenditure. The following are examples of functions that can be shared by both sides of the hospital:

- Pharmacy and laboratory: You might have a separate pharmacy for stocking bulk items directly onto trucks for the large animal/equine side but share a smaller dispensing pharmacy. The laboratory is a good space to share for cutting down on duplication of equipment.

- Doctors' stations.

- Pack/prep and scrub: It is not always practical to colocate this function to serve the equine and small animal surgery areas, but if there is an opportunity to do so, it would reduce the duplication of autoclaves, scrub sinks, etc.

- Administrative areas, offices, and meeting rooms.

- Restrooms.

- Janitorial and mechanical rooms.

- Storage and loading.

- Laundry, utility, and food prep.

ORGANIZING STRATEGIES

If your practice plan will accommodate multiple species, it is important not just to identify areas that can be shared between the two halves of the building but also to develop strategies that allow both halves of the practice to grow. These include the following:

- Locating the building on the property so the two halves can both expand.

- Anticipating more growth on the small animal side. This is true in most cases, so it is especially important for the small animal area to have room around it where the building footprint can be enlarged.

- Locating medical areas on the perimeter of the building, as these are the most likely to expand.

- Developing a core that doesn't require expansion. Laundry, utility, and other shared core spaces should be oversize from the beginning so they will not require future expansion. These spaces are constrained by their location, wedged between the two sides of the practice.

The figure below is a bubble diagram that illustrates the adjacencies and flow of the shared spaces in a mixed animal hospital. The floor plan design shows how the bubble diagram can be transformed into a functional floor plan.

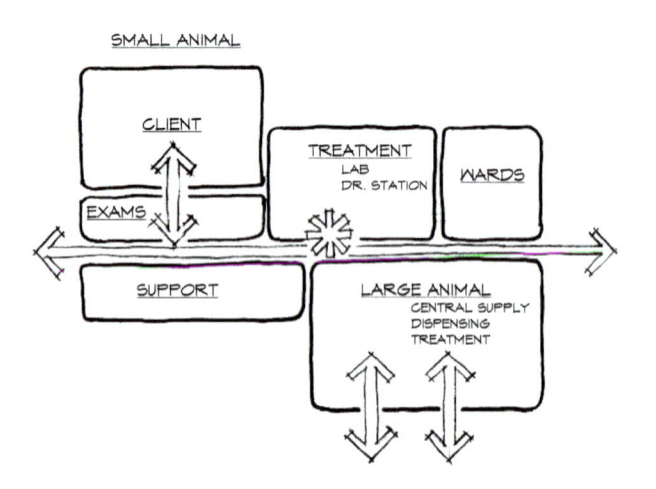

▼ ▼ ▼

A MIXED ANIMAL practice can be a very effective business model. The key to success is to plan to share as many spaces as possible. This will also help to create a culture of cooperation between large animal and small animal staff and practitioners.

Rather than thinking of a mixed animal practice as an older style of business, it is important to recognize the continued value that mixed animal practices bring and to embrace the efficiency of shared physical resources, financial resources, and staff.

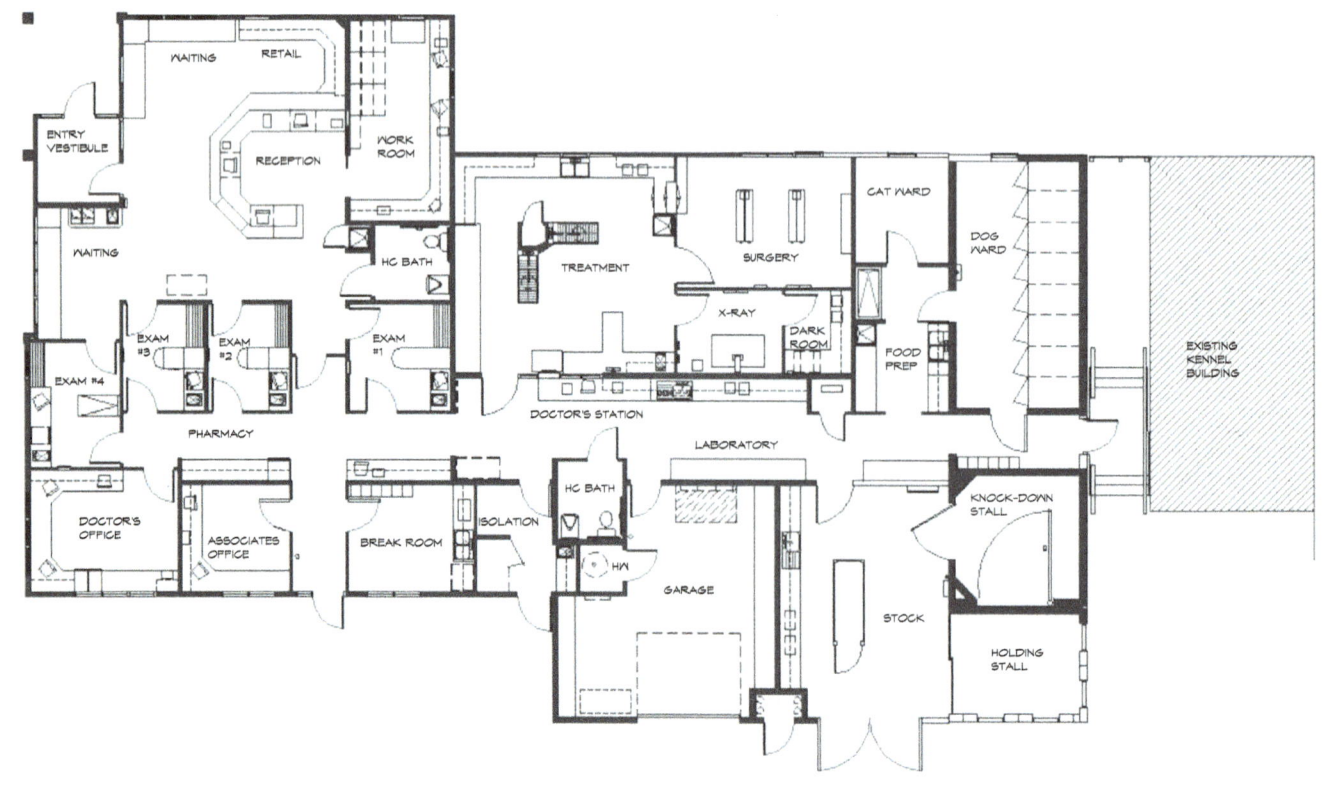

SECTION **THREE**

The Design of Veterinary Spaces

CHAPTER 26

RECEPTION AREAS

As was discussed in Chapter 14 on branding and curb appeal, the first impression that you communicate to your clients when they walk through the front door of your hospital can and will shape their perception of the quality of medicine you provide to their pets.

This is why following through with your branding decisions from the curb into your reception and client service areas is so important. It's also important to carefully consider how these spaces can help you engage with your clients, carry out your practice philosophy, and enhance the services you provide.

There are as many options for designing a reception and waiting area as there are veterinary practices: one desk, no desk, multiple desks, separate waiting areas, with retail, without retail, and so on. The options you choose will depend on a variety of other choices that you make about the medical and ancillary services you will provide. They will also depend on your customer service methodology, the level of transparency you wish to have, whether your practice is paperless, and so on.

ENTRY VESTIBULE

If you have the available square footage, usually a minimum of about 7 × 7 feet, including an entry vestibule in your hospital can have practical advantages.

For one, it can help to prevent any animal escape artists from making it out the front door and onto the street, as mentioned in the chapter on feline hospitals.

An entry vestibule has the added practical purpose of acting as a thermal barrier, helping to keep the elements, both cold and hot, from infiltrating your reception area.

The inside door of the vestibule should include glass at the client's eye level so clients can see and avoid other animals that might be present in the reception area near the doors. The vestibule can also be a safety feature for hospitals in urban areas or during overnight hours.

TRAFFIC FLOW

The design of your reception space is in part dependent on how you choose to organize traffic flow. Start by thinking about how your clients will enter and exit the building. It is important to visually align your reception desk with the entrance so that clients know exactly where to go when they walk in. If you wish to have separate entrance and exit doors, the traffic flow within the space must be very well defined, as people are naturally inclined to try to leave the same way they entered.

If your clients are greeted and moved quickly to an exam room, you may be able to minimize the size of your waiting area. However, if they are likely to wait for longer periods of time, the waiting area should be more spacious and comfortable. Calculate how many seats your waiting area should have based on your number of exam rooms, the number of treatment appointments you schedule in an hour, and any seating you think you might need for people waiting for ancillary services, such as grooming. Keep in mind that one client with a large dog, a cat in a carrier, or multiple pets may occupy two or more seats. You could also include a long-term waiting area for clients whose pets are receiving longer treatments or surgery. These waiting areas are usually more private and have more of a living-room feel.

The placement of the reception desk relative to other hospital functions can affect how you design and use it. In a typical traditional layout, it is common to align the reception desk with the exam rooms, with staff-only circulation behind it. This type of layout works well for small hospitals, but in larger hospitals it may create too much activity in one location.

If you prefer to have circulation around the desk, you will most likely want either an island reception desk or one placed on a wall opposite the exam rooms. A benefit of this layout is that it tends to minimize the times when clients and pets cross paths with other clients and pets. The drawbacks are that it is not as easy for the receptionist to dash into the back areas to fill a prescription or to track down a staff member, and that it takes up more floor space.

SIZE AND VOLUME

Traffic—and a certain amount of commotion—in your reception area will increase as the size of your hospital grows. This is especially true of "rush hour" practices that have many people dropping off or picking up animals at the beginning and end of each day. If you are planning a large hospital, consider the following:

- Have separate desks for separate services: If your services are divided into distinct categories, such as inpatient and outpatient, or

The half-height walls that separate the seating in this reception area help reduce stress while clients and pets are waiting. (Foto Imagery / Tim Murphy. Courtesy of Woodhaven Veterinary Clinic, Edmonds, Washington.)

boarding and medicine, separate reception areas or desks can help alleviate crowding and confusion. However, be sure your wayfinding is clear so your clients understand where they should go. Otherwise, you may end up adding to the confusion you are trying to alleviate.

- Design function-specific reception areas: Instead of having a one-size-fits-all desk, you may find it helpful to have separate check-in and check-out functions. The check-out function can be divided into individual cashier stations for efficient processing and space usage.

- Employ seating alcoves: Design your seating in alcoves so that people can naturally separate themselves or separate their pets by species. With this method, you can provide a variety of seating options. One way to reduce stress for animals while they are waiting is to provide clearly delineated spaces for cats and dogs where the animals' views of each other are blocked. You may wish to have an alcove dedicated to cashier waiting as well.

- Build an outdoor, covered waiting area: In favorable climates, covered outdoor porches can provide a comfortable and

A conceptual drawing for an outdoor waiting porch. (Courtesy of Donte's Den, Myakka City, Florida.)

less stressful alternative for clients and their pets waiting to be called into their appointment. For proper functionality and comfort, the porch should be at least 7 feet wide. If possible, position the porch to be south facing to make it useful during most of the year in Northern Hemisphere locations.

PHILOSOPHY

Veterinary reception areas have changed considerably over the years. A few decades ago, it was common for the receptionist to be in a separate room, greeting clients through a small window that opened into the waiting room. The tone this kind of reception area set was very different from the tone set by today's open and airy reception and waiting areas. The newest trends are continuing to reduce the physical barriers between clients and staff. Some practices are using the following:

- Greeter's station: With a greeter's station, the phone-answering function is removed from the front desk. The greeter's only job is to assist clients as they enter and exit the hospital. This method of receiving clients can lead to better service and allows you to minimize the size of the reception desk. Greeter's stations work well in practices with a high use of mobile technology, tablets, etc., as it is easier to physically separate the greeter, phone, and cashier functions while maintaining a virtual connection between them.

- The concierge: As discussed in Chapter 16, the next step in the evolution of the reception area is to establish a concierge relationship with your clients, essentially eliminating the physical barrier of a desk and making your clients feel like they are your first priority. Additionally, if your concierge is liberated from a desk, he or she can provide other services, such as facilitating curbside drop-off and pickup or sitting with, comforting, or educating clients while they wait.

- Views to other spaces: Views into other areas of the hospital from the reception area can reduce psychological barriers between the front and the back. Some veterinarians choose to open up views into exam rooms, surgery, special procedure rooms, or cat and dog boarding areas. This level of transparency creates a unique reception environment and can help educate your clients about the services you offer.

FINE-TUNING THE DESIGN

The layout, look, color, and materials of your reception area can create various impressions. Designs can range from a space where clients feel comfortable enough to settle in with a book or a laptop to that of a high-tech medical center. As you work through the details of your reception area design, consider the following possibilities:

- Minimize the number of steps between the reception desk, file shelves, business office, work room, and treatment area.

- Allow enough space around the reception desk for several people and their animals to check in and out at the same time. A minimum of 7 feet of clear space between the desk and seating areas should be maintained.

- Consider your space requirements for computers, telephones, printers, and credit card machines. Find solutions that minimize crowding and clutter on the surface of your reception desk. The more you rely on technology, the easier this will be.

- Give yourself adequate lighting at all work surfaces. Under-cabinet lighting can be very effective for task lighting. Overhead lighting, as well as pendant lights, can help to highlight the desk.

- Provide conveniently located cubbies for prescriptions, handouts, and forms.

- Choose durable materials for the reception area, especially where you expect the most wear. Clients and their pets can be hard on a reception desk, so installing a solid surface, such as plastic resin or quartz resin, in lieu of laminate may be a better investment. Protect all outside wall corners in the reception room with corner guards, and choose easily cleanable, durable furniture. Remember that durable does not have to look clinical or be uncomfortable.

- Incorporate colors that exemplify your branding or that help create the atmosphere you want to engender in the space, whether that means bright and cheery or calm and soothing. Put colors where they are easy to redo, such as on the walls, and keep the cabinets, which you are likely to have for a long time, a more neutral shade.

- Provide amenities for your clients such as a coffee bar, an information station, and access to Wi-Fi.

▼ ▼ ▼

THERE IS NO set formula for designing a reception area. The design should be a direct reflection of your individual practice philosophy and the way you run your hospital. Before you get started, take some time to think carefully about what you want these areas to say about the quality of care you provide. Remember that your clients will base their idea of what happens in the treatment area of your hospital on their experience when they first walk through your front door.

CHAPTER 27

EXAM ROOMS

The exam room is the most fundamental space in a veterinary hospital. It is the space that shapes the relationship between the practice's staff members and the clients and their pets. Exam room square footage is coveted because of its importance in helping to craft the client experience.

In the early history of full-service veterinary hospitals, the exam room was an open, multipurpose space that could also be used for treatment and surgery. There was very little separation between doctor and client, and the room was finished in a practical and durable manner. This approach was so pragmatic partly because a much larger percentage of pets visiting the hospital were injured or ill compared to today.

With the growth of wellness and specialty care, exam rooms became enclosed spaces, separated from medical areas, where doctors and clients could converse privately. Greater emphasis was placed on client comfort as well, and over the years exam rooms became larger and more elaborate.

As the veterinary industry continues to evolve, exam rooms are changing again, becoming more reflective of the needs of individual practices, the types of medicine and services they provide, and the images they wish to project to their clients.

Traditional exam rooms typically measured about 8 × 10 feet, with all equipment located against one wall. This size exam room may still work in a feline hospital, but most doctors prefer exam rooms that are larger, perhaps 9 × 10 feet or 9 × 11 feet in size, to accommodate more creative layouts, Fear Free examinations, or larger groups of people in the room.

Regardless of the shape, size, and style of the exam rooms in your hospital, there are some basics elements that should be included:

- An examination table with a surface that can be easily disinfected.
- Cabinetry to store items for easy accessibility and a counter to provide a writing surface.
- Comfortable seating for your clients.
- Adequate lighting to perform examinations, and convenient power outlets for equipment and computers.
- Other items that should either be in each exam room or easily accessible to each exam room include a computer monitor for viewing X-rays, a scale, and a sink. Refer to EF06 of the AAHA standards for the list of items AAHA recommends be in or convenient to your exam rooms.

EXAM ROOMS IN FLOOR PLANNING

A functional and efficient exam room layout within your hospital floor plan is one of the most important aspects in the design of your facility. Carefully consider how you want these spaces to function while laying out your floor plan with your architect.

One Door or Two?
Initially, exam rooms had one access door. In the 1970s, two-door "flow-through" exam rooms became the norm. Recently trends have been changing again. Part of the reason for the two-door design was the idea that clients and doctors should have separate circulation paths, and part of the reason had to do with safety. But as more clients began to come into practices with cats and lap dogs, the escape route became less necessary. Today there are many economic factors to contend with, and the one-door exam room is a great way to do more with less space. Ironically, a benefit of moving back to one door is that clients and doctors *do* enter from the same side of the room, which sets a precedent for the informal relationships that many clients prefer.

In-Line or Pods?
In small hospitals with two to four exam rooms, they can be positioned in the floor plan in a straight line, side by side. As the size of the hospital and the number of exam rooms increase, it becomes more important to consider the organization of the exam rooms. Because one veterinarian can typically work two to three rooms at a time, it makes sense to group exam rooms in twos and threes. It is also a good idea to group exam rooms, and specifically the entries to the rooms, so that the doors are visible from the reception area.

This exam room pod concept is used in many forms in human medical facilities and is effective in veterinary hospitals that focus on outpatient care. The pod concept allows a doctor and tech team to work a series of exam rooms simultaneously in conjunction with high-density scheduling. The advantage of this one-door approach is that it eliminates double circulation, which allows you to save significantly on square footage.

Closed or Open?
If you have logged lots of hours in an exam room, you know that most of them are not much better than solitary confinement. As small,

This exam room in the front of the hospital has frosted glass on the lower half of the window to ensure privacy while still allowing ample daylight into the space. (Foto Imagery / Tim Murphy. Courtesy of Melrose Animal Clinic, Melrose, Massachusetts.)

closed spaces, they offer little to look at, and not much to listen to other than the panting of an anxious pet. The perception of privacy was the driving force behind the creation of these spaces, and for some clients that is certainly what they expect and want.

The polar opposite of this concept is an exam room that is completely open, with a large window looking out to the sidewalk along a busy street. No walls, no problem? While it can be a good idea, the open exam room is likely too radically different to catch on. There are also some very real practical concerns, such as lack of privacy, escape possibilities for the pet, and distractions.

Perhaps there is a middle ground. How about a room that maintains privacy while still letting clients see out? The industry is seeing more exam rooms with some degree of visual connection into or out of them. For privacy, windows can be frosted or partially obscured while still maintaining an open feel.

EXAM ROOMS 145

The hospital of the future will likely have an even more inviting exam room environment, with subtler lighting, better seating options, and more exam rooms that connect to outdoor gardens. Ultimately, it is these larger questions of a client's experience in the exam room that will shape the hospitals of the future.

BEYOND THE BASICS

Consultation Room

One way to enhance customer service in your hospital would be to set aside one of your exam rooms as a consultation room. This room can be used for difficult cases, consultation, and pet visitation. Some hospitals also choose to use this room for euthanasia. This space should be close to a side exit to allow your clients to leave the hospital and proceed to their cars without having to pass through the waiting room. Consultation rooms need to be generous in size, at least 9 × 11 feet, and sometimes 10 × 12 feet, to allow for clients to feel comfortable and to accommodate family members.

Multipurpose Exam Room

In multipurpose exam rooms, it isn't the client services that are being added to the space but rather medical procedures. In many veterinary hospitals, exam rooms are not used to full capacity during the midday hours. A multipurpose exam room can be created by designing a folding or "operable" wall at the back of the room. With the wall closed, the room can function as an exam room in the morning and evening rush hours. With the wall open, the room can be used as an additional treatment area during the rest of the day.

Oversize Exam Room

Depending on the size of your hospital, you may want to consider including a larger than normal exam room that can accommodate several family members or multiple pets, or that could be used for floor examinations of larger dogs. This room will be similar in size to a consultation room.

Specialty/Referral

Specialty/referral hospitals have unique requirements for exam rooms. These rooms need to be set up to support the types of services being offered. They require space for longer consultations as well as room for more family members. Individually, the exam rooms can be set up for specialties, such as dermatology, ophthalmology, oncology, neurology, and ultrasound, with each containing the specific equipment, storage, lighting, ventilation, and mechanical requirements necessary. These specialty exam spaces are usually 10 × 12 feet as a starting point. Neurology exam rooms require close access to a large space or hallway for walking pets in order to assess their gait.

Emergency

Emergency and trauma services, whether they are being offered at a dedicated facility or in a separate area of a larger hospital, require unique exam rooms. The room should be located adjacent to an easily accessible entrance, be visually separate from nonemergency areas, and be in close proximity to treatment, radiology, and surgery services.

Trauma exam rooms are typically larger than a standard exam room due to the specialized care performed in these spaces that generally requires more people and more equipment.

Also important to note is that emergency facilities can be open at all hours. Thus, the safety of the staff and the security of the closed portion of the hospital should be considered when contemplating the location, layout, visibility, and accessibility of emergency services and their exam rooms (see Chapter 22).

Run to Back Room

The run to back room is an outpatient treatment room adjacent to the exam rooms. An exam light, medical gas, dedicated power, and more clear floor space are needed here. A good starting point for this area is 12 × 12 feet. This space works well with the pod concept and high-density scheduling. A technician can do minor procedures in the run to back room, allowing the doctor to go on to the next exam room. At the same time, the client can be moved back to the waiting room, thus freeing the exam room for another client and patient.

Exam Room Checkout

Many veterinarians want the capability to use their exam rooms as a place for clients to check in and out. The advantage is that the clients and their pets are already in the room, allowing all involved a comfortable place to discuss charges and other concerns.

▼ ▼ ▼

FROM THE MANY options described here, it should be clear that there is no set formula for designing exam rooms or their layout, other than maximizing their number, staying flexible, and following appropriate size recommendations. Before you get started with the actual design, take some time to think carefully about how the exam rooms in your practice can help you develop the best possible relationships with your clients and their pets.

CHAPTER 28

LABORATORY, PHARMACY, AND CHARTING

The spaces described in this chapter serve as the connection between client services and the medical functions of the hospital. This area comprises the laboratory, pharmacy, charting stations, and, frequently, office areas as well. In many facilities, the laboratory and pharmacy form a physical buffer between the exam rooms and the treatment area. This becomes the place where doctors and staff gather and where most of the charting and impromptu consultation takes place. As a buffer, the lab/pharmacy cuts down on noise and visual clutter that can otherwise be transferred from the treatment area to the exam rooms.

If you feel your practice does not require this buffer, you can create a more efficient, faster-moving floor plan. In this model, veterinarians and staff can move directly from the exam rooms into the treatment area, speeding up the traffic flow. Keep in mind, however, that whatever happens in the treatment area will probably be seen and heard in the exam rooms, so you might want to consider other methods of controlling sound (see Chapter 46). It is important to understand the pros and cons of different floor plan types before you decide what will work best for you in terms of operations, noise control, and space constraints.

Oftentimes, as alluded to above, it is most efficient to group the laboratory and pharmacy areas into one space, for example, by providing cabinetry and counters within the hallway that forms the buffer between your exam rooms and the treatment area. But this isn't always the best solution. The answer depends on the size of the pharmacy and how

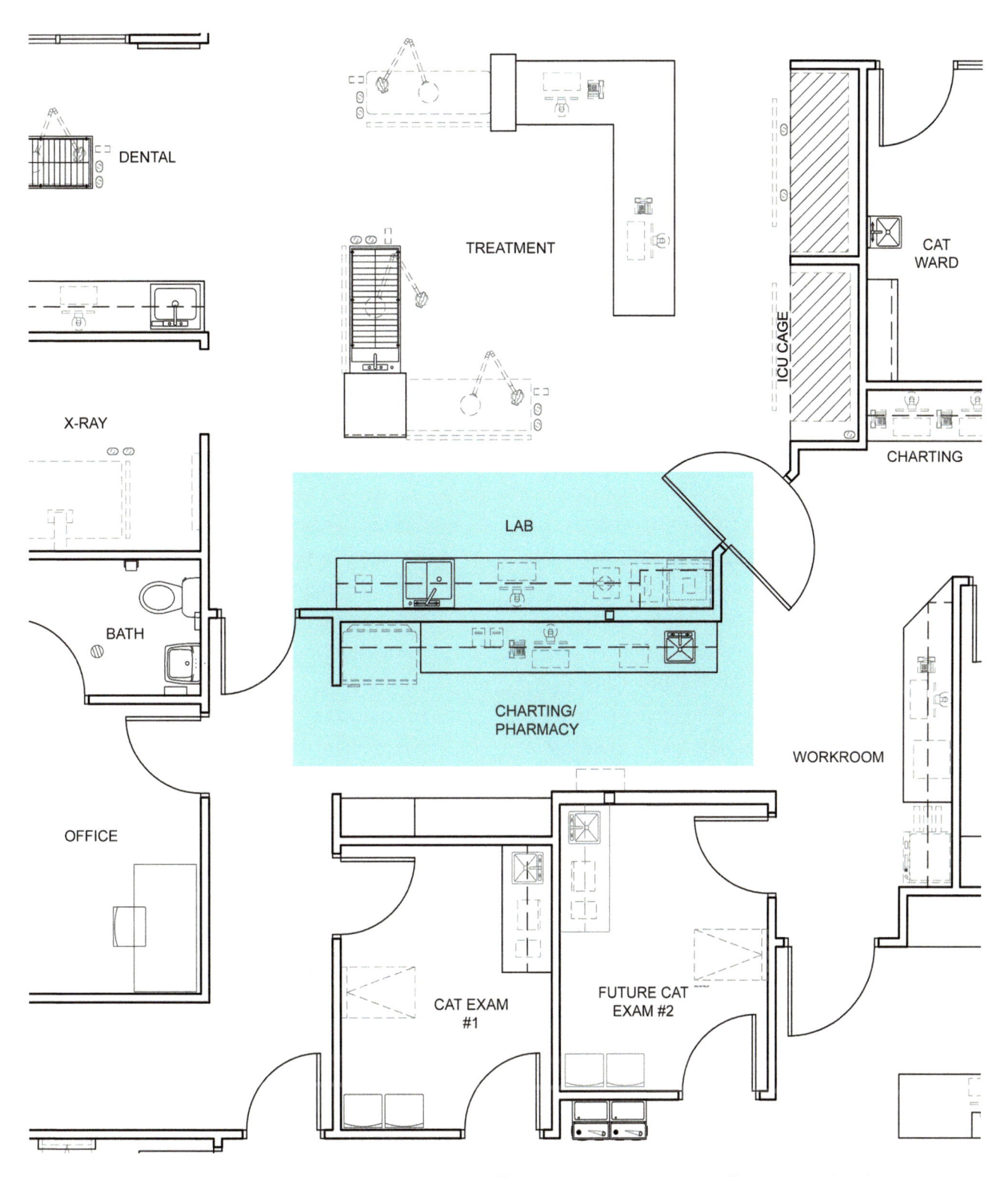

A floor plan illustrating how the laboratory, pharmacy, and staff work stations can act as a buffer between the client zone and treatment. (Courtesty of Pablo River Veterinary, Jacksonville, Florida.)

LABORATORY, PHARMACY, AND CHARTING **149**

much lab work and equipment your hospital will need. Some doctors like to do a wide variety of in-house lab work to cater more quickly to client needs; others prefer to do only basic lab work in-house, such as viewing fecal samples, and send more extensive lab work to an outside facility. If you plan on doing only simple lab work in your hospital, consider the grouped approach to these two spaces. Otherwise, separate spaces may be more beneficial in terms of staff efficiency.

If a separated lab and pharmacy is the better approach for your practice, there are several ways to handle the design and layout of these two spaces. The usual approach is to locate your pharmacy toward the front of house so that you can access medications quickly for clients waiting in the lobby or an exam room. Your laboratory would then be located closer to, or even within, the treatment area, proximal to where the more intensive medical procedures are performed. If you prefer your lab space to be in a separate room, the best approach is usually to create an alcove off of the treatment area, so that it remains close to the action but still self-contained. With this approach, the lab should be designed as a three-sided alcove without a door in order to allow your staff to quickly dart in and out as needed.

When it comes to larger facilities, such as specialty/referral or emergency hospitals, it is almost a given, based on the sheer volume of work performed in each space, that the laboratory and pharmacy areas will be separate. Furthermore, because of the greater distance between functions within these larger hospitals, there is often a need for "satellite" laboratory spaces. These are typically small counter areas with only a few pieces of equipment, such as a microscope, sink, computer, centrifuge, and refrigerator. They are best located in or near ICU or surgery, where quick lab analyses are often critical.

LABORATORY DESIGN

As you plan your laboratory, start with a reasonable amount of floor space to allow for staff to be able to work comfortably and enough countertop real estate for your equipment and additional workspace. Below are some basic recommendations.

Counters

- Be sure to include enough space for all needed equipment, including microscopes, centrifuges, blood chemistry analyzers, incubators, and so on.

- In addition to equipment and work area requirements, the counter size should also account for the sink width and a splash area.

- Verify the clearance requirements between upper cabinets and countertops for computers and larger equipment. Some equipment is top loading or requires access to the top. Two feet is a reasonable amount of vertical clearance for most items in your laboratory.

- The area where microscopes are placed should be isolated from the centrifuge and any computer keyboards to avoid vibrations. The microscope counter is generally lower, at a comfortable sitting height.

Cabinetry

- Like all spaces in a busy veterinary hospital, the counters and cabinets in your lab will need to be very durable. Choose high-quality cabinetry with durable finishes.

- Think about workflow and storage needs when planning cabinets with doors, drawers, and knee spaces.

- Consider installing some open shelving or cabinets with glass inset in the doors to make it easier for staff to locate items and track supplies.

Equipment

- Equipment can vary tremendously in terms of type, size, required clearances, and electricity and water needs. Choosing your equipment early in the design process will ensure that the laboratory is designed appropriately to suit your needs.

- Each piece of equipment will likely have unique requirements and connections for power, data, water, and sewer.

- Refrigerators come in all shapes and sizes. Choose the refrigerator you will need early enough in the planning stage to ensure there is a place for it around your cabinetry.

- Install a kitchen-type vent hood over the sink to remove odors during fecal sample testing.

Power

- Provide dedicated circuits as needed and required by code. These are separate circuits intended to avoid overloads and to keep the power supply clean and free of interference from other equipment.

- Any quad boxes (with four places to plug in) and power strips need to be sized by an electrical engineer for maximum expected loads.

- Electrical and data connections can be challenging to locate in island or long peninsula counters. Avoid installations that are flush with or recessed in the countertop and pop-up outlets that can get wet or collect dirt and hair.

Sinks

- Plan for a large, deep, single- or double-bowl sink with a drain board.

- Specify high gooseneck faucets with wrist blade controls.

- An eyewash station is typically required by code. Flip-down fixtures that attach to the sink faucet should be adequate for most veterinary laboratory accidents. However, some jurisdictions require a separate free-standing eyewash station.

- Allowing for space for drying racks or surfaces nearby is a plus.

Work closely with your design team to lay out and optimize the space and flow of staff and work. Keep in mind that equipment takes up much of the required counter area and that appropriate lighting and sufficient power for equipment are a must. Plan for plenty of storage, as there is never enough.

Remember that, like everything else, veterinary medicine is constantly changing. Some equipment might shrink while at the same time additional space may be needed for the latest and greatest gadget. As much as you can, plan for maximum flexibility in all the components of your laboratory, including the ability to add more connections for power and data.

PHARMACY DESIGN

The design of the veterinary pharmacy is reflective of the hospital's size and the type of medicine practiced. Regardless of your pharmacy design, controlled substances are required to be under double lock. Many hospitals keep their primary drug safe secured in a locked room and then provide a small drug lockbox in the treatment area. Larger hospitals may have more than one drug lockbox.

- In smaller hospitals, a small locked closet may be enough to keep control of expensive products. This can also help to prevent opportunistic break-ins, as these products (and controlled drugs) are more likely to be targeted for thievery.

- In medium-size hospitals, an enclosed pharmacy may be more appropriate. In this case, the pharmacy is no longer in the

The roll-down window provides security for the pharmacy when the hospital is closed to the public. For further security, an automated inventory control system lines the back wall. (Foto Imagery / Tim Murphy. Courtesy of VCA South Shore Animal Hospital, South Weymouth, Massachusetts [VCA, Inc.].)

circulation space and is surrounded by four walls. Ideally, an enclosed pharmacy should be placed where it can have window access to the lobby for client pickup. A pull-down grille or locking pharmacy window can help secure the front window after hours. A second window or Dutch door can provide back-of-house access for staff working with hospitalized patients or in the exam rooms.

- The largest hospitals may find that they benefit from an inventory control system such as a Cubex or a Pyxis machine. These systems can also be used for containing controlled substances. Inventory control systems can be located either in a pharmacy or in circulation spaces.

Enclosed pharmacies are particularly important for hospitals that have large or bulky inventory. Large animal and equine hospitals typically have enclosed pharmacies with convenient access for ambulatory services.

To prevent confusion about what has already been dispensed and what is ready for pickup, the hospital can provide a dedicated area for storage of products and medication prepped for clients. Hanging bag storage systems can be particularly useful for smaller items, as they take up little space.

DESIGN FOR CHARTING AND OTHER WORK AREAS

Charting and other staff work areas, including offices, often work well as part of the buffer between the exam rooms and treatment. In this location, they allow doctors and staff to have

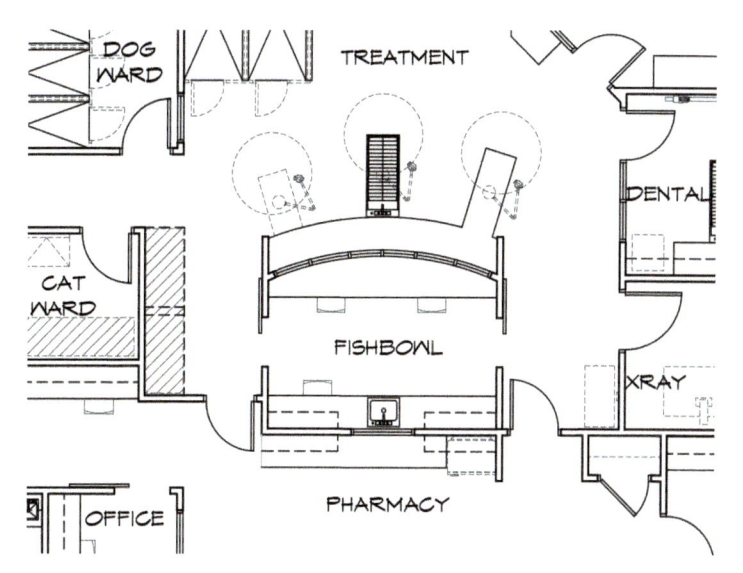

A floor plan excerpt showing the generous sightlines and connectedness you can achieve with a fish bowl approach. (Courtesy of Callbeck Animal Hospital, Whitby, Ontario.)

quick and easy access to all of the major medical spaces of the hospital. Providing charting stations at a wall of cabinetry in the hallway behind the exam rooms is a common and efficient approach.

One unique design element within this area that has become popular over the years is the fish bowl approach to doctors' or tech stations. This concept essentially creates a glass box or enclosure adjacent to the treatment space that contains workstations for charting, private conversations, or even just a quick mental break for the doctors and staff while still providing a visual connection to the treatment hub for monitoring of patients and in case of emergency.

This area of the hospital is so important for the efficiency of the daily workflow and has great potential to facilitate communication between doctors and staff, particularly if it is designed with this opportunity in mind.

▼ ▼ ▼

LABORATORY, PHARMACY, AND CHARTING

REGARDLESS OF WHERE you choose to locate your laboratory, pharmacy, and charting areas, they will serve as both a buffer and a link between the client services and the medical functions of your hospital. In designing their details, remember to consider how they will be used by your staff members and how they can benefit your clients and patients.

CHAPTER 29

TREATMENT AREAS

Treatment rooms are the hub of activity and the primary workspace in veterinary facilities of all types and sizes. There are a few exceptions, such as practices that focus solely on diagnostics, but even large and specialty/emergency/referral hospitals with numerous zones or departments have treatment areas at the hub of each of the departments.

Treatment areas in today's state-of-the-art animal hospitals are all about minimizing steps, optimizing efficiency, and condensing spaces to reduce expensive square footage. To achieve these efficiencies, spaces such as exam rooms, the laboratory, the pharmacy, radiology, surgery prep, pack/prep, surgery suites, wards, etc. are commonly located in close proximity to or combined with treatment. An open layout maximizes the use of square footage by including circulation paths that pass through the treatment room instead of around it in hallways. As it is the center of activity, a large percentage of the doctors and staff will spend a significant amount of their day working in or close to the treatment area.

Treatment rooms can also be congested, noise-filled spaces that are stressful for both staff and patients. Significant efforts to reduce room sizes, or include too much overlap of workspaces, can lead to bottlenecks and negative interactions between patients. These problems multiply as the practice grows, as more staff is added, and if the facility starts to be used beyond its design capacity. Also, as the center of activity, treatment rooms tend to be buried in the middle of the hospital, which leaves few opportunities to include windows or other visual connections to the out-of-doors.

SPACE CONSIDERATIONS

The layout of treatment areas can vary significantly between different veterinary hospitals and practice styles, but there are some solutions and recommendations that can be incorporated into the design of any hospital.

Combining some functions such as charting/doctors' station, laboratory, dental, ICU/recovery, surgery prep/induction, and pack/prep/scrub with treatment can help to reduce steps, optimize the use of square footage, and, in some instances, require less staff to manage the space. For example, an open-plan treatment area will allow a doctor or technician to enter information at a charting station and simultaneously monitor a critical patient in ICU or quickly assist with a fractious animal. Depending on the size of the facility and the functional needs, the treatment workstations can be used for multiple purposes, including minor or "dirty surgeries," surgery prep/induction, dentals, endoscopy procedures, etc. In an open treatment room, congestion and conflicts between staff at workstations and others circulating through treatment can be common. The following general rules can help you estimate your hospital's treatment room needs:

- The number and type of workstations in treatment are based loosely on the number of exam rooms and on whether the stations will be utilized for multiple functions. If based on the number of exam rooms, one station can generally support two exam rooms.

- Provide approximately 150 square feet (12 × 12 feet) of space per workstation when planning a basic treatment room. This figure does not necessarily account for other shared functions, such as the laboratory, a large charting area, or a large ICU.

- Avoid circulation paths that run through the middle of treatment, encroach into required space at the ends of workstations, pass too close to the front of cages and runs, or create bottlenecks at critical locations. A minimum pathway width of 5 feet is recommended.

- Many procedures in treatment take place with staff and equipment located at the sides or outboard ends of workstations. Provide a clear area of about 5 feet in diameter at the ends of tables and, where possible, a minimum of 6 feet between workstations and nearby obstructions such as walls, cages, and other workstations.

- The most efficient layout in terms of space usage is to design the workstations as peninsulas perpendicular to counters or walls. An island arrangement of workstations allows for a greater degree of circulation but also requires more floor space. Typical arrangements of workstations include configurations that are H-shaped, X-shaped, U-shaped, T-shaped, linear (I-shaped), and L-shaped.

FEATURES AND EQUIPMENT

One of the most common complaints among veterinary staff is that there is no connection to the out-of-doors from treatment. Staff members can spend their entire day in the treatment area and not know if the sun is shining or if it is

"H" layout

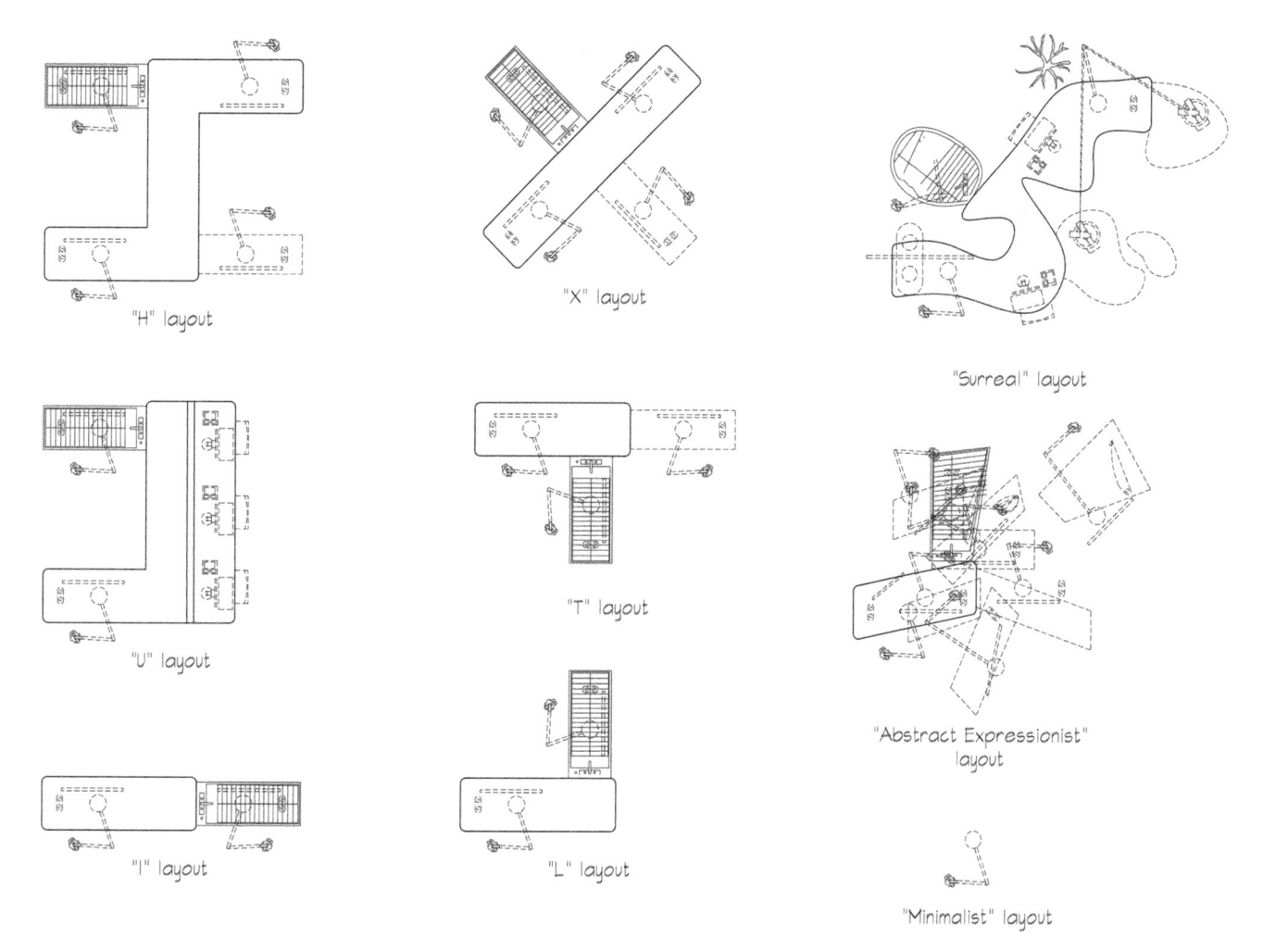

"X" layout

"Surreal" layout

"U" layout

"T" layout

"Abstract Expressionist" layout

"I" layout

"L" layout

"Minimalist" layout

A compendium of treatment table layouts.

pouring rain. Functionally, treatment requires cages and cabinets that use up available wall space, and related rooms need to be located in close proximity. As a result, the treatment area, as the heart of the hospital, tends to be buried in the middle of the building, leaving little or no opportunity to have direct visual access to the outside.

Installing lots of interior windows can help to counteract some of these issues by visually opening up the treatment area while still allowing staff to keep an eye on the activity in other rooms, such as ICU. To improve the connection to the outside, consider using windows—or "borrowed light"—between treatment and adjacent rooms with outside walls, and, where practical, provide windows from those rooms to the outside. Surgery suites, specialty rooms, wards, and other rooms frequently have walls devoid of cabinetry, equipment, and other obstructions. These walls, with some control of light and privacy, offer an excellent opportunity to bring daylight and views in from the outside.

Treatment is the primary location where patient care is organized. A well-thought-out doctors' station, or several charting stations scattered around, can reduce bottlenecks and competition for space. Standing stations or knee

TREATMENT AREAS   157

spaces can be as narrow as 30 inches but are more comfortable at 36 inches and wider. Space should be provided for a monitor, a keyboard, a computer, medical books and journals, paper charts, and a phone. Plan to provide enough wall space for large TV monitors to be used as patient status boards and for viewing X-rays, among other purposes.

Even though many of today's animal hospitals have gone mostly paperless, some practices still find it practical to have dry-erase boards for quick visual access to patient status, for reminder notes, and to easily jot down information. Reserve enough wall space to install boards, which are commonly 3 feet tall and 4 feet or more in width.

Equipment and cabinetry are what primarily fill up space and make up most of the cost in veterinary facilities. The layout of treatment is largely based on the use and placement of equipment.

Plan to provide some out-of-the-way space to park mobile equipment such as anesthesia machines, gurneys, dental machines, and carts, as well as space for fixed equipment such as a floor scale. When not entirely thought out, mobile equipment frequently gets parked in surgery. When floor scales are placed in inconvenient locations, they can end up using precious circulation space, becoming serious trip hazards.

Veterinary equipment and cabinetry are unique, intended for specific purposes and difficult to replicate. Rather than having custom casework and furnishings built, consider installing modular, off-the-shelf, premanufactured components that are easily obtained from manufacturers specializing in animal care equipment. For example, built-in treatment tables are commonly cantilevered at their outboard ends to provide knee space for a seated person to work on a patient. Combined with a drop-in tub, the details and support of the tables can be complex to build and fraught with potential problems.

The actual workstations come in a range of options, including drop-in metal sinks (wet tables, or tub tables), "hard-top" counters, freestanding lift tables, rolling scissor tables, and gurneys. Most tables come in heights that match standard counter heights, in lengths of 4 to 6 feet and widths of 2 feet.

When treatment counters are installed in an island arrangement, they are typically attached to or parked against floor-to-ceiling utility columns. Besides serving as a surface to butt the workstation against, utility columns are used as a conduit for and place to mount power, data, sewer/water, oxygen, gas scavenging, and central vacuum. Task lights, patient monitors, TV monitors used for patient status boards and viewing X-rays, and other equipment can be hung from the face of the column, and cubbies can be installed to allow for quick access to tools and other stored items. Purpose-built utility columns are also available from manufacturers of veterinary equipment.

Note that utility columns, while useful, can obstruct views across a space. These columns can be fed from below and capped at half height to provide for a more open view.

Be sure to provide adequate and easy-to-access handwashing sinks in addition to the sinks in wet tables, as well as additional electrical outlets for unforeseen needs.

Ceilings are the logical location for the installation of sound-absorptive materials in treatment. Suspended acoustic tile ceilings are very effective at sound control and should be installed throughout the space. Oxygen, gas scavenging, clippers, electrical power, treatment lights, and IV tracks can be supported within

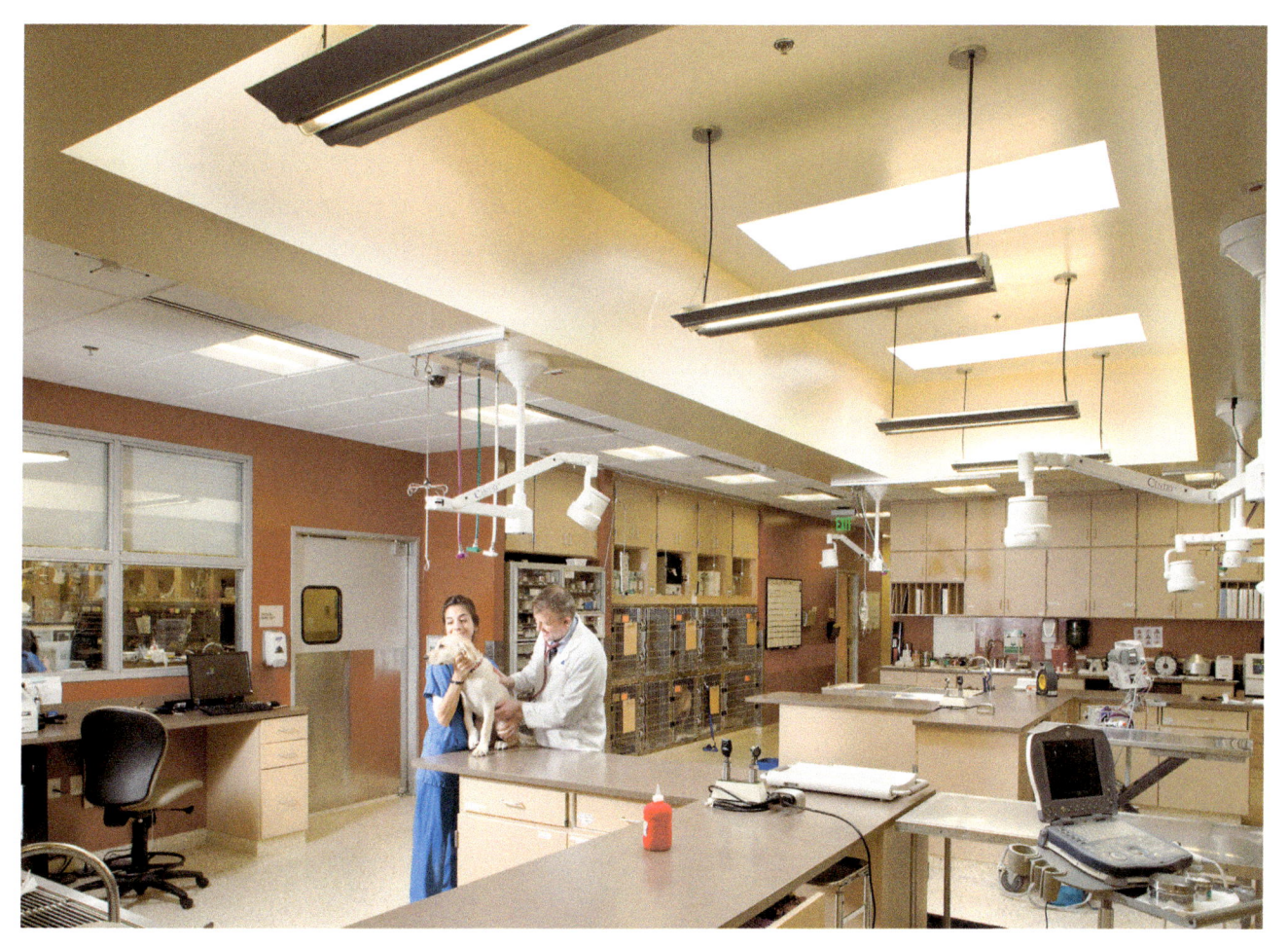

The racetrack-shaped soffit provides a place to hang exam lights, IV tracks, and medical gas drops in line with the treatment tables. Skylights located in the center of the track bring natural light into the space. (Foto Imagery / Tim Murphy. Courtesy of VCA South Shore Animal Hospital, South Weymouth, Massachusetts [VCA, Inc.].)

drywall soffits directly over the tables. It is easier and cleaner to attach these fixtures to drywall with structure behind rather than using somewhat irregular metal tracks and acoustic tiles, which have to be cut and notched around ceiling penetrations.

Where and how patients recover following surgery varies significantly by doctor and by practice. Some doctors want to be able to see and hear their patients, and therefore choose to have them recover in nearby cages or on the floor immediately adjacent to where they are working in treatment. Others prefer to have them recover in a well-situated, glass-enclosed ICU ward. A compromise is to have some combination of these options, which may include cages and recovery runs or beaches in treatment as well as a glass-enclosed ICU.

When estimating capacity for any caging, consider the number, size, and type of patient, as well as medical needs. Kittens, cats, puppies, and other small dogs do not need to be housed in 3 × 5-foot runs; conversely, it may not be appropriate to recover large dogs in too-small cages. (See Chapters 30, 38, and 39 for more information on caging and ward design.)

Instead of recovering large dogs on the floor in treatment, where they can be a trip hazard,

TREATMENT AREAS   159

recovery beaches—dedicated floor space or raised floor nooks located off to one side—can be used. Beaches are sized roughly 4 × 4 feet or 6 × 6 feet to allow room for both the patient and a staff member to work with them or provide comfort. If you choose to use these, include nearby hook-ups for power and oxygen, storage shelves or cubbies for monitors, patient warmers, oxygen equipment, and storage for blankets.

Minor procedures, such as blood draws and nail trims, that are not always appropriate to perform in an exam room, but also do not require a trip to the primary treatment room, can be performed in a small outpatient treatment area. An outpatient treatment area, sometimes referred to as a run to back room, can be conveniently located in an alcove between treatment and the exam rooms. This space can reduce steps, minimize congestion in treatment, and reduce the amount of time clients spend in exam rooms. Outpatient treatment can range from a simple short counter in a hallway, in smaller hospitals, to an elaborate, multiple-table triage space in large, specialty/referral, and emergency hospitals.

RECOMMENDATIONS

If you're uncertain about your needs, talk to your colleagues and tour other hospitals to learn about their preferences and experiences. To help visualize a particular layout, use an open space, such as a parking lot, to tape off features you are considering in your layout. This exercise really helps if you are having difficulty visualizing sizes and clearances of rooms, tables, and equipment. Cardboard boxes can help to further delineate counters and other features.

Consider where bottlenecks occur in your hospital—or in other hospitals where you have worked—and think about what may have caused them and how they might be prevented. The annoyances of having to wait for an opening between people, having to wait for another dog to pass by, and jostling someone in the middle of a procedure can easily be avoided through proper planning.

▼ ▼ ▼

AS THE HUB of the hospital, a properly designed treatment space will maximize efficiency, safety, communication, and comfort for the team, the patients treated, and the clients served. Before finalizing the design of your treatment area and the adjacent spaces, talk through your understanding of how this area will be used with your architect and carefully consider the wide range of options and how they might complement your practice philosophy.

CHAPTER 30

INTENSIVE CARE UNIT

Every second counts, from the instant an accident or illness occurs to the moment the patient is stabilized. When designing for a hospital that sees critical patients, careful consideration must be given to more than just the intensive care unit (ICU) or critical care unit (CCU) itself. Easy-to-read site and building signage, dedicated emergency parking spots, and an efficient staff will all help to move the patient quickly into the triage or intensive care area of the hospital. Quick access once inside the building is also required through a main corridor or direct path to the ICU. Triage can occur in an exam room, in treatment, in ICU, or in a dedicated triage space. In most practices, it is hard to justify staffing a separate triage room. As such, this function generally blends into the main treatment area or ICU space.

Within this framework, the ICU can be designed as an open alcove off of the treatment area, making it immediately accessible and visible, or it can be glassed in to minimize commotion. There is no right or wrong design answer. That said, with a large patient demand, you will likely need a dedicated room with dedicated staff to be most efficient.

The present-day veterinary ICU is a reflection of changes in how and why animals are housed in veterinary facilities. In years past, most animals being treated or cared for could look forward to an extended stay. This is no longer the case. With the advent of minimally invasive medical procedures, quicker and more effective treatment, and modern prescription drugs, oftentimes patients do not stay as long as they once did for the same illnesses or injuries. In addition, most general practices now refer their overnight cases to emergency hospitals, reducing or eliminating

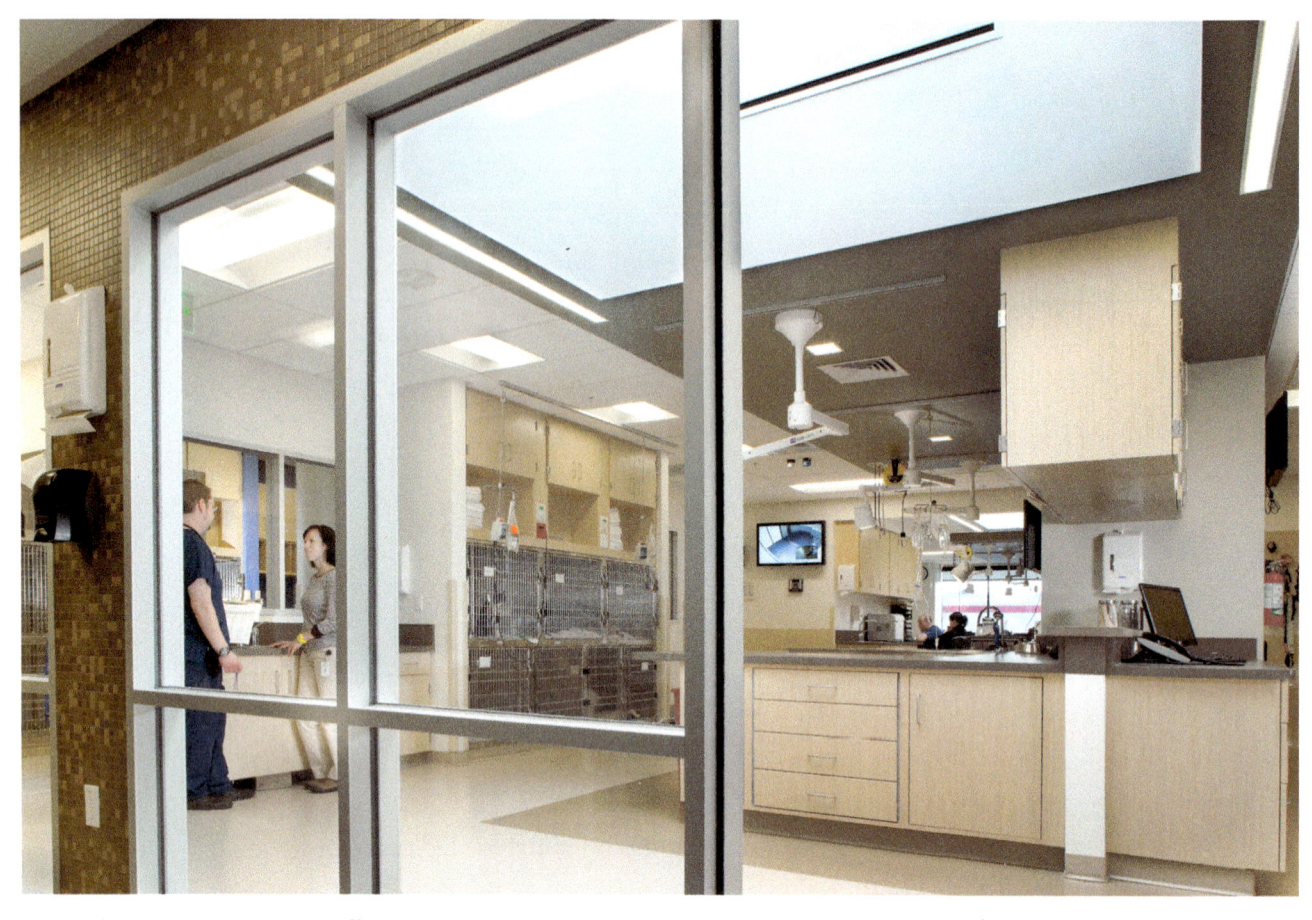

Large glass windows provide staff with the ability to easily monitor ICU patients. (Foto Imagery / Tim Murphy. Courtesy of VCA West Los Angeles Animal Hospital, Los Angeles, California [VCA, Inc.].)

the cost of overnight staffing and removing the need to get up in the middle of the night to care for housed animals.

Many veterinarians have also come to depend on the medical expertise an emergency hospital can provide. In many cases, this means that the total amount of animal housing in the general practice veterinary facility has been reduced. Animals that are housed are up front and accessible, because only the most seriously ill or injured animals are kept for extended stays. Specialty hospitals are growing, and the growth and refinement of the ICU is a direct product of this trend.

While a well-designed ICU is akin to the treatment area, there are several differences between these two spaces. The first is the need to keep the ICU as calm as possible. Treatment rooms are the center of the practice, where everyone quite literally comes together. ICUs, while still best located at the core, also need to be positioned such that circulation does not cross through them. The ICU's location in the overall plan is therefore key. It must touch the treatment area; it must be adjacent to the surgery and radiology suites; and it must be in close proximity to the general ward area of the hospital.

The ICU should also be designed with multistage or dimmable lighting. Sound walls or acoustical dampening materials between the ICU and any adjacent ward areas can assist in

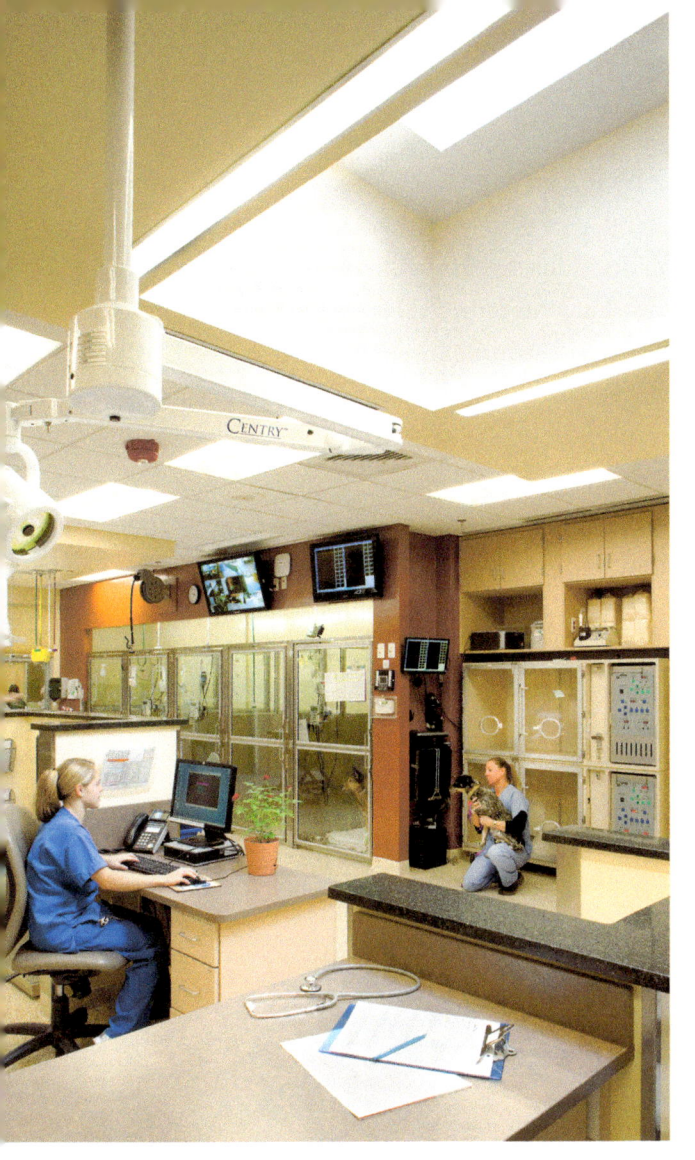

Daylighting has been integrated into this ICU through a large skylight in the ceiling. (Foto Imagery / Tim Murphy. Courtesy of VCA South Shore Animal Hospital, South Weymouth, Massachusetts [VCA, Inc.].)

keeping the space quiet and calm. When space allows, the actual triage room should be kept separate from the main ICU area. Capturing any capacity to keep the ICU itself quiet and calming will aid in the healing process for your patients.

Below are a few additional concepts you can employ to foster healing in this environment:

- Include sound-dampening measures at cages and runs. This includes selecting a manufacturer that uses quiet latches and hardware. Sound-dampening materials can also be added to run panels by the manufacturer or individually between cages.

- Provide adequate space for the patient to promote healing, but it is important to note that in an ICU setting this may mean slightly smaller enclosures than what is typically recommended, in order to minimize mobility and the risk of an animal further injuring itself. Neurology patients in particular often require their movements to be restricted.

- Whether introduced by proximity to an outside window or a skylight, daylighting creates a more natural, healing space. As a side benefit, if designed properly and integrated with your electric lighting system, it can also decrease energy costs.

- Plan for concentrated areas of care within the ICU space to create a calmer environment. For example, you might incorporate a dedicated ventilation table either off to the side of the main space or in an alcove. Patients on a ventilator need twenty-four-hour care and observation, so a quiet, dedicated space for them can be extremely beneficial.

- Some animals can be quite vocal when in the ICU. For these patients it is beneficial to be able to isolate them to a quiet run that is still integral to the rest of the room. The run should have a full-glass door for patient visibility, along with adequate power and medical gas for proper care. A cleanable floor and wall surface, along with a highly sound-absorptive ceiling tile, is necessary. This run will assist in keeping the rest of the room quiet while still providing a space to adequately care for the animal.

The second main design difference between ICU and treatment is the increase in power and medical gas needs. The power required in the ICU is typically two to four outlets per patient. Power will be required for infusion pumps, hot air blankets, and oxygen cages. Oxygen, anesthetic scavenge, and medical suction are also integral to a modern-day ICU. One oxygen drop is usually provided for every three to four cages. In the run areas it is typical to provide one oxygen drop for every two runs. Power and oxygen should be positioned to hang in between a pair of runs so they can be easily accessed by either run. These can also be provided on the wall, depending upon the hospital's preference. Note that oxygen and ICU cages will significantly affect the quantity of oxygen used by the hospital. Medical suction and anesthetic scavenge should be provided at the treatment tables.

As with most spaces in the hospital, proper planning for specific equipment in the ICU is key. Ideally, locate patient housing and storage cabinets along the walls. This will increase patient visibility and allow the center of the room to be used as a general workspace. Here are some additional considerations:

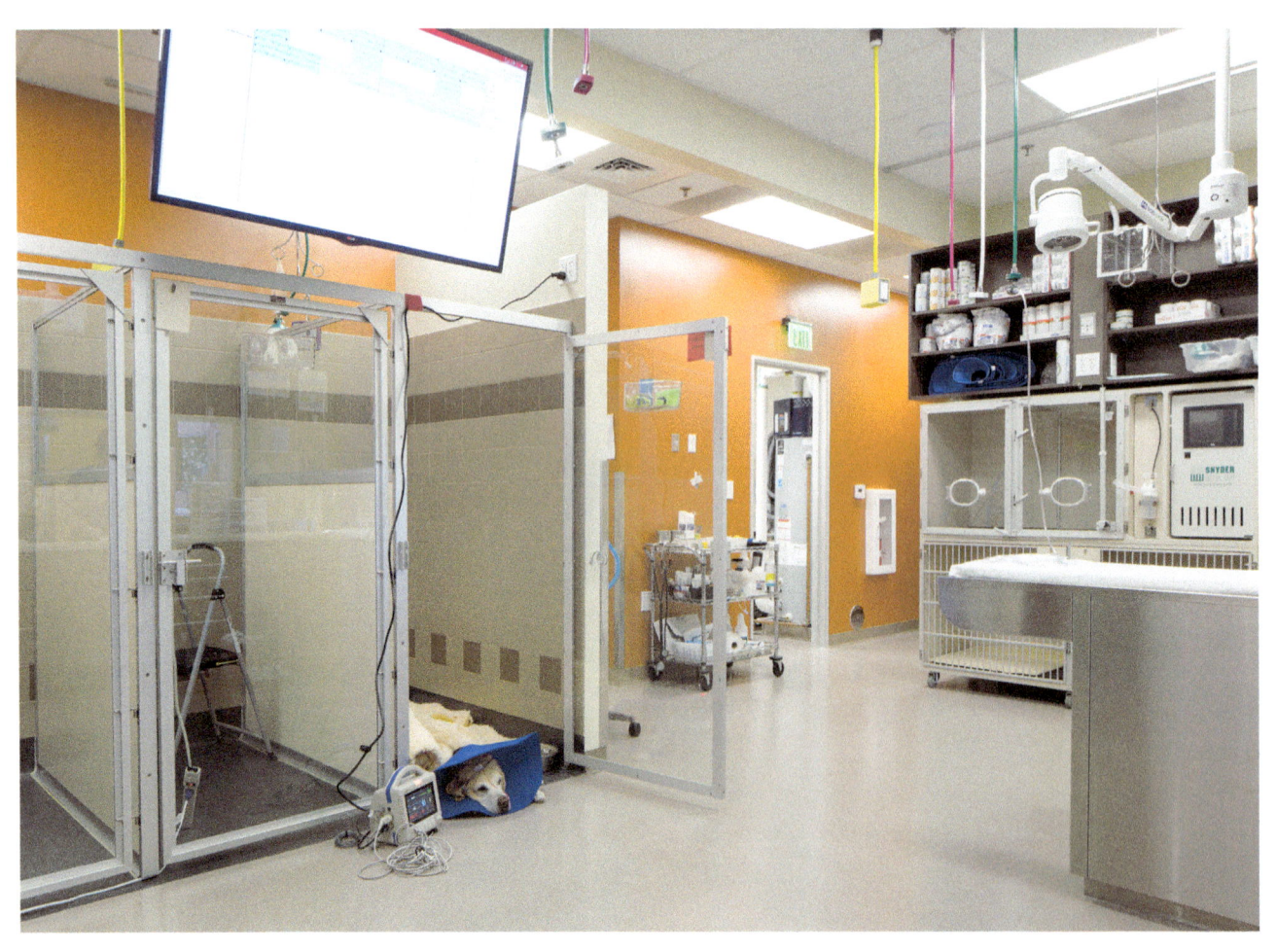

This large patient status board provides an efficient means for staff to stay current on their patients' treatments. (Courtesy of Four Seasons Veterinary Specialists, Loveland, Colorado.)

- A variety of treatment tables should be included for flexibility: gurney, wet, and dry. Either pass-through drawers or proper delineation of left-hand versus right-hand placement of the drawers on the wet and dry tables should be determined to allow for the most efficient access to supplies within the tables.

- The placement of scales (floor, feline, and exotics) should minimize the need to move patients for weighing. As in all other areas of the hospital, species should be separated to reduce stress whenever possible.

- In-room charting and computer workstations need to be situated such that sight lines are maintained to hospitalized animals.

- The ICU should be equipped with climate-controlled intensive care/oxygen cages with dedicated power and oxygen lines. Remember to keep clearance around these units or make them movable to allow for maintenance and cleaning.

- Patient status boards (electronic or old-school dry-erase boards) should be strategically placed in the space to provide easy visibility to patient information and treatment protocols. Telemetry viewing equipment can also be included adjacent to the status board.

- A table designed and intended for crashing patients should be centrally located to aid in critical care measures. This crash table should have adequate overhead lighting provided by an exam or procedure light, an IV track or pole available for running fluids, and dedicated power for a defibrillator cart.

▼ ▼ ▼

INTENSIVE CARE UNITS are intense. They require extensive planning defined by equipment and patient needs. Each hospital will have its own requirements based upon the level of care that needs to be met. Whether your ICU is part of your treatment space, an alcove off of treatment, or a full-fledged dedicated room, identifying and understanding your hospital's unique needs during the design process will help you to create an efficient and healing space.

CHAPTER 31

DENTAL SERVICES

There is no one-size-fits-all approach when it comes to dental spaces. They are usually an extension of the treatment room—for example, a nook in the corner. In other cases, a dedicated room is used for dental services. Wherever you choose to locate dental, it is useful to keep it in close proximity to treatment, to share staff and allow the veterinarian to know when a patient is ready for examination. In addition, because most practices utilize anesthesia for dental procedures, it is important for the staff and patients to be located in a central area of the practice. That said, it is also important to have some separation, whether it be physical or just with ventilation, to prevent the spread of disease.

According to the *AAHA Standards of Accreditation* for dental care, DE07, dental procedures with the potential for aerosolization of infectious debris should be performed in a properly ventilated area set apart from other patients and practice team activities (AAHA, 6). The extent to which the area is required to be "properly ventilated" or "set apart" is open to interpretation, so individual practitioners should work with their medical staff and their architect to find a balance suitable to their specific practice needs. Some practices install an exhaust fan or provide additional mechanical exhaust over the table where dentals are performed.

For most practices, the amount of space allocated to dental procedures is not large enough to warrant the installation of a dedicated ventilation system. Careful design of supply and exhaust airflow in the vicinity of the dental treatment tables should minimize the risk of aerosolized debris spreading to other areas of the hospital.

SIZE OF THE SPACE

The space required for a dental alcove or suite will depend on both the number and arrangement of treatment stations necessary and the desired extent of separation from other hospital activities. Designs with higher degrees of separation for dental suites will require more hospital square footage than those with dental areas integrated within general treatment spaces.

Dental procedure stations located within a general treatment room are best limited to brief, nonsterile procedures. A dedicated dental area with more separation is best for longer nonsterile procedures under anesthesia. A surgical operatory would provide the most appropriate space for sterile and lengthy procedures using anesthesia. While ideal, this is not always practical for smaller practices. Both the available square footage and the quantity and type of predicted patient procedures in dental services will help dictate space decisions.

LAYOUT RULES

In a typical peninsula-type layout, treatment tables should be approximately 7 feet apart from center line to center line, with 5 feet of clearance in between tables. Additionally, there should be a maximum 3-foot reach to any adjacent work counters. The minimum distance between treatment tables and adjacent walls or counters should be 5 feet to allow for technicians to treat patients and for staff circulation.

You may want to consider a shorter table for better reach, or adding an extension arm to the dental X-ray unit. Another option to consider is locating the X-ray unit on a bump-out that is centered on the wall to provide better reach. Provide as much space as possible at the head of the table, where you will need the most maneuverability.

DETAILS FOR A DENTAL SPACE

As with any medical space, the equipment that will be used in a dental room will help to dictate its overall layout. Below is a list of the big items that will be important factors in the design of your space.

Dental X-Ray Unit

A dental X-ray unit needs to be able to reach the head of the patient. It could be on a mobile stand, on a side wall, or centered between two tables on the wall at the counter end of the table.

X-rays can be developed in a traditional method using chemicals or they can be developed digitally. Most of the practices designed today utilize a digital system. There are two main types of digital systems: digital radiography (DR) and computed radiography (CR). DR systems include a sensor and software that works with your existing machine, whereas CR systems involve the use of phosphor screens that are scanned to produce an image. Both systems have pros and cons. DR is less expensive and faster in terms of image processing, but CR allows for the use of larger films, and the phosphor screens are not as easily damaged as the sensors for the DR systems. DR is currently the system of choice for most practices. (See Chapter 32 for more information about diagnostic imaging equipment.)

Proper support for a wall-mounted dental X-ray system will need to be provided by your

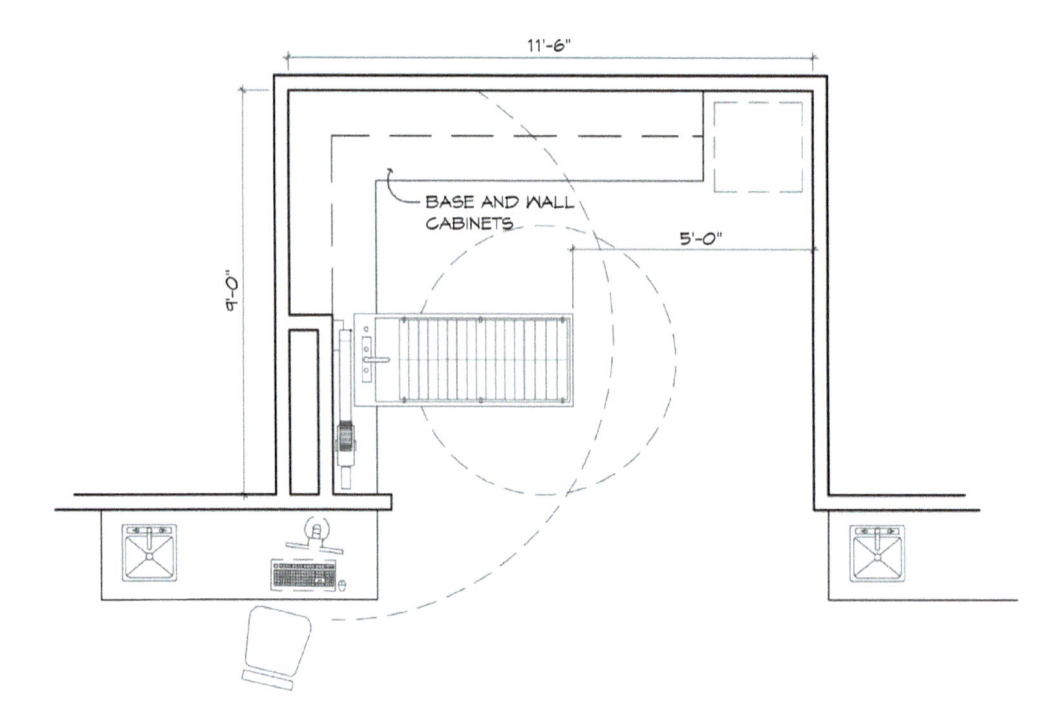

A floor plan for a one-table dental alcove.

contractor. In unique cases, such as seismic zones, it is important to have your architect coordinate with your structural engineer on any special bracing that may be required for the installation of the unit.

Dental Delivery Systems

Dental delivery systems come with or without compressors built in. You will want to try to locate a remote compressor where you can provide sound attenuation. Most remote compressors tend to be larger and louder than their quieter, smaller counterparts. Dental delivery systems can have water bottles that you fill or dedicated, hard-plumbed water lines. Your design professional should coordinate plumbing and electrical needs, as well as any necessary blocking in the wall or cabinetry to help to properly support these wall- or cabinet-mounted systems.

Optimal placement in the room is necessary to allow easy access to the equipment. If the unit is mobile, it is best to provide an alcove in which it can be placed when it is not in use. The type of dental equipment you own, or want to own, will help determine space, sound mitigation, and safety requirements.

Shielding

Most people assume that a physicist's radiation shielding report is not necessary for the use of dental X-ray machines. This is true, *unless* your workload is very high. A busy two-table dental suite that is taking many X-rays throughout the day may need lead in the walls of the room. What constitutes a high level? The safest answer is to ask a physicist. For less than $500 you can have an expert analyze your specific case and provide a professional decision on whether you need additional shielding for the

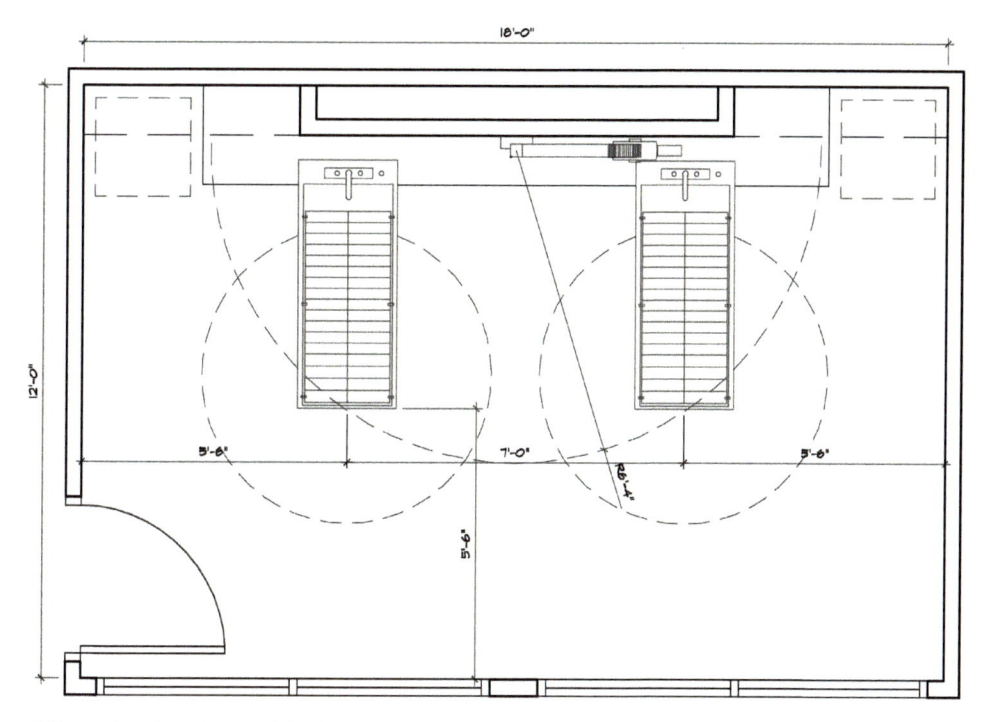

A floor plan for a two-table dental suite.

room. It is best to do this prior to finishing your construction documents so that if lead shielding is required in the walls, you (and your contractor) will be able to budget for it and your design team can include the details in the drawings. If you find out that your practice does enough X-rays to warrant additional shielding, and you have an alcove in which your dental table is located, you can often use a portable lead shield to meet the requirements.

Computer Stations

Computer stations are required both for general use and for interface with the dental X-ray unit. A strategically placed flat-screen monitor, in direct view of the veterinary staff, will make it easier for them to review images while still keeping a close eye or hand on the patient under anesthesia. A second station, or a laptop, is also handy for updating charts.

Medical Gas and Power

In a dental procedure, the head of the patient is where all of the action is. This makes the head of the table a very congested area. It is important to be strategic about the location of the oxygen, gas scavenging, and power. There are two optimal locations for these items—directly above the head of the table or within the knee space of the table. Each has its pros and cons. Locating the power and medical gas drops off to one side of the table is ideal, preferably on the opposite side from where the staff will be working.

▼ ▼ ▼

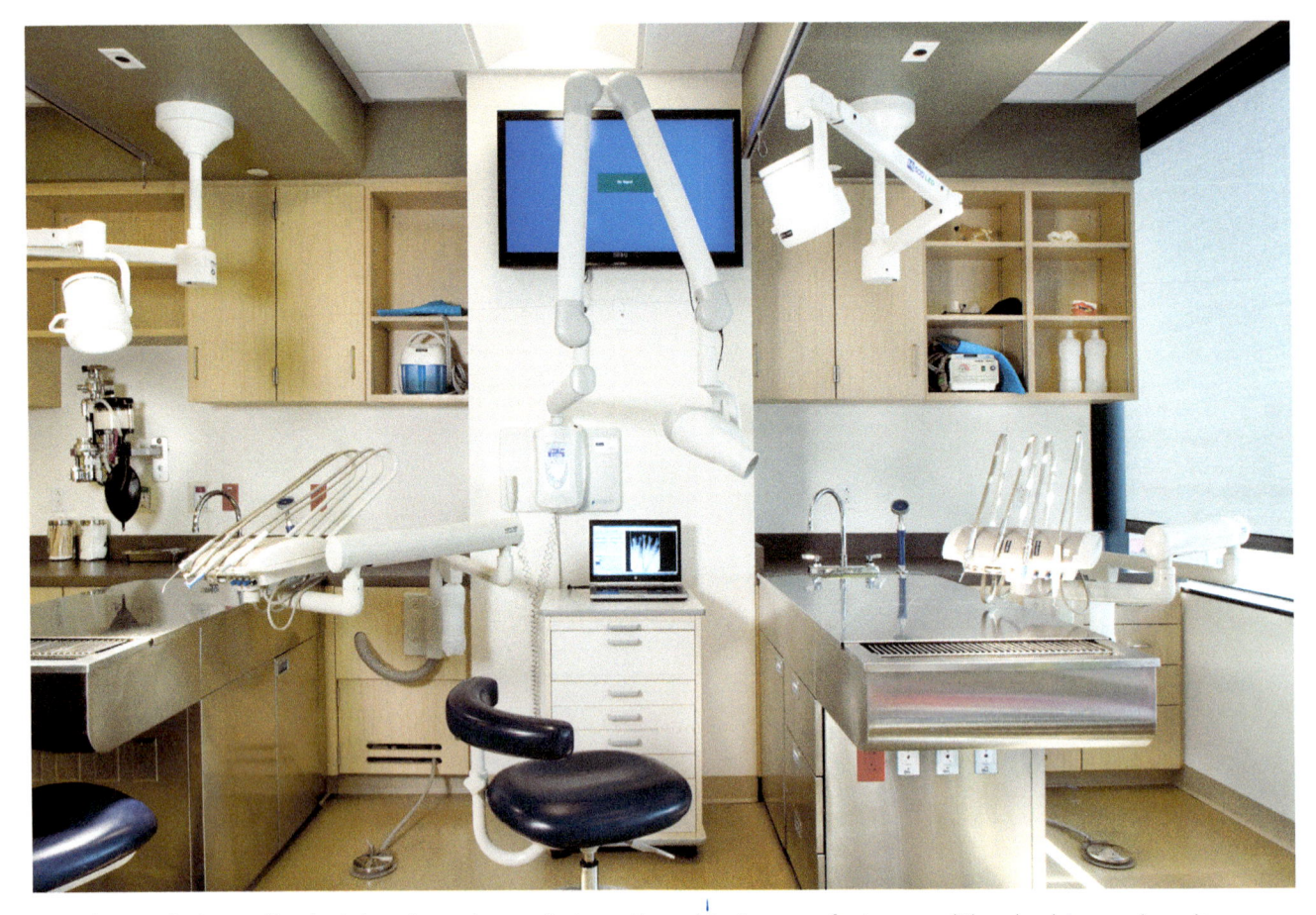

Coordination between the dental equipment manufacturer, the cabinetry manufacturer, and the plumbing engineer is essential to the design of a dental suite. (Foto Imagery / Tim Murphy. Courtesy of VCA West Los Angeles Animal Hospital, Los Angeles, California [VCA, Inc.].)

DENTAL SUITES CAN be a great resource for your hospital. They can range from small, single-table nooks off of the main treatment room to dedicated rooms with multiple tables and access to the specialized equipment required for dental surgery. Proper planning will help to ensure that your space meets your practice's needs.

CHAPTER 32

DIAGNOSTIC IMAGING

In veterinary medicine the modalities used for diagnostic imaging are digital radiology, ultrasound, computed tomography (CT), and magnetic resonance imaging (MRI). Most, if not all, veterinary hospitals have a radiology suite. It is a mainstay of the modern veterinary practice and is typically found in the core of the hospital design. Ultrasound rooms, while incredibly useful, are not always seen in a general practice hospital. Specialty hospitals will have single or multiple ultrasound rooms as well as MRI and/or CT suites to help better care for the specialty patient's needs.

RADIOLOGY

Gone are the days in which radiographic images (X-rays) were developed using caustic chemicals. Most veterinary practices now utilize digital imaging equipment. This is good for your staff's health and good for your floor plan. Without the need for a darkroom to develop film, this valuable square footage can be absorbed back into your practice. In the renovation of existing practices, darkrooms are usually the first spaces to get nabbed as an office or an additional exam room, depending upon their size. Today, there are two types of digital X-ray systems on the market, CR and DR. (See Chapter 31 for more on the differences between the two systems.)

The first step in laying out the radiology room is to decide on the equipment you wish to incorporate into the space. Table sizes and electrical requirements for X-ray machines can vary widely. X-ray tables can have two-way float tops, four-way float tops, and wall-, ceiling-, or table-mounted tube stands. At a minimum, you will want to start with a room that is 8 feet wide and 11 feet long, with the X-ray machine located parallel to the long dimension. If you have the space, a larger room, perhaps 9 × 12 feet, will work even better. You should also have enough space to circulate around three sides of the table (the long approach side and the two ends). Practice staff will utilize physical restraint by either positioning a technician on each end of the table and physically holding the animal's front and hind limbs or by sedating the animal and mechanically restraining them. In either case, staff will need to access both ends of the table for proper restraint or positioning of the patient.

In addition to the layout of the table and the space to circulate around it, consideration needs to be given to the supporting elements required in the room. These elements include racks to hang protective lead-lined aprons, gloves and thyroid/neck covers, a digital capture station, an additional computer station, a phone, oxygen and anesthetic scavenge, and dimmable lighting. All of these elements will need to be properly located for the overall function of the room. Blocking must be provided in the wall at the appropriate locations for the apron rack, any cabinetry, and a wall-mounted tube stand for the X-ray machine, if selected. Building codes generally require that the X-ray machine's electrical disconnect be located within the X-ray room. This panel requires clear space around it, but it can be located in an unobtrusive corner.

Shielding is also an important design consideration for your radiology suite. Early selection of your equipment will allow the shielding to be designed earlier in the process. A radiation shielding physicist can provide a shielding report outlining lead requirements for the design team. Be aware that if there is occupiable space above or below the X-ray room, shielding may be required on the ceiling and/or floor. If there is no occupiable space above or below the radiology suite, typically the shielding will only be required to extend to 7 feet above the finished floor surface. Your physicist will require the specific equipment information as well as information on usage, room size, and adjacencies in order to complete his or her report. The information provided in the shielding report should be incorporated into your construction documents prior to finalizing pricing with your contractor so that you can account for this cost. An "X-Ray in Use" light should be mounted outside the room above the door to aid in the safe use of the space.

In terms of adjacencies, the radiology room should be located near the main treatment area, with easy access to the exam rooms and to surgery, if possible. In larger hospitals, this is not always feasible. In these cases, two or more radiology rooms are often needed. One is typically designated as an outpatient radiology suite and placed closer to the front or client area of the building, and the other, as an inpatient radiology room, located farther into the back or medical area, in close proximity to surgery. It is beneficial to have a radiology suite located close to surgery when X-rays are needed during or after surgery.

Hospitals large enough to require a second radiology suite often include a fluoroscopy unit or a traditional X-ray machine with fluoroscopic capabilities. Fluoroscopy uses X-rays but intensifies them, allowing for a higher-resolution real-time image. This type of machine is useful for contrast studies of the gastrointestinal or cardiovascular systems. As a fixed unit, spatially, the radiology room would need to increase in size to accommodate the footprint of the fluoroscopy machine and the proper clearances around

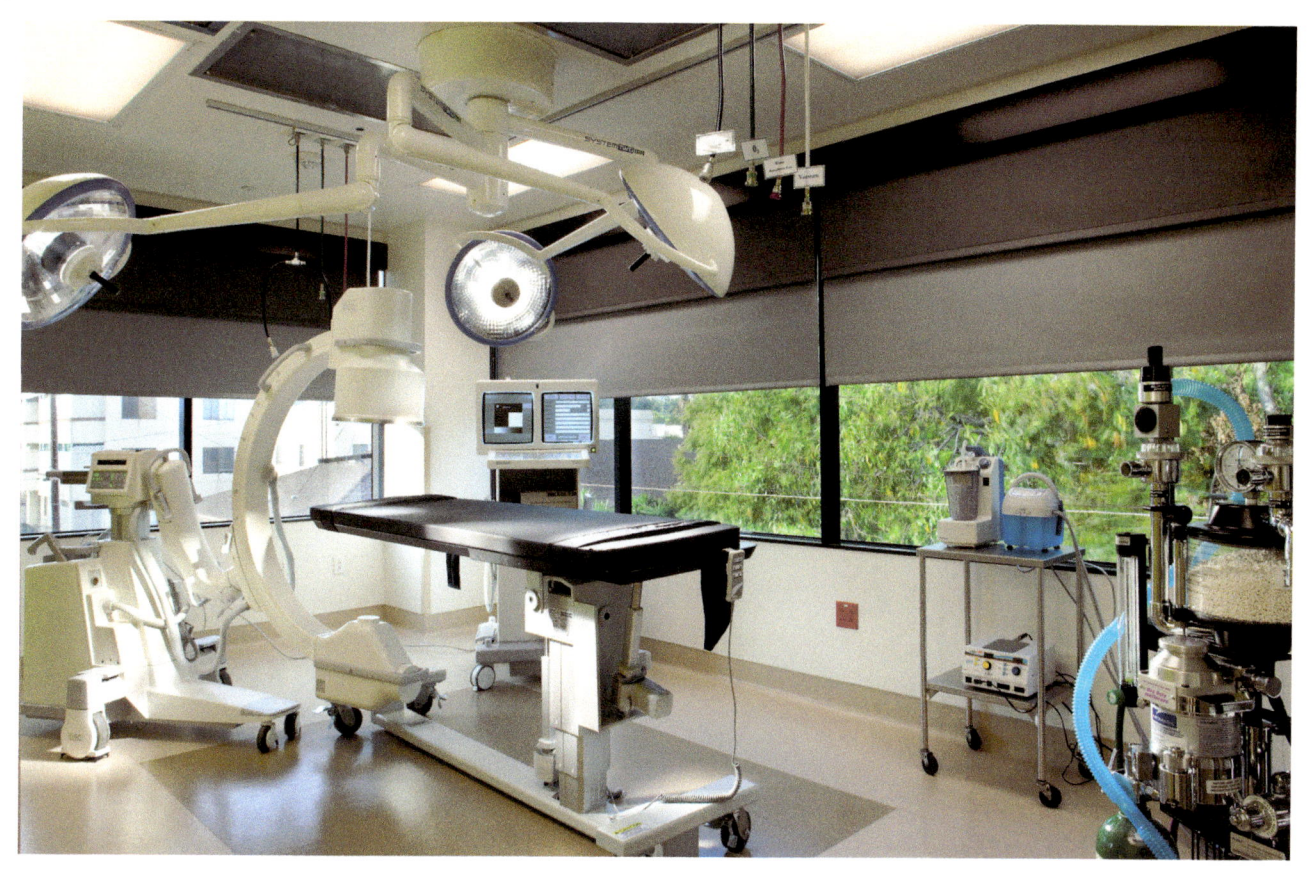

A C-arm in a specialty surgery suite. The size of the equipment, and the need to be able to maneuver it around the surgical table, necessitates a larger surgery room. (Foto Imagery / Tim Murphy. Courtesy of VCA West Los Angeles Animal Hospital, Los Angeles, California [VCA, Inc.].)

it. Additional electrical requirements as well as a separate capture station will also be necessary.

A fluoroscopy unit can be either fixed or mobile. Mobile units are also referred to as C-arms. In larger specialty hospitals, C-arms are used intraoperatively and replace the need to move the patient out of the surgery suite to check the success of the surgery prior to waking the patient. The use of this technology has allowed for faster recovery times as well as better treatment outcomes (Weisse, 61).

Spatial accommodation of the C-arm typically requires the operatory to increase in size by approximately 25%. In addition, dedicated power and a data outlet will also be needed. Some jurisdictions require additional signage outside the room to indicate to staff that X-ray technology is in use. A lead apron rack is also required for proper radiation safety within the room. Not all C-arms require the room itself to be shielded. Just as with the traditional radiology room, a radiation shielding physicist should be consulted to verify if lead protection is needed in the walls, the floor, or the ceiling.

ULTRASOUND AND CARDIOLOGY SPACES

The second modality for diagnostic imaging is ultrasound. Ultrasounds are a very useful tool in the veterinary setting. They can be performed in treatment areas when a dedicated room cannot be provided. Because ultrasounds utilize sound waves and not ionizing radiation, the exterior walls do not require shielding.

Ultrasound workspaces, including for cardiology, can be dedicated to that purpose or can double as consultation or exam rooms. Practices that have an advanced cardiology department may also require multiple cardiology exam rooms, as well as a treatment space and work area specifically dedicated to them.

As with most special procedure rooms, in ultrasound the layout starts with the functional needs of the procedure being performed. Most ultrasound rooms are not much larger than an oversize exam room (10 × 12 feet or 12 × 12 feet). In larger specialty hospitals, multiple rooms can be used for ultrasound, or perhaps one larger room with multiple tables. Ultrasound rooms can also be designed to double as other specialty rooms that generally have the same space requirements, such as cardiology or dermatology. To conserve space, an ultrasound room in a smaller practice can also double as an overflow exam room.

In general, the following four spatial elements make up an ultrasound suite:

- Space for the ultrasound machine: These machines can range from small table units, which are much more portable, to large freestanding units on casters. The location of the ultrasound machine depends on the staff members who will be using it. Ideally, the room will be designed to allow for flexibility and customization for both right- and left-handed individuals.

- Space for the ultrasound table: To keep the room flexible, the table is usually oriented so it acts as a peninsula, up against a wall or a base cabinet. Tables generally consist of a gurney or mobile stainless steel table with an ultrasound exam table on top. There are also tabletops that can double as cardiology exam tables. If you will be using your room as a more flexible space, you may want to consider this dual-purpose tabletop option. These tabletops allow for easier access to the underside of an animal during an examination. V-troughs or foam positioning devices are also useful. Install a few oversize shelves on which to store these items.

- Space for the sonographer and staff to circulate: The sonographer needs a stool or chair to sit on that is easily adjustable, so they can ergonomically reach both the machine and the patient on the table. Staff will also need space to assist with restraint and monitoring of the animal during the procedure. To ensure adequate space, allow for 4 to 5 feet between tables in a multiple-table room and 3 to 4 feet to a back-up counter.

- Space for storage and a back-up counter: A back-up counter or cabinetry should be provided on both sides of the room, so staff and doctors can access computers and position devices for accessibility during a procedure. A counter space for laying out medical supplies and a sink for handwashing are also recommended. Sometimes space will not allow for cabinetry on both sides of the room. Mobile supply carts, as well as shallower cabinetry, may be utilized instead. In addition to general storage needs, patient-monitoring equipment and access to medical gas are required in these spaces. This is usually done on a mobile cart or on shelves located at the end of the table that abuts the wall. Medical gas can come from the ceiling or can be wall mounted, depending upon the preference of the practice.

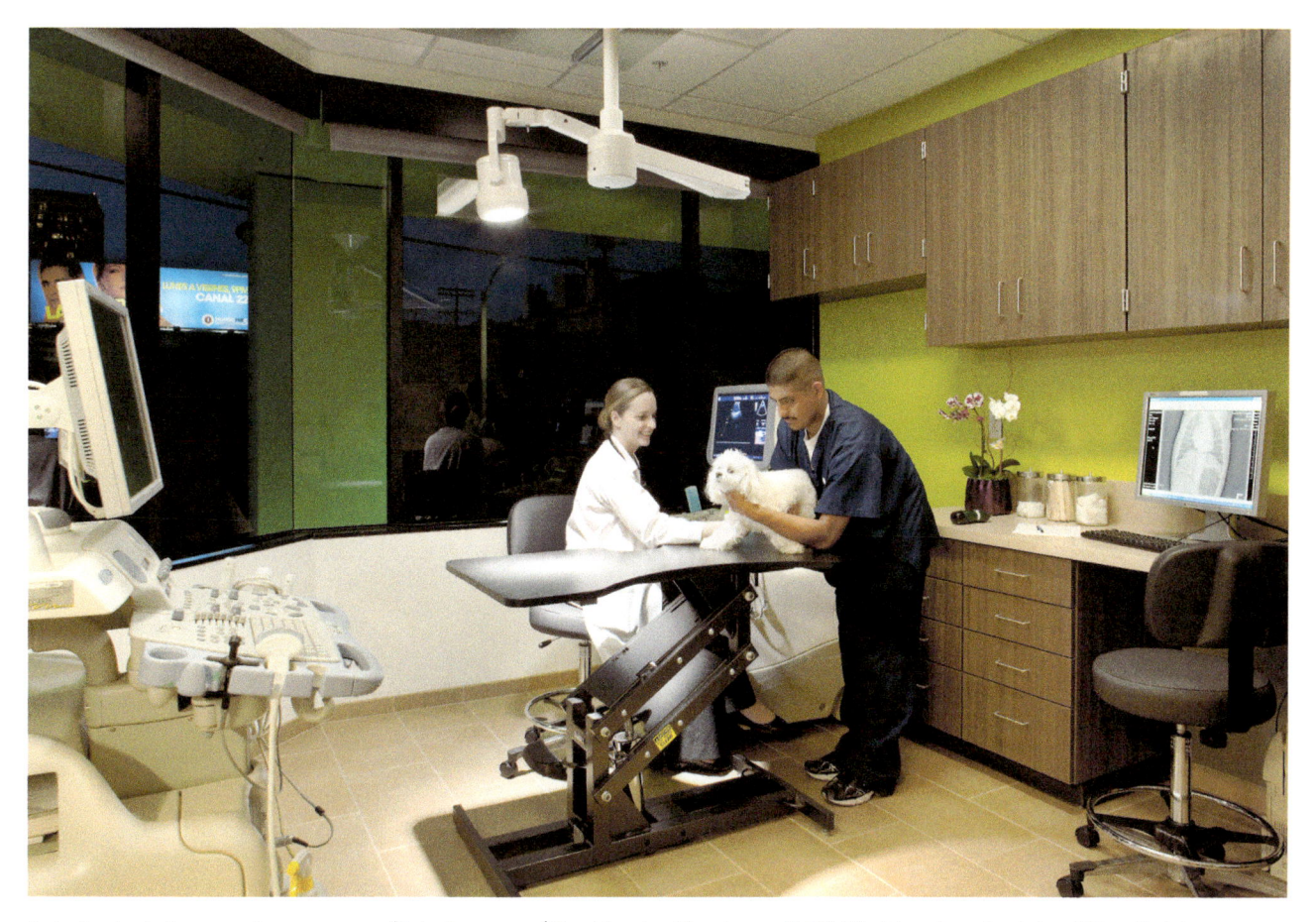

A dedicated ultrasound exam room. (Foto Imagery / Tim Murphy. Courtesy of VCA West Los Angeles Animal Hospital, Los Angeles, California [VCA, Inc.].)

Ultrasound rooms also require dimmable lighting and an exam/procedure light, and it is useful if the dimmable light has a controller in reach of the ultrasound table. The exam/procedure light, like the medical gas equipment, can be mounted from the ceiling or from the wall. Power is usually provided at the wall the table backs up to as well as at the counters. Additional ceiling power drops can be added as needed.

Keep in mind that ultrasound procedures require low-light conditions. Skylights, solar tubes, and windows without adequate coverings are not recommended in these rooms.

▼ ▼ ▼

RADIOLOGY AND ULTRASOUND

modalities are fundamental to most veterinary practices for diagnosis. They are traditionally located in the core zone of the hospital to provide easy access to all areas of the facility. If diagnosis cannot be achieved by the use of one of these two modalities, additional diagnostic imaging may be required. In these cases, a general practice can refer clients to a facility with more advanced imaging technology, such as CT and MRI. The following chapter discusses design requirements for these two tools.

CHAPTER 33

SPECIALTY IMAGING

It takes a village to raise a child.
—*African proverb*

It also takes a village to design and construct a specialty imaging area in a veterinary hospital. There are a multitude of responsibilities and detailed coordination involved in a successful MRI (magnetic resonance imaging) and/or CT (computed tomography) unit installation. From the owner who selects, purchases, and eventually uses the equipment to the contractor who works hand in hand with the shielding company, imaging consultant, engineers, and architect, it literally does take a village. As with any other area of the hospital, selecting the equipment is the first critical task for designing the appropriate space. Determining whether you will have both a CT unit and an MRI in your facility will hinge on such parameters as case load, the type of diagnostic services you plan to offer, and economic considerations. In very general terms, CT machines are better for capturing bone images, while MRIs are better for soft tissue. These two machines capture information in very different ways.

As you know from your training, CT machines use ionizing radiation to capture "slices" or views of the body that are then combined via the use of a computer to produce either a two- or three-dimensional image for diagnostics. An MRI, on the other hand, "uses strong magnetic fields to induce resonance at the nuclear (atomic) level" ("MRI Design Guide," 2-2). "As the orientation of the magnetic field is manipulated and atoms are

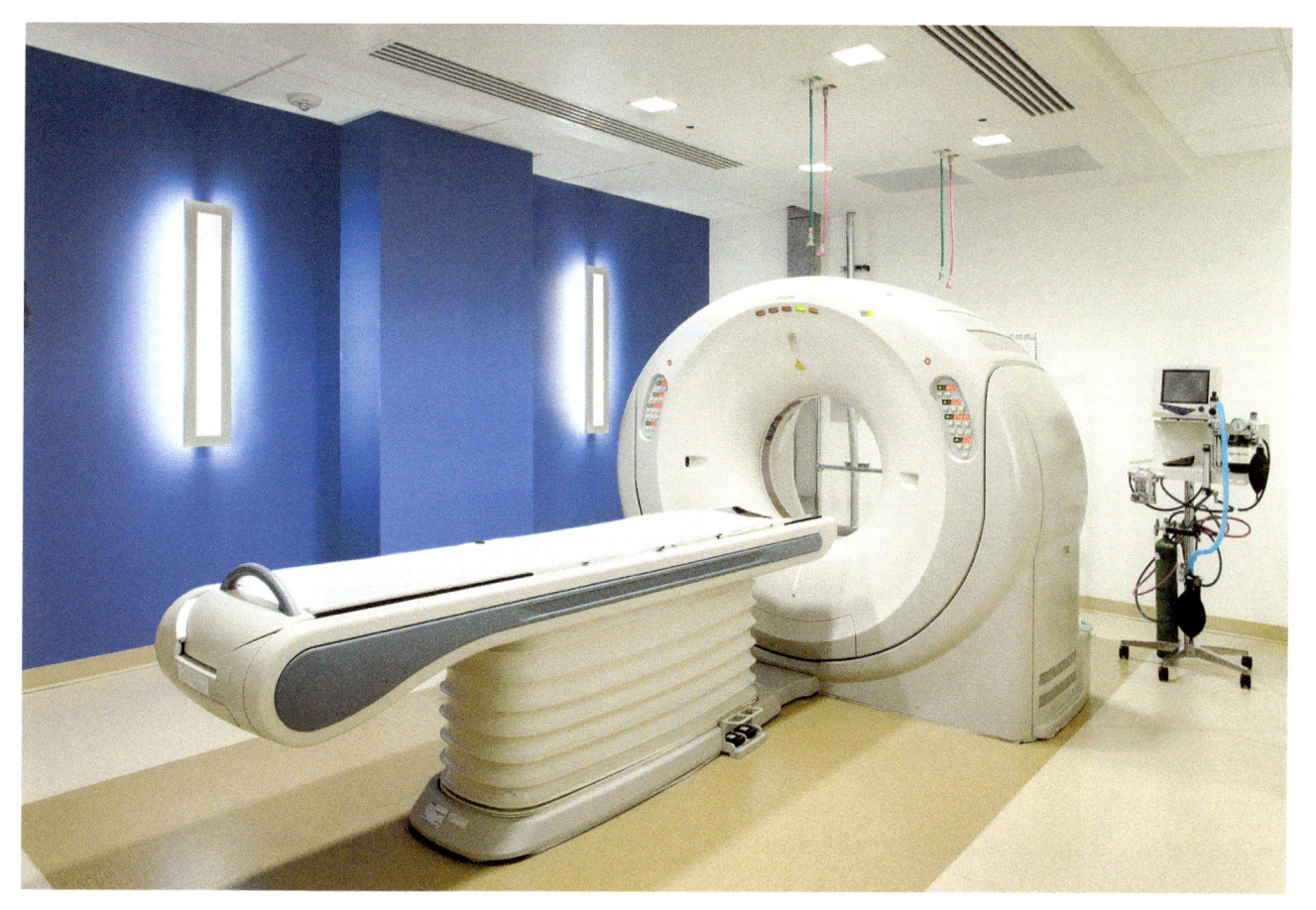

The CT suite in a specialty hospital. (Foto Imagery / Tim Murphy. Courtesy of VCA West Los Angeles Animal Hospital, Los Angeles, California [VCA, Inc.].)

knocked off axis, they emit faint radio frequency (RF) energy as they return to their polar orientation. These emissions are measured and allow a computer image to be created by the analysis of the frequencies emitted by resonating atoms comprising cell structure" ("MRI Design Guide," 2-2).

Therefore, the goal in shielding for CT machines is to prevent radiation from leaving the room, whereas for MRIs, we are shielding for two separate conditions. The first is a radiofrequency shield and is typically installed in the perimeter walls of the room. Its purpose is to prevent incidental RF energy from entering the room and interfering with the MRI scans. Second, it is sometimes necessary to provide shielding to reduce the size of the magnetic field to keep it contained within the room. There are two types of magnetic field shielding: active (contained in the machine) and passive (via steel alloy plates). Many machines on the market now come with an active shield built in. This does not eliminate the need for the RF shield at the perimeter walls. The passive shield is usually only used to modify the shape of the field to prevent external undesired obstructions from interfering. These external obstructions can be things like cars driving by or adjacent equipment that cannot be located elsewhere in the building.

The most prevalent MRI format currently used in both human and veterinary medicine is the "bore" format. The bore is the open cylindrical center portion of the magnet. The magnetic field generated by this type of machine is shaped like an acoustic guitar without the neck. This magnetic field is tens of thousands of times greater than the Earth's own magnetic field and its strength is measured in gauss (G). As a result of the strength of the MRI field, there are certain safety concerns that need to be addressed, including a health risk to those with implants and pacemakers inside what is called the "5-gauss line." The 5-gauss line is sometimes marked on the floor to show where this area falls around the machine; within this perimeter, the magnetic field exceeds 5 gauss. Ferromagnetic objects cannot be brought within this space. It is important for this exclusion zone to fall within the confines of the room itself. Proper siting of the MRI suite within the building and both active and passive shielding techniques help with the confinement of the 5-gauss line.

Outside of the 5-gauss line, there are other concerns. Vibrations from surrounding buildings, existing building conditions (for example, out-of-balance HVAC or chiller systems, or elevators), highway traffic, and even railroads and airports can affect image quality. It is important to evaluate how adjacent spaces and equipment relate to the various gauss lines of the MRI to minimize interference with the field. Due to the sensitivity the MRI system has to vibration, it is wise to complete a vibration field test prior to finalizing the location of the MRI suite.

Because most of the CT and MRI equipment that goes into veterinary practices these days tends to be previously used, little to no assistance will be provided by the manufacturer on the facility design or installation of these rooms. As such, hiring an imaging consultant will be the most valuable step you can take toward a successful project. A qualified imaging consultant should be brought on board during equipment selection and should continue to be a part of the team until after construction is completed. The image consultant can assist with the following tasks:

- Equipment selection.
- Coordination of specifications supplied to the design team.
- Review of proposals from shielding consultants.
- Sequencing, quality control, and review of installation details and progress.
- Coordination with the rigging company for equipment delivery.

Once the floor plan has been finalized for the CT and MRI areas, it is time to bring on the shielding consultant to determine the scope of the necessary lead shielding for the CT room and of the RF shielding for the MRI room. Most larger companies are able to design the shielding for both types of spaces as well as any other imaging areas of the hospital. The sooner this is completed, the more time your design team will have to integrate this information into their drawing set.

DETAILS FOR CT AREAS

Room Size and Location

- Generally, spaces of 15 × 20 feet for the scan room and of at least 8 × 8 feet for the control area will accommodate most CT machines and their associated equipment. Follow the recommended floor plan dimensions

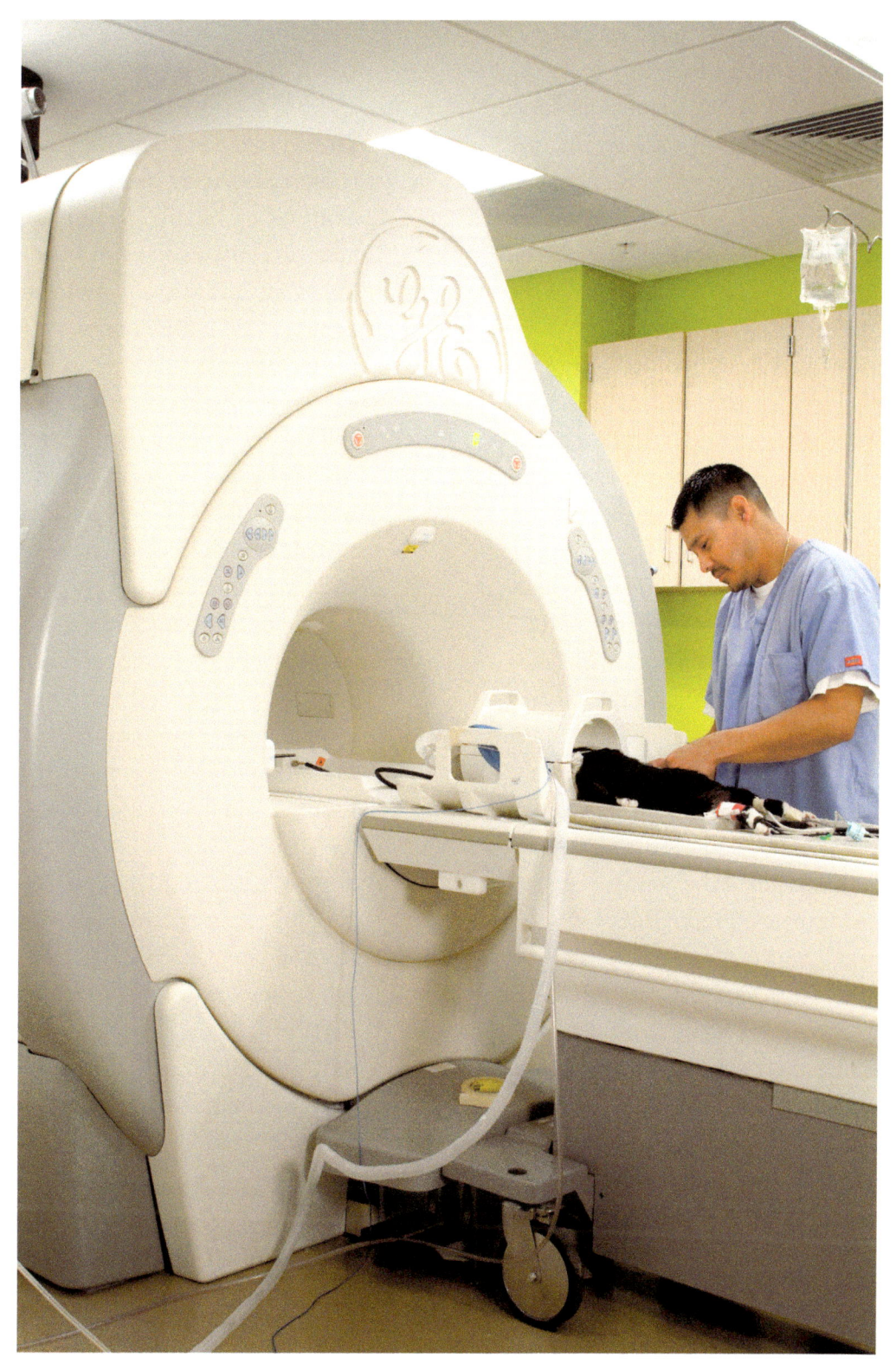

An MRI machine in action. (Foto Imagery / Tim Murphy. Courtesy of VCA West Los Angeles Animal Hospital, Los Angeles, California [VCA, Inc.].)

SPECIALTY IMAGING 179

provided by the manufacturer of the equipment as closely as possible. If you can predict what kind of replacement machine you might purchase in the future, you can provide shielding, power, space, and mechanical systems for this potential scenario. (This suggestion also applies to the MRI room.)

- There are some CT units with rotating gantries, the donut-shaped part of the machine. Be sure to provide the recommended clearances to account for the space the unit will take up when rotated.

- You will want to locate the CT room in close proximity to the areas of the hospital that will be using it the most. This is usually near treatment and/or the surgery department.

- It is ideal to locate the control area so that it has a direct view of the patient table and through the center of the gantry. (This is also true for the MRI room.)

- If the CT (or MRI) room is not located near an induction or treatment space, a small area may be needed in close proximity for this purpose.

Path of Entry for the Gantry into the Building

- The gantry is wide and tall. It can be brought in through the building into the scan room as long as the doors and hallways are sized to accommodate the equipment. Usually a door that is 3 feet, 6 inches wide to 4 feet wide and a hallway that is 5 feet wide are required. Have your design team check your specific equipment manuals for dimensions.

- The rigging company that will deliver the equipment should protect your floor as the gantry is moved in. The unit is very heavy and can cause damage to existing finishes if they are not properly protected.

- CT machines are heavy and sensitive to movement. The floor area in the scan room will need to be structurally reinforced, and the gantry should be anchored to the floor with bolts. Placement typically involves a thickened slab directly under the gantry and patient table. If the CT machine is located on a raised floor system, additional steel- or wood-framing members will be required to support the unit and to keep it level and free from warping or sagging. It is important to involve your structural engineer early in the design process.

Power and Lighting

- Careful planning and consideration will need to be given to the power layout in the room. Recessed floor and wall ducts, or, alternatively, surface-mounted floor and wall ducts, can be used to help accommodate the large number of cables that will need to be run. Because most CT machines purchased by veterinary hospitals are refurbished units, there can be limitations in cord length. Thus, cord length should be verified prior to finalizing the design to prevent any issues with the installation.

- Most CT machines require a dedicated 100 amps (A), 480 volt (V), 3 phase (PH)

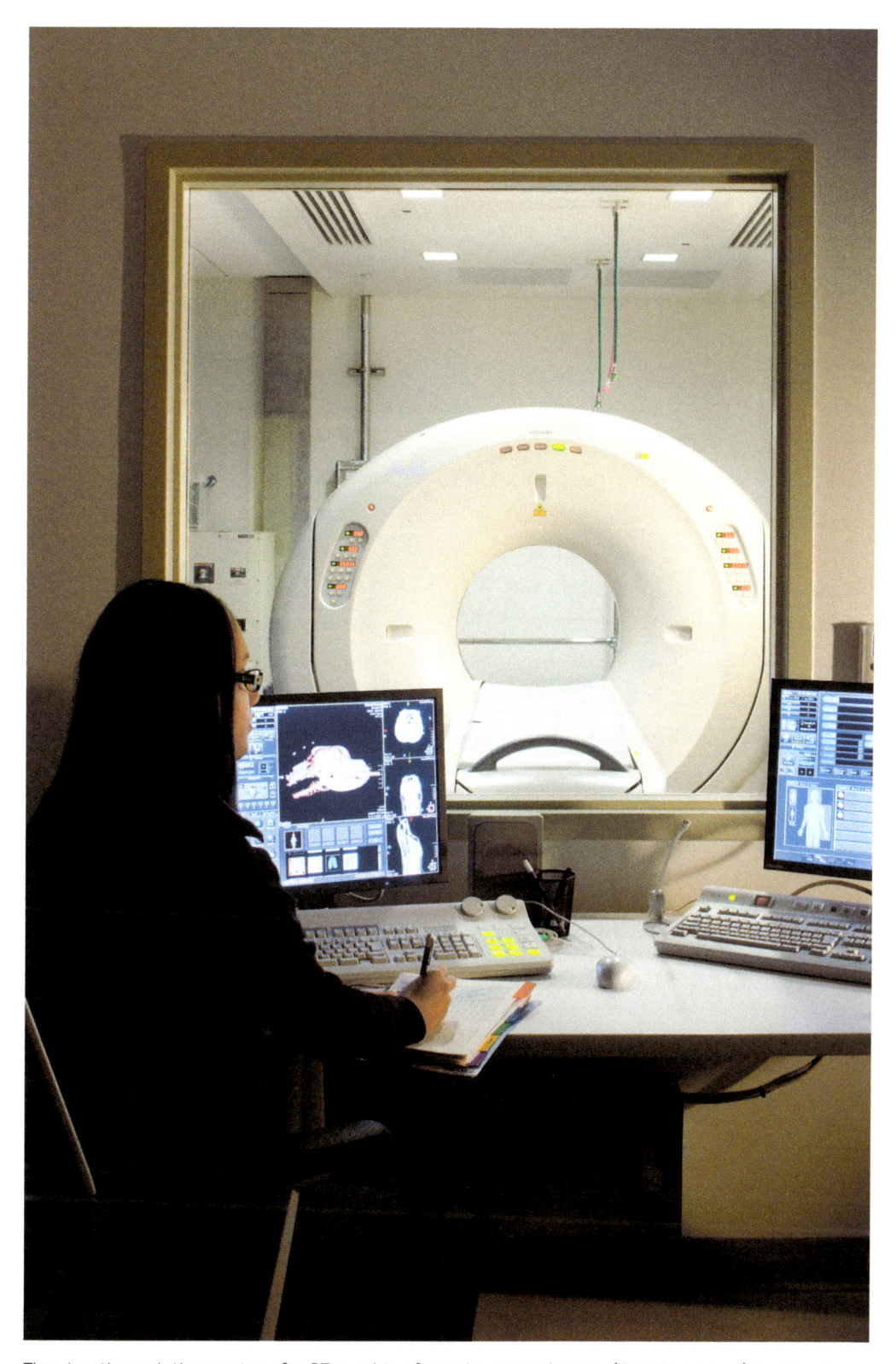

The view through the gantry of a CT machine from the control room. (Foto Imagery / Tim Murphy. Courtesy of VCA West Los Angeles Animal Hospital, Los Angeles, California [VCA, Inc.].)

electrical connection. Often a smaller facility will be provided with 120/208 V, 3 PH power and may require a step-up transformer or a building electrical service upgrade to accommodate the requirements.

- Don't forget "X-Ray in Use" signs outside the room, as well as emergency power-off (EPO) buttons to allow the machine to be quickly turned off in case of an emergency. Both the signs and the EPO buttons are usually located directly outside the CT room in easy reach of the control station.

- Lighting for the room should be designed to allow for an even amount of light on the patient table. The recommended lighting level is 50 foot-candles (fc). (See Chapter 47 for more information on foot-candles.) Adding dimming controls to this room is optional. The lighting should be controlled at the entrance to the room as well as at the operator's workstation.

- CT and MRI procedure rooms and control rooms can produce excessive amounts of heat, so it may not be practical to utilize the base building HVAC system and supplemental equipment may be required.

Shielding

- Shielding for this room is dependent upon the occupancy and use of the adjacent spaces, the type of machine, and the predicted usage. Lead is almost always required in the walls to a height of 7 feet above the finished floor. If there is occupiable space above or below the room, lead will also need to be added to the ceiling or floor. It is helpful for your structural engineer to have an understanding of the shielding requirements before designing the floor system so that this can be coordinated.

- Doors and windows will also require lead shielding. The windows should be oriented for the view from the control area into the scan room, and the doors should be positioned to allow for efficient patient flow.

- Lead-lined wall penetrations as well as leaded junction boxes will be required for power entering or leaving the scan room through a wall below the 7-foot height.

Don't Forget

- Medical gas and medical gas scavenger outlets/drops will be required in this room. It is helpful to locate them both in front of and behind the gantry to provide more flexibility.

- IV tracks on the ceilings allow for a cleaner layout and should also be located both in front of and behind the gantry.

- Storage cabinets can be located inside the scan room, if desired, along with a sink for convenient cleanup of contrast materials.

DETAILS FOR MRI AREAS

Room Size and Location

- Generally, 16 × 24 feet for the magnet room and no smaller than 8 × 8 feet for the control area will accommodate most MRI machines. In addition, the MRI has a large amount of equipment that will need to be housed in a separate room adjacent to the magnet side of the scan room. This equip-

An example of the rigging process for an MRI being moved into a new emergency hospital in Vancouver. Note the large magnet access panel required for delivery. (Courtesy of VCA Vancouver Animal Emergency and Referral Center [VCA Canada].)

ment room usually measures about 16 × 8 feet. All dimensions should be checked against the typical floor plan layouts supplied by the equipment manufacturer.

- The magnet and equipment rooms need to be oriented to allow for easy delivery and removal of the magnet and associated equipment. This typically means the magnet room should have one or two exterior walls. A magnet access panel—that is, a large, removable wall panel—will need to be designed, and its removal and final installation will need to be coordinated with the contractor and the shielding company. The use of access flooring in both the scan room and the equipment room can help to organize and make the rooms more functional.

- In addition to the control desk, there also needs to be an area dedicated to patient monitoring. This can be a small desk adjacent to the control area with a clear view into the scan room. If a clear view cannot be obtained, a video camera and monitor

SPECIALTY IMAGING 183

can be used. Medical gas, anesthetic gas scavenging, and patient monitoring cabling are brought into this area through wave guides. These wave guides, or RF filters, allow only specified frequencies to pass, thus reducing the possibility of affecting the MRI image.

- Like the CT room floor, the MRI floor slab needs to be reinforced, and in this case, the isocenter—the center of the magnetic field—needs to be clearly identified. The entire room design is based on the isocenter. The MRI floor slab is usually about twice as thick as the slab required for the CT room. This slab, depending on findings from the vibration test, may need to be isolated from the surrounding slab.

Power, Lighting, and Mechanical Needs

- Careful planning and consideration will need to be given to the power layout in the room. Most of the power that runs from the magnet to the equipment room will go from the machine into the access floor area and through the panel that is detailed for penetration through the shielding.

- An EPO is also required for this room and should be easily accessible from the control area.

- All cabling, including for power, lighting, the fire alarm, and cameras, must pass through wave guides or RF filters as it goes through the shield.

- Most MRIs require a dedicated 150 A, 480 V, 3 PH electrical connection just for the MRI machine. Additional power will be required for the chiller (see next bullet point), the equipment room air conditioning, and the MRI room itself. Often, a smaller facility will be provided with 120/208 V, 3 PH power and may require a step-up transformer or a building electrical service upgrade to accommodate these requirements.

- The magnet itself requires cooling. A chiller, with either a remote condenser or a built-in condenser, is necessary for this task. The chiller unit can be large and have very specific maintenance access requirements that can sometimes make it difficult to locate even for a new build, but finding space for it can be especially difficult for a renovation to an existing facility. There are also limits to the length of the cable from the chiller to the MRI equipment that require coordination. It is always preferable to locate the chiller on the ground. If this is not possible, the unit can be mounted above grade, but it will need a structure to support it.

- As in the CT room, lighting in the MRI room should be designed to allow for an even amount of illumination on the patient table. The recommended lighting level is 50 fc. Adding dimming control to this room is an option, though if you choose to do this, it is recommended that a DC lighting controller be utilized. Normal building power (AC) can produce electromagnetic interference, which could affect image quality. Lighting should be controlled at the entrance to the room as well as at the operator's workstation.

- MRI procedure and equipment rooms, like CT rooms, can produce excessive amounts of heat. It may not be practical to utilize the base building HVAC system; supplemental equipment may be required. Maintaining humidification levels may also be dictated by the MRI manufacturer and should be accommodated.

Shielding

- As previously noted, the magnet room will require RF shielding. This shielding is typically constructed of copper but can also be made from steel or aluminum. The shield must be contiguous on all sides as well as on the floor and the ceiling. It is best to recess the slab by the required thickness to account for the subfloor, shielding, and floor finish to create a flush condition at the door threshold into the suite. If this is not practical, the floor will need to be sloped outside the scan room to get back down to the typical finished floor height for the building.

- The construction of the walls for the magnet room truly takes a team. The walls are composed of multiple layers. The contractor and shielding company must work closely with one another to build the room. The contractor is responsible for the main framing elements, and the shielding company is responsible for the remainder of the wall structures.

- Doors and windows into the scan room must also be RF shielded. The shielding company typically supplies the door and windows for the scan room. The door for the scan room should always swing out of the room. In the case of a quench event (described below under "Don't Forget"), the pressure inside the room could drop lower than the pressure outside the room. If the door swings in, it would not be physically possible to open the door from inside the room.

Don't Forget

- Nonferrous gurneys (those made with little to no iron) and medical equipment should be used near the MRI. One of the greatest safety risks for an MRI area is the missile/projectile effect. This occurs when an attractive force is applied to a ferromagnetic object by the magnetic field. Even the most common objects can become a life-threatening safety hazard in this setting. Warning signage should be used, and access control should be necessary to gain admittance to the MRI area whenever possible. A change in finish or color can assist in delineating the "safe zone." For example, you might alter the wall paint color or the flooring material or color.

- Any other metal objects in the room that have the ability to move even after installation need to be made of nonferrous material. Typically, this includes the sprinkler system, access flooring, and the ceiling grid and the wires from which it is hung.

- The quench is the other large safety hazard with the MRI. The quench is an event in which the liquid cryogen that cools the magnet rapidly boils either deliberately or spontaneously. The correct design of the cryogen vent is critical for safe operation. If a quench event were to occur, this venting system provides a pathway for the cryogen to escape as a gas.

- Built-in cabinetry is generally needed inside the MRI room for coil storage. The coils are used to assist in the imaging process. The coil storage cabinetry in veterinary medicine is usually 7 feet long, with upper, lower, and full-height storage areas.

- Flooring in MRI rooms should be astatic or static-dissipative seamless sheet vinyl. A seamless cove base is also preferred for sanitation but is not essential.

- MRI machines can be noisy. The noise comes from a variety of sources, from the low-frequency, relatively quiet noise produced by the helium pumps to the potentially loud vibrations caused by the electrical currents passing through the coils. It is important to remember that this noise may spread beyond the confines of the room. Consider how you might use noise control and isolation in the construction of the room.

MRI TRAILERS OR MOBILE UNITS AS AN ALTERNATIVE

Mobile MRI units have all of the same components and work the same way as standalone units, but with the convenience of being self-contained inside a 60-foot-long semitrailer. They can be a great alternative to their more permanent cousins. The first steps for siting an MRI trailer involve obtaining approval from the local authorities that have jurisdiction and providing adequate electrical power for the unit. Sound control, mainly on the HVAC side of the unit (head of the trailer), should be considered. If the unit is positioned in close proximity to a property line, the jurisdiction may have specific sound-control requirements. A trailer is also considered to be temporary, and as such, permits will only be granted for a few years at a time.

There are several benefits to using a trailer for MRI imaging. The economic investment is lower, it involves less commitment than a permanent installation, and it gives you the ability to change your equipment more easily in the future. MRI trailers are also sometimes easier to run as an outside company that is separate from the rest of your business. Two of the disadvantages to the trailer setup are, one, the potential difficulty of locating the trailer in close proximity to one of the doors of your hospital and, two, the inconvenience of transporting patients from the building to the trailer unit and back. Typically, a small built-in lift or stair is used to gain access to the trailer.

Confirmation of available building power should be performed by an electrical engineer. Most MRI trailers require a 200 A, 480 V, 3 PH connection. This connection is made via a large specialty receptacle that is often specified by the trailer manufacturer.

The exclusion zone around the magnet can also be a little trickier with trailers because they are often located in parking lots, where both pedestrians and automobiles can pass through or around the field. Signage and secured fencing is critical for any successful trailer installation. There are still specific areas that need to be avoided, such as the cryogen vent and any area within the 5-gauss line. Maintenance clearances need to be maintained, and rigging or parking of the trailer needs to be coordinated.

▼ ▼ ▼

WHILE THERE ARE certainly a few overlapping design needs between CT and MRI spaces, there are far more differences between the two than similarities. CT rooms require a certain level of experience related to equipment planning and shield design. MRIs require a village for a successful outcome. It is critical for the owner and design team to understand the capabilities of the equipment as well as the coordination required and to work as a team from beginning to end to ensure the proper design, construction, and installation of all equipment.

CHAPTER 34

ONCOLOGY

Out of all of the specialty veterinary equipment that architects plan for, linear particle accelerators (LINACs) are the most complicated of the bunch. It is important to rely on a team of experts to ensure the proper design of the room to house this equipment. Like MRI and CT machines, it takes a group effort to get it right. Before diving into the design needs for LINACs, let's take a look at the larger oncological picture. Oncology is a diverse and complicated field of veterinary medicine. Within the three areas of care—medical, surgical, and radiation—oncology offers many challenges to the design of the modern-day veterinary specialty practice.

CHEMOTHERAPY

In the past, chemotherapy drugs were minimally regulated in the veterinary world. With the advent of new standards from United States Pharmacopeia (USP), entitled "<800> Hazardous Drugs—Handling in Healthcare Settings," from the United States Pharmacopeia Conference, this will no longer be the case as of December 1, 2019. New requirements will then be in effect for the receipt, storage, compounding, dispensing, administration, and disposal of hazardous drugs. USP <800> specifically addresses the veterinary field in these standards, whereas in the past they dealt primarily with human healthcare settings. This is significant for veterinary medicine in a variety of ways, including operations and the design of your facility and building systems. All antineoplastic drugs (Group 1) requiring manipulation must follow all containment requirements of these new standards. While USP is the standard-setting organization, enforcement will be carried out by other regulatory bodies and accreditation organizations.

What does this mean for you and your hospital? The answer to this question will vary drastically for each practice. The major variables involve sterile versus nonsterile compounding, maximum beyond-use dates for the drugs that you are handling, and what type of risk these drugs pose to your staff. The best place to begin is with a thorough reading of the USP <800> chapter, followed by the National Institute for Occupational Safety and Health (NIOSH) listing of hazardous drugs. In addition, you should also familiarize yourself with USP <795> and <797>, as some of these standards will also now apply to veterinary settings. With this information you should be able to create a plan and protocols for executing these standards.

As of this writing, how precisely these standards will change veterinary facility design is still being evaluated, but the following paragraphs provide some information on two different design options based on the hazardous drugs you plan to administer.

Basic layout: If all your antineoplastic drugs are received in their final form, are low to medium risk, and are used by their maximum beyond-use date, you will most likely be able to design for a two-room oncology area.

- The first room will be your sterile compounding room, in which your biological safety cabinet is located. This room will need to be externally vented, have a minimum of 12 air changes per hour, and be negatively pressurized. This room can be a non-ISO space if it meets the standards established for an unclassified containment segregated compound area. ISO refers to standards for clean room classifications set by the International Organization for Standardization. These ISO classes are determined by the number of particles permitted by volume of air in a space.

- The second room will be your administration room. If possible, the administration room should be directly adjacent to the compounding room. The chemotherapy administration room is the special procedure room in which the patient receives chemotherapy drugs. This room should be located in a quiet area of the hospital to help keep patients calm and undistracted during treatment. Treatments can range from quick subcutaneous injections to eight-hour infusions. The administration room should be a minimum of 10 × 12 feet, with temporary housing for patients in the room.

Advanced layout: If you manipulate your antineoplastic drugs in any manner, such as expelling air or hazardous drugs from syringes, constituting or reconstituting powdered or lyophilized hazardous drugs, or weighing or mixing components, you will need at least a three-room setup.

- The first room again will be your compounding room. If you engage in nonsterile compounding only (medications given orally in pill form or applied as a topical treatment), you will only need one compounding room. This room will need to meet ISO class 5, be negatively pressurized, and have HEPA filtration.

› If you also require sterile compounding for medications that are used in the eye or are injected, you will need an additional compounding room that meets ISO class 7. There are provisions to provide both sterile and nonsterile compounding within one room, but the ISO requirements are significantly higher and more expensive to meet.

- The second room required is a dedicated anteroom. This is an area that allows for proper access into the compounding room and allows for a pass-through into the administration room. This room will need to have positive pressurization, have HEPA filtration, and attain an ISO level of 7.

- The third room in this scenario is the administration room, as described above.

A few additional notes about the biological safety cabinet. You should verify that any Class II biological safety cabinet you are looking to purchase meets USP <797> requirements. These cabinets will be a 100% vented hood with a built-in HEPA filtration system. The exhaust stack for this ducted unit is 10 feet tall. Because of its extreme height requirement, positioning it on the roof of the hospital in an inconspicuous location is sometimes a challenge. Attention should be paid in the early design phase to the exact location of the room to minimize views of this vent stack from the street. All manufacturer ventilation and electrical specifications should be followed. USP <800> also recommends that the biological safety cabinet be placed on the emergency generator, if possible.

There are very specific requirements related to USP <800> that specify ISO standards for the design of the hood and the room where the hood is located. Be sure your design team is aware of them as early as possible. Proper layout of equipment is essential, and this equipment needs to include a dedicated refrigerator and biohazard waste receptacles. USP <800> also clearly states how the Group 1 drugs should be stored within your facility, including a provision for an exhaust fan near the compressor on the refrigerator.

The administration room should include proper lighting and an ergonomic treatment space. The treatment table can vary from a straightforward flip-down table to a wet table. Some clinicians may prefer to administer treatments while the patient is safely contained inside a run or cage. A sink and a computer station are recommended for this room. Because chemotherapy drugs are cytotoxic, an emergency eyewash station is required under both Occupational Safety and Health Administration (OSHA) standards and USP <800>.

LINAC

In human medicine, a linear accelerator is the equipment used to administer radiation therapy. There are various types of linear accelerators, and some can be more accurate for certain types of treatments than others.

LINACs are also used for radiation treatment of cancer in animals. The machine can be directed to destroy cancer cells while sparing the surrounding healthy tissues.

LINACs are a bit of a bear to design for. You should start at the very beginning, during the site selection process. Have the soil condition of the site examined to determine if the foundation system that will be required for the LINAC vault will be economical to construct. If the soil is unforgiving and extraordinary foundation systems will be required, it may be worth walking away from a given site to avoid the high construction costs that will be required.

As with most of specialty veterinary hospital design, the next step will be equipment selection. Once the equipment has been determined, an extensive specification and installation guide will be provided by the manufacturer. Your design team should then review the specific electrical, mechanical, and spatial requirements of the equipment. Most LINACs in the veterinary industry, like MRIs and CTs, are refurbished from the human healthcare marketplace, and you may find there is time-limited support from the secondary market vendors.

In addition to your engineering team—inclusive of your electrical, mechanical, and structural engineers—you will also need to hire a radiation shielding consultant who will design the actual vault. This consultant will work with your given site conditions, as well as with your architect and engineers, and the selected equipment to design the best vault for your project. The vault is typically constructed of extremely thick concrete, sometimes 3 to 6 feet thick at the walls that flank the isocenter of the machine. In tight quarters, steel plates or lead brick can be utilized. Both of these materials are traditionally more expensive.

In addition, the door into the vault must be properly shielded. In order to keep the door size down, a maze can be used. The downside of a maze is that it uses up a lot of square footage. Your design team must also ensure that the path of travel into the vault, whether through a maze or not, is large enough to handle the width of the LINAC itself and gurney and patient traffic.

The following are some power considerations:

- LINAC equipment typically requires a dedicated 150 A, 208 V, 3 PH electrical service. Approximately another 150 A, 208 V, 3 PH electrical service is required for the supporting spaces and HVAC equipment. So a LINAC suite will require a 400 A, 208 V, 3 PH service.

- The linear accelerator manufacturer should provide installation drawings, whether typical or site specific, that the electrical engineer will use to closely coordinate the process. There are several special installation requirements necessary for the system to function properly.

- Dimmable lighting fixtures that are controlled from the control workstation are recommended within the vault.

- Installation of an electrical service entrance rated surge protection device is also recommended to protect the linear accelerator machine equipment.

Support space is also needed outside the vault. This includes an induction area with treatment tables, equipped with medical gas, exam lights, and power. A mold/cast room to fabricate the molds that will be used for each unique patient to help position the patient and the beam accurately is also required. A room measuring 8 × 8 feet should be sufficient. A small patient-holding area, either separated from or integral to the induction area, is also useful.

In existing hospitals, LINACs added onto the building usually end up being remote from the rest of the facility. In large new veterinary specialty hospital construction, there is a benefit to having the LINAC area closely related to the

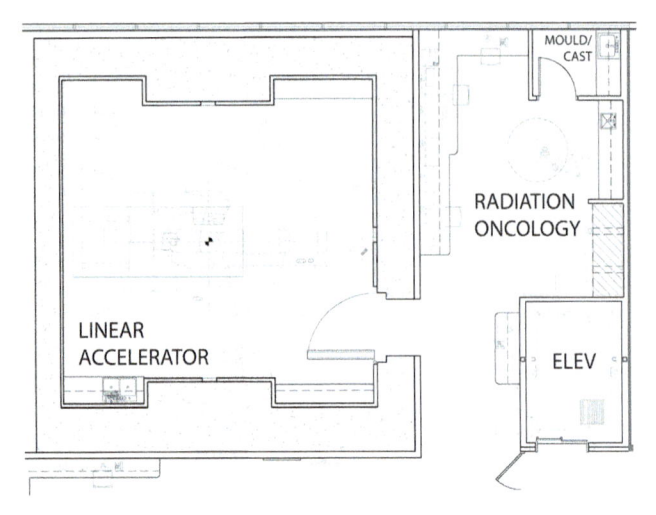

A floor plan for a LINAC vault. Induction and the mold/cast room are conveniently located adjacent to the vault. (Courtesy of VCA West Los Angeles Animal Hospital, Los Angeles, California [VCA, Inc.].)

oncology department. Construction of a LINAC above grade is not recommended due to the extensive foundation system required for the vault.

IODINE-131

Another treatment related to radiation oncology is the administration of I-131 for feline hyperthyroidism. In I-131 treatment, radioiodine is injected subcutaneously into the patient. Most cats are cured with one treatment. In humans, I-131 is used to treat thyroid cancer, thus its connection to oncology.

Patients that receive the injection are literally radioactive until the isotope leaves the body. As a result, they need to be housed for several days, with limited contact, until it is safe to return them to their owners. Because of the high levels of radiation in this area of the hospital, a radiation shielding physicist needs to be consulted to determine the shielding that will be required for this room. In some cases, if high numbers of animals are to be treated and held in the room, the required lead shielding can reach a thickness of 1 inch. If the lead requirements are high enough, the excess weight will need to be accounted for by a structural engineer. Concrete block walls can sometimes be used in combination with lead to provide a more economical way of meeting the shielding requirements.

There are generally two or three required areas in an I-131 suite. The first is the anteroom or vestibule. This area acts as a staging area for supplies that need to be brought into the room and provides a spot for gowning prior to entering the main treatment space. It also allows for more division between a main hallway and the treatment room itself. This anteroom is a good area in which to locate a workstation with a computer and phone for general administration purposes.

Just past the anteroom is the treatment room, or, in some cases, the holding or housing area. A separate treatment area can be a small space adjacent to where the cats will be housed. This area can include a small treatment table and general cabinetry for storage of medical supplies.

The holding area will consist of stainless steel cages with shelving for the storage of biological waste. Urine and feces are bagged and stored until they reach the half-life in which they are safe to discard with the rest of the building waste. Some facilities will store the animal waste in freezers or sealed containers. This storage is sometimes done in a separate, fourth area. The hospital owner and design team should verify the requirements for waste disposal with the company that will be operating the I-131 area or with the local authority that has jurisdiction over this type of room occupancy. If cost allows, a security camera in this room to monitor the cats

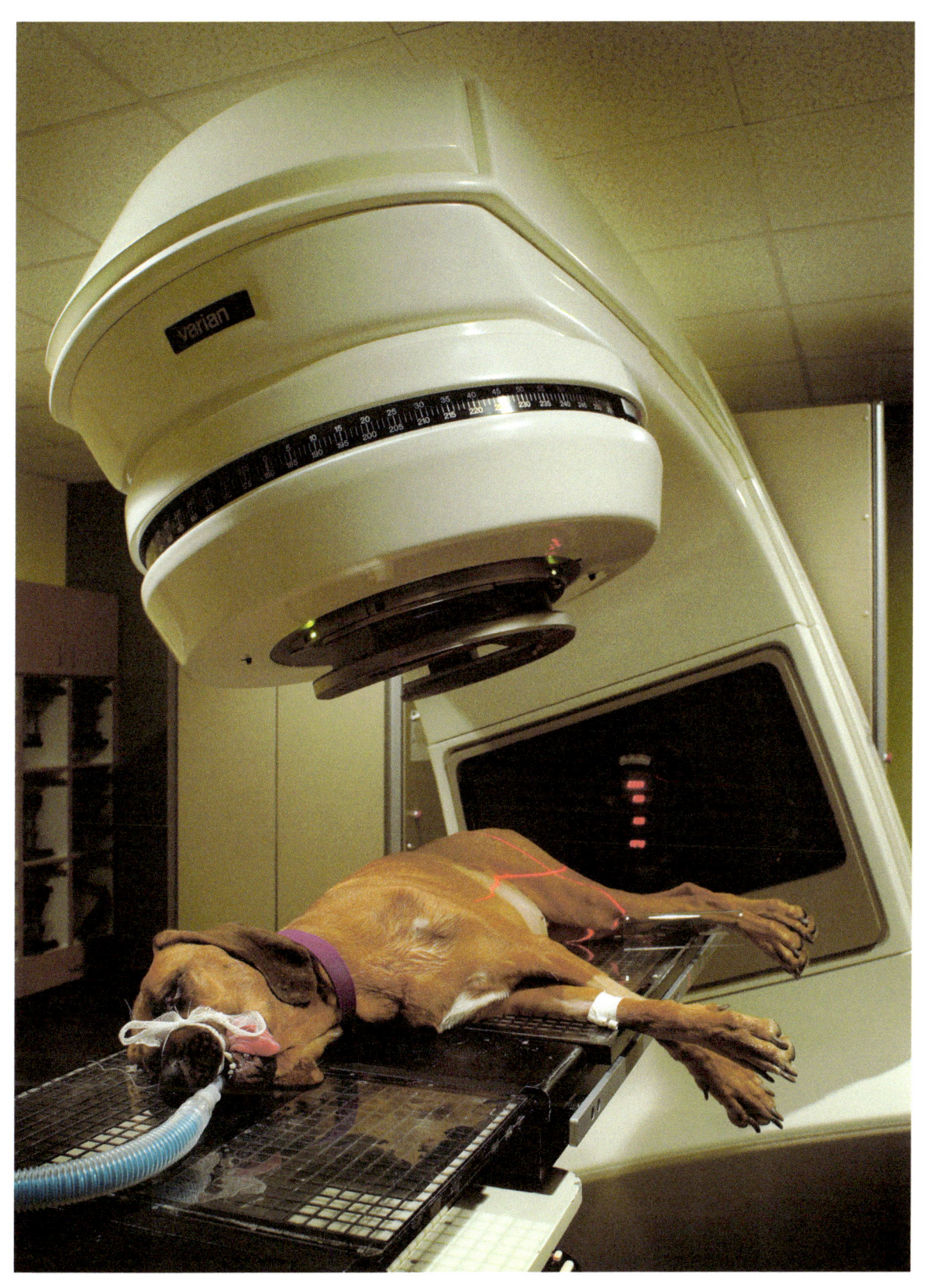

A LINAC in operation. (Foto Imagery / Tim Murphy. Courtesy of Upstate Veterinary Specialists and Emergency Clinic, Greenville, South Carolina.)

is useful to limit the frequency with which staff members have to enter the space.

Overall, I-131 suites should be located in a remote area of the hospital. They are now typically operated by an outside company in specialty hospitals, and as such it is useful to locate them near an exterior door to allow the separate staff members more direct access in and out of the building.

BONE MARROW TRANSPLANTS

In rare instances, and usually in a veterinary teaching hospital setting, oncology departments are able to perform bone marrow transplants. This type of transplant is done to replace damaged bone marrow with normal stem cells. It is used for the treatment of blood-cell cancers such as lymphoma and leukemia.

Similar to the I-131 suite, the bone marrow transplant area needs to have an anteroom or vestibule for gowning and staging. Just past the anteroom is a treatment area with separate housing, typically for canines. The two key elements for the design of this area are visibility to the rest of the main oncology treatment area and the capacity to provide an environment that is as clean as possible for the patient. Animals receiving transplants are immunocompromised and highly susceptible to nosocomial infections during the transplant process. The HVAC system in this area must be designed with this in mind—it's critical to prevent cross-contamination. Special attention should be paid to the selection of materials and finishes as well.

Because bone marrow transplantation is a highly intensive and hands-on treatment process, it is not within economic reach for most people. There is, however, a small market for this service, particularly in some metropolitan areas.

▼ ▼ ▼

IN THE END, early selection of equipment, careful planning, and an educated design team can help you to build a successful oncology department. Listen to the unique demands that oncological veterinary staff members bring to the design table in order to ensure a design that will function efficiently and effectively for many years to come.

CHAPTER 35

ADDITIONAL SPECIALTY SERVICES

In addition to diagnostic imaging, cardiology, and oncology, specialty practices also have spatial needs for the plethora of additional services they may offer. Every practice is unique and could have a combination of any of the previously mentioned services as well as any of the specialties covered in this chapter: endoscopy, nephrology, dermatology, and neurology. The effective design of the rooms relating to these specialties starts with understanding the physical needs of the clinical staff and the necessary equipment. There is no one-size-fits-all layout, but the following room descriptions will help as a starting place.

ENDOSCOPY

Similar to many special procedure rooms, endoscopy rooms are designed around the equipment and procedures that occur in the room. They do not require any type of shielding because endoscopy does not use X-rays. For smaller practices with the need for only one endoscopic table, a room with a minimum size of 10 × 12 feet will work. Busier practices can either have multiple single-table rooms that also double as ultrasound or cardiology rooms or a multitable room. A two-table endoscopic room should have a minimum footprint of 12 × 15 feet.

As for the spatial needs of the layout of this room, 5 feet between tables and 3 feet to a back-up counter should still be adequate. A 5-foot circulation area is also required at the end of the table. Most practices prefer to set up the tables as peninsulas due to spatial constraints. Endoscopic procedures can be very messy, so a wet table is recommended. To provide the most flexibility, a 5-foot-long wet table is usually used. The wet table also serves a dual function. In addition to catching bodily and procedural fluids, it can be used to clean the scopes once the procedure is completed.

Dimmable lighting, exam lights, medical gas, and monitoring equipment can be laid out in a similar manner to an ultrasound room (see Chapter 32). In addition, endoscopy rooms require medical suction. Some larger facilities may also like to have the ability to house a few animals in the room before and after the procedure. The main difference between this room and an ultrasound room is the equipment. The scopes, like other sensitive medical instruments, need to be stored properly. A premade scope cabinet can be purchased as a piece of furniture or it can be custom made by your cabinetry contractor.

In addition to the scope storage area, there must also be a scope tower. This tower is a mobile cart with multiple shelves and built-in power. This is where all of the capture devices reside, along with a viewing monitor. The tower needs to be stored in the room so that it is easily accessible during procedures. Ideally, when not in use, the design should allow it to be tucked back into a corner or within the cabinetry in the room. There are usually multiple scopes and one tower dedicated to each table.

Endoscopy rooms also have more storage needs than some of the other special procedure rooms as there are more medical supplies associated with this type of procedure. It is typical to see one solid wall of cabinets, upper and lower, in this special procedure room.

As with all specialty procedure areas, it is best to start with a broader analysis and discussion with the specialty team to understand how each special procedure room will relate and work with other specialty rooms from an operations perspective. How will patients and staff move throughout the day based upon their procedural needs? In endoscopy, for example, locating a scope cabinet in an easily accessible area, so that a staff member can grab a different scope while a procedure is going on, will greatly help the efficiency of the team. Spatially, it is also important to consider how animals will enter and exit the space and how they will be situated within the room. Always be sure to prevent animals from coming into close contact with each other.

The procedures performed here can be very interesting to the medical staff, and a window to a main hallway can provide the ability for multiple staff members to view procedures. Strategic positioning of the viewing monitors, angled toward the window, will allow for easy viewing outside the room. A remote viewing station somewhere else in the building can also be a good addition to your hospital. There will be times, however, when a sensitive procedure will occur. In these cases, the addition of blinds on this window can be useful. Window coverings should be on the outside of the suite to minimize dust collection in the aseptic suite.

NEPHROLOGY

Currently, veterinary hemodialysis centers capable of caring for animals with diseased kidneys are rare, but nephrology as a specialty is likely to become more common in hospitals in the future.

The hemodialysis procedure room's spatial needs are similar to those of the endoscopy room, with treatment tables, equipment storage, and a large amount of cabinetry. Some centers may prefer more clear floor space in lieu of a treatment table to allow the patient more room in case they move during treatment. The ability to contain the animal inside a low-gated space or crib-like enclosure can also be desirable. If space allows, separate areas for various species are also very beneficial to keep stress levels lower. Dimmable lighting and an overall calm space can contribute to better patient outcomes.

Animals who are undergoing hemodialysis may also require critical care, so close proximity to the hospital's ICU is beneficial. The hemodialysis center will always have staff by the patient's side to closely monitor them during treatment. Larger areas of floor space are needed not only for the hemodialysis equipment but also for the additional monitoring devices that will help the staff keep a closer eye on the health of the patient. Patients are generally allowed to move, eat, and sleep during the procedure, so extra floor space is good to have.

DERMATOLOGY

The dermatology area of the hospital, similar to ultrasound and endoscopy, can function in one oversize room within smaller practices. In higher-volume hospitals, multiple rooms are required. Ideally, one or two exam rooms and a treatment room directly adjacent to them will be dedicated only to the dermatology patients. Some dermatological conditions can be contagious and even zoonotic, so it is important to isolate this service. A separate entrance/exit and check-out area are ideal. In addition, a dedicated dermatology lab and bathing area are essential in busier practices.

Exam rooms should be equipped with good lighting to assist with the exam. Use lighting in a wide variety of spectra and color temperatures in order to see all of the features of skin lesions. A wall- or ceiling-mounted exam/procedure light is preferred, along with the ability to dim the overhead lights when the use of a Wood lamp (black light) is needed. A small refrigerator under the counter and cabinetry for culture plates are also required. The exam table can range from a stainless steel flip-down table to a mobile gurney station.

The dermatology treatment area will also need examination tables. At least one of the

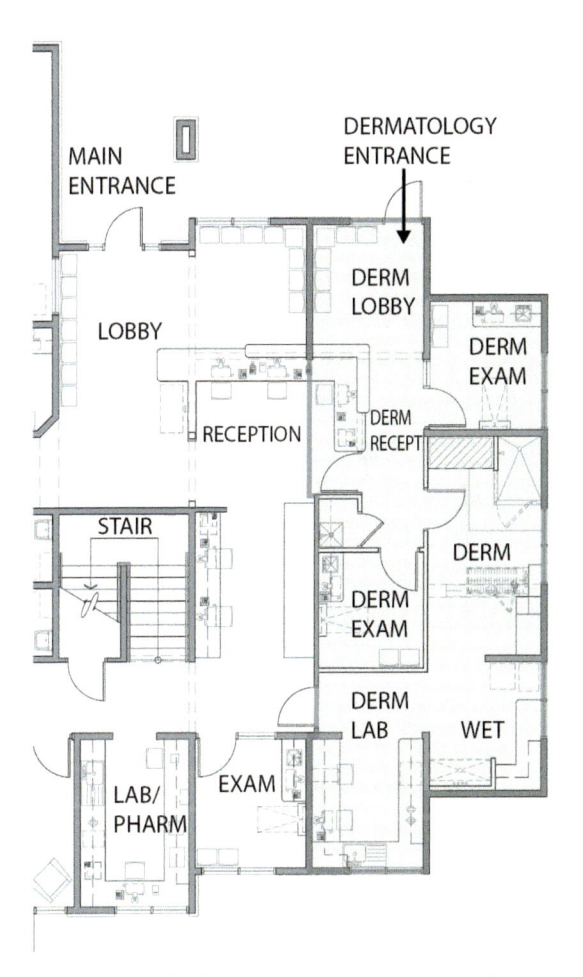

An example of a dermatology suite inclusive of a separate entrance, reception, exam rooms, laboratory, and treatment space. (Courtesy of VCA Northwest Veterinary Specialists, Clackamas, Oregon [VCA, Inc.].)

ADDITIONAL SPECIALTY SERVICES 197

treatment tables should be a wet table. Proper clearances around the tables include 5 feet for circulation and 3 feet to a back-up or support counter area. A single microscope or a dual-head teaching microscope, along with an additional under-counter refrigerator, is needed as well in the treatment area, or in the lab space if one is provided. Each treatment table should have an exam or procedure light that provides 50 fc of illumination. Establish the level of treatment that will be provided in this area to determine the medical gas requirements. Where space allows, a small cage bank or run is helpful for patient load management.

NEUROLOGY

Animals suffer from all sorts of disease conditions related to the nervous system, and neurology departments are in high demand. The fundamental spatial component in the hospital for this specialty is the generously sized exam room. Neurology examinations require ambulation, and an animal must be able to express a normal range of movement. Many neurology patients are larger-breed dogs, and the extra space is especially useful for them.

In addition to the larger room sizes—ideally 20 feet long by 10 to 12 feet wide, the flooring must be nonslip. Since neurology patients typically already have challenges walking, a slippery floor will not allow the clinician to complete a proper examination. Storage for medical supplies and counter space for staff computer workstations are also desirable. Although most patients are examined on the floor, a flip-down table is useful to have in this exam space.

Due to mobility issues in these patients, neurological examinations and treatment should be located close to the front of the hospital. If the practice also has a physical rehabilitation service, it is practical to have the neurology space close to the rehab area. Other complementary spaces that should be nearby are the main treatment room and a radiology suite.

Though neurology is itself a nonsurgical specialty, it does have a corresponding surgical specialty. This is neurosurgery, which will be covered in Chapter 36.

▼ ▼ ▼

SPECIALTY VETERINARY MEDICINE is always evolving, and the demand for better and more specialized care is on the rise. Many of the specialty rooms covered here have similar elements—it's the procedures and associated equipment used in each room that set them apart from each other. There are numerous special procedure areas that will be used by the same department, e.g., internal medicine. Sufficient support space, treatment areas, and doctor and staff workstations should be built for the optimal function of any department. Selecting equipment early, gathering information from the clinical staff on how they will use the room, and dialing in the details is what will make the layout of your specialty spaces a success.

CHAPTER 36

THE SURGERY ZONE

Surgery zone design is well defined and highly prescriptive. Maintaining sterility and good process in this area of the hospital is part of providing proper patient care. The surgery zone is defined as surgery prep and induction, pack/prep, scrub, and sterile corridors (where applicable) and includes the radiology area serving surgery, surgery rooms, and patient recovery. Hospitals that provide extensive surgical services may have an entire surgery department, whereas small hospitals may have only one induction table, a small pack/prep/scrub, and a surgery room. These basic design principles apply regardless of the size of the surgery zone:

- Primary hospital traffic flow should be separated from the surgery area. This is why surgery rooms should have only one door; traffic should never flow through a surgery room.

- Dirty procedures should be placed at a distance from surgery. For example, dental procedures tend to aerosolize bacteria, and therefore dental rooms should be placed away from induction tables.

- Air pressurization is an important tool for maintaining a sanitary environment. Surgery rooms should be positively pressurized relative to the spaces around them so that no air flows into surgery.

- The surgery zone should be designed with cleanable materials and finishes.

- The surgery room should be dedicated to surgery. Pack/prep activities and scrubbing should be done in a separate space. Likewise, dirty procedures should be performed in a separate space.

- Design criteria become more rigorous depending on the type of surgery that is being performed. For example, orthopedic surgery rooms need to be designed to higher standards than soft tissue surgery rooms. Neurological surgery rooms need to be designed with the utmost care.

With an understanding of the basic ideas, below are the design requirements for the different rooms in the surgery zone.

SURGERY PREP

Surgery prep and induction is the area where animals are induced, clipped, and prepared for surgery. This space is significantly dirtier than surgery itself, so in larger hospitals where more specialized surgical services, such as orthopedics or neurosurgery, are performed, surgery prep may be separated from the surgery rooms by a sterile corridor.

The basic requirements for surgery prep include oxygen and scavenger, an overhead medical light, clippers, and storage for supplies. The veterinarian will also need to review how the animal is being transported into the surgery room. The patient may be moved directly from surgery prep to surgery on a mobile gurney or may be moved on a stretcher. Small animals may be hand carried, but keep in mind that hand carrying may not be the best solution for cleanliness.

Because animals are clipped in surgery prep, this room can be difficult to keep clean. Many practices use shop vacuums or central vacuum systems to get rid of hair. Central vacuums are preferable because the motor can be located in a remote, sound-insulated closet, in order to preserve a quiet atmosphere in surgery prep. A handwashing sink is also good to have in surgery prep, as the scrub sink should be used solely for scrubbing for surgery.

PACK/PREP

In small hospitals, pack/prep and scrub are often located in the same space. Even in a small hospital, an alcove-style pack/prep and scrub area that places these functions out of the primary traffic flow of the hospital is the best option.

Pack/prep should be organized to consider clean and dirty zones. See the diagram for an example of how the flow may work.

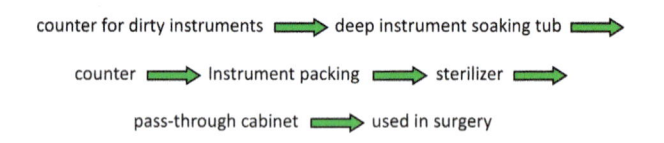

counter for dirty instruments ⟶ deep instrument soaking tub ⟶
counter ⟶ Instrument packing ⟶ sterilizer ⟶
pass-through cabinet ⟶ used in surgery

It is a best practice to provide a separate washer and dryer for surgical items. They may be installed in pack/prep or in another location near surgery prep.

The design of pack/prep rooms must be carefully coordinated with the equipment to be used in this space. For example, small autoclaves typically require counters that are deeper than the standard 24 inches. Large autoclaves may be stand mounted and can take up a lot of space. Some autoclaves may also trigger a code requirement for a hood over them to capture steam. In any case, it is not practical to locate upper cabinets above autoclaves, both because they would not be reachable and because the heat and moisture may destroy them. Gas sterilization equipment requires even more coordination as it must vent to the outside of the building for safety.

As the size of the hospital increases, so may the need for counter space in pack/prep. Larger hospitals may require large pack/prep spaces with center islands to provide enough counter space for the supplies and processes that occur in this space. It is common for larger hospitals to also separate scrub and to place it within a sterile corridor outside surgery, which is a better place for scrub to be located, since the scrub sink should remain clean.

The scrub sink itself should be outfitted with a touchless system such as an electric sensor or a knee or foot pedal. Gowns, gloves, and antiseptic solution should be kept nearby.

RADIOLOGY

It is a good idea to locate radiology, and sometimes MRI and CT, near the surgery room so that images can be taken before, during, or after surgery. Larger hospitals may locate dedicated radiology within the surgery zone itself to provide the most convenient circulation and to keep the surgery zone clean.

In addition to general radiology, some hospitals use imaging equipment in the surgery room itself. A good example of this is C-arm fluoroscopy, which provides continuous imaging during surgery and is helpful with minimally invasive procedures. There are two issues with incorporating fluoroscopy into a surgery suite:

- Shielding may be required around the surgery room, depending on the state where your hospital is located and the equipment requirements.

- This equipment is large, and the room should be sized appropriately to accommodate it. Dedicated power and data will also be required.

PATIENT RECOVERY

The most critical time for surgery patients is between completion of the procedure and extubation. During this time, patients need to be kept warm and closely monitored by staff. Many hospitals use a "beach" for this temporary holding of surgery patients. A beach is a flat or slightly raised semienclosed and dedicated floor space set apart as a recovery area. It can be outfitted with outlets for patient monitors and radiant-heated floors for the patients' comfort. It's best to dedicate space for a beach rather than counting on informal floor space, as, in the latter case, patients will end up in the way.

Some hospitals prefer to place postsurgical patients in runs or cage wards. Runs are more practical for big dogs, and big dogs are overrepresented in surgery recovery areas because a lot of orthopedic work is done on them. Post-op wards should be readily viewable from surgery or surgery prep for the safety of the patients.

SURGERY ROOMS

The surgery room itself must be planned with the greatest care. Here are the general rules for surgery room design:

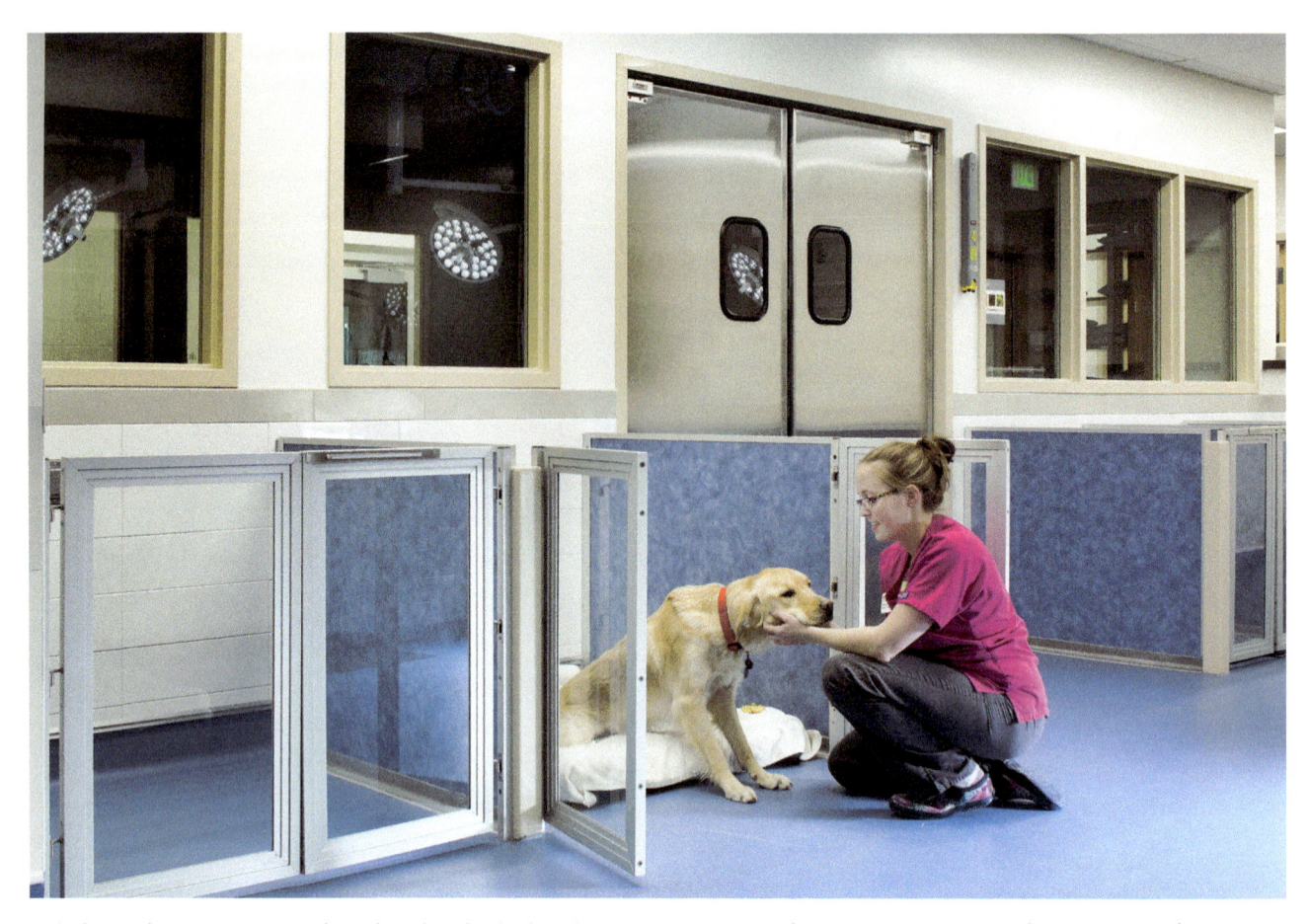

A dedicated surgery recovery beach with individual enclosures was designed for this treatment area. (Foto Imagery / Tim Murphy. Courtesy of Larimer Humane Society, Loveland, Colorado.)

- Cleanable flooring: A surgery room must have a sealed and cleanable floor. This is an AAHA standard and it is common sense for a room that must maintain sterility. A cleanable floor is a seamless product, such as welded sheet vinyl, rubber, or linoleum, or a resinous floor such as epoxy. The joint between this floor material and the wall is of particular importance. The floor material must be run up the wall a few inches for sanitation reasons, and there should be a concave transition between the floor and the wall (known as an "integral" or "flashed" cove base). Concrete surfaces should not be exposed in surgery rooms as they are never sterile, especially at the transitions between the floor and the wall.

- Cleanable walls: Like the floor, the walls must be cleanable. A smooth, water-based epoxy paint is a good solution. Some people prefer a wall liner product, such as a plastic, up to a specific height. If using a wall panel, ensure that all the joints are well sealed.

- Cleanable ceiling: Acoustical tile ceilings should not be used in surgery rooms. They are not well sealed and are known for dropping bits of fuzz over time. Hard drywall ceilings should be used in surgery rooms and painted with a wipeable paint.

- No sinks, base cabinets, or pack/prep supplies: Surgery rooms are for surgery and nothing else. They are not for scrubbing, cleaning tools, or storing supplies, with the exception of sterile, packed instruments. When storing sterile, packed instruments, glass upper cabinets work best for viewing the packs and keeping them free of dust and airborne particles. Packs should be dated and resterilized when past the expiration date.

- One door: There should never be more than one way in and out of a surgery room in order to avoid through traffic.

- Separate airflow: Surgery should be positively pressurized and should not share air with other rooms. It is recommended to boost filtration in all surgery rooms as well the incoming air. For hospitals providing orthopedic or neurologic surgery, HEPA filtration is highly recommended. Surgery rooms also typically need to be in their own thermostatic zones because they have higher lighting and power loads and therefore need more cooling.

- Boosted air exchange: For general surgery rooms, 12 to 14 air changes per hour is acceptable. For specialty surgery rooms, 15 to 20 air changes is recommended. Keep in mind that human hospital surgery rooms require 20 to 25 air changes per hour, so the veterinary standards are already slightly dialed back from what is ideal.

- High-lighting levels: Fifty foot-candles is the minimum lighting requirement for a surgery room, and 75 fc is recommended at the tables. This can be achieved with a specialized surgery light fixture. LED lighting fixtures allow surgery rooms to be well lit without as much heat.

Surgery rooms can vary in size. Below are some typical examples that are acceptable:

- Smallest general surgery room with circulation around three sides of the table: 10 × 11 feet.

- Smallest general surgery room with circulation around four sides of the table: 11 × 12 feet.

- Smallest general surgery room with two tables (common in simple spay/neuter clinics): 12 × 18 feet.

- Small orthopedic surgery room: 12 × 14 feet.

- Large orthopedic surgery room or room for other special surgeries, such as neurological surgery with operating scope or C-arm fluoroscopy: 14 × 16 feet.

Finally, like all rooms in veterinary hospitals, surgery rooms require careful coordination of the equipment, including the following:

- Blocking for surgery light fixtures: These fixtures are subject to a lot of torque stress due to their weight and the lever action of the long arm for the light fixture, so they require very sturdy blocking.

Blocking in a ceiling to support surgical lighting.

- Room to accommodate special equipment such as a laser.

- Possible inclusion of nitrogen for surgical tools, if required by the hospital.

- Location of monitors and computers.

- Counters for layout space.

- Small but important features such as a wall-mounted clock.

In general, due to the need to maintain a cleanable floor surface, power for equipment should be located on the walls (and sometimes the ceiling), but not from the floor.

CREATING GREAT SPACES TO WORK

Surgical staff may spend a lot of time in the surgery room, and the work may be long and tiring with many hours of standing. It is easy to focus on the technical requirements of the surgical zone, but do not forget to make it a wonderful place to work.

One way to achieve this is for a surgery room to have a nice view to the outside. Ideally this would be toward the north, to prevent glare. Provide glass from the room into other spaces as well so that the surgical staff can remain connected to the rest of the hospital.

▼ ▼ ▼

THINK ABOUT COLOR schemes in this space as well. Traditionally, mint green was used in human surgery rooms because it is restful to eyes continuously looking at red blood. Most people are tired of mint green, however, which now evokes an institutional feeling, but other soft, light colors can be used in the surgery zone. An ideal color is one that minimizes glare and eye strain and projects a true hue so as to provide an accurate interpretation of patient mucous membranes and tissue color. Take the extra time to make this space functional, effective, and yet comfortable, as your ability to concentrate in this space will help you give your patients the best possible outcomes.

CHAPTER 37

PHYSICAL REHABILITATION

Physical rehabilitation is a useful tool that helps animals maintain, restore, and promote proper function after injury or surgery and reduces the effects of many chronic conditions typical in aging pets. Rehabilitation is also helpful for athletes and working dogs that need to stay at peak performance, for overweight patients, and for geriatric patients. Regardless of the patient and the specific goals, rehabilitation encourages proper movement and can reorganize body movements into more efficient, pain-free patterns.

This area is a new and fast-growing field within veterinary medicine. "Physical medicine and therapy" was added by the American Veterinary Medical Association to the definition of veterinary services in 2003. Since that time, rehabilitation service options have rapidly expanded across the US. As the field has grown, so has our knowledge about the best practices for creating effective and comfortable spaces for veterinary rehabilitation.

THE BASICS

The spatial requirements for rehabilitation areas vary widely depending on the specific services being provided. While basic services might be offered with as little as a single treatment room measuring 9 × 12 feet, more extensive services can require something as large and complex as a hydrotherapy center. The key is to develop a model that will work for your practice from the perspective of patient outcomes, considering the return on investment and potential local competition.

One option for developing rehabilitation services is to start small and build the services and the spaces over time. In smaller practices, an oversize exam room can work well as an area to perform treatment and evaluations. As long as there is enough space for the patient to lie fully stretched out on a mat on the floor, with one or two people on either side, this can be a starting point.

Dry rehabilitation areas allow rehabilitation professionals to perform gait analysis, therapeutic exercise, and often modalities such as therapeutic ultrasound, electrical stimulation, and laser therapy. Required equipment for such services typically includes physioballs, therapy bands, dry treadmills, ramps, stairs, and other devices that help to increase strength, range of motion, flexibility, and coordination for pets receiving care.

A comfortable size for a dry rehabilitation space in a larger specialty practice is usually around 15 × 15 feet of clear floor space. You may consider utilizing a nearby hallway for gait analysis, as long as the traffic flow is at a minimum. The room should be enlarged if the walls need to be lined for computer workstations, holding cages, equipment, and storage, as it is important to maintain the minimum clear floor square footage. Noise is also a factor when deciding on a location for this room. When treating several dogs simultaneously and at max capacity in the holding cages, expecting peace and quiet is usually not feasible.

Many rehabilitation programs also provide hydrotherapy. The natural properties of water buoyancy in a wet rehabilitation setting allow animals to experience low-impact exercise through the use of underwater treadmills and swim pools. Using wet rehabilitation therapy can enable an animal to transition more quickly to dry therapies by increasing muscle strength and endurance.

When planning a room for an underwater treadmill or swim pool, it is important to select your desired equipment first and then plan carefully around it. Points to consider are the positioning of the treadmill units, including the direction the dog is facing, and the clear floor space that may be required around each of them. A treadmill and the space around it will take a minimum of 8 × 13 feet, with adequate room on the sides of the treadmill for the professional to analyze the dog's gait and possibly to assist the dog or change an incline or decline.

In larger facilities where two treadmills are used, it is useful to place them parallel to each other with about 30 inches in between them to allow the clinician access to both patients simultaneously. Consider covering or darkening the middle sides of the units to avoid distractions while dogs are in the tank. Depending upon the underwater treadmill selected, it may also be desirable to recess the unit in the floor to allow the patient direct access without the need to step up (which can be difficult for patients with limited mobility). When a recessed unit is installed, special consideration should be given to how the "pit" is closed off to the treadmill unit, in order to prevent paws from getting stuck in the gap. Another option is to place a small ramp at the front of the treadmill to get dogs in and out of the unit.

A typical underwater treadmill requires a pump and water storage tank. These are usually located in a separate enclosed room of about 6 × 6 feet or 6 × 8 feet in area. It is critical to design for the actual treadmill you will use, as each manufacturer's requirements are a little different. Carefully consider where you place this room and equipment, as the pump and the treadmill can be loud. Additional considerations

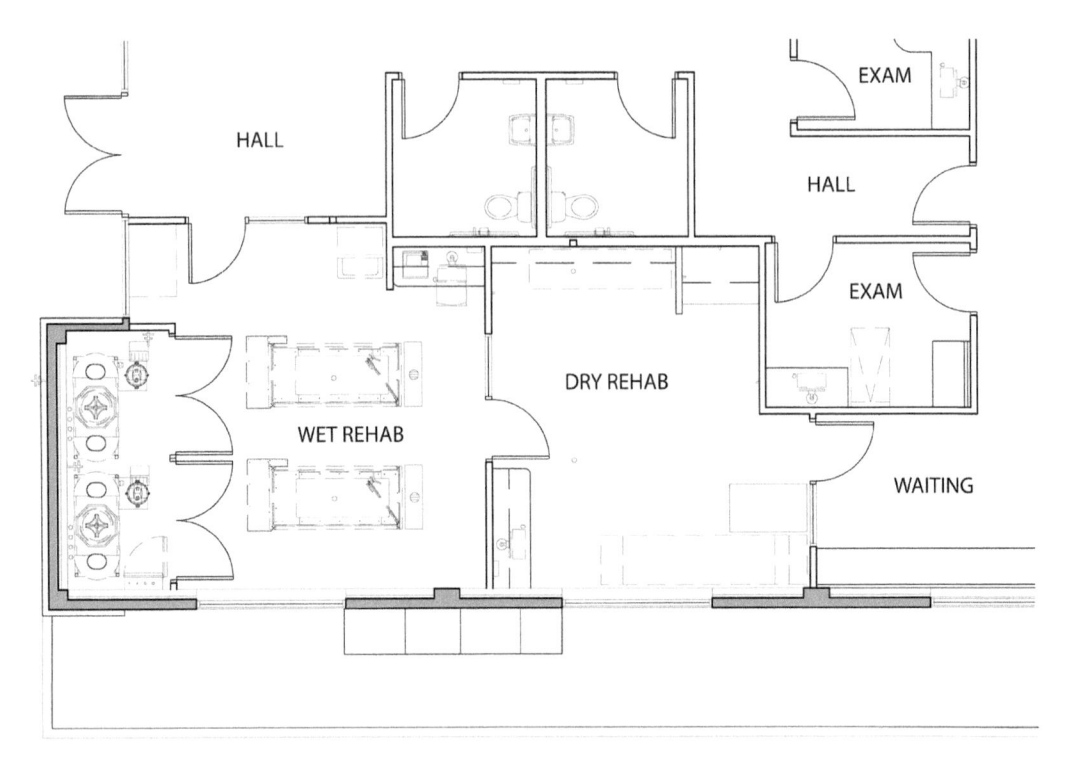

An example of a wet and dry physical rehabilitation floor plan in a large specialty hospital. (Courtesy of SAGE Centers for Veterinary Specialty & Emergency Care, Redwood City, California.)

include power, controller location, increased HVAC ventilation, dehumidification, general exhaust, connecting piping between the underwater treadmills and the utility room housing the equipment, hose bib water supply, floor drain locations and floor drain strainer configuration, and specific flooring needs for the wet therapy area.

Your electrical engineer should be involved in the coordination of the requirements for the rehabilitation equipment, such as the underwater treadmill, which will have special connection requirements and often will require conduits to be installed under the floor slab.

It is also recommended that a uniform lighting level of 50 fc be provided in the rehabilitation areas. It is beneficial for these lights to be adjustable with dimmers or switching to allow for flexible use of the space. The light fixtures in the wet areas should be enclosed to prevent humidity from entering the fixtures. If you plan to install a pool, be sure to provide proper electrical grounding/bonding around the pool and its associated equipment.

For psychological reasons, animals will move more readily toward an open area or window than toward a wall. For this reason, and because rehabilitation is inviting for people to watch, rehabilitation rooms are often designed to have visual access to the out-of-doors or to a lobby or public space, with the treadmills positioned so the animals can see out.

The desire to keep a rehabilitation room open should be balanced with the need to minimize distraction for the animals and for the people working with them. It is often preferable to place rehabilitation services in a quieter area of the building out of the primary traffic flow.

In some cases, larger pools are used for hydrotherapy. For example, a boarding facility

A hydrotherapy pool during construction. Coordinating the installation of a pool will involve your whole design team and the pool manufacturer. (Courtesy of Veterinary Referral Associates, Gaithersburg, Maryland.)

may offer canine swim therapies as an "a la carte" option for an additional fee. If a pool is used for these functions rather than for play, the setup should include a pool that is deep enough for dogs to swim in and wide enough for them to jump in without potentially injuring themselves by hitting the other side. Remember to provide a storage area for proper safety equipment, such as canine life jackets, an easy entrance and exit to the pool, and other safety features typical of swimming pools, such as security into the room to prevent accidents and safe footing around the pool. Facilities that want to add swimming along with boarding must have trained, professional staff to offer these services.

OTHER CONSIDERATIONS

As with other ancillary services offered in a veterinary setting, you should ask these important questions to understand how rehabilitation will integrate with the rest of the practice and the facility:

- Is the rehabilitation portion of the practice a separate business under the same roof? If so, will it have its own hours? Will it need a separate entrance? Who will greet clients? Who will provide the rehabilitation services?

- Where will clients wait?

- Will rehabilitation need to share any examination rooms with the veterinary facility?

- Is there a need for an outdoor rehabilitation area to allow for greater movement of the patients or additional exercise/agility equipment? Can the rehabilitation department be located so it has access to an outdoor fenced yard? Could this yard include a separate entrance and exit for patients and clients?

- Will the rehabilitation area need its own holding wards for animals awaiting therapies?

- How much storage will be needed? A wall of both open and closed storage in rehabilitation rooms can be more useful than an enclosed storage room, so that supplies such as towels and therapy balls are handy. Storage spaces should be designed for bulky supplies and equipment such as cavaletti rails, canine wheelchairs, harnesses, and any equipment required for the various therapeutic modalities.

- Will there be drying cages for post water therapy? Dedicated power outlets are usually required for these units, along with requirements for increased HVAC ventilation.

- Will a washer and dryer be needed for towels and wet clothing from staff?

- Will overhead support be required for assisting with the movement of patients? For example, should there be anchors in the ceiling to tether patients during treatments, or pool lifts attached to the floor or ceiling?

If so, special structural consideration will be needed.

FLOORING AND MECHANICAL SYSTEMS

There are two primary challenges in designing spaces for physical rehabilitation: mechanical systems and flooring. The first obstacle to address is the humidity and heat that will be produced by hydrotherapies and drying animals. Though they are often ignored, humidity and heat can wreak havoc upon a room. Proper air exchange rates and dehumidification should be designed to accommodate the loads in the room, with care taken to ensure that increased airflow rates do not overcondition the space. All steel in the room should be galvanized to minimize the deterioration that can be caused by wet conditions. Laminate cabinetry in the wet rooms should be minimized, if not eliminated. Stainless steel should be used where possible. In addition, think carefully about the placement of electrical equipment, such as phones and computers. The incorporation of a vapor barrier to minimize the transfer of the higher humidity from this room to adjoining spaces should also be considered.

The second primary challenge is flooring. The two best solutions for dry rehabilitation spaces are safety vinyl floors and rubber floors. For wet rooms, it is critical to use a floor that is slip resistant when wet as well as dry. Safety vinyl flooring is therefore the best solution for this type of space. Be sure to select a floor that is compatible with puddling and that can be terminated properly around drains. Specific floor drain strainers will need to be designed to accommodate the sealing of any rubber floor-

A well-thought-out rehabilitation room can be an important asset to your practice. (Foto Imagery / Tim Murphy. Courtesy of Coral Springs Animal Hospital, Coral Springs, Florida.)

ing material. For rooms where dry therapies are conducted, rubber flooring is generally preferred because it is cushioned underfoot and slip resistant when dry. Avoid rubber flooring that is porous, as it is important to select a hygienic floor for the clinical setting. There are numerous nonporous rubber flooring solutions on the market.

▼ ▼ ▼

PHYSICAL REHABILITATION as a service continues to grow and become a key resource for positive patient outcomes. Whether you are introducing a complementary service to an existing practice or opening a standalone business, careful consideration must be given to the program's spatial needs to successfully sustain your business model. Be sure to keep the specific equipment, finishes, and mechanical needs of these unique spaces in mind. It is best to start small and stay flexible so that you can expand in the future as the practice grows. This goal can be accomplished by placing the rehabilitation area on the perimeter of the building or simply by keeping future renovation ideas in mind as you complete the initial design for the hospital.

CHAPTER 38

ANIMAL HOUSING

CREATING A BETTER ENVIRONMENT FOR ANIMALS

Environment significantly affects the behavior and stress level of both animals and humans. In today's progressive veterinary facilities, design goals have shifted to consider the behavioral, biological, psychological, and social wellbeing of animals in order to improve health outcomes and reduce fear and anxiety.

A number of methods can be employed to create healthier and more pleasant housing environments for animals in veterinary settings. Stress is often caused by exposure to new and different environments. Therefore, the environment within a holding enclosure should seem as familiar and be as comfortable as possible. Below are some ideas for creating environments that reduce stress and promote wellness and healing:

- Avoid crowding too many animals in one room.

- Separate animals by species.

- Provide pleasant views, such as to outside spaces.

- Provide raised resting areas that are separated from the floor of the enclosure (when medically appropriate).

- Reduce odor and provide good air quality. If possible, provide the animals with access to fresh outside air.

While different species of animals benefit from specific conditions, there are some approaches from which everyone (including your staff) can benefit. These are explored below.

DAYLIGHTING

The benefits of daylighting in human medical spaces include maintaining natural circadian rhythms, reduced recuperation time—especially when combined with nighttime dimming—and even a reduction of pain. Daylight has also been shown to increase productivity among workers and improve staff morale. Animals have similar physiology to people, so daylighting may produce the same benefits for animals.

CHOICES

Research from the National Research Council's Committee on Recognition and Alleviation of Distress in Laboratory Animals shows that animals need to have some control over their environment in order to avoid stress and distress.

For a cat, 9.5 square feet is required for longer-term housing, such as healthy overnight housing, in order to maintain 3 feet between food and litter (Newberry et al., 8). The choice to get away from a toileting area is important, and it allows a cat to maintain more normal behavior. The goal of separating food and litter translates into an enclosure at least 4 feet long for cats.

Dogs that are housed for long periods also benefit from choice, including separate areas for resting, eating, and elimination. If given the choice, dogs will opt to eliminate away from eating areas, and long-term housing should be configured to provide two separate compartments (Newberry et al., 7). Exercise and play areas are also required for dogs that are being housed for any length of time.

In hospital settings, the above choices may be reduced out of medical necessity, but enclosures should still provide animals with as many elements of choice as possible given the patient's circumstances.

ENCLOSURE SIZES

Providing choices to animals in housing goes hand in hand with the sizing of the enclosure. In a hospital setting, there are situations where a pet's movement must be restricted out of medical necessity. In other areas, where this is not an issue, a pet should generally be housed in a way that allows for normal posture. The animal should be able to turn around without touching the walls and express common behaviors. Although studies have not yet been done in private veterinary settings, studies in animal shelter settings by the Koret Shelter Medicine Program at the University of California at Davis have demonstrated that allowing an animal enough space to exhibit normal behaviors is a basic requirement that helps to support an animal's physical and behavioral health.

NOISE CONTROL

One of the major questions to be answered in the design of any veterinary facility is how to effectively control noise from barking dogs. The conventional focus has been on absorbing reverberant sound, and secondarily on keeping the noise from being broadcast throughout the rest of the facility. Both of these methods will be discussed more thoroughly in Chapter 46. While all of the traditional sound control techniques still need to be employed, it is most important to prevent the factors that cause barking in the first place.

Some of the causes to be considered are fear and stress, people and animals passing enclosures, the social facilitation that spreads barking, and mechanical noises beyond the range audible to humans. Beyond the basics of providing appropriately sized, enriched housing for dogs, consider other suggestions to help reduce barking:

- House dogs according to their behavioral needs. Having at least two dog wards can help to separate dogs when necessary to reduce overall stress.

- Avoid long, straight runs of dogs to prevent having to walk too many dogs past each other. Wards can be configured with a door on each end.

- Place mechanical areas away from housing to minimize the effect of the very high- and low-frequency sounds that only animals can hear.

Don't forget that dog noise affects cats. Cats should be housed in areas that are physically separate from dog areas and away from other loud areas of the hospital.

AVOIDING SENSORY ISOLATION

While it is important to reduce overstimulation in your ward areas, it is equally important not to put animals in sensory isolation, especially when they are trying to understand and process a new environment. Follow these general rules:

- If you will be using glass on the front of cages or runs for visibility, provide a sniff hole or a section of bars so the cat or dog may use its nose to explore its surroundings.

- Dogs who are extremely stressed may benefit from additional visual blocking on the front of their enclosures, but all dogs should have a section of unobstructed view at eye level so they do not need to jump to see out, as the latter behavior increases stress and may result in injury.

- Provide soft music to help mask unpleasant sounds. *Through a Cat's Ear* and *Through a Dog's Ear* are soundtracks designed specifically for animals. The ASPCA also recommends soft classical music (McConnell).

CATS

Cats are particularly susceptible to the negative effects of stress, so it is especially important to design enclosures that support their wellbeing. Primary stressors for cats include dogs, noise, new experiences, diminished control of personal space, uncomfortable surroundings, and unnatural social situations. Since cat housing is one of the stressors veterinarians can have some control over, it should be designed to be as stress-free as possible. Specific suggestions for cat housing include the following:

- Provide larger cages, even for cats being held for short-term medical care. Very small

This cat housing area is located on the "cat only" side of the hospital and provides views out to the cat waiting area. (Thomas Winter Photography. Courtesy of VCA Hillsboro Animal Hospital, Coconut Creek, Florida [VCA, Inc.].)

Vertical housing provides cats with room to stretch and play. (Courtesy of Mason Company.)

cages seem to be stressful for cats. Better enclosures allow cats to stretch their bodies to full length.

- Provide enough vertical height to allow the cat to move naturally, or about 30 inches. For healthy cats, it might be more appropriate to house them in vertical rather than horizontal enclosures.

- Provide enriched enclosures. You may not be able to do a lot to enrich the enclosures in a medical environment, but here are some concepts that others are applying:

> Quiet cage latches prevent the loud slamming noise of cage doors.

> Horizontal bars are thought to be more calming than vertical bars. Horizontal bars should only be used for cats, as dogs can hurt themselves by biting horizontal bars.

> Provide natural light and views to the outside.

> Include materials that allow cats to retain their body heat.

> Bump up ventilation further in cat wards as they tend to be smaller rooms.

ANIMAL HOUSING   215

Horizontal bars are thought to be less stressful for cats. When medically appropriate, providing a hiding space by adding a box or covering part of the cage door can also help cats feel less stress. (Courtesy of Snyder Manufacturing, Inc.)

› Avoid housing cats across from one another.
› If medically appropriate, provide cats with a resting platform or partial hiding box.

Here are some other possible improvements for the design of cat wards:

- Ventilate through the cat cage when possible to provide cats with fresh air.

- Design wards with highly absorptive ceiling materials to reduce reverberant noise.

- Provide windows in the backs of cages for views and to keep cages from feeling claustrophobic.

DOGS

In medical areas, it may not be possible or even desirable to provide a housing solution with separate compartments for eating and toileting, but consider what can be done to make dogs more comfortable. Exercise yards or walking areas should be designed for dogs so they do not need to eliminate inside. A dog with a lifetime

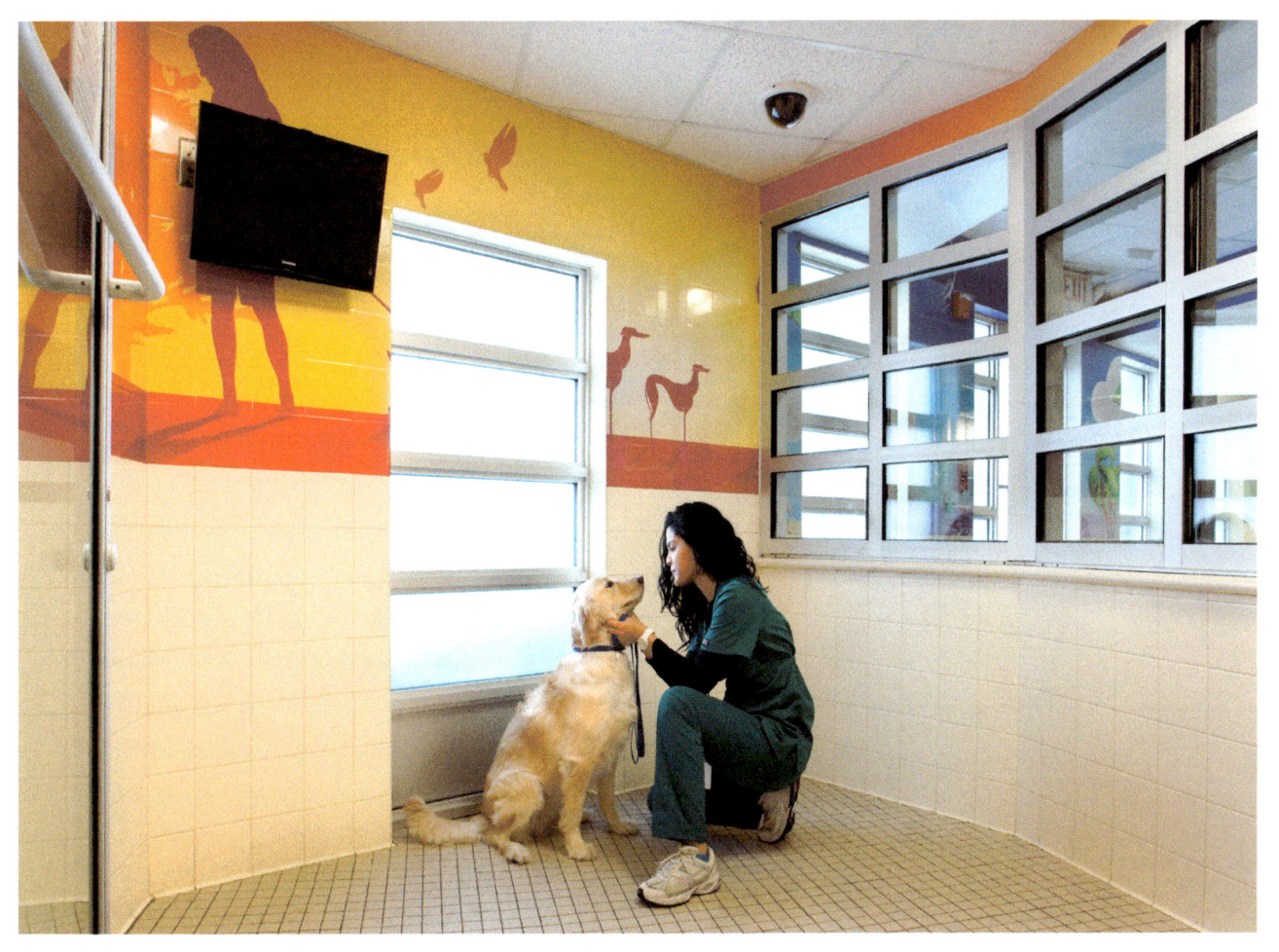

Larger enclosures/runs allow staff to easily interact with and care for dogs. (Foto Imagery / Tim Murphy. Courtesy of Coral Springs Animal Hospital, Coral Springs, Florida.)

of house training finds relieving itself in its own living area to be extremely stressful.

Appropriately sized enclosures need to be based on the individual sizes and species of the dogs being housed. The standard one-size-fits-all approach to run design ignores these differences. Most dogs will require a run that is at least 4 feet wide, but for larger dogs this size may not be adequate. What is comfortable for a Maltese can be uncomfortable for a Great Dane.

The narrow shape of traditional runs can also contribute to discomfort. In the typical long, narrow run, dogs cannot move and circle in the same way they would in a free environment. These runs are stressful and promote undesirable behavior in dogs, such as barking, fence fighting, lunging at gates, and soiling the enclosures. When dogs are individually housed, this is not a significant concern, but when another dog or a staff member is in the run, some dogs will feel trapped and display abnormal levels of aggression. You see the same dynamic at work when dogs pass each other in narrow hallways. For these reasons, a square enclosure is better than a long, narrow run.

Consider all the pets you might care for when designing animal housing for your hospital.

These methods of making dog housing more familiar and less stressful can decrease patient recovery times, reduce stress-induced barking, and improve staff-dog interactions.

SMALL ANIMALS

Your small mammal, aviary, and reptile housing needs probably depend on how often you treat these species. It is ideal to have them in species-separate rooms with their own temperature and climate control. Ferrets can be housed in the same room as cats, but they should not be housed with other small mammals because ferrets are predators. It is important to note that rabbits cannot be housed in traditional cat housing, as they can chew through anything but stainless steel. They also require more space. As with any animal, they require enough room to move naturally, which could mean 3 to 4 feet. Reptiles require warm and humid enclosures, which can be achieved with individual lamps; therefore, it is best to have extra outlets in a space that is planned for reptile housing. Birds may also require additional heating.

THE SMALLER DETAILS

Animals housed in hospitals are hypersensitive to the various aspects of the enclosure, just as you would be in a human hospital ward. Pay attention to the details that will help animals feel more comfortable and calm. Here are a few suggestions:

- Provide a soft surface to lie on, such as a towel or blanket.

- House animals in caging with nonreflective surfaces when possible.

- The insides of cages should be a light color, but avoid white plastic as it will appear to fluoresce to the pet.

- Use LED lighting where possible in housing as it is better attuned to the way animals see.

- Specify dimmable light fixtures so you can turn the ward lights down when appropriate.

- For surgery recovery, consider using radiant heating in the bottom of the enclosure to create a therapeutic surface. Be careful to use heating specifically designed for animals, and be sure it does not get too hot.

▼ ▼ ▼

ONE VETERINARY HOSPITAL in California saw a 90% reduction in postsurgical sedation rates for their dogs as a result of moving to their new hospital, where postsurgical housing was designed to be quiet, calm, enriching, and supportive. The right housing really can support the right behavior, and ultimately the right result for your patients and your practice.

CHAPTER 39

GENERAL WARDS

While more specific approaches to reducing stress in animal housing are covered in Chapter 38, all hospitals must also achieve the basic requirement of keeping patients safe and medically supported while they are in care. This chapter covers the fundamentals of effective animal ward design.

PLACEMENT OF WARDS

A great mantra for the patient-centered practice is "Everyone should watch patients." In older hospitals, it was typical to see floor plans that placed patients in remote back areas. Today it is more common to place wards adjacent to treatment. Patients can be placed behind glass enclosures to reduce their stress while still keeping them visually accessible to doctors and technicians. At-risk animals should be placed where they can most easily be seen and where staff can react to emergency situations.

Especially critical patients can be placed in half-height runs or beaches in the treatment areas, where they are immediately accessible to staff. While this may seem contrary to stress-reduction principles, in certain cases it is more important to have animals within close proximity so they can receive the care they need.

Large hospitals may develop a variety of wards based on the level of monitoring each patient requires. These ward types include the following:

- Immediately accessible open runs or cages for the most critical patients.

- Fully visible wards for ICU, surgery recovery, and isolation.

- Step-down wards—intermediate-care wards for animals that are less critical but still require rigorous monitoring. These may be placed where they are easy to see, but not necessarily with a direct view.

- More remote wards for healthy patients, especially loud dogs.

Practices that do a better job of watching patients report that they are more successful with patient outcomes and more efficient with staff time.

HOUSING SOLUTIONS BASED ON THE TYPE OF WARD

The art of good ward design involves a diversity of solutions. Below are some useful points to consider:

- Some enclosures may intentionally restrict patient movement for their safety. For example, some types of surgery, such as neurological surgery, require movement restrictions during the recovery period. These cages can be smaller.

- On the other hand, in many ICU settings it is important to create wider runs and cages that allow staff members to sit with and attend to patients. The typical ICU run is wider than 4 feet to allow for this requirement. Deep runs are undesirable, as they make the patient harder to reach.

- Cats vary more in physical size than is typically acknowledged. Providing different sizes of cages allows for comfortable and safe housing for tiny kittens and larger adults. The largest ones should allow for healthy cats to move normally without touching the walls of the cage, which means a vertical height of at least 30 inches, preferably 36 inches.

- Most adult cats dislike being housed in lower cages. To make cat wards more comfortable for your feline patients, cages can be raised off the floor onto curbs.

- Because small dogs are used to being carried, some are more comfortable when they are housed off the floor in cages.

- It is rarely desirable to stack cages more than two units high. The highest cages are not as visible and are harder to use.

The bottom line is that because of the diversity of patients and their medical and behavioral situations, it makes sense to provide a variety of housing options.

CONFIGURING WARDS

Some spatial configurations are better than others for the wellbeing of the patient. Follow these guidelines for designing the space:

- Unless space is at a premium, avoid placing traditional dog runs in configurations where dogs face each other across a narrow aisle. If runs must face each other, then use glass fronts that prevent the spread of disease and consider partial visual blocks so that dogs are not looking at each other across the aisle.

- Avoid housing cats across from one another as well to avoid social anxiety in short-term housing solutions. If they must be housed across from one another, create at least a 6-foot-wide aisle between the cages and provide hiding spaces within the enclosures.

MATERIALS AND SYSTEMS

One major factor to consider when it comes to the design of animal care wards is noise control. Do not design your cat ward and your dog ward to share a common wall. Design full-height sound walls all the way around the ward rooms. These walls should extend all the way to the underside of the roof structure above and be filled with sound batt insulation, which will help limit noise transmission to the adjacent spaces. In dog wards, also consider providing an acoustical ceiling tile with a high Noise Reduction Coefficient (NRC) in order to help further dampen sound transmission. NRC refers to the percentage of sound absorbed by the material within a tested frequency range. (For more details, see Chapter 46.)

Wards are typically cleaned more thoroughly than any other space within the hospital, which means they should be designed with durable and cleanable finishes. For rooms such as dog run wards that are hose cleaned, highly durable materials, such as tile and epoxy floors and wall systems, are the preferred finishes. Avoid installing base cabinets in any ward that you hose clean. The water will cause failures and warping of lower cabinets.

Consider how floor drains and hoses play a role in your ward design. When it comes to floor drains, individual drains within each enclosure are preferred so as to prevent any potential cross-contamination among patients. In small wards, it is usually sufficient to provide a hose bib and a wall-mounted hose rack within the room. In larger wards with lots of runs, for ease of handling it is preferable to use a self-retracting, coiling hose reel that can be mounted high on the wall or ceiling.

▼ ▼ ▼

IN GENERAL, DESIGN the wards for your practice with the same level of care as the client services spaces. Your clients' pets will fare better if the wards incorporate a variety of housing solutions with the common theme of encouraging every staff member to help monitor patients in order to keep them safe and well.

CHAPTER 40

ISOLATION WARDS

Biological risk management in the veterinary setting is vitally important to the health of all patients visiting the hospital. Creating and maintaining a proper isolation space is also a requirement for AAHA-accredited hospitals (AAHA, 5).

It is important to know the disease incidence and prevalence of your area and design your isolation space accordingly. Also, if your practice will be working with rescue groups or local shelters, the likelihood and frequency of contagious patients with ringworm, mange, and upper respiratory infections (URIs) are a greater concern.

The first question any practice should ask is how many patients would need to be isolated concurrently in a worst-case scenario. The isolation areas should be sized for this worst case. For most practices in more northern latitudes, the worst case may only result in one or two isolated patients. For practices in warmer climates where infectious disease is more prevalent, several patients may need to be housed at once. There might be unusual circumstances to consider as well. For example, for mixed animal practices in Canada, scouring calves may be brought inside during the spring for proper care and treatment.

Isolation spaces should be divided by mode of disease transmission if the possibility of several isolated patients exists. For example, fecal/oral transmitted diseases, such as parvovirus, should be separated from respiratory illnesses. This may mean setting aside two rooms with an airlock between them.

LOCATING YOUR ISOLATION ROOM

There is some debate within the industry about where to house isolated patients. Since isolated patients may be the sickest patients in the hospital, it is desirable to have an unobstructed view to them; this implies that the isolation room should be located off a primary working space within the hospital. Others believe that it is more appropriate to house isolated animals out of the flow of traffic to minimize the risk of tracking pathogens through the hospital. In truth, the best location meets all of these criteria. It must be out of the traffic flow and yet visible. Consider these factors when deciding where to place the room:

- Position the room on an outside wall and provide an exterior door that can be used to separate traffic when needed.

- The exterior path to the isolation area should not share traffic with other exterior uses.

- The room should be closer to the "dog side" of the hospital to shorten the distance a sick dog has to travel to reach it, thereby minimizing the distance that a pathogen may be tracked. Cats are generally moved in carriers, so traffic flow is less critical for them.

- Provide view windows from staff areas to allow for proper monitoring.

- Locate the room away from other patient wards or pet boarding rooms.

- Do not place isolation within a common-use space like laundry, as this is a high-traffic area.

DESIGN CONSIDERATIONS

Once you have decided where to place isolation and how large it should be, it is time to design the room itself. The first consideration is a careful sequence of protocols. It is generally helpful to have a place for personal protective equipment (PPE) on the wall just outside the isolation room. The staff member can then don the equipment before entering the room. Once in the room, staff members should care for the patient and then remove soiled equipment, sanitize footwear, and thoroughly wash their hands before exiting the room.

Handwashing sinks should never be omitted from the design of isolation rooms. They are important for these reasons:

- Nonenveloped viruses are not killed by hand sanitizers, even when the sanitizers are medical grade.

- Hands soiled by handling potentially contagious animals cannot be cleaned properly without a sink.

This said, be sure the sink itself is designed to boost sanitary procedures. Isolation rooms should be equipped with touchless sinks and paper towel dispensers.

Footbaths are sometimes used for sanitation of footwear, but they should be used with caution, or not at all. Disinfectant deactivates over time, and in the presence of organic matter, footbaths can become ineffective, or worse, they can help spread pathogens ("Sanitation in Animal Shelters"). Many facilities now use disposable booties instead of footbaths for this reason.

For hospitals requiring larger isolation areas, it is helpful to have a vestibule or airlock at the entrance to the isolation zone. This helps to separate the isolation zone and to reinforce the need for isolation protocols to be followed when entering or exiting these rooms. A vestibule or airlock is also a convenient place to store isolation supplies and laundry.

The isolation room itself should be designed to be completely cleanable. It must have seamless flooring and wall materials. If you are also installing a floor drain, the floor and wall materials should be designed for hose cleaning, so that they maintain durability and sanitary conditions over time. Cleaning supplies, such as hose bibs, disinfectants, clean towels, and janitorial sinks, should be located within isolation, so the room can be cleaned without dragging cleaning supplies from other places in the hospital.

CAGING

Caging in the isolation area either should be designed to roll away from the wall, for total room sanitation, or should be sealed and built into the wall in such a way that the cage can be sanitized in place. For built-in caging, remember that it is not feasible to completely seal all gaps between cages, so a built-in solution should only be used when a wipe-clean protocol is in place. It is not acceptable to allow water to get in, around, and behind the cages. Runs should be hose cleaned from the front to the back of the run toward the drain.

The prevention of disease transmission should influence every detail of caging design. For the containment of respiratory illness, it is helpful to use some glass on the front of the enclosures. For containing fecal/oral disease, and especially canine parvovirus, it is imperative to be able to use caging or runs that contain waste within the cage so that the remainder of the room is not contaminated. Because canine parvovirus is often seen primarily in puppies, caging may be more practical than runs for housing these patients. Some cage manufacturers design specific cages for the containment of canine parvovirus or other contagious waste.

VENTILATION

While cleanable caging is important, proper ventilation in isolation is also critical. Although there is little useful information about the spread of specific diseases through air systems, we know from research in human hospitals that fungal diseases are most likely to spread, followed by bacterial diseases, and then viruses, via this method. The best way to minimize this risk is to directly exhaust the isolation room without connecting it to other air streams and without recirculating it within mechanical equipment.

Air pressurization is a commonly used tool to reduce the spread of airborne contaminants. Isolation rooms should maintain negative pressurization, meaning that more air is exhausted from the space than is supplied.

Finally, it is important that isolation room design considers ease of use. If protocols are cumbersome and difficult, they will be less likely to be performed correctly. For example, sinks should be located in convenient locations.

▼ ▼ ▼

A GOOD ISOLATION room design will help the hospital contain infectious patients efficiently, effectively, and with minimal risk to other patients in the hospital.

CHAPTER 41

ANCILLARY SERVICES

The majority of Americans consider their pets to be an important part of the family. One of the outgrowths of this societal trend is the rise in the number of veterinary hospitals that are now offering boarding and grooming services within their facilities.

BOARDING

Offering boarding services can provide many benefits for veterinary practices, including the following:

- Boarding provides an additional profit center.

- It brings in income at times when veterinary service revenues drop, such as during the summer months.

- It reinforces the veterinary practice by offering medical or specialized care for boarded dogs and cats, thus providing services that veterinary clients need and value.

While these benefits are promising, it is important to note that the business of boarding requires capital expenditure, expertise, and finesse to ensure profitability. Weigh the pros and cons during the early stages of project development in order to determine whether offering these services is the right choice for you and your practice.

An example of a boarding area with stud-wall enclosures for noise control and a more homelike feel. The floor-to-ceiling tile allows for easy cleaning of the space. (Foto Imagery / Tim Murphy. Courtesy of VCA PetCare Veterinary Hospital, Santa Rosa, California [VCA, Inc.].)

From an economic standpoint, it is important to have a good picture of investment versus return before committing to including boarding in your business. How many animals do you want to be able to board, and how much will it cost? What options for boarding already exist within your community? Is there a need for additional boarding? It is essential to do your research and answer all of these questions before making your decision.

As a general rule, to calculate the size of the housing and support areas of a boarding facility, use the ratios of 100 square feet per dog and 75 square feet per cat. Then add the desired square footage of large spaces, such as dog playrooms.

Boarding spaces are not inexpensive to construct. They require a decent investment in order to accommodate proper HVAC design, durable materials and finishes, and the costs of caging, runs, and equipment. With this in mind, there are other important questions to consider: First, do you have the square footage to spare, or will you need to take space away from the primary services you provide with your veterinary practice? And second, do you have adequate funding to build a boarding facility that will be profitable on its own? If the answer to this second question is no, a third question arises: Will the boarding services bring other benefits to the practice, such as client loyalty, growth in other services, or an enhanced community presence?

Many clients do not have the expectation that their veterinary hospital will have a high-end luxury boarding setup. Rather, they know you and they already entrust their pets to your care, and therefore your boarding services will often sell themselves. However, in order to cater to all of your clients and potential clients, and to compete with any luxury facilities in the area, it is best to offer a variety of boarding options, ranging from more traditional to luxury, with varying price ranges.

For dogs, these options may include the following:

- Fully enclosed luxury suites, which should be a minimum of 6 × 6 feet for small dogs and 6 × 8 feet for large dogs or pairs. These can be constructed out of prefabricated dog run/kennel panels or, better yet, can be actual stud-wall enclosures that create a true "room" where noise can be mitigated well.

- Luxury runs with a minimum size of 4 × 6 feet.

- Smaller basic runs of 3 × 5 feet.

- Standard caging.

The other key aspects of designing dog spaces within a boarding facility have to do with reducing stress and providing high-quality spaces designed to support the psychological and physiological wellbeing of dogs. While discussed in more detail in Chapter 38, some of the key design features to remember include these:

- Avoid housing dogs across an aisle from each other.

- Use caging with a more square shape instead of long, narrow enclosures.

- Create environments free from unpleasant auditory stimulation.

- Provide natural daylight with views to the outdoors if possible.

- Provide adequate air flow.

- Include radiant heat in a portion of the floor for a choice of a warm or cool space.

- Provide plenty of outdoor time with staff members.

Along with actual dog boarding, some veterinary hospitals also tap into the "doggy daycare" concept as another way to reach potential clients and generate revenue. If your practice is located in an area that can support a drop-in daycare, then adding this service can be very profitable.

At the most basic level, doggy daycare requires:

- A large, open, dividable play space that can be easily and thoroughly cleaned and sanitized.

- Time-out areas. These can be as simple as dog crates in a separate room.

- Shade or weather protection if an indoor play area is not provided or available during times of inclement weather.

It should be noted that clients are less likely to board their cats than their dogs, so in a veterinary hospital setting, do not make the mistake of creating cat boarding areas that are larger than necessary. If possible, design the cat boarding area to be expandable, so that you can gauge the popularity of this service before investing a lot of money or square footage.

For boarded cats, methods to avoid and reduce stress are the biggest factors to consider. All of the considerations mentioned in the chapter on animal housing should apply. Place special emphasis on these considerations for boarding cats:

- Allow enough space (at least 9.5 square feet) for cats to fully stretch out and have a separated litter compartment, a hiding box, and multiple levels.

- Provide housing in a quiet area away from noise and commotion, particularly away from dog boarding areas or wards, and select caging that utilizes quiet latches.

- Select cage fronts of glass or horizontal bars rather than vertical bars.

- Select cages with a window in the back and provide a view to the outside if possible.

- Provide natural light.

- Provide ventilated cages for odor control and for the health benefit of fresh, uncontaminated air.

- Incorporate a catio into your facility for outside play. Catios must be fully enclosed and can only house one cat, or multiple cats owned by the same client, at a time.

GROOMING

Another opportunity for generating revenue is through grooming. The main challenge with offering grooming services is in deciding whether to hire a full-time, on-staff groomer or to provide the physical grooming space within your building and then lease it out to an established groomer.

Each option comes with pros and cons. With an on-staff groomer, you can control profit margins more effectively, as the service will be an integral function of your hospital. But if the grooming services do not take off, you are stuck paying a salary to a groomer who may not be consistently busy. With the lease option, the pressure is on the groomer to bring in work; however, in this scenario you are bound to a landlord-lessee relationship, which has its own risks and potential shortcomings.

For the design of your grooming space, there are several things to consider. First is the layout of the space. There are two basic approaches. For smaller grooming rooms, planning for all of the functions to occur in one space is often the most efficient option. The bathing tub, cages/dryers, and grooming table are all in the same room and laid out within easy reach of one another. For larger grooming spaces with multiple tubs and grooming tables, it is often best to divide the grooming area into two separate spaces: one room for bathing and drying, and the second for grooming, holding cages, and general storage. The benefit to separating these

This prefabricated tub has a door and stairs to make it easier for dogs to climb in and out. (Foto Imagery / Tim Murphy. Courtesy of VCA PetCare Veterinary Hospital, Santa Rosa, California [VCA, Inc.].)

functions is to create separation between the noisy tasks and the quieter ones, making the actual grooming experience less stressful for the animals and staff.

Additionally, the bathing process produces a lot of humidity and heat, and therefore requires special HVAC considerations. One way to combat the heat and humidity is by using a DX cooling air handler within the room. Regardless of the method chosen, however, separating the actual grooming tables and work areas from the bathing and drying area allows for a much more comfortable environment.

As in other areas of your practice, it is important to determine the equipment you will use within the space during the design process. Grooming tables are a pretty straightforward selection. There are two primary options when it comes to drying. Drying cages can be purchased as standalone units with fans/dryers built into them; however, many groomers prefer the flexibility of standard cages with a separate portable cage dryer. Portable cage dryers can be bought with octopus-type nozzles that have multiple outlets, allowing them to be hooked to the front of several cages at once. Either drying style works—it simply comes down to personal preference.

Once you have selected the equipment you will use, share this information with your design team. The heat, odor, and humidity generated in this room will require far more mechanical infrastructure and venting than other rooms.

The final consideration is bathing tub selection. There are a variety of options: 4-foot-wide tubs, 5-foot-wide tubs, tubs with stairs, tubs with ramps, and even hydraulic tubs. When making your choice, consider your canine clientele. Large dogs are the hardest to deal with, so choose something that will make getting a large dog into the tub as easy as possible for your staff and as stress-free as possible for the dog. Or, as many veterinarians have done in the past, consider a standard bathing tub for small and medium dogs, and then build a walk-in shower stall with a hand sprayer for bathing the larger dogs. Note that prefabricated tubs are more ergonomic and easier to maintain than standard bathing tubs.

▼ ▼ ▼

IN THE END, boarding and grooming are service-based businesses. Regardless of the quality of the facilities, just like a veterinary business, a boarding or grooming business cannot be successful without well-trained staff and outstanding customer service.

CHAPTER 42

HOSPITAL SUPPORT SPACES

Storage is the bane of all veterinarians. Even when there seems to be plenty of storage space built into a brand-new hospital, it is never enough. Storage issues also top the list of complaints architects hear from veterinarians about their existing facilities. Combine storage areas with other support spaces, such as laundry and utility rooms, janitors' closets, offices, and even staff support areas like the break room, and now you have a grouping of spaces that, while often an afterthought, are critical to the proper design of any animal hospital. In order to address these needs, it is best to develop an effective strategy based on the flow of goods and materials through your hospital. But how is this done?

STORAGE

Think for a moment about the enormous number of things that move through a veterinary hospital every day—items such as food, drugs, money, medical supplies, retail supplies, dirty laundry, trash and sharps, and deceased animals. In addition to all of these, if you offer boarding, you will also need space for items such as cat carriers, food, toys, and the other things that owners leave with you. You can quickly see that virtually all of your storage needs have a direct relationship to material handling.

The first step in organizing all of the categories described above is to visualize a flowchart for how items move from place to place. As an example, let's follow a roll of gauze through the typical hospital:

- Receiving: The gauze arrives with a shipment of other items in a box.
- Staging: It is stacked in the pharmacy or in a medical supply closet.
- Use area: It is moved to treatment or an exam room to a cabinet where it is handy.
- Intermediate disposal: The used gauze is disposed of in medical trash.
- Final disposal: It is taken out in the trash to the trash receptacle.

As you can see, even a simple item follows a complex path and demands storage through each stage. The trick to solving the storage problem is to design effective solutions for every item as it moves in, occupies, and moves out of your hospital. This sounds like a lot of effort, but by thinking of storage in terms of material handling, you can create more efficient solutions. This is critically important, because storage space does not bring in any income, and wasted space compromises your revenue-generating capacity.

Another important reason to properly understand the flow of goods and materials through your hospital is to have a good handle on inventory control and security. If you have no idea where something is, chances are you won't notice when it goes missing. Nor will you have it at your fingertips when you need it. So how can you make sure to utilize storage space in the most effective way possible while still maximizing your profitable space?

First, keep it simple. If your storage is inconvenient, it will become cluttered and unorganized and will take up more space in the end. You may be tempted to store something in every nook and cranny of your hospital. However, some locations, such as inside waiting or exam room benches, or above dog runs, are not convenient or workable. You and your staff should not have to bend over to get something, stand on a tall ladder in a run with a Rottweiler, or move a client off the bench to access the storage. What you should try to achieve instead is storage that is convenient to the place where the item will be used. One larger storage room is better than lots of small ones. Likewise, avoid storage in attics and basements. These areas are just difficult and inefficient to access. Once something goes into a basement or attic, it rarely comes back out.

When thinking about storage solutions, focus on methods of organizing things that are both specific and efficient. Since people do not want to crawl on their hands and knees to get items they use every day, spaces below counters do not get used as efficiently as over-counter cabinetry. Therefore, strive to maximize your upper cabinet storage space and install drawers in your lower cabinet space to make them more accessible. You can also use the space below your counters to store bulky items that are used less frequently, or leave the space open to park equipment, trash cans, and carts out of the way.

In addition, be sure to design for the size and mass of the items you are storing. As mentioned above, one large and more centralized storage room often functions better than lots of small ones. If this room is instead located way in a back corner of the hospital, your staff will have to drag big, heavy items from one corner of the facility to the other, decreasing their efficiency. It is also important to be strategic about how you store items in this room. Invest in solutions that help to maximize your storage space, especially in bulk storage areas.

For larger items, consider high-density storage solutions with deep, adjustable shelves that allow for modification depending on what is being stored. Resist stacking larger items on the floor, as this just creates more clutter and less organization. This general rule is especially important when it comes to food, as food on the floor can be enticing to small rodents and insects. And while the ability to store large quantities of supplies is important, it is also important to make sure you can find everything you need. For numerous smaller items, use high-density storage bin systems that will fit on the shelves and can be labeled. These can be very effective for categorizing items and creating easy-to-access bulk storage.

OTHER SUPPORT SPACES

Beyond storage areas, the other major support spaces to consider and make sure to effectively design are your laundry and utility spaces, bathing areas, food prep areas, staff offices, break room, and meeting spaces. For these areas, think about the daily flow within each room, not just of materials but also of the people using the spaces. For example, in the laundry area it is usually best to treat the flow of laundry in the same way you would treat the clean and dirty flow of a pack/prep room. Dirty laundry comes in one side and clean laundry exits out the opposite side. This really helps to keep things organized and prevents any potential cross-contamination. A similar approach can be used for food prep areas with regard to dirty bowls and clean bowls.

Be sure to provide adequate counter and workspace within laundry, utility, and food prep rooms. Consider providing deeper-than-normal countertops and/or wall shelving. You will need an adequate area for folding laundry and storing towels and blankets. You will also want to make sure there is space to spread out while you work, and for food storage in a food prep area. It is important to ensure that all of these work surfaces are durable. Stainless steel countertops and stainless steel wire rack wall shelving are optimal, because these rooms tend to endure a lot of use and abuse over time. Stainless steel is easy to clean and is resistant to water damage, making it a good choice for rooms where heavy cleaning or bathing may occur. Ultimately, these utilitarian-type support spaces don't need to be pretty, but they should still be carefully designed so that they will be effective in promoting an efficient daily workflow.

SUPPORT SPACES FOR STAFF

Staff support spaces include those with critical business management functions such as break rooms, conference or meeting rooms, and offices. Just as we envisioned the flow of goods through the space, consider the flow of people. Your staff break room does not need to be right in the middle of your hospital, where it would take up important medical space, but it should not be located in a back corner, either. Most of your staff will use the treatment area as their hub. So while the break room should be a place to retreat and truly take a break, you want it located close enough to the action that you can quickly grab staff if an urgent issue arises. Locating the break room not far from treatment will also keep your staff peripherally engaged in what is going on in the hub of the hospital during their breaks. Try to also locate the break room close to an exterior door.

The tables in this conference space can be easily rolled to the side of the room and the chairs stacked to provide an open space if required for trainings. The room also takes advantage of the wooded area that the hospital backs up to. Nature sets the backdrop for this staff and client education space. (Foto Imagery / Tim Murphy. Courtesy of VCA South Shore Animal Hospital, South Weymouth, Massachusetts [VCA, Inc.].)

Your staff will generally enter the hospital through a separate, nonpublic door, drop their personal items off at the staff lockers (which can be located in or near the break room), put their lunch in the break room refrigerator, and clock in for the day. By locating the break room and lockers near a door, you are giving your staff the chance to jump into their workday more quickly.

Similar rules apply for designing the conference or meeting room. Not all hospitals have a dedicated conference room. In fact, when square footage is limited, many hospitals allow their staff break room to double as a conference room. But if your hospital operations warrant a dedicated meeting room, go through the same thought process about workflow to determine where it should be located. Because conference rooms tend to need to be quieter, it usually makes sense to locate them more remotely to provide some level of privacy. They may be near your break room but farther from your central treatment area. It may also make sense to put the conference room near your offices, so that like functions are grouped together. The best approach is to map your day-to-day use and see what makes the most sense.

Some veterinary hospitals like to use their conference rooms as gathering spaces in which to offer classes, behavior training, etc. to staff, the general public, or visiting veterinarians. This can be a great outreach opportunity in your community. If you want your conference room to function as a dual public space, consider locating it closer to the front of the hospital, so that you can have both public and staff access, depending on what is going on in the space each day. Ultimately, the conference room is an area whose location is mostly dependent on the anticipated use and function.

Office areas have shifted over the years for veterinary hospitals. Decades ago, it was common to see large, private offices for veterinary owners, often with their own meeting areas and private bathrooms. As hospitals have become more expensive to build and more diversified in terms of ownership structure, large owners' offices have become less common. Instead they have been replaced by shared offices and even open work areas.

While shared spaces save square footage and diminish the hierarchical structure in a work environment, the problem is the lack of privacy this creates. Veterinarians have a difficult and communication-intensive job, and many of them prefer to have a quiet space in which to make client calls, and where they can get away to recharge. The challenge of a veterinary hospital design, then, is to find a balance between the need to minimize office space and the need for privacy. The following are some common strategies for achieving the right balance:

- Separate shared offices; provide one for owners and the other for associates.

- Create a small separate meeting room for private conversations or sensitive phone calls.

- In shared workspaces, utilize sound baffles between workstations to cut down on noise and give each person a greater sense of privacy.

- Establish charting and doctors' stations throughout the medical areas so that quick computer tasks can be completed during the day without the need to run back to an office. The office can then be a true retreat for end-of-day paperwork and tasks requiring longer periods of concentration.

- Open the office to the outside with windows, so that shared workspaces feel open, connected, and peaceful. Burying offices in the center of the building can make them feel uninviting.

- See Chapter 52 on furnishings for information on how to equip your office spaces.

OTHER CONSIDERATIONS

Below are a few miscellaneous considerations to keep in mind as you design the back-of-house support spaces within your hospital:

- Be sure to provide multiple janitorial closets in strategic places around your hospital. The last thing you want is for a patient to have an "accident" in an exam room that requires you to run to the far back corner of the building to get a mop to clean it up.

- Consider how pickups and deliveries will occur at your hospital. You probably do not want them all coming through the front lobby. Be sure to provide an easily accessible back entrance near your storage or receiving areas.

- Though it is never fun to think about, make sure you look at the path that deceased animals will take through your hospital. Is there a direct path from your comfort/euthanasia room to where your freezer is stored that is out of sight of the general public? Also, try to keep your freezer close to the back door for easy pickup and also away from any animal wards, because dog noses work a lot better than ours do.

▼ ▼ ▼

DESIGNING EFFECTIVE SUPPORT

spaces and storage solutions for your practice is ultimately an exercise in understanding material handling and workflow. It is easy to get caught up in the details of designing your treatment room cabinetry, but without a good idea of how things move in and out of your treatment area, you may find yourself with spaces that are not as useful as you hoped.

Once you understand your storage flowchart, the real challenge is to keep the storage solutions simple and efficient. If you are to succeed in doing this, you may spend more money on shelves, cabinets, and storage systems, but you will save yourself square footage. Most importantly, you will save time and energy for yourself and your staff in the long run.

SECTION **FOUR**

Building Systems and Finishes

CHAPTER 43

HVAC DESIGN

Mechanical (HVAC) design for veterinary hospitals must achieve two main objectives: creating a comfortable environment, and maintaining and promoting animal health. And both of these objectives must be met within the context of building, mechanical, and energy codes, which mandate minimum standards for airflow, contaminant removal, and energy efficiency.

However, the design of the hospital mechanical systems typically goes far beyond code compliance. This is because veterinary environments have unusual requirements that necessitate a rigorous and sophisticated approach. This chapter reviews the basics of mechanical design for veterinary hospitals.

To begin with the first objective—comfort—the building must maintain the following:

- A temperature of 70°F to 76°F.

- A humidity level of 20% to 60%.

- Six to thirty air changes per hour (depending on the situation).

- Air velocity at head level of 10 to 50 feet per minute.

Several different types of systems can be used to successfully create this comfort zone, but any design must use some level of forced air in order to maintain proper air exchange. Four main types are available:

- Rooftop units (gas-fired furnaces or electric resistance and refrigerant cooling systems): These systems are very effective for veterinary hospitals and are the most commonly used. They require flat roofs or large exterior grades for placement.

- Residential furnaces (with remote condensers and evaporators): Residential furnace systems can be located in an attic, crawl space, or closet, making it more flexible than a rooftop unit. However, this equipment cannot typically provide the outside air needed for medical spaces and may not be able to meet energy code requirements. These systems are not appropriate for larger projects.

- Two- or four-pipe fan coil systems (gas-fired boilers and remote chillers): In a two- or four-pipe system, hot and cold water are run to fan coil units, which are usually mounted above the ceilings of individual rooms. Each fan coil unit can provide either hot or cold air as required. A two- or four-pipe fan coil system is probably the Cadillac of systems, but it is not typically cost effective in terms of initial capital expense for any but the largest hospitals.

- Heat pumps: A heat pump system provides refrigerant cooling, and by running the pump system in reverse, it can also heat. Heat pumps can be incorporated in rooftop units or furnaces. While they are cost effective in temperate climates where air conditioning is the primary use, they are not ideal for cold climates.

In selecting equipment for hospitals, most engineers land on rooftop air-handling equipment because it is cost effective and can accommodate specialized outside air requirements.

In addition to the typical choices for equipment, many veterinarians ask about other systems that may supplement their mechanical design, including these:

- Radiant heating (in floor): Because veterinary hospitals must maintain a certain level of air exchange for animal health, radiant heating is used simply as a means of boosting comfort. Radiant heating cannot respond quickly enough or maintain a high enough temperature to be used as space heating. It can be used in dog run areas, for example, to dry the floors quickly and provide the dogs with a comfortable surface. When used in spaces like this, keep in mind that it needs to be kept at a temperature low enough that it will not overheat the animals.

- Geothermal systems: Geothermal heating and cooling systems use the constant temperature of the earth or of groundwater to provide a heat sink or heat source. They utilize heat pump technology and they can provide an excellent way to reduce the costs of mechanical systems for certain types of buildings that have lower mechanical loads, such as office buildings and libraries. The efficacy of geothermal systems is entirely location dependent. If you are in a location where geothermal systems are common, then they can be cost effective. However, veterinary hospitals have large demands for heating, cooling, and ventilation, and therefore utilizing a geothermal system may not be workable or may be cost prohibitive in some cases.

MECHANICAL ZONING

Your mechanical engineer will review the major design requirements for different areas of the hospital. This review will inform how the hospital should be separated or zoned by mechanical unit. In the big picture, hospital zones should be separated as follows:

- Client zone: reception, waiting, retail, exam rooms.
- Medical zone: treatment, surgery, lab, pharmacy.
- Patient zone: wards, runs, isolation, food preparation.

This separation helps to prevent airborne odors and contaminants from spreading throughout the building. The shaded floor plan on the following page illustrates this typical arrangement. If the hospital is very small, such as a 1,200 square-foot lease space, it may survive with two zones (one for client and office spaces and one for the other areas of the hospital). As the hospital grows, it may need more mechanical units. The need for upgrades will be defined by the limitations of heating and cooling a volume of air on a single unit.

Thermal Control: The Key to Comfort

In understanding how zoning a system relates to comfort, it is important to understand that veterinary hospitals work best as constant air volume systems. These systems deliver defined, constant volumes of air to each space depending on the sanitation and pressurization requirements of the space. The opposite of this is a variable air volume system, which delivers varying volumes of air to spaces with the purpose of temperature control, but at the expense of sanitation and pressurization.

As an example, it is not acceptable to have the airflow fluctuate in a surgery room, as this would compromise sterility as well as the air pressure relationships that are so critical for cleanliness and odor control. Without the ability to vary the air in some portions of the hospital, the engineering team must have means of controlling air temperature differentially in specific spaces. Imagine two identical animal housing spaces, one on the outside wall and one in an inside space. These two spaces are both on the same mechanical unit. Because of their different exposures, one space is likely to feel uncomfortable most of the time. This situation can be solved by providing supplemental cooling or heating to one of the two rooms.

Some hospital spaces require supplementary cooling in specific areas simply because these areas have far greater heat loads than the surrounding spaces, such as MRI rooms, CT rooms, and IT/data rooms. Surgery rooms typically require supplementary cooling systems because of the lights, gowns, and patient warming systems that make these spaces hot and stuffy for the surgeon and technicians. Grooming and bathing rooms can also get very hot and stuffy and often require supplemental cooling for the comfort of the staff working in them. A DX cooling air handler can be installed to allow staff additional temperature control in these spaces.

A HEALTHY ENVIRONMENT

Creating a healthy environment and minimizing biological risk are also primary goals of veterinary hospital mechanical design. Most of the ventilation standards that have been developed

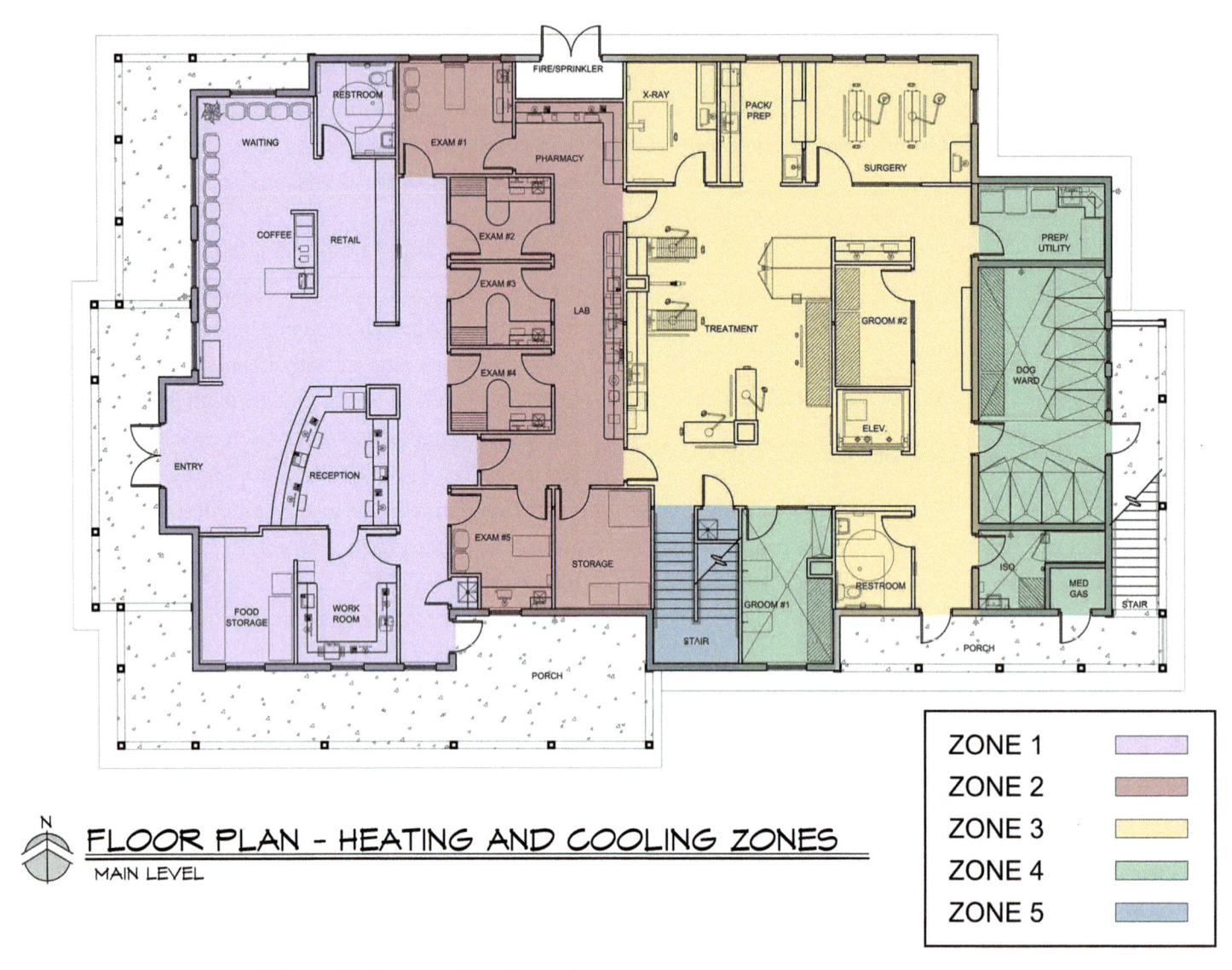

FLOOR PLAN – HEATING AND COOLING ZONES
MAIN LEVEL

ZONE 1	
ZONE 2	
ZONE 3	
ZONE 4	
ZONE 5	

A floor plan showing different HVAC zones within a hospital.

for animal hospitals are based on odor control, for the following reasons:

- Odor is an indicator of airborne contaminants.
- Airborne contaminants may be unhealthy for animals and staff, based on studies in human healthcare environments.
- Odor is off-putting to staff and clients, and it is likely to be uncomfortable for animals as well.

Little definitive research has been done to indicate whether pathogens are successfully spread through air handling systems in veterinary hospitals. In human hospital studies, however, there is some indication that fungal spores, including ringworm, spread readily, followed by bacteria, followed by viruses (Fencl). This research supports the goal of reducing recirculated air in veterinary environments.

Besides rigorous cleaning and maintenance, the best way to control odors is to achieve separate mechanical zones, as discussed earlier in this chapter. Each of these zones should have its own air handling units and supply and return. This approach keeps air from crossing from one zone into another and keeps odors originating in the patient zone from being drawn into the client zone.

PRESSURIZATION

Variations in air pressure can also work to isolate odors. Exhausting more air than you put into the medical and patient zones creates negative air pressure. Putting more into the client zone than you exhaust creates positive pressure. The positive-pressure air in the client zone will keep odors moving toward the negative pressure in the medical and patient zones. Below are some typical pressure relationships for spaces within most hospitals:

- Lobby: positive.
- Treatment: neutral.
- Surgery: positive.
- Dental: slightly negative.
- Wards: negative.
- Isolation: very negative.

In the most negative environment, isolation, the space should exhaust 15% more air than is supplied and transferred from adjacent spaces combined.

EXHAUST REQUIREMENTS

The simplest method of ensuring an odor-free indoor environment is to utilize 100% exhaust in animal wards and 40%–60% exhaust in medical spaces. By moving air to the outside of the building, odors and contaminants are also removed.

Some engineers prefer to boost exhaust rates less and to treat the air with air treatment systems. There are two types of air treatment systems: ultraviolet germicidal irradiation, or UVGI, and ionization. Ionization is not used in human hospital settings and is not recommended. Do your research before choosing a UVGI system:

- Find verified studies concluding that the air treatment system works for the application, as there are some ineffective systems on the market.
- Find out about the engineer's proficiency with the system.
- Obtain good references for use of the system in animal care settings.

UVGI is becoming a reasonable supplement to the overall mechanical design in human hospitals, but do be careful. If you are considering using UVGI to help clean the airstream, keep in mind that there are some technologies and products that can, in combination with air filtration, produce the desired results, but there are imposters in this field as well. Make sure any system you are considering has been proven to be effective in hospital environments. (For further reading on this topic, refer to ASHRAE's website at ashrae.org.)

Regardless of your engineer's specific approach, be aware also that boosted exhaust rates can cause other problems for facilities, such as the introduction of moisture from the outside in humid climates. To combat this problem, dehumidification should be included with any high outside air system except in the driest of climates.

AIR CHANGE RATES

In addition to exhausting more air than a typical office building, hospitals must also move the air more quickly in order to maintain fresh and odor-free spaces. Air change can be measured in cubic feet per minute (CFM) or as air change per hour (ACH). Here, for simplicity, we will use ACH, even though it does not account for volume. This information also assumes a 9-foot ceiling, which is standard for commercial medical spaces. The following are typical ACH requirements for different spaces in a hospital:

- Medical spaces: 8 to 10 ACH.

- Surgery: 12 to 15 ACH. In this case, this is an air change recirculation rate, as this air does not need to be exhausted because of odors. The purpose here is to filter contaminants out of the air to preserve the aseptic environment.

- Dog ward: 12 to 15 ACH nominally, and up to 20 ACH depending on the number of dogs housed in the space.

- Cat ward: 20 to 25 ACH nominally, and up to 30 ACH depending on the number of cats housed in the space.

- Isolation rooms: 25 to 30 ACH.

Ventilation rates—the amount of outside air brought into any space—are driven by the mechanical codes but are often boosted above levels required by code to maintain animal health.

DIRECTIONAL AIRFLOW

It is important not only to control airflow throughout the building but also to control the direction of airflow within specific rooms. The following are some examples:

- Provide exhaust over cages, and supply over the space in front of cages, to prevent odors within wards.

- Supply a laminar (nonturbulent) flow of air over surgery tables to keep them clean and uncontaminated.

- Ventilate through cages, if possible.

VENTILATED CAGES

The practice of aggressively ventilating an entire room does accomplish odor control, but it is not necessarily bringing much benefit to each animal being housed. By exchanging air through cages instead of around them, it is possible to achieve room odor control while reducing overall room air exchange rates. This method also increases the effective air exchange rates in the patients' breathing zone.

Cages don't have to be built in to be ventilated. A rolling cage has many advantages—it can be cleaned easily, can be reconfigured based on need, and can be rolled from room to room. But how does one ventilate a rolling cage? There are two options: installing a dryer-type vent to the back, or using vent grilles.

The dryer vent solution is simple enough to apply in some cases (see photo). But for stainless steel cages, this solution isn't practical. Instead,

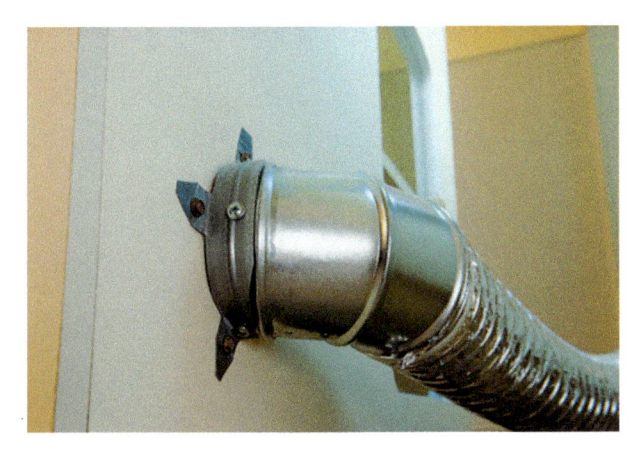

An air vent leading from the back of an enclosure. (Courtesy of Mason Company.)

for a low-tech solution, caging can be ordered with vent grilles in the backs from the manufacturer. Exhaust ducting is provided in the wall directly behind where the cages will be located. Supply air in front of the cages and exhaust from the wall behind them to draw air through the cages with very little effort. You can mount a bumper to the tops and bottoms of the cages so they fit snugly against the wall when in place. This reduces the possibility that air will simply rush around the cages rather than through them.

For built-in cages, most manufacturers now offer ventilated cage solutions. These are straightforward and merely hook up at the top to the building exhaust system.

A mechanical engineer should be able to use volume measurements to calculate the air in cubic feet per minute (CFM) that will flow through the cage and adjust the overall volume of room air exchange accordingly. Depending on the size of the cage, 20 to 30 CFM per cage works as a guideline, because this volume of air exchange provides sufficient odor control without creating a feeling of air rushing through the cage. Even if you use less than this amount, the result will still be more satisfactory than in a typical ceiling-ventilated room, because the air will be flowing in the direction that most benefits the occupants. The use of vented caging allows for the reduction of overall room air exchange because of the directional flow of the air.

AIR FILTRATION FOR MEDICAL AREAS

Filters are helpful in creating a cleaner indoor environment. They can be purchased based on the level or size of the particulates that you want to screen. For most spaces in the hospital, filters that are 80% efficient (MERV 8) are more than adequate. Filters that are 90% efficient (MERV 13) on the air supply to the surgery suite will screen out almost all significant particulates. Filters with an efficiency beyond 99% are called high-efficiency particulate air (HEPA) filters. These remove virtually all contaminants, including many viruses, but are not usually used in veterinary surgery rooms except in cases where the hospital provides neurosurgery or a large number of orthopedic surgeries. Increased filtration percentages will have a direct effect on the fan horsepower of the mechanical equipment and operating expenses. High filtration also requires more frequent maintenance and a higher maintenance expense.

ENERGY REDUCTIONS

To reduce utility costs, many hospital systems are constructed with energy recovery systems that precondition the incoming airstream with energy from the outgoing airstream. Some energy recovery equipment can achieve the trans-

An example of a cage system vented from the top of the enclosures.

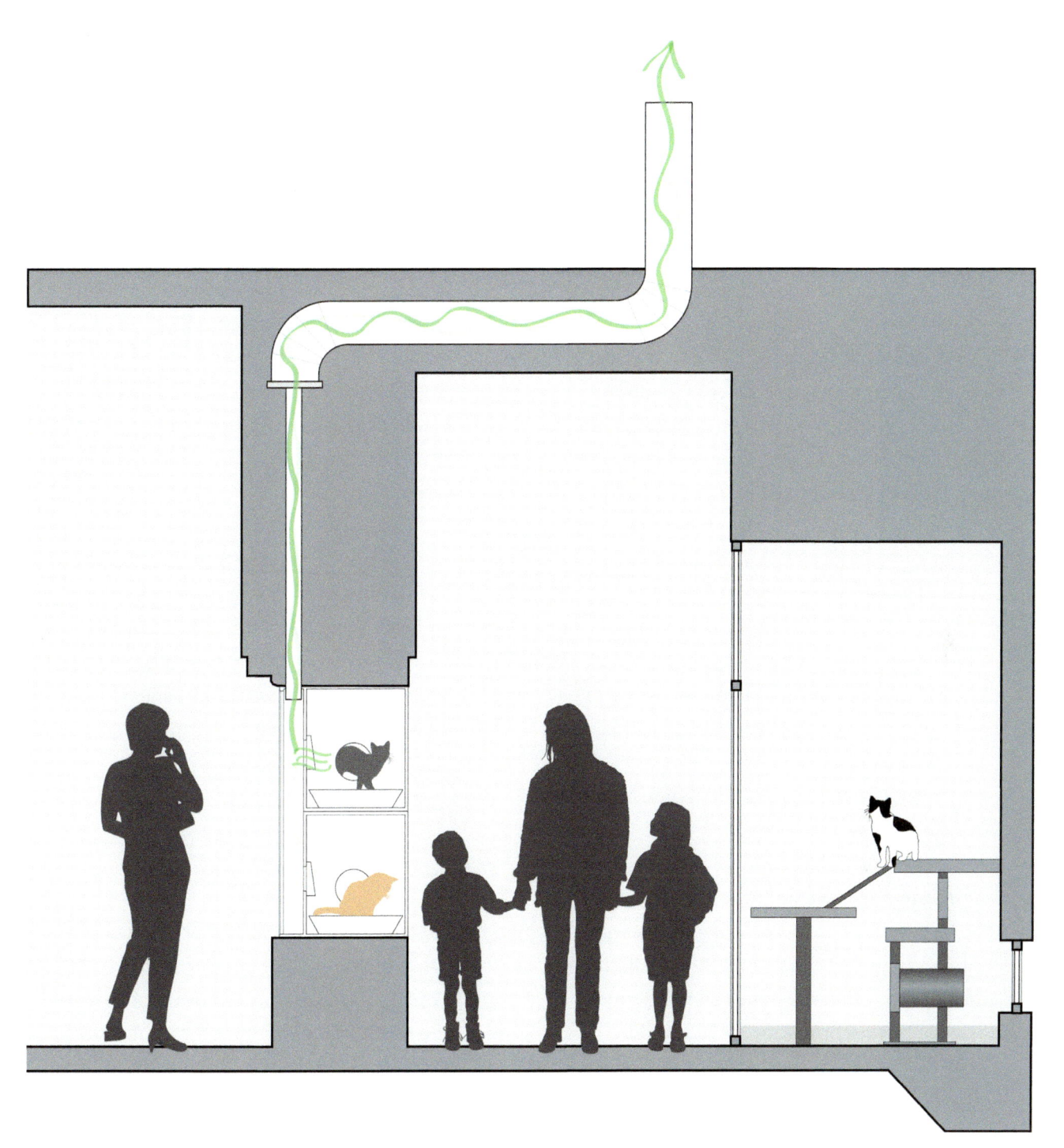

A section view of a ventilated cat enclosure. The air is carried directly from the cat's elimination area through the vent and out of the building.

HVAC DESIGN   **249**

fer of energy with no cross-contamination of the airstreams, while less expensive equipment, such as a heat wheel, may allow a small amount of cross-contamination. Discuss your expectations with your mechanical engineer so that he or she can select the most appropriate equipment.

Another way to reduce the amount of energy that a system must use is to harvest excess air from clean spaces to help supply air to dirtier spaces. For example, it is acceptable to transfer some positively pressurized air from the lobby to assist in providing some of the supply for a negatively pressurized space such as a dental room, as long as noise control strategies are not compromised.

SPECIAL CONDITIONS

To ensure the proper design of your building mechanical system, consider these specific cases:

- Laboratory: Install a 150 CFM exhaust fan over the sink.

- Chemotherapy: If chemotherapy drugs are being prepared, install a biological safety cabinet to meet USP and OSHA regulations for the drugs that are being administered. Specialized roof-mounted fans should be used to provide discharge from the roof—which means that they push contaminated exhaust air off the roof to prevent it from being reintroduced into the building through the outside air intakes on adjacent mechanical equipment. (For more details, see Chapter 34.)

- Exam room: Install a 90 to 180 CFM ceiling-mounted exhaust fan to prevent stuffy air and remove odors. Each fan should be on a timed switch, which will allow them to be used intermittently to help minimize the effect on the mechanical equipment.

- Isolation: Install direct and dedicated exhaust fans to the outside.

- Autoclaves: Some large autoclaves require hoods over them because of the amount of steam that is released. Check the manufacturer's requirements.

- Commercial dryers: Commercial dryers have their own makeup air requirements and can affect the entire room and surrounding space. Ensure that your mechanical engineer reviews the cut sheets (the manufacturer's equipment specifications) for the specific dryer.

▼ ▼ ▼

UNLIKE MANY OF the other aspects of a veterinary hospital, the HVAC system is not something you move through or touch every day, and so it is easy to forget how important it is. Yet the proper design of this system is absolutely essential to maintaining and promoting animal health and ensuring a comfortable work environment for you and your staff. Work closely with your architect and your mechanical engineer to ensure the special requirements of this system are met in your new facility.

CHAPTER 44

PLUMBING DESIGN

Good plumbing design is a vital part of creating a hospital that is clean and easy to sanitize. The best approach is a carefully considered balance of the right plumbing systems located in the right areas. Including more drains than necessary increases the expense of the building mechanical systems needed to expel humidity as well as the expense of the materials and finishes needed to stand up to hose cleaning.

Good plumbing design starts at the floor. First, identify areas that need to be cleaned with a hose. Isolation spaces and dog run wards, for example, are typically hose-down spaces, equipped with floor drains. In hose-down areas, the floor slab must be designed with care. Follow these guidelines:

- Drains should always be located in the back of a run, as the best protocols are to clean from front to back toward the dirtiest areas.

- Slope floor drains at a minimum of 0.25 inches per foot in runs and a maximum of 0.25 inches per foot in walking areas.

- Maintain a minimum thickness in the concrete slab as required by the structural engineer. This may mean making slabs thicker in areas with drains.

- The height of the drain and the direction of the slope should be indicated on your architect's drawings.

Dog runs can be equipped with individual drains or trench drains. Individual floor drains in each dog run are typically a better choice than trench drains in medical areas because they minimize the risk of cross-contamination. Individual drains may be round, square, or long and rectangular. For many projects, the long, rectangular individual drain is an economical design because the concrete may gently slope toward it in one direction, minimizing the need for multiple slopes to a point drain. The grate configuration with either floor or trench drains should be discussed with the design team to ensure that the correct grate is selected for the area and the animals being housed. Dogs, cats, and puppies all have specific needs pertaining to grate configuration. Most drain manufacturers offer many grate styles, such as slotted, perforated, or hinged solid covers, along with optional sediment buckets.

For projects that require greater budget control, trench drains may be the best option, because they minimize drain connections and therefore can be more economical. If your design team chooses trench drains, follow these recommendations to maintain the most sanitary environment:

- Flush the drain at the top with a water inlet. The water inlet can be activated via a push button, or it can be on a timer for more automatic rinsing. This will require flush valve assembly on the water feed to the drain, or the water can be piped from a nonpotable water source through a solenoid valve.

- Keep the drains covered with a solid hinging cover that is produced by the run product manufacturer in order to prevent dogs from having contact with the drain.

- Again, trench drains should not be used in areas where parvovirus or other fecal/oral transmitted diseases are being isolated. Use individual drains in these spaces instead.

Regardless of your final decisions about draining the dog runs, provide aisle drains as well so the walking surface may be sanitized as the last step in the cleaning process.

HANDLING SOLIDS

Removing solid waste prior to cleaning runs is considered to be a best practice for the following reasons:

- It has been proven that leaving solids in a run sabotages the effectiveness of disinfectant chemicals.

- Forcefully spraying feces can splatter other surfaces and aerosolize contaminants.

- Forcing solids down drains uses a tremendous amount of water.

- Drains that are designed to accept solids may trap other items, such as toys and blanket scraps, and may be prone to clogging.

Dealing with solid waste can be unpleasant. Consider the number of runs your hospital will have, and if you can justify the expense, a great solution is to include a "poop closet" in your design. This special janitorial closet is designed with a large flushing rim sink like those used in nursing homes and hospitals, an exhaust vent to control odors, and a hose and floor drain for cleanup.

WATER PRESSURE AND CLEANING

Pressure does not necessarily equate to better cleaning. On the contrary, it has been shown that "high-pressure spraying . . . may aerosolize microorganisms and spread contaminants" (Petersen, 57). However, appropriately selected pressure cleaning systems do have some benefits, such as reducing water usage and properly dispensing disinfectants and other cleaning chemicals. If you decide to use a pressure system, follow these guidelines:

- Select a medium-pressure system.

- Select rigorous wall and floor finish systems to withstand the water pressure.

- Remove solids before spraying to minimize the risk of aerosolization of contaminants.

- Choose a pressure system that has a long track record in animal care facilities.

- Involve the manufacturer early in the design process to ensure that the system is designed correctly.

WET/DRY VACUUM SYSTEMS

There are several wet/dry vacuum systems now on the market that are designed specifically for animal care. These systems can be used in full hose-down spaces and spaces you might not hose but want to sanitize, such as cage wards.

The limitations of wet/dry vacuum systems are as follows:

- They should *not* be used in areas where infectious animals are housed, such as isolation. Pathogens will be sucked up into the canister and potentially be spread to other areas of the hospital.

- They should not be a sole means of cleaning. If something breaks and you are waiting for service, you will need a backup hose to drag from somewhere and a floor drain somewhere.

- They're not for sucking up feces.

Central vacuum systems must be compatible with the cleaners and disinfectants you use. For example, if the hospital chooses to use accelerated hydrogen peroxide, even at diluted ratios, it cannot be pumped through a central cleaning system unless fittings and pumps are specified with stainless steel instead of brass. Therefore, it is best to align your intended disinfectant protocols with the design and specifications of any centralized cleaning system.

THE SCIENCE OF DISINFECTION

Understand how cleaning chemicals work and work for you before settling on protocols for your hospital. Chemicals are tested for efficacy against various pathogens by many credible groups, such as universities and the Centers for Disease Control and Prevention (CDC). Human pathogens are equivalent to veterinary pathogens as long as they are within the same genetic group. For example, testing for norovirus can be considered equivalent to testing for other similarly virulent nonenveloped viruses. Before using a disinfectant, be sure it is tested by one of these reputable organizations for the pathogen you are trying to kill, or an equivalent one. Most importantly, ensure that disinfectants are used at the proper dilutions. Always dilute chemicals as directed and rinse them thoroughly to prevent unnecessary corrosion of surfaces.

Using hot water to disinfect rooms is an anachronism that is unnecessarily persistent in the industry. It is impossible to disinfect or degrease using hot water unless the water is at least 180°F. Water this hot is scalding and unsafe. While some disinfectants are more effective in warm water, there are equally effective protocols that work for cool-water disinfecting and degreasing. Therefore, it is not necessary to plumb rooms with hot water for cleaning.

HOSE BIBS AND REELS

There is nothing more likely to recontaminate recently cleaned surfaces than dragging a hose around on a floor. The level of sophistication of your hose equipment should relate to room size and the effort needed to clean the room properly. Here are some solutions for different room sizes:

- Large dog run room: Use a ceiling-mounted hose reel with a clutch to control the speed of return of the hose. This system keeps hoses off the floor and out of the way so the room can be cleaned effectively and quickly. The clutch keeps staff members safe in case they get in the habit of letting the hose rewind itself.

- Medium-size hose-down room: Install a small, manual-wind hose reel mounted on the wall at user height.

- Small hose-down room: Install a hose bib with a hose mounted on a bracket on the wall. In small rooms, hose reels are expensive and not necessary.

- Outdoor spaces: Use exterior wall hydrants or hose bibs to assist with the cleaning of outdoor walking areas and outdoor kennels.

HANDWASHING SINKS

The most important consideration for cleanliness in the hospital environment is providing staff members with the opportunity to wash their hands. Handwashing is essential because it decreases the probability of fomite transmission of disease. Hand sanitizers are not to be a replacement for handwashing with soap and water because they are ineffective against nonenveloped viruses.

Handwashing sinks should be placed in isolation wards, in close proximity to other patient housing, in medical spaces, in surgery scrub areas, in utility and prep areas, and in specialty spaces, such as endoscopy, where messy procedures are performed. The choice to place sinks in each exam room is a personal preference, but at minimum doctors and staff need convenient access to a centralized handwashing sink.

Stainless steel, heavy-duty 18-gauge sinks are durable enough to hold up to daily use in animal care facilities. Faucets should have wrist-blade handles or electronic sensors.

OTHER PLUMBING FIXTURES

- Mop closets: At least one janitorial mop sink basin is required for a veterinary hospital. Mop sinks may be located near

An example of a wall-mounted hose reel with a clutch control. (Foto Imagery / Tim Murphy. Courtesy of Denver Animal Shelter, Denver, Colorado.)

the front for cleaning up accidents in the lobby, in the surgery zone—but outside any surgery suites—for cleaning this area separately, and near the back of the hospital for other cleaning.

- Public bathrooms: In most veterinary hospitals, public bathrooms will be required, and in larger facilities, based on the number of occupants and model building codes, one bathroom for each sex will be required.

- Lab: A stainless steel, large bowl sink with a stainless steel drain board is useful in the laboratory. The lab is also a convenient place to install an emergency eyewash station. Eyewash stations should be located in this room and in other spaces as required by OSHA.

- Treatment room: A combination of peninsula and island workstations that incorporate both dry and wet tub tables works well in the treatment area. Tub tables come in 4-foot and 5-foot lengths and can be freestanding stainless steel units, sinks that drop into cabinetry, or sinks that are already in the cabinetry. Tub tables come in different depths and configurations. Order your unit with a handheld spray hose that can easily reach to the other end of the table.

- Specialty rooms: Depending upon the specialty, these rooms can require a range of plumbing fixtures. In a room that is used for ultrasound, for example, a small sink in the corner is handy for washing off instruments.

- Pack/prep and scrub: A deep, oversize sink for washing utensils and a stackable washer and dryer can be included in the pack/prep area. The scrub sink should be separate from the instrument-washing sink. Scrub sinks come in a variety of sizes, shapes, and configurations. Size them based on the number of people that may need to scrub at any one time. An infrared sensor is the best control mechanism for a scrub sink.

- Employee lounge: Include a handicap-accessible sink in employee areas.

- Staff bathrooms: If you decide to install a shower in a staff bathroom, remember to make it handicap accessible, which may mean that you separate it from the toilet rooms themselves so that you are not required to have a shower for each gender.

- Grooming/utility/food prep: A back room or utility room is a good place for a grooming tub, a utility tub, and a sink for food prep. The best grooming tub is a premanufactured, raised, stainless steel tub with stainless steel surrounds. Grooming tubs are available with ramps, fold-down access, and many other features. A simple utility tub and an oversize kitchen sink can also be helpful.

- Electric water cooler or drinking fountain: Most jurisdictions will require your hospital to have at least one ADA-compliant drinking fountain or an electric water cooler.

CLEANING GARAGES

Service garages have their own unique cleaning requirements. Trench drains in garages and loading areas work best because they help to collect oil and sand and shuttle it to a central sand/oil interceptor that is typically located outside the building. Pressure washing systems work well in garages for removing oil and properly cleaning the floor slab.

▼ ▼ ▼

TAKE THE TIME to go room by room with your architect and plumbing engineer to locate and design every drain and fixture in your facility to ensure the needs of every space in your hospital have been properly accounted for based on room function and your desired cleaning protocols.

CHAPTER 45

MEDICAL GAS DESIGN

Any hospital that performs procedures under anesthesia requires medical gases. Understanding the design requirements for medical gas systems is integral to creating successful veterinary workspaces.

OXYGEN SYSTEMS

Oxygen is the most ubiquitous medical gas in veterinary hospitals. Very small facilities may not have centralized oxygen systems, but most hospitals that require multiple oxygen outlet locations will need a centralized oxygen system with a manifold and pipe distribution.

Oxygen systems for veterinary use do not have to comply with the same codes that human hospitals must follow. However, they should be distributed within medical-grade "L" copper piping that is brazed rather than soldered, and the piping must also be purged and tested to ensure that it does not carry any contaminants, such as lead, to patients. Copper piping is expensive, so it is best to locate your centralized oxygen storage close to the areas it will serve.

Oxygen may be stored in tanks that contain compressed gas or in sub-cooled vessels that store the oxygen in liquid form. Oxygen itself is not flammable, but it is an oxidizer by definition, so it can rapidly feed a fire that is consuming other fuels. For this reason, oxygen storage is limited by codes, including mechanical, plumbing, fire, and fuel and gas codes. Facilities with a limited amount of stored oxygen may not need a fire-rated closet, but these closets will be required for medium to large hospitals. As the amount of oxygen storage increases, other codes may require mechanical ventilation of the oxygen closet. In some climates, it is acceptable to store liquid oxygen outside the building, but it is important for your architect to review all of the applicable national and local codes, as in some jurisdictions this could be considered bulk storage, which can create other design concerns.

For larger hospitals or hospitals that use a lot of oxygen, an oxygen generator may reduce long-term operating costs. When sizing an oxygen generation system, do not forget to consider ICU oxygen cages, as these are the largest consumers of oxygen in the hospital. Oxygen generators require larger spaces for storage of the generator itself, along with expansion tanks and backup oxygen tanks. Oxygen generators also produce heat and require climate control and ventilation, and therefore they are stored inside. System delivery pressure may be a concern with oxygen generation, as these systems typically can only deliver oxygen at 20 to 50 pounds per square inch (psig), compared to bottled systems that typically deliver oxygen at 50 to 85 psig.

In addition to the considerations of sizing, storage, and oxygen source, the following system features require planning:

- Location of oxygen outlets: Outlets or connection points may be in the ceiling, at the ends of tables, in walls, or plumbed into cabinetry. Your plumbing engineer should indicate Diameter-Index Safety System (DISS) connection plates for these outlets, along with specifying hose drops from ceiling outlets with a quick-connect outlet on the user end. You will also need to determine the defined height above the finished floor for the drop terminations; this typically ranges from 6 feet to 6 feet, 6 inches.

- Decisions regarding zones: If it is unacceptable for your hospital oxygen system to be down, then consider more than one oxygen zone to provide backup and flexibility. Your engineer can define the zones utilizing master valve boxes in order to provide isolation of a portion of the medical gas system and protect employees and patients.

- Alarms and zone valves: The manifold should automatically switch oxygen when it gets low from one set of tanks to another. If the entire system runs low, an alarm should sound to warn personnel. Zone valves allow shutoff in one zone while another zone is working, and can provide an easily accessible location to isolate a zone in the event of a problem at a given outlet. Zone valves should be located in an egress path close to the outlets being served, as these are typically used for emergency conditions to protect patients and employees. Oxygen alarms should be located in the main treatment area, where they can be monitored regularly.

GAS SCAVENGING

Anesthetic gases produce potential health risks to personnel. Even in the smallest hospitals, it is advisable to utilize active anesthetic gas evacuation to the exterior of the building in lieu of passive canisters to adequately protect staff members from inhalation of the gases. Active scavenging systems, or scavenger systems, are simple and inexpensive to install. They typically consist of a schedule 40 PVC or CPVC piping system connected to a pump that expels gas to the building exterior through an outlet shaped like an exterior dryer vent or a gooseneck elbow pipe outlet. All piping sizes should be per the manufacturer's recommendations.

In selecting an active scavenging system for a veterinary hospital, it is important to choose one designed specifically for veterinary use and to follow the manufacturer's instructions for installation. Scavenger outlets should be located adjacent to the oxygen outlets in every location where anesthesia is to be used. The outlet plates should be specified by the scavenger equipment manufacturer and are not exactly the same as oxygen outlets.

Hospitals with surgical suction systems can utilize this system to provide a vacuum similar to that of the scavenger system described above. This type of system is called a waste anesthetic gas disposal (WAGD) system. Here, a centralized pump provides suction to the suction line and the active scavenging line. Each line is regulated before the outlet to provide the level of suction required. For practices that do not want to have a centralized surgical suction system, the active scavenging system should be utilized.

OTHER GASES

Other gases that may be used in veterinary medicine include nitrogen for operating surgical tools and nitrous oxide. Nitrous oxide is not used much today. Nitrogen is piped like oxygen systems. However, nitrogen is inert and is not an oxidizer, so it can be stored in higher quantities than oxygen. Nitrogen systems should also contain a pressure regulator that can be easily controlled by the end users. In some instances, multiple regulators may be needed to provide different pressure zones. Each room utilizing nitrogen should have, at a minimum, an accessible isolation valve or regulator and valve to allow the end users to turn off and relieve the pressure prior to disconnecting tools after any procedure.

▼ ▼ ▼

MEDICAL GAS SYSTEMS need to be carefully designed by someone who is not only familiar with medical gases in general but also familiar with the requirements of veterinary systems. Most designers for medical gas systems follow standards set by the National Fire Protection Association (NFPA), the American Society of Plumbing Engineers (ASPE), and the American Society of Heating, Refrigerating and Air-Conditioning Engineers (ASHRAE). These standards are designed around human healthcare, but pipe sizing and outlet capacities will be similar. The manufacturers of reputable veterinary medical gas and anesthesia equipment can also be very helpful, so consult with them, if necessary, in making decisions about your equipment and medical gas storage layout.

CHAPTER 46

NOISE CONTROL

Noise has long been an issue in veterinary hospitals. It causes additional fear, anxiety, and stress for patients and affects how clients experience the practice. A quieter environment also makes for a more enjoyable workplace for staff. So what can be done about noise? Here are the five traditional noise reduction strategies:

- Absorption: Choosing materials that stop sound waves in their tracks.

- Isolation: Constructing well-thought-out spaces that contain sound in specific areas.

- Dissipation: Designing the space to give sound the room it needs to die off on its own.

- Good HVAC design: Providing a system that does not add mechanical noise to the building.

- Masking: Utilizing calming white noise in the background to disguise some sounds.

Though these strategies are all important aspects of helping to mitigate noise within veterinary hospitals, they only deal with the problem once it has occurred. The best line of defense is a good offense. In other words, the best approach is to prevent noise from occurring in the first place.

NOISE PREVENTION

There are two types of noise we can work to prevent: the noises made by equipment, and the noises made by animals.

Do you still notice the sounds of slamming cage doors, of the running dishwasher, of the washer and dryer spinning, or of the crackling of the paging system just before an announcement? Probably not. These sounds have become white noise to you, but that doesn't mean your clients and patients are used to them. Methods for preventing common, familiar noises include these:

- Specifying quiet latches on all cages and dog run doors.

- Specifying soft casters for chair and equipment wheels.

- Purchasing newer appliances designed for quieter performance.

- Requiring silencers or, better yet, gasketing on doors to prevent them from slamming shut.

- Specifying lighting fixtures that avoid the hum of the old ballasts. Although you may not even notice the noise, the high-pitched hum of these ballasts is well within the frequency range that cats can hear.
  › LED fixtures with the correct dimmer or driver provide not only quiet operation but also energy savings.
  › For retrofits, replace existing magnetic ballasts, or ballasts with a noise rating other than class A, with a new ballast with a class-A sound rating.

As discussed in the chapter on animal housing, generally the biggest source of animal noise within a veterinary hospital is the barking of dogs. While some dogs will never cease to bark completely, barking does tend to increase when an animal is stressed and aroused. The following strategies have been proven to help prevent excessive barking:

- Provide kennels and caging of appropriate sizes and shapes. As discussed in Chapter 38, consider creating enclosures that are almost square in shape, rather than long and thin. Dogs move more naturally and have better interactions with staff members when housed in wider enclosures.

- Choose housing for dogs that allows them to see out of their enclosures. Dogs are typically quieter in glass enclosures than in barred or chain-link ones. If you are opting to use glass run doors, remember to specify doors equipped with a small barred area at the bottom of the door to encourage airflow and provide the dogs with a sniff hole that will help them use their noses to acclimate to their new environment.

- Design a layout that does not have dogs facing each other across a narrow aisle.

- Create comfortable spaces for dogs. Supply their enclosures with bedding, a warm surface, natural light, and proper ventilation.

NOISE ABSORPTION

Since it is not possible to stop all noise, the best strategy is to mitigate the noise that does occur through sound absorption techniques. It is best to absorb noise as close to the source as possible. This can be achieved by providing materials with a high Noise Reduction Coefficient (NRC) rating on the walls, floors, and ceilings of spaces where the noise originates.

The NRC rating quantifies the amount of noise a material absorbs. For example, an NRC rating of 1.0 means the material absorbs 100% of the reverberant noise that hits it. A ceiling tile has an NRC rating of 0.65. In contrast, concrete block walls and concrete floors have an NRC rating of 0.00 to 0.1. It is reasonable to aim for materials with an NRC of approximately 0.75 to 1.0.

Unfortunately, the typical absorbent materials are not very cleanable or durable, which can make them less than ideal for veterinary hospital use. So how do you absorb sound while providing a clean, aseptic environment?

The following materials can be used to absorb sound and are at least somewhat cleanable:

- Moisture-resistant ceiling tiles: NRC of 0.70.
- Nylon hanging sound baffles: NRC of 0.75.
- Cementitious spray-on soundproofing: NRC of 0.85.
- Rubber flooring: NRC of approximately 0.50, depending on the specific product.
- Acoustic wall panels: NRC varies depending on material and thickness.

While it is true that the more surface area of absorbent material you have, the more noise you will absorb, the efficacy of simply adding more absorptive material reduces as you add more material. A doubling of absorptive material in a room will only reduce the sound in the room by 3 decibels (dB). This means that if you have a 10 × 10-foot room with an acoustic tile ceiling—which provides you with 100 square feet of absorptive material—adding an additional 100 square feet of absorptive material to the wall will only reduce the sound level in the room by 3 dB, which is a barely perceived threshold. You can expect absorptive materials to reduce the noise level in a room a maximum of approximately 10 dB, which will sound as though the noise has been halved.

ISOLATION OF SOUND

Sound is a wave, and as such, it travels. In fact, it travels both through air and through materials. One of the most effective ways of controlling noise is to isolate it in the space where it originated. Sound isolation requires two ingredients: mass and space. Mass traps the airborne sound waves, whereas space stops the structure-borne sound waves. This is the principle behind construction types such as double-stud walls. The creation of two masses with an air space between them is the most effective construction for stopping sound.

A Sound Transmission Class (STC) rating is used to describe how much noise passes through a given assembly. The STC rating is equivalent to the number of decibels of sound the assembly screens out within a given frequency range. For example, a wall with an STC of 45 screens out approximately 45 dB of sound, or the equivalent of a normal person talking. To provide some perspective, a dog barks in the range of 100 or more decibels. This means that to effectively screen out all sound from a run, you would need to build a wall with an STC of 100. While this is not feasible, it is also not necessary.

Acoustical wall panels are hung on the wall in a play area to absorb sound. (Courtesy of Tails of Terra Linda Pet Resort, San Rafael, California.)

The highest effective STC that can be gained in a normal wall is approximately 55 to 65. For the most part, this is workable, because the remaining sound that escapes, approximately 35 dB, will be masked by normal background sounds.

But rooms are not composed of walls alone. Providing a double-wythe (a vertical stack of masonry one layer thick), concrete-block-wall construction with a 4-inch air space filled with insulation will not stop you from hearing the dog bark in the room next door if the sound can travel through either the floor or the ceiling.

A single, continuous concrete floor slab throughout your hospital will carry sound from the front of the facility to the back with no consideration for the well-constructed walls you built on top of it. There are a few options that can help improve this situation:

- One of the simplest solutions is to add absorptive material to the surface of the floor that will decrease the sound the floor is transmitting.

- Recall the earlier discussions about creating client versus medical zones within your building. These zones make for good locations to provide isolation joints in your slab. An isolation joint is simply a break

NOISE CONTROL 263

in the slab filled with an elastomeric filler. The locations for these breaks need to be carefully coordinated with flooring options and wall locations.

Your ceiling is the other area where sound will leak from one room to another via the structure. Floors and roof trusses stretch across spaces, so you need to decouple that structure from the ceiling in the room. A gypsum board ceiling structure on resilient channels is the best option. Insulation above the ceiling will help to absorb sound before it is transmitted to the structure. This type of ceiling above suspended acoustic ceiling tiles is often referred to as a "sound lid" and should be provided over noisy spaces such as wards.

In all cases, your wall, floor, and ceiling systems are only as good as their joints and connections. If the top of your wall is not sealed to the structure above, sound will travel over the wall directly into the adjacent room.

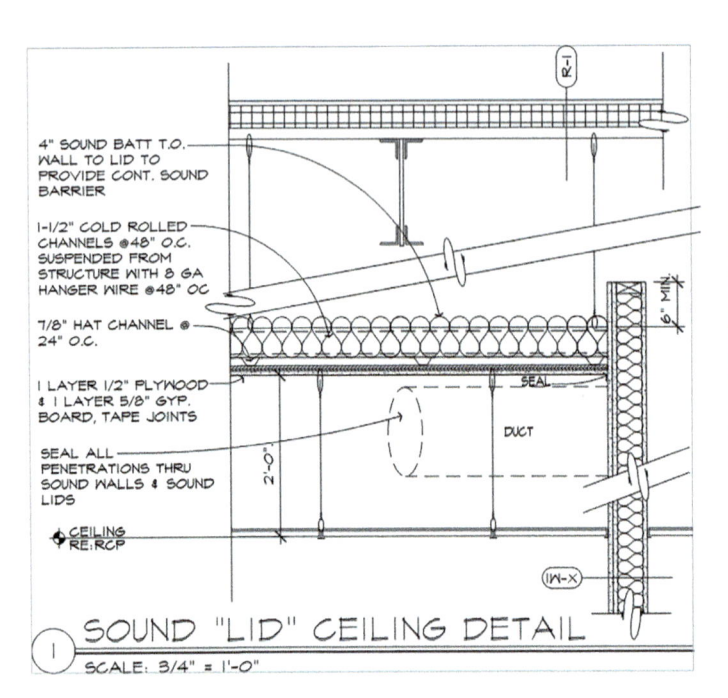

An example of a sound lid detail for sound attenuation above a noisy animal space such as a large dog ward.

Back-to-back electrical outlets within the same stud bay create a direct path through even the best-designed walls and allow sound to transfer seamlessly. HVAC ducts, which will be discussed in more depth shortly, are another pathway for sound to travel through a well-designed sound isolation wall.

The biggest culprits, however, are doors and windows. Even if you provide the perfect wall with a standard door and hardware, there will be a gap at the bottom of the door for direct transmission, and the door itself will stop only a very small percentage of the sound. If you are attempting to isolate sound in a space, you will need to be sure your architect specifies a door rated for the same STC as your wall, and that sound isolation hardware, such as a door bottom and closer, are provided.

DISSIPATION OF SOUND

The good news about dissipation is that it occurs without you needing to do anything about it. The bad news is that it is not typically very useful for reducing noise within a single room due to the lack of distance between walls.

Sound, if not provided with surfaces to reverberate off of, dissipates quite quickly. The inverse square law is a useful tool for understanding the basic relationship between decibels and distance. For every doubling of distance from the source, the sound decreases by approximately 6 dB. What this means for practical planning purposes is that an option that locates kennels 40 feet away from the lobby will provide a lobby area that is approximately 6 dB quieter than an option that locates the kennels 20 feet away from the lobby. This may not sound like a lot, but a change of just 5 dB is noticeable.

In conjunction with the other aspects of sound control discussed in this chapter, dissipation can provide a reasonable boost to your sound control efforts.

HVAC DESIGN FOR NOISE CONTROL

An HVAC system can add a significant amount of noise to your building in a variety of ways.

- Duct penetrations between sound-isolated spaces provide a highway for sound to travel between these two spaces. Ideally, HVAC zoning should be designed to mimic sound isolation zones. Though the ideal is not always possible, here are a few options for mitigating the sound transmission if a duct needs to pass between two sound-isolated rooms:
  › First, an attenuator can be installed in the duct at the wall location where a duct penetrates the sound isolation barrier.
  › Second, the duct can be lined with an absorptive material to reduce the amount of sound traveling between the two spaces.
  › Last, the penetration in the wall should be well sealed with an acoustic elastomeric sealant around the duct to stop a direct leak between the two spaces.

- The movement of air through a duct creates noise. To avoid the whoosh of air through a duct, the large masses of air need to be moved at a slower speed. The shape of the duct also affects the noise level. While most ductwork tends to be rectangular, a round duct is the most efficient shape for air movement, which also means it is the quietest of the duct shapes, as the air is not forced to work as hard to move through. Proper sizing of both the duct and the diffuser or register is also important. Trying to push large volumes of air through a small duct or diffuser will increase the velocity of the moving air, and therefore also the sound it makes. Larger duct and opening sizes, and fewer bends, will keep the noise level down significantly.

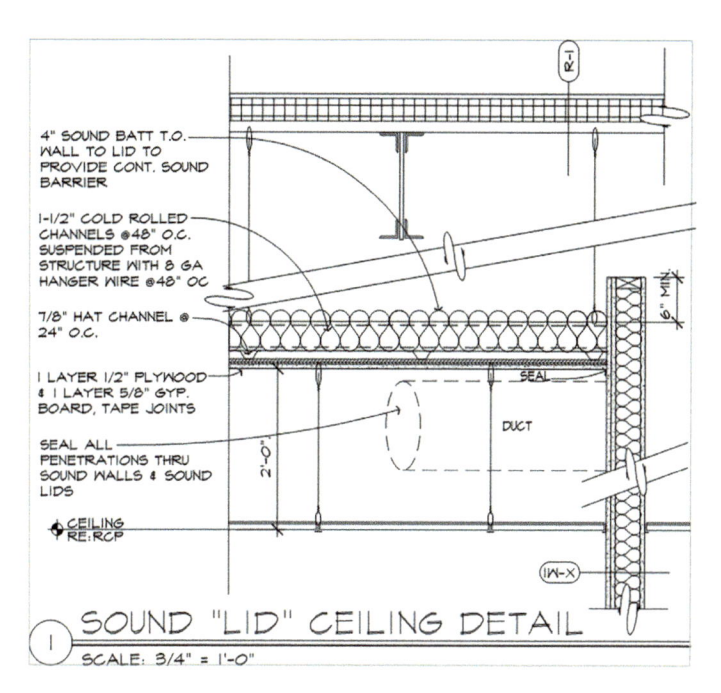

An example of a duct penetration detail.

- Equipment noise is the last of the issues to be aware of when it comes to HVAC design. Choose an appropriate size of fan—that is, as small as possible—to get the job done in order to keep fan noise to a minimum. You can also ask your mechanical engineer to specify an internally isolated fan, which reduces the noise coming off a fan significantly. HVAC equipment should be located as far away from animal holding areas as possible to take advantage of the noise dissipation discussed earlier. Provide isolation pads or spring isolators for all mechanical equipment. These are rubber pads or springs on which the equipment sits. The pads are useful for seismic situations as well as sound isolation. They keep the vibrations of the equipment from transferring noise through the building structure.

NOISE MASKING

When all else fails, use music or white noise. This is said only somewhat facetiously, as noise is not additive. Turning on soft music, nature sounds, or species-specific music does not add to the existing noise level; instead it masks a background noise problem. This can be an effective way to reduce stress in exam rooms and ward spaces, provided that the right type of masking noise is selected.

▼ ▼ ▼

AS IS THE CASE with most issues that must be "controlled," the best method of control is preventing the issue altogether. Keeping animals and their humans as calm and as comfortable as possible will go a long way toward reducing the noise threshold in your facility. You can then deal with mitigating the remaining noise.

CHAPTER 47

LIGHTING DESIGN

Lighting a hospital well is a matter of responding to the special requirements of each veterinary space. In the lobby, lighting can help with accenting a front reception desk or a retail area. In medical areas, overall illumination is important, as is task lighting on work surfaces. In patient areas, lighting should be tuned to the way animal patients perceive the space. The key is to understand how lighting can enhance your overall design goals.

Before discussing the lighting needs of different spaces, it is important to recognize that lighting design is constrained by the applicable building and energy codes. In fact, lighting is a central focus for today's energy codes, because lighting systems have traditionally accounted for up to 30% of an average commercial building's energy usage. Newer codes require designers to utilize more efficient fixtures and lighting control systems. Balancing energy codes with the requirements of veterinary lighting can be tricky, but it can be done!

LIGHTING LEVELS

The term "illuminance" is often used to describe the relative lighting level in a space and is simply the number of lumens per area. Lumens are part of the International System of Units, and in the US we also use a measure called foot-candles. One foot-candle (fc) is equal to one lumen per square foot on a work surface. For a point of reference, a bright, sunny summer day will generate an illuminance of around 10,000 fc, and an overcast day will generate approximately 2,000 fc. Lighting in a building is nowhere near the brightness of sunlight. Interior spaces are typically lit between 10 and 100 fc.

Recommended illuminance for veterinary spaces is as follows:

- 15 to 20 fc: hallways and utility spaces.
- 30 fc: office areas.
- 40 to 50 fc: exam and patient areas.
- 50 fc: medical areas.
- 75 fc: surgery rooms with all lights on.

Following these general illuminance guidelines in each space will help you create a functional and efficient lighting plan. However, illuminance does not describe the direction of light or the actual light perceived by the eye, and so to truly light a space well you should consider the locations of your lighting fixtures as well as views from space to space and to the outside. Follow these general rules:

- Light a space that you would like to see into more brightly than the space outside that room. For example, as shown in the photo, a doctor who is working in an ultrasound room has a view into a more brightly lit patient ward. This view is only effective as a result of the differential illumination between the two spaces.

- Light the animals well. As anyone who has worked in a veterinary space knows, it can

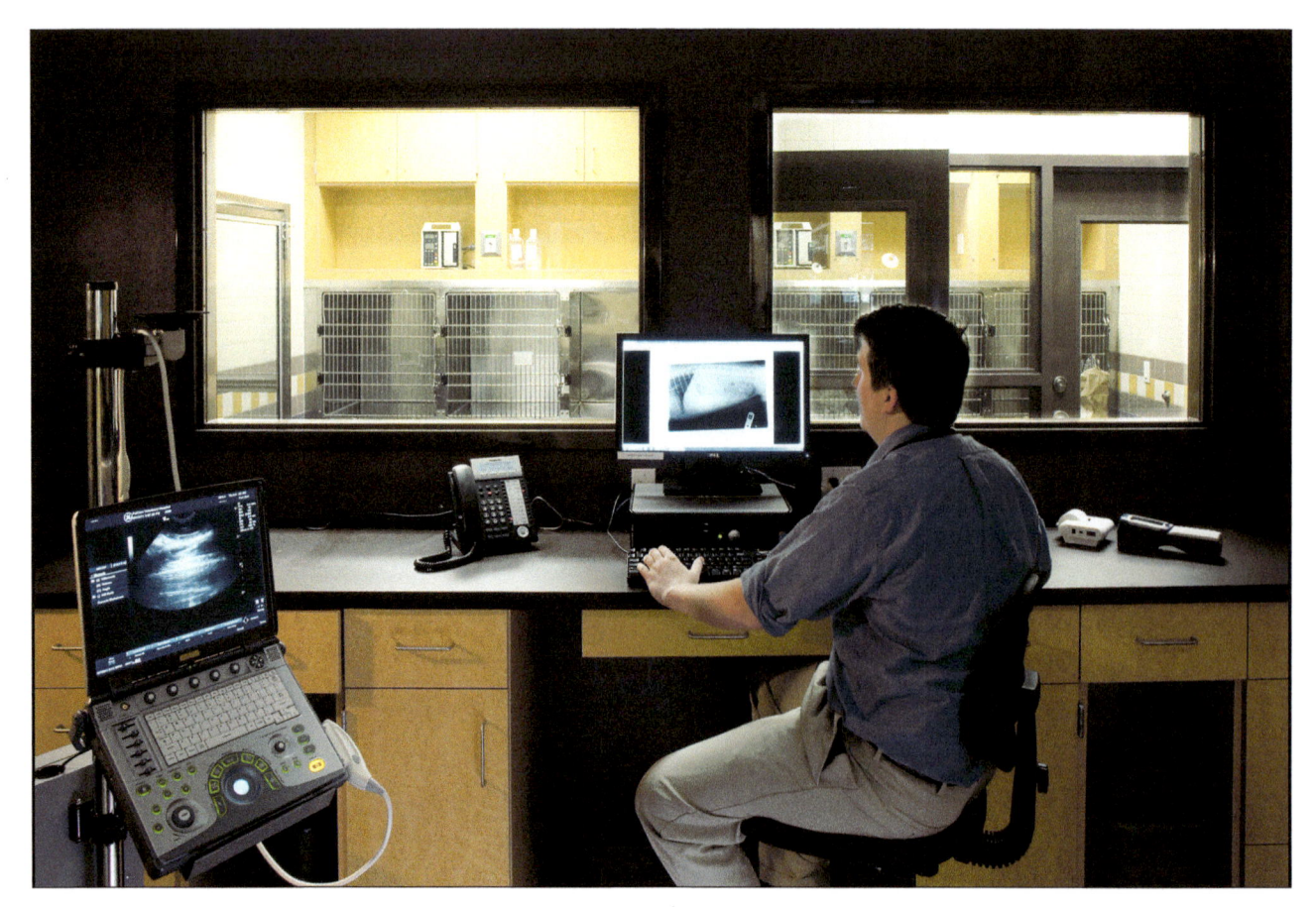

(Foto Imagery / Tim Murphy. Courtesy of VCA PetCare Veterinary Hospital, Santa Rosa, California [VCA, Inc.].)

be difficult to see into animal caging because the cages themselves block the light. To counteract this problem, place light fixtures close to the cages at an appropriate angle so that light can enter the front of the cages and reach into their interiors. It is ideal to be able to dim this light when it is desirable to keep the patients calm.

- In the future, cages may be individually lit. Some caging already allows for this feature.

Under-cabinet lighting used for task lighting. (Foto Imagery / Tim Murphy. Courtesy of Upstate Veterinary Specialists and Emergency Clinic, Asheville, North Carolina.)

Individual cage lighting can be even more helpful in specific spaces such as ICU, where it is important to keep a watchful eye on patients.

- Place lighting on either side of work surfaces such as exam tables and treatment tables in order to achieve cross lighting at the table. This helps to reduce shadows and provides an even lighting distribution.

- Use task lighting at desks by providing a small desk lamp. This technique concentrates the lighting where it is needed and allows the overall space to be less brightly lit.

- Use under-cabinet lighting for high-use areas such as the laboratory. This is another example of efficient task lighting.

LIGHTING EFFICIENCY

Efficient lighting fixtures are becoming increasingly important under today's building and energy codes. The term "efficacy" describes the light output (lumens [lm]) per unit of energy consumed (watts [W]) for a typical type of light fixture. Using this measure, a typical incandescent lamp has a very poor efficacy (approximately 16 lm per W [lm/W]). For this reason, incandescent lighting has not been used in commercial construction for some time. An equivalent fluorescent lamp has an efficacy of 60 to 100 lm/W and lasts about ten times longer than an incandescent bulb. Fluorescents are still used in commercial construction, although they will be used less frequently in the future.

LIGHTING DESIGN

The trend is to use light-emitting diode (LED) lighting for current and future commercial construction. LED lamps are indirectly mandated by code in certain jurisdictions. In other words, you may find that it is not possible to achieve the recommended veterinary illumination levels without using LED lighting, as the energy codes limit the number of watts that can be used overall. A typical LED lamp currently has an efficacy of anywhere from 60 to 120 lm/W and lasts 10 to 30 times longer than an incandescent lamp, according to the US Energy Information Administration. LED lighting is also rapidly advancing and is expected to improve to an upper limit of around 220 lm/W.

Fortunately, LED lighting is generally more pleasant than fluorescent lighting and can have better color balance. It can also be more easily controlled than fluorescent lighting. LED lighting offers many other advantages as well:

- It eliminates buzzing and flickering. Older fluorescent fixtures, particularly those with magnetic ballasts, often emit a buzzing sound and produce a noticeable flicker. Even if we can't hear these noises, animals can. Cats and dogs can also perceive flicker more easily because of differences between their eyesight and human eyesight. Flickering has been proven to cause a variety of health problems in humans, from seizures in certain individuals to general health effects such as headaches and problems with alertness. LED fixtures utilize a solid-state lighting technology that uses a driver to convert AC current to DC current within the fixture to power the LEDs. As a result, LED lighting fixtures do not flicker or buzz but simply produce even lighting distribution.

- Because of the driver that is already included in LED fixtures, they can be dimmed more easily than lighting using previous technologies. Dimming is achieved by reducing the DC current through them. LED fixtures easily accommodate dimming within individual fixtures without large cost increases.

- LED lighting is more compatible with the way dogs and cats see. While cats have trichromatic vision and dogs have dichromatic vision, neither species can see the lower end of the human visible spectrum, including oranges and reds. They do, however, see into the ultraviolet (UVA) end of the spectrum. LED lighting fixtures can produce a more balanced, whiter light that is closer to the blue end of the visible spectrum. This means that dogs and cats will perceive colors to be truer and more natural under LED lighting than under other types of artificial lighting.

- LED lighting is more like natural sunlight. In the chart, note the distribution of spectra produced by various types of lighting in comparison to natural sunlight. While LED lighting does have a strong peak in the far blue end of the visible spectrum, it is generally more evenly distributed across the visible spectrum than fluorescent lighting. In fact, it is apparent why fluorescent lighting feels so unnatural to many people; it has strong spectral peaks and valleys that make it feel harsh and alien to our eyes—and to the eyes of animals.

The bottom line is that LED is the lighting of the future for commercial buildings. We are fortunate that this superior technology is so compatible with veterinary care.

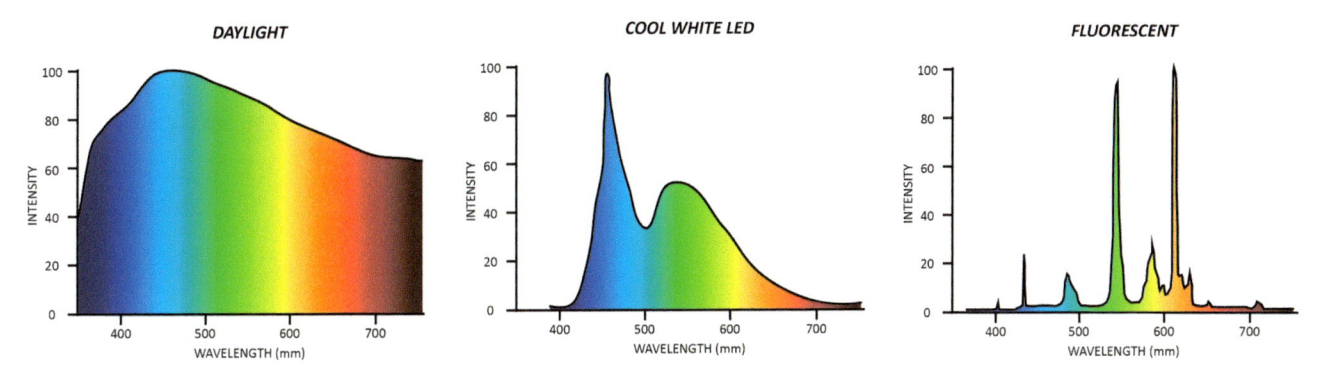

The spectra in the illustrations above show how much closer LED light is to natural daylight than fluorescent lighting is.

LED lighting in this lobby mimics the color and feel of daylight. (Thomas Winter Photography. Courtesy of VCA Hillsboro Animal Hospital, Coconut Creek, Florida [VCA, Inc.].)

COLOR TEMPERATURE

One of the questions you may have if you are selecting lighting fixtures for your building is how to interpret the term "color temperature." If you have been to the home improvement store lately, you have probably noticed that some light fixtures are marketed as "cool" and others as "warm," even within the same lighting technology. The color temperature of the lighting,

LIGHTING DESIGN 271

in technical terms, is the temperature at which an ideal black-body radiation source would emit light of a comparable hue to that light source. Color temperature is measured in kelvins (K). Unless you have a physics background, that explanation may not make much sense. All you need to know is that color temperatures from 4,000K to 5,000K are perceived as cool (more bluish), while color temperatures from 2,700K to 3,000K are perceived as warm (more yellowish or reddish). At a home improvement store, LED bulbs of about 2,700K are marketed as warm, and LED bulbs of about 5,000K are marketed as cool.

When incandescent lighting was the main source of lighting in our homes, most veterinarians also preferred warmer lighting in their hospitals. Now that home lighting is being replaced with fluorescent and LED technologies, people are becoming more accustomed to cooler, whiter light. Fortunately, cooler lighting is also more like sunlight. The sun emits a color temperature that is measured on Earth at about 5,800K.

While a warmer color temperature is often preferred and can be more comforting, using a color temperature on the cooler and whiter side, around 4,000K, will make your veterinary space feel cleaner and brighter. This lighting will also integrate better with daylight. This is particularly important because integrating daylight is a critical concept for a comfortable and effective hospital design.

If you're using more than one type of lighting fixture in a space, be sure that the fixtures are lamped with bulbs producing equivalent color temperatures. Variations in color temperatures throughout a hospital will feel visually discordant.

The one special case for introducing fixtures of different color temperatures within the same hospital is in the dermatology suite or alcove. Sometimes it is easier to see skin lesions with lighting of one color temperature than it is with another. Providing warm and cool light within the same space can create a superior examination space for this specialty.

INTEGRATING DAYLIGHT

There are many good reasons to integrate natural daylight into your hospital design strategy. From a practical standpoint, daylighting can reduce your energy consumption. Daylight has an efficacy of anywhere between 90 and 130 lm/W outside and up to 220 lm/W inside, making it more efficient than any artificial light source. Introducing natural daylight is also a good way to create more natural environments that are more connected with the world outside the hospital.

Your architect can assist you with integrating daylight into a hospital design. Ideally, daylighting opportunities will be considered from the beginning. In Northern Hemisphere locations, take the following into account:

- Appropriately size and place windows on the south side of the building and include shading-control elements that allow low winter sun to enter but shield the interior from high summer sun.

- Introduce northern lighting high on the wall or through high windows to bring in the soft, white, neutral lighting that occurs on the north side of structures.

- Minimize and appropriately place openings on the east and west sides of the building to minimize heat gain. However, windows on the east side are useful for certain spaces that benefit from warm morning sun, such as staff break rooms.

- Daylighting strategies work best when the light penetrates deeper into the interior space, allowing for softer, more diffuse lighting. High windows, combined with strategies such as light shelves, can bounce light off the ceiling, bringing the daylight deeper into workspaces. (A "light shelf" is a horizontal surface, usually above eye level, that reflects daylight into the space.)

- Avoid direct solar beams on work surfaces to reduce glare.

Veterinary hospitals are not the easiest building types for integration of daylighting strategies. They tend to be driven by operational considerations over other considerations. While it is a good idea to keep daylight strategies in mind when developing your plans, there will likely be at least one feature that is not optimally located based on what works internally. For example, a hospital may need to locate its front door based on how traffic approaches rather than on what is best for the daylighting design. Hospitals also tend to have bulky footprints. The larger a hospital is, the more difficult it is to get daylight into the interior from the perimeter. In some cases, you may find that daylighting from above is a useful strategy.

Many projects default to utilizing skylights and tubular daylight systems (also known as light tubes or solar tubes). The issue with skylights is that poor-quality skylights can introduce heat and glare into the space and cause additional heat loss at night. If you choose to incorporate skylights, select ones designed to minimize glare and heat gain. Translucent insulated panels work best for this purpose. Tubular daylight systems bring light from the roof down in reflective tubes. They work well but almost always give an underwhelming psychological impression to the building occupants, as they often look like banal, glowing light fixtures on the ceiling. Despite this, they still provide the physiological benefit of natural daylight to both people and animals. Tubular daylight systems are also generally pretty easy to integrate into a variety of roof geometries.

When a hospital is well designed for utilizing daylight, it becomes reasonable to turn artificial light fixtures off, at least during some portions of the day. This can be done manually or can be mandated by building codes. You should be aware of this potential code requirement, because occasionally daylight sensors can work against hospital operations. A good example is a surgery room, where operational requirements trump energy conservation. In human healthcare, this type of priority is understood and codified. Animal healthcare does not have the benefit of codified standards, so your team may need to ask for certain exceptions from building code officials, using human healthcare environments as a reference.

CLIMATE AND LIGHTING DECISIONS

The movement to reduce energy and integrate daylight into design is creating healthier, more pleasant indoor environments. While your hospital is likely to be a more comfortable workspace than one that was designed thirty years ago, it is still important to use discretion, as dictated by your climate, with any of these ideas.

For example, in a hot locale such as Arizona, it is very important to minimize or shade openings to the west. The sun is so brutally hot, and the light so intense, that daylight must be integrated into the work environment with a certain finesse. On the other extreme, in far northern locales, north-facing windows may simply lose more energy than they provide. You may have noticed an unpleasant chill if your workspace has ever been adjacent to a shaded, north-facing window. In cold climates, maximize southern exposures to take advantage of passive warmth on sunny winter days and use high-performance glazing (and seal the windows carefully) to prevent the chill on overcast days.

THE FUTURE OF LIGHTING DESIGN

We are entering an exciting frontier for lighting in commercial buildings. The term "human-centric lighting" is just entering our vocabulary. This is the science of matching lighting to human vision and perception, human physiology, and human comfort. As this field is developed, those of us in animal healthcare should apply what is understood about the biological and physiological differences between humans and animals to create lighting environments that specifically support the wellbeing and comfort of animals.

CHAPTER 48

FLOORING

"What is the best flooring for my veterinary hospital?" This is one of the most commonly asked hospital design questions. Because there are so many options, flooring can be a difficult decision to make. Many veterinarians and their team members have heard about flooring failures and fear making the wrong decision. Fortunately, we can also learn from thousands of successful veterinary flooring installations. This chapter outlines the basics of selecting the best flooring products for your hospital.

THE MECHANICS OF FLOORING FAILURE

It is helpful to examine the hows and whys of flooring failures before jumping into the many available flooring options.

Seamless flooring products are common and appropriate for veterinary hospitals because they are sanitary and easy to clean. However, they are also more prone to failure because they are not breathable. In order to avoid an expensive mistake, it is important to understand the causes and mechanics of floor product failures:

- Changes to chemical formulation: For decades, floors adhered better to their substrates because they were manufactured with solvent-based adhesives and formulations. Solvent-based products were replaced over time with water-based products as a result of the environmental laws regulating volatile organic compounds (VOCs) enacted in 1999.

- Vapor drive: When there is a moisture vapor gradient, moisture vapor will migrate toward areas that are less humid. The inside of a building is usually cooled and dried by an air conditioning system. This means that even in dry climates, moisture will tend to migrate through the damp underlying earth and find its way through a concrete slab, where it will be trapped by seamless flooring products. This moisture has a very high pH, as it typically brings with it the alkali salts (calcium hydroxide and sodium hydroxide) that are contained within the concrete slab. The resulting basic mixture may re-emulsify the water-based adhesives or low-VOC formulations of many flooring products, causing the floor to delaminate from the substrate.

- Lack of knowledge about vapor barriers: To combat these phenomena, designers began specifying plastic vapor barriers under slabs to prevent moisture migration. Unfortunately, the thin 6-mil vapor barriers that were specified in the past do not stop enough moisture migration to be effective. Failures may occur years after the flooring products are installed and long after the manufacturer's warranty expires. (For further reading, see the document from the American Concrete Institute titled "302.2R-06: Guide for Concrete Slabs That Receive Moisture-Sensitive Flooring Materials.")

Flooring failures can be dramatic and difficult for everyone involved. Over the past fifteen years, industry groups, building scientists, and product manufacturers have made a tremendous effort to get ahead of the flooring failure problem. This effort has resulted in the following standard recommendations:

- Specify a 15-mil, Class A polyolefin vapor barrier that complies with less than 0.01 Perm, which is a rating of the vapor permeance of the material. The polyolefin material is more chemically stable than polyethylene sheeting, and the 15-mil thickness is required to ensure the vapor barrier does not get unnecessarily punctured during installation. Vapor barriers should be installed according to the manufacturer's instructions.

- The concrete slab should be placed directly on top of the vapor barrier. Because the slab will release mix water from one side when placed directly on a vapor barrier, experts advise that the water-to-cement ratio of the slab should be lowered to 0.45, which is slightly lower than typical. This mix will cure more evenly and more quickly than wetter concrete.

- The slab should be tested for moisture vapor emission prior to installation of any seamless flooring product, according to the manufacturer's written instructions. The most pertinent test of a slab is a relative humidity test that uses a wet bulb thermometer inserted into the concrete slab.

- If a slab is too wet to comply with the manufacturer's requirements, architects should seek assistance from the manufacturer. Topical vapor barriers may be added to the slab to reduce moisture vapor emissions so the flooring material can be installed.

The bottom line is that successful flooring installations depend on a team effort. The architect, contractor, flooring installer, and manufacturer must work together to make sure the slab is designed and installed properly, prepped properly, and ready for the installation of the chosen seamless floor.

FLOORING FOR HEAVILY CLEANED AREAS

The most limiting factor for flooring materials is their ability or inability to stand up to the use of water. This is why it is important to identify the hose-down areas of the hospital before you choose your flooring. Floor choices are limited to three types of products in these areas:

- Exposed concrete floors.
- Resinous products (epoxy, urethane, acrylic).
- Tile.

Of these three choices, exposing the concrete is by far the most economical approach. Before embracing this solution, however, consider that exposed concrete is porous and less sanitary than the other choices. All concrete slabs crack, and cracks may add to an unsanitary condition. Also consider the way the concrete floor will meet the wall. This joint must be easy to clean and waterproof.

Of the other two choices, most people agree that properly installed resinous products are the best products for hose-down areas. The problem with these products is that they are difficult to predict, as they depend on so many variables, from their chemical composition to the installation method. To add to the confusion, the products are always changing. This is why general rules are more useful than specific advice when it comes to choosing high-performance resinous flooring products:

- Resinous floors come in three basic chemical compositions: epoxy resin, urethane resin, and acrylic resin (also known as MMA, for methyl methacrylate). Most hospitals use epoxy or urethane resin floors. Acrylic floors dry very quickly, but they require very experienced installers and tend to be more expensive and are therefore used infrequently.

- Regardless of whether your project uses epoxy or urethane resins, use the thicker products. Thin products will fail under constant impact, hosing, and chemicals. The best veterinary products are 3/16 of an inch or more thick.

- If you plan to clean with hot water, use a urethane-based product instead of an epoxy-based product, as epoxies cannot withstand thermal shock.

- The top coat of either an epoxy- or urethane-based product must be urethane. Epoxies yellow in the presence of uric acid.

- Have the manufacturer provide physical samples of the standard floor textures. Smooth floors can be too slippery. Rough floors can be difficult to clean. A physical sample can help you decide how textured the floor should be.

- For reasons of durability and sanitation, resinous floors should be installed with a "coved" base, which means the product is troweled up onto the wall a number of inches. If possible, the top of this base should be "keyed in" to the wall substrate to provide a durable and thick termination that will survive the test of time. A coved base is labor intensive and will add to the overall cost of the floor installation.

USING TILE EFFECTIVELY

Properly specified, installed, and grouted tile floors are excellent for veterinary projects. For some projects, including renovations over existing concrete slabs that may or may not have effective vapor barriers, they are the superior choice, because they are far less prone to moisture failure than other durable floor products. A leveling and patching compound can be applied prior to a tile installation to cover a variety of slab irregularities. Therefore, tile is a great choice for a difficult remodeling project. Another benefit of tile is that it can be installed in sections and does not off-gas during installation, so it can be installed while a building is occupied.

If tile may be right for your project, shop for color-body or through-body porcelain floor tiles over any other type of tile. Porcelain tile is extremely durable. Porcelain tiles come in

Wood-look plank tiles give this lobby a warm, natural feel. (Courtesy of Four Seasons Veterinary Specialists, Loveland, Colorado.)

278 PRACTICAL GUIDE TO VETERINARY HOSPITAL DESIGN

a variety of sizes, from small 1 × 1-inch mosaic floor tiles to oversize tiles that may be up to 48 inches wide. Tiles also come in wood-look plank sizes. For most projects, avoid the extremely large sizes, as they are more prone to breakage. For floors that slope to a drain, choose smaller sizes to avoid the complexity of cutting numerous tiles to fit a floor slope.

You will also want to choose a tile with a smooth finish, but be careful that it does not become slick when wet. Measurements of "coefficient of friction" (COF)—which calculate the amount of resistance a surface exerts on anything moving over it—are confusing to building owners and designers alike. These measurements are currently in flux in the industry. The best source of information is the tile manufacturer's technical representative, who can recommend a tile product that is both cleanable and slip resistant.

Many people worry about grout. This is a legitimate concern, as grout can compromise the sanitation of a tile floor. For a sanitary and cleanable floor tile installation, use a 100% solids industrial epoxy grout. This type of grout requires an experienced tile installer.

FLOORING FOR MEDICAL AREAS

Although it is acceptable to install resinous or tile flooring in medical areas, many hospital

The flooring in this treatment space was installed with 100% solids epoxy grout to ensure proper sanitation in the room. (Foto Imagery / Tim Murphy. Courtesy of VCA PetCare Veterinary Hospital, Santa Rosa, California [VCA, Inc.].)

owners choose to select a less expensive product for these areas, as sanitation is still the primary driver of product selection. To comply with AAHA accreditation standard SX07d, flooring in surgical prep and surgical areas must be made of smooth, nonporous materials that are easy to clean and maintain (AAHA, 14). Sanitary and affordable products include these:

- Sheet vinyl.
- Sheet safety vinyl.
- Sheet rubber.
- Sheet linoleum.

Sheet vinyl (also generically encompassing PVC flooring) must be heat welded for long-term performance of the seams. Choose a high-quality commercial sheet vinyl with a pre-finished top surface. Be careful about choosing products designed for human healthcare facilities, as some of these are made to be waxed on a more regular schedule than most veterinary hospitals can afford.

Safety vinyls are sheet vinyl floors that incorporate aluminum oxide particles for slip resistance. These products used to be difficult to clean, but newer safety vinyls have more moderate textures and can be specified with clear

The owners of this hospital chose a wood-look vinyl for their rural hospital, which is coved and heat welded at the seams. (Edmunds Studios, Inc. Courtesy of Veterinary Village, Lomira, Wisconsin.)

aluminum oxide particles that do not detract from the aesthetics of the floor. Safety vinyls are excellent in certain applications, such as in dog training rooms, ramps, and walking surfaces, and in other generally dry areas that need some level of safety and slip resistance.

Sheet rubber products are made from naturally derived virgin rubber. Rubber flooring is naturally slip resistant, comfortable to stand on, and antimicrobial; it is also the only product that has inherent noise-reduction properties. It is a great product, but it does have a couple of shortcomings. First, it is more expensive than vinyl, so it often gets culled from projects during a value engineering process. Second, and more seriously, it is very moisture sensitive and can bubble in the presence of vapor pressure under the slab. Careful testing must be done prior to installation of this product.

Linoleum is assembled from tree resin, linseed oil, wood flour, and calcium carbonate over a jute backing. As a product made from natural materials that are byproducts of wood manufacturing, it is a greener product that may be used in place of vinyl in a veterinary hospital. Linoleum must be installed by a qualified installer. It can be seamed and coved up the wall like other medical flooring products, and it is also used in human hospital settings. The primary concerns veterinarians may have about linoleum are that the product must be cleaned more gently than some other products and it does not hold up well in the presence of water. Linoleum also costs more than sheet vinyl.

All sheet products benefit from periodic waxing or installation of a manufacturer's finish wear surface. Rubber floors can be left unwaxed, and they will get harder and glossier over time.

FLOORING FOR OTHER AREAS OF THE HOSPITAL

Concrete

In areas of the hospital where sanitation is less critical, practices have more options. Stained and sealed concrete floors are popular and inexpensive. Like sealed concrete, stained and sealed concrete will expose cracks and joints in the concrete surface. Stained floors can look very irregular and more like the floor of a coffee shop than a hospital, so it is important to adjust your expectations before choosing this product.

Stained and sealed concrete floors are not recommended in hose-down areas, as the stain will wear off over time. Integrally colored concrete integrates color into the concrete mix. If colored concrete is aesthetically important to the project, this is a more durable option.

Polished concrete floors are buffed with resins and mechanical action for a smooth, mirror-like surface. Polished concrete is popular in grocery stores and car dealerships. Some veterinary hospitals install them, but they can be both physically and psychologically slippery, so use caution when specifying this product. Fortunately, the polishing process does yield a more sanitary, sealed surface.

Carpet

Carpet is not an appropriate choice for any area where animals will be present because it is not very cleanable. However, some hospitals do use carpet in offices and conference rooms. Of the products on the market, the best ones are vinyl-backed carpets, as they are much easier to clean than carpets with traditional carpet pads. Vinyl-backed carpets are also used in schools and nursing care settings.

The stained and sealed concrete floor in this reception area plays off well against the wood-clad ceiling. (Foto Imagery / Tim Murphy. Courtesy of Woodhaven Veterinary Clinic, Edmonds, Washington.)

Recycled Rubber

Recycled rubber tile and sheet products are granulated rubber adhered with resins. These products are porous and not recommended for medical areas, but they may be used as an inexpensive floor cover in dry rehabilitation rooms and large recreational spaces where healthy animals are playing.

Vinyl Tile

Vinyl tile is a common, inexpensive flooring product often used in inexpensive office buildings, grocery stores, and drugstores. Typically the tiles measure 12 × 12 inches. Vinyl tile is brittle and requires frequent waxing, and its numerous joints and short lifespan make it a less popular choice for most veterinary hospitals. It is not sanitary enough to use in medical areas, and it performs poorly in the presence of moisture or water.

Vinyl Plank

Vinyl plank floors, also known as luxury vinyl tile, or LVT, are growing in popularity. The planks are thick and made to look like wood and snap together tightly to create a more monolithic finished surface than would be expected given the numerous seams. It is accept-

Product Families	Cost	Sanitation	Slip Resistance	Durability	Lifespan	Wet Area Use	Maintenance	Notes
Concrete Products								
Sealed Concrete	$	N	P	N	N	G	Yearly Reseal	Seal Visible Floor Cracks
Stained/Sealed Concrete	$$	N	P	P	P	N	Yearly Reseal	Seal Visible Floor Cracks
Colored/Sealed Concrete	$$	N	P	N	G	G	Yearly Reseal	Seal Visible Floor Cracks
Polished Concrete	$$$	N	P	G	G	P	Periodic Reseal	Seal Visible Floor Cracks
Resilient Tile and Plank								
Vinyl Tile	$$	P	N	P	P	B	Three Month Wax	
Vinyl Planks	$$$	P	N	N	N	P	Periodic Finish Restorer	
Rubber Tile	$$$	N	G	N	N	P	Periodic Floor Finisher	
Recycled Rubber Tile	$	P	E	N	N	P	Cleaning Only	Not Sanitary for Medical Use
Carpet								
Broadloom Carpet	$	P	G	P	P	B	Clean and Stain Protector	Not Recommended
Carpet Tile	$$	P	G	P	P	B	Clean and Stain Protector	Office Areas Only
Vinyl-Backed Carpet	$$$	P	G	N	N	B	Cleaning Only	Office Areas Only
Sheet Flooring								
Vinyl	$$	G	N	N	P	P	Six Month Wax	Flash Cove Base in Sanitary Areas
Safety Vinyl	$$$	N	E	G	G	N	Six Month Wax	Flash Cove Base in Sanitary Areas
Sheet Rubber	$$$	G	G	G	N	P	Periodic Floor Finisher	Flash Cove Base in Sanitary Areas
Recycled Sheet Rubber	$	N	E	N	N	N	Cleaning Only	Not Sanitary for Medical Use
Sheet Linoleum	$$$	G	N	N	P	B	Six Month Floor Finisher	Flash Cove Base in Sanitary Areas
Resinous Flooring								
Broadcast Epoxy	$$$	E	N	G	G	G	Re-Apply Top Coat +/- 10 Years	Integral Base in Sanitary Areas
Troweled Epoxy	$$$	E	N	E	G	G	Re-Apply Top Coat +/- 10 Years	Integral Base in Sanitary Areas
Self-Leveling Urethane	$$$	E	N	E	G	G	Re-Apply Top Coat +/- 10 Years	Integral Base in Sanitary Areas
Cement Urethane	$$$$	E	N	E	E	G	Re-Apply Top Coat +/- 10 Years	Integral Base in Sanitary Areas
Acrylic (MMA)	$$$$	E	P	E	G	G	Re-Apply Top Coat +/- 10 Years	Integral Base in Sanitary Areas
Tile								
Porcelain Tile	$$$$	G	N	E	E	G	Cleaning Only	Use 100% Solids Epoxy Grout
Ceramic Tile	$$	N	P	N	N	N	Cleaning Only	Not Recommended

Key	
E	Excellent
G	Good
N	Neutral
P	Poor
B	Bad

able to use this product in the lobby and office areas, but it is not sanitary enough for medical areas.

For a summary of the numerous flooring materials and their relative costs and features, see the chart. Use this chart as a tool for selecting the right product for your application.

AVOID COMMON MISTAKES

Despite the knowledge available to architects and veterinarians about flooring selection, some mistakes are more common than others. Here are five typical errors that are made in flooring selection for veterinary hospitals:

- Using paint on a horizontal surface: Any product that is paint-like, including rolled garage flooring, is not durable enough for the horizontal floor surfaces of a veterinary hospital. Hundreds of practices have learned this the hard way.

- Using residential-grade products: Products purchased at home improvement stores or from residential product lines are not durable enough to hold up to the wear and

FLOORING 283

tear that veterinary hospitals receive. It is important to select commercial-grade products for every hospital project.

- Installing without testing: It is easy to assume that an existing slab will be fine for the installation of a new product, but without the flooring manufacturer's involvement, this is just an assumption. If something goes wrong and no testing was done, the manufacturer's warranties will be invalid. This is why it is so important to have all floors tested and inspected prior to the installation of new products.

- Installing very light-colored floors and grout: Veterinary hospitals do not have the maintenance budgets of human hospitals, so it is best to set aside a desire for a highly aseptic look and to choose products that have some color. Color helps to hide a few scuffs and scratches. Similarly, it is best to use richly colored grout products. Even epoxy grout will collect dirt and dust.

- Using products that are misaligned with desired cleaning protocols: For example, if it is important to the hospital to bleach the floor in the isolation room, then the floor material selected for this room must stand up to the use of bleach.

Overall, while veterinary projects are challenging, flooring choices become clearer as the parameters are defined. For remodels, tile floors are often the best choice. For projects with budgetary constraints and an urban aesthetic, owners may choose concrete floors. For the most sanitary and durable hose-down conditions, resinous floor products are a clear favorite. And for an affordable and sanitary approach to medical areas, a sheet product such as heat-welded vinyl with a flash-coved base is a tried-and-true solution.

▼ ▼ ▼

INVOLVE YOUR TEAM in flooring decisions. Once you have made preliminary choices, contact the manufacturers of the products that interest you. These professionals will represent the products, answer your questions, and help you ensure a successful installation.

CHAPTER

49

WALLS AND CEILINGS

While flooring is typically the material asked about most often when it comes to hospital design, wall and ceiling materials should not be overlooked. Due to the high level of use and abuse that veterinary hospital finishes suffer, it is important to ensure that all of the materials you install are appropriate for the space and the amount of wear and tear they will receive. For example, in hose-down or wet animal housing areas, a waterproof wall system and moisture-resistant ceiling finishes are imperative. Even in some of the more standard-use areas, it is important to keep the small details in mind, such as using paint that is both cleanable and durable.

INTERIOR WALL FINISHES AND MATERIALS

Interior wall finishes include paints, integral wall materials such as glazed block, and materials that can be applied to walls to make a wainscot, such as vinyl wall coverings.

Painted Coatings

In a veterinary hospital, walls are typically constructed out of wood or metal studs with drywall on each side and the appropriate paint, finish, or wall covering over the drywall. It is perfectly acceptable to specify a commercial-grade, latex-based paint or coating for the front of the hospital. This will create a cost-effective and functional finish that can be easily wiped down. However, latex paint should not be used in medical wards and run areas or in spaces that are hosed down or require higher levels of cleaning.

In the medical spaces and nonhosed wards, consider using a slightly more durable and cleanable paint option, such as a water-based, epoxy, high-performance coating. On masonry walls in run areas, where the walls will be exposed to daily hosing, use a high-build, high-performance organic instead that is recommended by your industrial coatings representative.

Other Wall Materials and Treatments

In animal housing areas or very high-use areas, walls may be constructed of concrete masonry units (CMUs). When using CMUs, the proper paint finish should be specified as described above under "Painted Coatings." However, there are a couple of other block units that can be used that have a more aesthetic feel to them.

The first is glazed block. Glazed block is a very durable, maintenance-free wall material. The block is a regular gray block of concrete masonry with a permanently bonded, glazed face on one or more sides of the block. It comes in a wide variety of colors, much like tile, and is a good material for wards and run areas. Use glazed block in conjunction with epoxy grout for a wall that is resistant to stains and odors.

The second type of more aesthetically pleasing block is glass block. Glass block is a good material to use in exterior walls where you wish to let in light but also restrict views and maintain durability. Glass block works well in wards and run rooms.

Tile over cement backer board and waterproofing is a tried-and-true solution for heavily used walls in runs and wards as well as in restrooms. As with all tile installations, specify an epoxy grout to ensure it is sanitary. Not only does tile provide a waterproof finish material, but it also provides a higher-end, aesthetically pleasing look in your wards and boarding spaces.

Wall Protection

If some wall protection is required in the front and working areas of the hospital, using a simple vinyl wall covering to about half height on the walls will be the most cost effective while still being sufficient to provide a light level of protection. This can be used in lieu of wainscoting to provide wall protection in the medium-traffic areas of the hospital that take lower levels of use and abuse. Be sure to use a healthcare-quality product so it lasts longer.

Instead of a generic vinyl wall covering, a rigid PVC covering—a heavy-duty, semirigid vinyl—can be used. This material is resistant to bumps from handcarts and equipment. It can also be used as a wainscot. It is usually applied directly over drywall, but it can also be applied over plywood or particleboard. Because rigid PVC is flexible, it can also be formed around curves, and because it is textured, it doesn't show scratches. It is available in a wide range of colors, trim pieces, corner guards, and rails that are compatible with most contemporary interior color schemes.

Glassboard, or fiberglass-reinforced plastic (FRP), is a virtually indestructible plastic panel that can be used for wainscoting or full-height walls. It is used most extensively in commercial kitchens and food processing plants. Unfortunately, it is not the most visually appealing material. Therefore, it is often used in more utilitarian, back-of-house spaces, such as storage and utility areas. It should not be used in animal housing areas because, due to the frequent joints between panels, it is not very waterproof.

With any of the above finishes or wall protection options, install corner guards. Corner

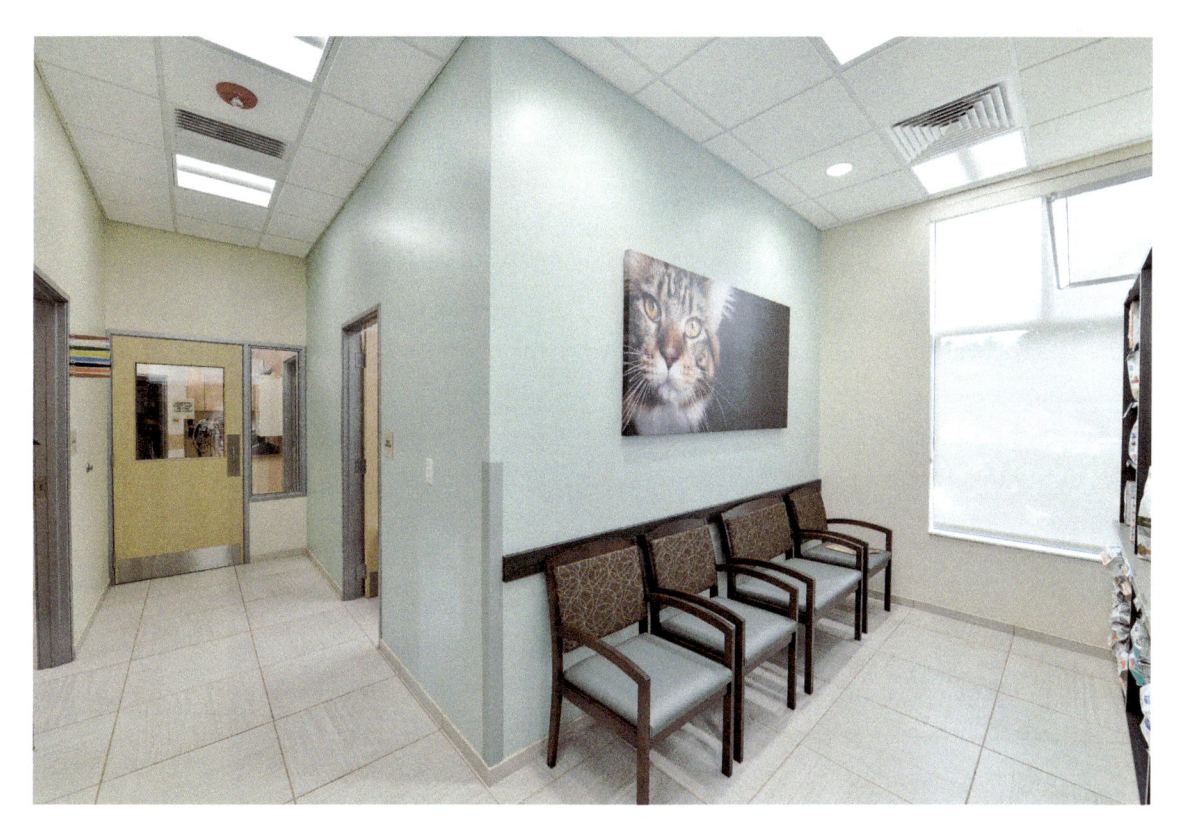

A PVC corner guard and plastic laminate (PLAM) chair rail provide aesthetically appealing wall protection in this lobby space. (Thomas Winter Photography. Courtesy of VCA Hillsboro Animal Hospital, Coconut Creek, Florida [VCA, Inc.].)

guards work great to defend against carts and dog leashes wearing away at those edges. They can be made from stainless steel or rigid PVC. Stainless steel corner guards have a crisp, sterile feel to them. Rigid PVC corner guards, in contrast, come in a large variety of colors that can usually be selected to match the PVC wainscoting or even the wall paint. They also have a softer look, as they tend to blend in with the wall. Either option works well to provide protection at the outside corners within your hospital.

CEILINGS

In a veterinary hospital, there are two basic types of commonly used ceilings: painted drywall ceilings and acoustical panel (tile) ceilings. Each has advantages and disadvantages, and each should be used where appropriate based on the function of the room or area of the hospital. When choosing a ceiling type, remember to consider both your lighting fixture options and the available height of the room based on the above-ceiling functions, such as ductwork and wiring that need to be accommodated.

Interior Ceiling Finishes

Most ceilings within a hospital are designed with acoustical panels suspended in a metal grid. Acoustical ceilings provide effective noise reduction and hide all the stuff that goes above the ceiling. They can be used throughout the hospital except in certain areas, such as surgery rooms, where drywall ceilings are preferred for sanitation reasons. They are available in designer styles, in panels with high sound-absorbing abilities, and in panels that can be used in high-moisture and clean-room areas. In choosing these materials, the most important quality to look for is a high Noise Reduction Coefficient (NRC) to assist in reducing reverberant noise in the rooms where the ceiling is installed. A general recommendation is to use panels with an NRC of 0.70 or greater, which means they absorb 70% of the reverberant sound that hits them. In damp rooms, use an aluminum grid to prevent rust stains and sag-resistant ceiling tiles.

There are some locations in your hospital where drywall ceilings are more appropriate than grid ceilings. One example would be in surgery rooms, where drywall can be used to promote sterility and to prevent ceiling fuzz from falling into your surgery space. Likewise, drywall ceilings work well in bathrooms, which have high cleaning needs. Other areas where drywall ceilings might be appropriate include tiny spaces, such as janitor closets, in storage areas, and featured areas such as dropped soffits over your reception desk. The downside to painted drywall ceilings is that they do not allow for flexibility or immediate access to the spaces above the ceiling, which can be important for maintenance issues involving mechanical duct work, overhead plumbing, and electrical wiring. They also do not absorb any noise; in fact, they can cause spaces to be louder due to the reverberation that they can sometimes cause.

Ceiling Heights

The most useful ceiling height for a hospital is 9 feet. Anything shorter than this makes the rooms feel oppressive, and anything taller makes it difficult to use ceiling-mounted equipment. However, there are exceptions to the 9-foot rule. The first is in larger rooms or spaces such as lobby areas or open treatment rooms. Here, the height of the ceiling should be raised to create the proper proportions in the space. The other area where ceiling height may vary or can be manipulated is in areas where you are trying to make a design statement. For example, while it is nice to have a higher ceiling in a reception area, you might consider dropping the ceiling over the reception desk to create a focal point.

Open Ceilings

In contrast to the typical drywall or acoustical tile ceilings that are generally used, there is one other option that can be considered in special cases. This is to leave a ceiling completely out of a space for an industrial-looking aesthetic. Consider the following before committing to an open ceiling:

- Open ceilings work well in high spaces with exposed steel joists. If you have a low space, or a wood-framed structure, then an open ceiling will not work well for your project.

- If you plan for the space to be open, your architect and structural engineer can specify acoustical metal decking, which is a roof-decking material that achieves an effective NRC.

- An open ceiling costs more than a grid ceiling. The plumbing, fire sprinkler, electrical, and mechanical work has to be installed neatly, and the round spiral duct associated with an open ceiling is more expensive than rectangular ductwork.

This suspended cloud ceiling was designed both to be architecturally interesting and to absorb noise in this conference room. (David Dietrich Photography. Courtesy of Upstate Veterinary Specialists and Emergency Clinic, Greenville, South Carolina.)

WALLS AND CEILINGS 289

- Consider how to mount infrastructure such as lighting fixtures, oxygen drops, etc. These may need to be mounted on walls and columns or on supports that are dropped below the joists.

- Be aware that an open grid will create some cleaning problems. Light fixtures should be designed with closed tops.

▼ ▼ ▼

IN THE END, your wall and ceiling materials and finishes are as critical to the quality, function, and experience of your hospital as any other surface. Remember to spend enough time envisioning each room and "walking on your ceiling" to imagine what you want to achieve.

CHAPTER 50

DOORS AND WINDOWS

Veterinary hospitals have evolved over time from light commercial buildings to specialized, high-performance buildings. When searching for performance door and window products, keep in mind that there are some tried-and-true solutions for complex facilities like veterinary hospitals. These solutions can be combined in ways that minimize costs, create a specific look, and place durable solutions where they are needed the most.

DOORS AND FRAME TYPES

Wood Doors

Many hospitals use solid-core, commercial-grade wood veneer doors. They are attractive and relatively affordable. Wood doors are appropriate for most locations in a hospital, with the exception of specialty doors or doors in hose-down locations. Wood doors can be stained or finished with a clear urethane. For uniform results, it is best to order them prefinished.

Wood doors can be prone to wear and tear. It helps to install a kickplate—a metal plate affixed to the bottom portion of the door to prevent damage from shoes, dogs, carts and gurneys, and floor-cleaning equipment.

Wood doors can sit in wood frames or metal frames. Metal frames are preferable for the wear and tear the frames will take in a veterinary hospital setting.

Hollow Metal Doors

Hollow metal doors are made of steel. As their name suggests, they are hollow inside, but the core of the door can be filled in the shop with insulation for fire resistance, thermal insulation, or sound insulation purposes. Hollow metal doors are extremely durable. They are used most often either when utility is the biggest driver of door selection or on the exterior of a building.

When hollow metal doors are used on the exterior of the building or in damp rooms, they should be shop galvanized (zinc coated) prior to being primed and painted; otherwise they will rust. There are several types of galvanized coatings. The one that is most practical for veterinary use is an A60 coating, which is a "galvannealed" coating that holds paint well. Hollow metal doors are painted on the jobsite after installation.

Hollow metal doors are framed with hollow metal frames. These frames are fully welded and assembled before they arrive at the project site. They must be set in place before or during the framing of the walls. Hollow metal frames can be coated with galvanized coatings and painted to match the hollow metal doors. Hollow metal frames can also be used as the frame for wood doors.

Aluminum Storefront Doors

Aluminum storefront doors are typically used on the exterior of buildings where a stylish storefront look is desired. They are constructed as a frame holding a piece of glass. Usually,

Storefront doors provide a crisp and open feel at the main entrance to this hospital. (Foto Imagery / Tim Murphy. Courtesy of VCA West Los Angeles Animal Hospital, Los Angeles California [VCA, Inc.].)

an aluminum storefront door is full glass from top to bottom. The frame is known as a "stile." Narrow stile doors look very classy because the frame is minimized. However, wide stiles that are at least 5.5 inches in dimension are more practical for mounting the types of durable door hardware sets that are required for veterinary hospitals.

Aluminum storefront doors are always set in aluminum storefront frames. These frames come in a variety of thicknesses. The most common thickness is 2 inches in width and 4.5 inches in depth.

Aluminum storefront doors can also be used in interior applications where doors are exposed to moisture frequently, such as on the front of a dog ward. In extremely wet locations, aluminum storefront doors tend to hold up over time better than hollow metal, which will eventually rust. The issue with using aluminum storefront doors is that the frames are designed to be set within an opening rather than to wrap the edge of an opening. This can create an opportunity for water intrusion. Therefore, if you plan on using this product inside, it must be detailed with care by your architect.

PRODUCTS FOR INTERIOR USE ONLY

There are a couple of commercial-grade products that are not appropriate for exterior use but are durable enough for interior use in a veterinary hospital. These are knock down (KD) steel doors and frames and interior aluminum doors and frames.

KD steel doors and frames are constructed of prefinished steel. They arrive at the project site disassembled and are assembled in each opening. The advantage of the frames is that they can be placed after the walls are finished, which sometimes helps speed up the sequence of construction. The doors and frames can be galvanized as well, and this is done in the shop prior to prefinishing. KD frames can also be used to frame wood doors, and this is a common assembly for veterinary spaces such as exam rooms.

Interior aluminum doors are lightweight, aluminum, office-front systems that can be used throughout a hospital. Like KD frames, these are assembled onsite and designed to wrap a finished opening. They can also hold either aluminum/glass doors or wood doors. Interior aluminum systems can be used for sliding doors and all glass openings to help create a minimalist aesthetic.

Sliding glass doors open this exam room up to treatment to make the space multifunctional. (Edmunds Studios, Inc. Courtesy of Veterinary Village, Lomira, Wisconsin.)

SPECIALTY DOORS AND OPENINGS

The following are the most common specialty doors and windows that may be used on veterinary projects.

Residential-Style Windows

For hospitals wanting less of a commercial look, the exterior windows can be a residential style. Of the products on the market, fiberglass windows that look like residential windows, but still have the durability inside and out of a commercial product, are the best option.

Sound Control Products

Around dog wards and other loud rooms where a view into the room is desired, sound control doors and windows may be used. This typically entails insulated doors, gaskets around the door opening, and double-glazed windows. Two layers of tempered glazing is preferable, rather than using laminated glass, which is not break resistant.

Lead-Lined Doors

For radiology rooms, hollow metal doors are most common. These can be lead lined to the coating thickness that is required for shielding the space. For spaces that need higher levels of shielding, such as doors to linear accelerator vaults, these doors are made specifically for the machine and its use and installation. The doors to these rooms are extremely heavy.

These commercial windows were crafted to add to the Old Florida style of this practice in Port St. Lucie, Florida. (Thomas Winter Photography. Courtesy of Morningside Animal Hospital, Port St. Lucie, Florida.)

Traffic Doors

Some hospitals like to use double-swing traffic doors like those typically seen in restaurant kitchens. Traffic doors can be made of stainless steel or they can be wood clad. They can contain large glass openings to make them more practical in a veterinary setting. While these doors are a joy to use because they are lightweight, self-closing, and extremely resistant to abuse, they do little to control noise because of the way they are constructed. Traffic doors are used most frequently for surgery suites. Keep in mind that they do not seal air well, so any hospital that is very fastidious about maintaining aseptic environments should consider other types of doors.

ICU Doors

Automatic sliding doors manufactured specifically for ICU settings save space and are a joy to have. However, they are extremely expensive, so price them before deciding to add them to your project.

NOTES ON DOOR HARDWARE

The door hardware in veterinary hospitals gets used hard and should be durable and functional. The best hardware for veterinary use should be heavy duty or extra heavy duty depending on the wear and tear expected for that particular door. Below are a few general rules for selecting door hardware:

- Avoid any door hardware that is mounted against the floor because it creates cleaning problems. Floor-mounted hardware also tends to rot over time from the cleaning products used on flooring.

- In rooms occupied by dogs, keep the hardware out of the way. For example, dogs love to eat rubber wall stops. What dog can resist a wall-mounted chew toy?

- Use gasketing around the door and a sweep at the bottom to control sound in rooms where sound control is important. Rubber sweeps are better than brush-type sweeps because they are easier to clean.

- Use metal kickplates or armor plates (stainless plates that extend half height on the door) in areas of high traffic.

- Avoid door handles that lift up or down to open, as large dogs can potentially manipulate them and escape.

▼ ▼ ▼

DURING THE DESIGN of your project, set aside time to carefully consider the doors, frames, and hardware. Identify all the special requirements of the door opening, such as "needs to be lead lined," so that your architect can select durable products where they are needed. In other locations, your choices may be guided by a balance of economy and aesthetics. In all cases, your hardware should be able to put up with a lot of use. If you select them carefully, your doors and windows will last you a lifetime.

CHAPTER 51

COLOR PALETTES

Everyone has a favorite color, but did you know that colors that appeal to you may appear dull or visually jarring to animals? This is important to consider when designing your veterinary hospital to cater to both your clients and your patients. Color theory and the science behind vision can guide you when making decisions about flooring, wall paints and coverings, and furnishings for your hospital. What type of mood are you trying to convey? Do you prefer something a little upbeat and trendy, or something warm and natural? The primary goal should be to create a sense of comfort and wellbeing.

Animals perceive their environments differently from humans. When choosing colors, keep in mind that dogs and cats do not see reds and oranges well. Instead, their vision extends into the ultraviolet spectrum of light. Humans do not see ultraviolet light, although it is possible to mimic the way a dog or cat sees it by shining an ultraviolet light over a surface. Because they can see in the ultraviolet spectrum, animals naturally see items that for humans fluoresce under UV light, namely, materials containing phosphorous, such as urine. These organic materials are unavoidable in veterinary hospitals, but it is possible to avoid compounding the issue. Materials that are predominantly white or clear that glow brightly in the UV spectrum can be visually unsettling to animals. These are particularly important to avoid in areas where caging or long-term occupation occurs.

CHOOSING A COLOR SCHEME

In order to design an environment that is comfortable for animals, choose light color schemes that are centered on the blue, green, or violet end of the spectrum, or a scheme that is inspired by nature. This allows animals to perceive their environment well even when the lights are dimmed or off. These colors also work well with a neutral base selection and can be accented with darker furnishings.

In color theory, humans often associate certain colors with certain emotions. For example, the human eye is most attracted to the color red and associates it with strong emotional feelings as well as active thought processing. Following along this end of the spectrum, orange and yellow are happy associative colors that can brighten a room. For dogs and cats, however, these colors will be perceived in the dull gray range, which will make it difficult for them to differentiate surfaces. The red-orange-yellow end of the spectrum is warm. These colors are better as accent colors than as base colors.

On the opposite end of the spectrum are the cool colors, which are better base colors when paired with neutral colors. People associate

A lobby space designed with natural tones to bring the outside in. The wood cladding from the exterior of the building flows into the space, which is accented with warm yellow paint. (Foto Imagery / Tim Murphy. Courtesy of VCA PetCare Veterinary Hospital, Santa Rosa, California [VCA, Inc.].)

COLOR PALETTES

This hospital wanted to evoke a calming, spa-like feel by using greens, blues, purples, and grays in their color scheme. (Posh Pooch Portraits. Courtesy of Adobe Animal Hospital, Los Altos, California.)

green with nature. It creates a peaceful environment with a sense of wellness and mindfulness. Blue and violet are also more emotionally calming and can help to reduce stress levels. These colors are preferable in the veterinary setting because they appear in lighter tones to animals and do not seem as abrasive as white or as dull as gray. By understanding and applying these ideas throughout your hospital, you can advertise your own practice philosophy, brand, and style to your clients and reduce stress in your patients.

Once you decide on a certain color scheme, many variations of tint, shade, and tone can provide some flexibility even in the more neutral shades. Neutral shades vary through the browns, grays, and light tints of colors. Brown tonal neutrals create an earthier aesthetic for a more traditional effect, although going too light or too dark with these can create a dulling visual effect. Grays are better at creating a more modern aesthetic with variations like charcoal, slate, or lighter cloudy colors. For example, blue is a great option for a primary color that can be paired with yellow as an accent color to create a complementary happy effect. To unify a room with a restrained color scheme and create some pizazz, choose decorative items such as paintings, photographs, or furnishings in the brighter accent color.

This practice opted to stick with a modern aesthetic, using gray tones throughout their hospital. They added this soft blue behind the reception desk as a complement to the overall feel. (Courtesy of Callbeck Animal Hospital, Whitby, Ontario.)

COLOR BEYOND THE WALLS

Color palette selections also include the finishes on cabinets and flooring, not just the painted walls. When making color choices, remember to harmonize colors with your material choices and the functions of your spaces. For example, as client-occupied spaces, your exam rooms may be more aesthetic, with accent wall colors and more high-end finishes. In contrast, treatment and surgery spaces should be more functional, with colors and finishes that can stand up to a lot of wear and tear. When you create a color palette for your hospital, keep the function of each space in mind and consider whether it will be occupied primarily by people or might be an area that should be designed more for your patients' vision. Having variations in animal versus human rooms can increase the visual appeal of the hospital and reduce mental overstimulation.

To create a holistic scheme, start with the flooring. You will be surprised at how limiting flooring color choices can be, but by selecting these colors first, you can achieve good visual coordination between all of the spaces. Slightly darker flooring colors show less wear and tear, and since it can be difficult to replace flooring, choosing something durable and flexible in color helps with longevity. Even if you like a light, bright, clinical look, choose a floor that

Darker cabinetry with lighter countertops add warmth to this exam room. (Foto Imagery / Tim Murphy. Courtesy of VCA West Los Angeles Animal Hospital, Los Angeles, California [VCA, Inc.].)

is darker than you might otherwise select and keep the light, bright colors higher up. Floor colors should also be neutral, not colorful, so that you will have more flexibility in choosing colors for the walls and furnishings.

Going too trendy in the design can be fun at first, but the results can quickly become tiresome and dated. Continue with neutrals in your cabinets, since they need to last a long time. Darker tones look classier and more modern while helping to create a grounding element with the flooring colors. There is some flexibility with the variations, depending on the functions of the rooms where the cabinets are installed. For example, you can select something brighter and more colorful for a conference room, public space, or break room, but stick with neutrals for medical zones. Cabinets with darker tones work well with lighter countertops. Speckled colors are more forgiving than solid colors and create a visual texture in the room. Flooring and cabinet color decisions should be weighted more toward functionality than aesthetics.

Wall colors are the most changeable when designing a space and thinking about long-term uses. Some ideas to consider when choosing wall paint colors are as follows:

- The color is going to be much more colorful on the wall than it looks on the swatch.

- Be very careful with light neutrals that are derived from brown. The swatch may appear beige, but the wall may turn out to look pink on a larger scale.

- The best blues have a lot of gray and some purple. Otherwise they tend to look childish.

- Avoid minty green. When working in any healthcare industry, too many other things are minty green, a color that can clash in room design.

- For the most calming environments, nature-inspired colors are the best options.

If you are intent on choosing bright colors, choose more flexible options that work well with various color palettes for changeability later.

If neutral-on-neutral colors just don't suit your personality and practice philosophy, accent walls painted in lively colors can be fun and energizing. For example, design your floors and cabinetry with darker tones and sophisticated colors, and then add punch with bright, colorful accent walls. Taken to the extreme, color everywhere is a possibility when done correctly. The trick with this approach is choosing colors that are a little less intense and within the same color family or general tone. Richer greens and grayish blues work well with this option. Your spaces will be expressive but not overpowering to you or the animals.

▼ ▼ ▼

IN THE END, it is important to make choices that appeal for the long-term aesthetic of your spaces. These color palette choices can be utilized to express your practice philosophy as well as to create certain moods, help reduce stress, or enliven a space. Have fun with accent colors in furnishings that can be altered later to accommodate newer tastes and trends. Choose brighter colors that complement the base neutrals for an overall balance and range of uses in different spaces. Add more pops of color in your lobby with artwork and pendant lights above the reception desk. Fabric choices are also an option for brighter colors and patterns to create an expressive lobby that can be easily altered later.

CHAPTER 52

FURNISHINGS

In the exciting process of outfitting a new or expanded veterinary hospital, the purchase of furnishing comes second behind purchasing the necessary medical equipment. It is easy to discount the importance of furnishings, but the effect they have on client and patient comfort and staff efficiency should not be overlooked. Well-selected furnishings can also help round out the design of the hospital and reinforce your overall practice image.

The best time to begin making decisions about your major furnishing items is early in the design process to ensure that the spaces in your hospital can accommodate the pieces you wish to include. In order to develop a smart budget for these furniture requirements, start by making a list of the items you will need in your new space. This list typically includes the following categories:

- Waiting room seating and tables (hospitality furnishings).

- Chairs, stools, and work surfaces for employees.

- System furnishings—these are "cubicles" and other manufactured workspaces.

- Conference room and break room furnishings.

- Outside furnishings, such as picnic tables and benches.

- Animal furnishings, such as dog beds and cat perches.

- Artwork and photography.

The list you create at the outset will be refined over time, but it will provide a framework for all the decisions you will need to make and guide your design team on the types of furnishing to be included in the facility. Your architect can often help you with these decisions and will coordinate your furnishings with the drawings. For example, your conference room table should be sized to fit inside the conference room.

Once you've created your list of furnishings, what next? If you want someone to help you through all of the steps, an interior designer can be a big help, as long as you can afford the additional services. Your architect may include interior design services as an option; otherwise, you can hire a designer separately. Interior designers can also assist with color choices and artwork selections, shaping the finish of the interiors into a cohesive package.

If you choose to make your way through furnishing selections on your own, then you should at least make use of any assistance that furniture company representatives can offer. They can help you with selection, budgeting, and the bundling of various pieces. It is best to find a company that sells products that are appropriate for spaces that receive a high level of use and abuse, such as human healthcare buildings and restaurants, as veterinary hospitals fall into a similar category. Your architect may be able to recommend companies and reps.

The first time you meet with a furnishings rep, it is important to articulate your budget. You might find that your budget is not adequate to furnish the entire hospital in the way you had hoped, in which case you will need to develop some priorities. It's best to prioritize your waiting room furnishings for the comfort of your clients, as well as your employees' chairs for their comfort and job safety. Once your rep has assembled a furniture list and the associated costs, you will be able to better understand your options. If there are some items that you can get elsewhere or reuse from your current facility, you can reduce your costs. Before mixing and matching, consider the importance of creating a cohesive look and a stable source for future furniture purchases. As you decide on the list of items to purchase through a single source, remember that you will need to maintain some of the budget for the other items on your list.

Let's review some general rules for each category.

WAITING ROOM FURNISHINGS

Before selecting items for your waiting area, put your practice image into words. This will make it easier to choose specific items. Is your brand urban and modern, or homey and comfortable? Also, take a moment to think about your clients. For example, older people often find it more difficult to rise from benches than they do chairs with arms. Here are some of the main decisions to be made:

- Built in or freestanding: If your reception area furniture is built in, it will probably be designed by your architect and will not be in your furnishings budget. It's easy to clean around built-in furniture, and it's easier to prevent tangling of leashes and other nuisances as well. However, built-in furniture is a lot more expensive than freestanding purchased solutions and leaves you with less flexibility for changing things in the future.

- Fabric or no fabric: Padded furnishings are more attractive and comfortable. But the

This spacious and daylit waiting area provides clients with the option to sit on the window seat with their pets. (Foto Imagery / Tim Murphy. Courtesy of VCA South Shore Animal Hospital, South Weymouth, Massachusetts [VCA, Inc.].)

fabric must be selected carefully. Fabric is rated based on its durability and applicability to various industries. Choose a fabric that is rated at the top end for durability and stain resistance. Patterns wear better than solid colors. Appropriately chosen fabrics add warmth and create a less clinical atmosphere in a waiting space and can be appropriate for the following practice types:

› General practices with an emphasis on wellness care.
› Alternative medicine practices.
› Feline hospitals.
› Some specialty practices.

Practices that provide emergency or critical care, or that see a fair number of infectious patients, should not use woven fabric in their waiting areas. For padded chair solutions, select a puncture-resistant vinyl that is easy to clean.

- Emphasize design and whimsy: The waiting area is a place to make your clients comfortable and to have fun with furnishings. Choose a signature piece, or provide a variety of seating that allows clients to choose a seating arrangement that feels comfortable to them.

- Think about the animals: In the waiting area, you are accommodating not only the clients but their pets. Provide convenient tables for clients to set their cat carriers. Include separate alcoves so that clients with cats can sit away from dogs, or so that people with big dogs can separate themselves. Remember that a welcoming environment can help to reduce stress in animals and their humans.

CHAIRS AND STOOLS FOR EMPLOYEES

In employee work areas, the most important consideration is ergonomics. Chairs and stools need to be designed to support healthy working postures in order to prevent injuries and to increase productivity. Use the following general rules as you choose furnishings for these areas:

- Adjustability: All seating should be easily adjustable to meet each employee's needs.

- Solutions for sit-down stations: Sit-down areas are typically designed with 30-inch-high work counters. In these areas, use chairs designed for desk heights that allow employees to place both feet on the floor. It is also good for chairs to include armrests, so staff can keep their shoulders and arms close to their bodies and to assist with rising from the chairs. Station counters or desks should have enough depth for computer monitors to sit back 20 inches and should allow for ample leg space underneath. Finally, sit-down stations should be designed in a manner that facilitates open communication.

- Solutions for higher counters: Where employees may be perched, such as at lab stations, you may provide either drafting-height chairs, which are designed for higher counters, or stools. Most people prefer stools, but because of the absence of backs on stools, and therefore the lack of lumbar support, they are not comfortable to sit in for any length of time. In veterinary work zones, at least one counter should be lower to accommodate employees with disabilities or those who find it difficult to sit on higher chairs or stools.

- Solutions for exam rooms: In exam rooms, stools are preferred for staff because they take up far less room. They should be very durable as they will be raised and lowered frequently.

- Solutions for dental stations: Dental stations are also typically provided with stools. Doing dental work can offer real ergonomic challenges. Provide adjustability in the dental table, if possible. If not, provide adjustable stools with footrests for employees and doctors, who may have to work in raised positions where their feet cannot rest on the floor.

- Casters: All chairs and stools should have casters to facilitate ease of movement.

SYSTEM FURNISHINGS

System furnishings are the manufactured furnishing solutions for office areas. Today we have moved far beyond typical cubicles. System furnishings can be configured for a vast array of options, including degrees of openness or privacy. Although many employees say they want to have a private workspace, Gen X and Gen Y individuals on the whole tend to value openness in the workplace. It's possible to find the best balance with partitions that rise only slightly above the desk surfaces, or glass walls that open up the view across a space. If possible, consider purchasing partitions that contain built-in sound absorption materials to help keep the noise from other areas of the hospital from intruding into offices and other workspaces.

One significant trend is the sit/stand workstation. There is new recognition of the health benefits of changing positions throughout the workday. Sit/stand stations allow for this flexibility. Though these can be purchased through furniture reps, they're also popular enough to be purchased economically from some larger retailers.

CONFERENCE ROOM AND BREAK ROOM FURNISHINGS

This category covers a wide range of items, but the following common themes will help you make good choices for these group assembly areas in your hospital:

- Choose tables that store easily: Many conference room and break room furnishings can be purchased with tops that flip and legs that fold for easy storage. This can allow you to use group areas flexibly and easily move the furniture out of the way when you want to.

- Choose stackable seating: Stackable seating is important for the same reason. Some manufacturers make seating that stacks almost vertically so that it takes up a very small footprint in storage areas.

- Choose cleanable seating: It's likely that you'll have more perpetual stains in your break room furniture than in your waiting area furnishings. It's fine to use attractive plastic chairs in areas where food is present to lengthen the lifespan of your furnishings.

- Choose comfortable seating for CE events: If you host continuing education meetings or other events where visitors or employees will be parked in chairs for a long time, ensure that the chairs are designed for this. Your conference room and break room chairs might be from the same line, but the conference room chairs may have arms and padding for comfort.

OUTDOOR FURNISHINGS

If there were a neglected furnishings category, it would be outdoor furnishings. Yet the outdoor furnishings you purchase for your hospital will likely need to last a lot longer than the ones at your home and potentially withstand greater exposure to the elements. You won't be as likely to cover them or care for them the way you do with home furnishings. If you have the budget to purchase outdoor furnishings from a commercial source, these items could potentially last the lifetime of your project. You can start by speaking with your furnishings rep. If he or she doesn't sell outside furnishings, search online for "site furnishings" in your area. Site furnishings run the gamut from heavy and austere concrete items used in heavily trafficked public spaces, such as downtown plazas, to pieces that are friendlier in feel, such as colorful benches and tables.

Alternatively, you could purchase inexpensive furnishings and replace them every few years.

ANIMAL FURNISHINGS

Some people forget to budget for the furnishings needed for animal spaces. Furniture reps will not be able to help with these, so you will be working through these selections on your own or with your architect. Typical animal furnishings include these:

- Raised, dog-bench-style beds, such as Kuranda beds. These are great for well-dog kennels or for boarding situations. The aluminum versions of these beds last longer than the plastic ones.

- Cat housing enrichments such as hiding boxes (well cats only), benches, litter pans, etc.

- Feline exam room enhancements, such as climbing structures.

You will likely think of a variety of small animal furnishings that you'll need to provide as well, such as orthopedic beds for surgery recovery areas.

ARTWORK AND PHOTOGRAPHY

Last but not least, well-selected artwork and photography can help you finish a space and really personalize it. Choosing artwork and photography can be the most fun part of the project. The hard work is done, and now you're making it your own! The following images demonstrate a few ideas, from using

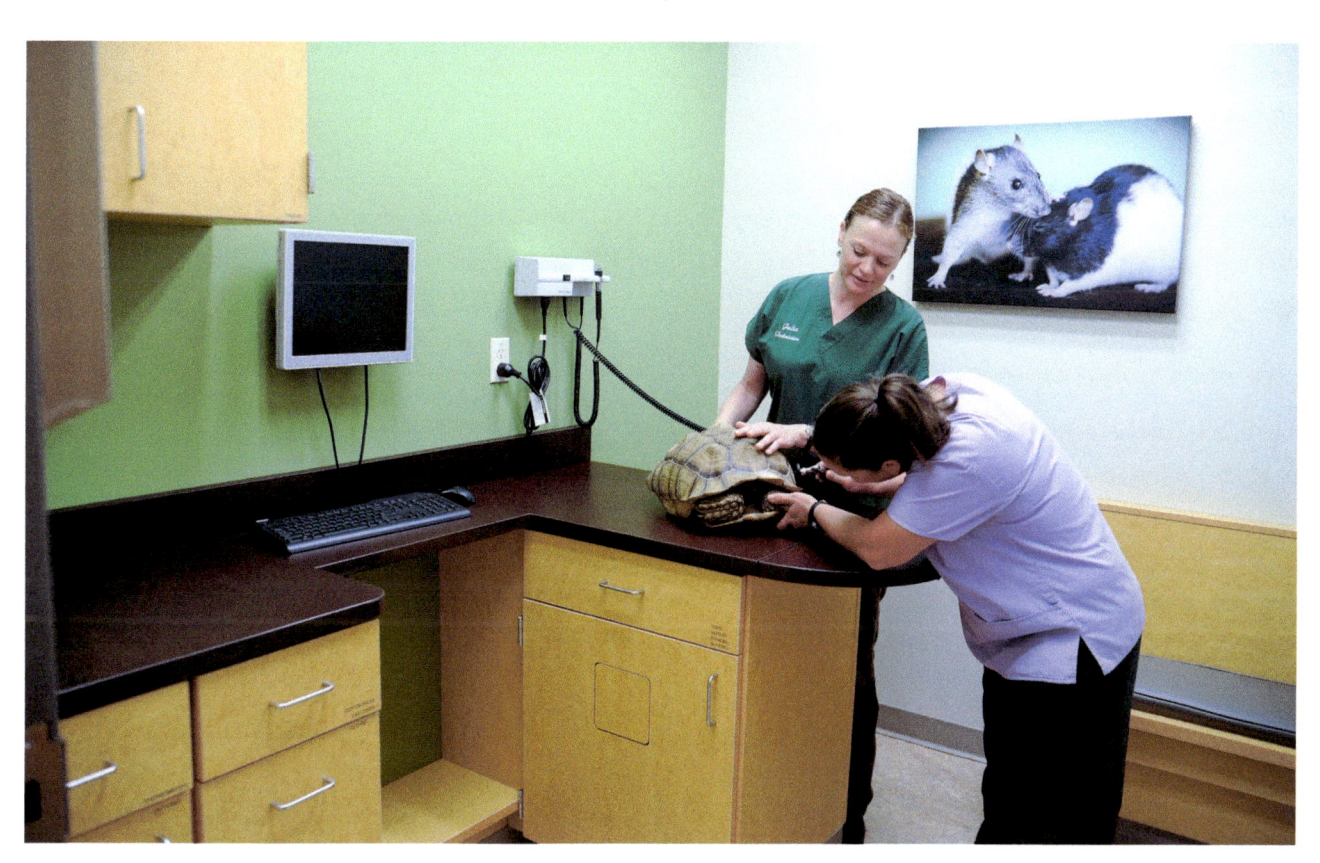

Art and photography can bring a playful element to any space. Only pets who are clients at this hospital get their portraits on the wall! What a great way to show how important your patients are to your practice. (Posh Pooch Portraits. Courtesy of Adobe Animal Hospital, Los Altos, California.)

Local artwork and vibrant colors are showcased in this new emergency and referral practice in Vancouver. It caters to its urban clientele with a welcoming spa-like feel. (Foto Imagery / Tim Murphy. Courtesy of VCA Vancouver Animal Emergency and Referral Center [VCA Canada].)

photographs of clients' pets to choosing pieces that complement a space.

SAVING MONEY ON FURNISHINGS

As your list grows, you will find that furnishing your hospital can be an expensive endeavor. Here are a few money-saving tips that other veterinarians have used to keep furnishing budgets under control:

- Consider used furnishings: When corporations go out of business or consolidate, they often leave vast seas of chairs and systems furnishings behind. If you want to save some money on these items, look for gently used ones. If you go this route, purchase enough to outfit the hospital, or at least purchase complementary items so that you don't assume a thrift store look.

- Purchase some pieces from less expensive sources: Many items can be purchased from furniture outlets. Look for high-quality items that are rated highly. Don't go inexpensive just for the sake of it, as you will sacrifice longevity and comfort, but use this strategy for items that aren't as critical.

- Reuse your own: If you're moving from an existing location, it's okay to reuse things that are in good shape. Before you do, look

Practical, inexpensive furnishings can work in your lobby space. Remember to choose pieces that work together. (Courtesy of Left Hand Animal Hospital, Niwot, Colorado.)

at them with a truly critical eye. If they look really long in the tooth, they're ready for charity. Remember that old items will look worse in new and shiny spaces. Reused furnishings should be used in back-of-house areas first.

▼ ▼ ▼

AFTER YOU OPEN your hospital, you'll interact with these pieces of furniture every day. You'll touch them, sit on them, and work with and on them. It is important to select furnishings that are comfortable, that are long lasting, and that make your employees and your clients feel at ease.

CHAPTER 53

EQUIPMENT COORDINATION

Take a moment to reflect on some of the day-to-day tasks that take place around your hospital. Not just the more obvious ones, like surgeries, but some of the basic tasks that, while small, are still a critical part of the overall operation of your hospital, such as sterilizing equipment and restocking supplies. Now think about how these tasks are affected by the design and layout of your spaces. Is your shelving at an easily accessible height? Are your countertops deep enough? Is equipment easily accessible, especially in an emergency?

Hopefully, this quick exercise opened your eyes to some of the small but important details that are often overlooked in the design of a new hospital. It is easy to get fixated on the bigger aspects of hospital design, like the overall look of the building or how spaces work and flow together. But successful hospital design also comes from designing for the small things—such as the proper coordination of equipment—that make workspaces effective and efficient. Coordination of equipment is an essential component that is often left until the end of a building project; but in fact, the sooner you begin to plan around equipment, the more successful your design will be.

DIVISION OF RESPONSIBILITIES

Equipment selection is your job as the owner. It is your task to make a list of everything you need in each room, to select manufacturers, and to follow equipment items through the design and construction process to ensure that each item is properly integrated. You will find it helpful to develop a spreadsheet for your equipment choices that you can add to as the design develops. Having this spreadsheet will also help you anticipate the price of your overall equipment package. Starting early will give you time to shop around in order to get the best value for your money.

It is your design team's responsibility to design for the physical needs of each piece of equipment, including power, data, ventilation, structural requirements, water, and gas. They should also verify that each piece of equipment can be brought into the building and that adequate clearances are maintained to operate and service the equipment.

GENERAL PROCESS

Here are the steps to take to help guide decisions regarding equipment.

Collect Information

If you are planning to reuse current equipment, start gathering your information ahead of time. Write down the model numbers and the dimensions of each item. Locate the operation manuals, which usually describe any required special conditions for installation. They can often be found online.

Shop in Advance

Make a list of the new equipment you need to purchase and become educated on the products available. In today's market, medical technology is constantly changing, and therefore so are the available products. Do your research. Talk to your colleagues about the equipment they use. Visit trade shows—there is no better place for one-stop shopping. You won't be expected to have all of your equipment purchased in advance, but having an idea of the specific

	Item	Equip. #	Long Lead Time Item	Furnished by GC	Installed by GC	Furnished by Owner	Installed by Owner	MEP Coordination	Generator	Notes:
GENERAL EQUIPMENT										
OFFICE										
	Rolling Carts for Food Prep	1-1.15				X				Must fit under counters
	Polymer Laundry Carts	1-1.16				X				Must fit under counters
	Polymer Trash Carts	1-1.24				X				Must fit under counters
	Hanging Storage Rack	1-1.18								
	Metal Filing Cabinet	1-1.19								
	Metal Lockers	1-1.03		X	X					
	Leash Hooks	1-1.09		X	X					Boat Cleats
APPLIANCES										
	Refrigerators (full size)	4-1.01				X	X	X		Need to verify count and locations
	Commercial Washer Extractor	4-2.04		X	X			X		65 lb load, confirm pricing with rep.
	Commercial Drying Tumbler	4-2.05		X	X			X		75 lb load, with overheat proection
	Commercial Dish Machine	4-4.03		X	X			X		
	Hood Vent	4-5.04		X	X			X		
	Walk-In Freezer	4-1.06		X	X			X		8x10
	Electric Water Cooler	4-6.02		X	X			X		
MEDICAL EQUIPMENT										
	Floor Scale	5-1.01		X	X			X		
	Cat Scale	5-1.03				X	X	X		
	Drug Lock Box	5-1.21				X	X			
	Stainless Steel Exam Tables	5-2.01		X	X					
	Gurney	5-2.04				X	X			
	Surgery Table	5-2.06				X	X	X		
ANIMAL HOUSING										
	Cubbies on Curbs	7-2.07 and 7-2.08		X	X			X		
	Cat Suites	7-2.04		X	X					
	Dog Runs	7-2.02, 7-2.06, 7-2.03, 7-2.04, 7-2.09		X	X					
	Dog Ward	7-2.02 & 7-2.03		X	X					
	Dog Iso Cages - 48"x30"	7-1.01		X	X					
	Dog Clinic Wards - 54"x30"	7-1.01		X	X					

A sample of a portion of an equipment schedule.

products you want can go a long way during the early design process.

Share with the Team
Compile all of the information you have collected in a folder or spreadsheet, or whatever works best for you. Be sure to give this information to your design team as early as possible to ensure that everyone is on the same page.

Ask for Help
Your colleagues can tell you what has and hasn't worked in their own hospitals. An experienced architect can be a good resource for you to understand how equipment and facilities relate to one another. The vendor or manufacturer of a piece of equipment is also a great source of information. You can also hire an equipment coordinator, who can help you select, design around, and purchase the equipment that will go into your hospital. If you go this route, purchase equipment that is tried and true in veterinary medicine and be very skeptical of human medical crossovers. Distributors can package a large equipment purchase, and these distributors often have good working knowledge of the performance and relative benefits of different brands of a product. This is very useful information. You can also consult with more than one vendor, which can be very helpful when making comparisons.

Despite your knowledge of medicine, you are unlikely to anticipate all of the pitfalls you may encounter when you purchase and install specialty equipment. In human medicine, equipment coordination is its own profession. Unfortunately, this is not the case in the veterinary market. Begin with the mind-set that you will be the leader of a team effort and will delegate responsibilities to accomplish the necessary tasks required to complete your equipment purchases.

OTHER CONSIDERATIONS

Which equipment items will be new and which will be reused from your current facility? Carefully consider your current equipment to determine which pieces need to be replaced in your new hospital. Do you need to purchase other items that you don't already have? Is there any equipment you plan to purchase in the future, as your practice grows? If so, how can you plan for those pieces and accommodate them in the design now?

It is important to decide ahead of time with your design professional which items you will be purchasing on your own and which are to be "included in the contract," or purchased and installed by your contractor. This is often determined based on whether something is built in. Before construction begins, sit down with your contractor to designate items that need specific coordination during construction. For example, many contractors feel intimidated by medical gas systems and need the support of the manufacturer and the owner during installation.

Many equipment items also need to be closely coordinated with various utilities. Most equipment requires power, and this needs to be integrated into the electrical design. Wet tables require water supply and drainage and need to be included in the plumbing design. Cages can be exhausted separately from the overall building exhaust, and this needs to be coordinated with the mechanical design.

Are you ahead of the curve on long-lead items? Some equipment is readily available for purchase, whereas other items need to be ordered and may take a long time to fabricate and deliver. Diagnostic imaging machines and cages and runs are good examples of items that

Any equipment built in, such as this floor scale, requires extra planning and care, including electrical and concrete subtrade coordination. (Foto Imagery / Tim Murphy. Courtesy of VCA PetCare Veterinary Hospital, Santa Rosa, California [VCA, Inc.].)

require a long lead time. Such items need to be selected early enough to avoid affecting the construction schedule.

MAJOR TYPES OF EQUIPMENT

Focus on major equipment purchases. Below are the items that should be high priorities.

- Any major diagnostic imaging equipment such as CT, and especially MRI. These technologies require thorough participation of the manufacturers, installers, architects, shielding designers, and mechanical engineers.

- Radiology: A digital X-ray machine requires some planning, including the location of electrical shutoff, room layout, and wall shielding.

- Items producing heat or humidity such as grooming equipment, laundry, and autoclaves.

- Medical lighting: Medical lighting needs to be supported structurally above the ceiling.

EQUIPMENT COORDINATION

Be sure your architect, structural engineer, and contractor are in contact with your lighting vendor for details about the support of medical lighting.

- Anesthesia and medical gas: Coordination of this equipment requires several decisions, including locations of drops (ceiling or wall); selection of oxygen and gas scavenging equipment; design of the manifold, zone valves, and alarms; and design for compliance with code requirements such as fire rating. Your medical gas vendors should be in close contact with the design team during the design of the project.
  › Centralized storage closets for oxygen tanks typically require special construction for fire safety. It is always best to locate medical gas closets on an exterior wall for fire safety reasons as well as for convenient tank delivery.

- Caging and runs: Animal caging and runs represent a large cost for most projects. Do your shopping well ahead of time in order to select the products and manufacturers with whom you're most interested in working. Be sure that you compare the durability and quality of materials, and ask for references. Don't hesitate to connect the equipment manufacturer with your architect to review the plans. These items can have long lead times, so have your contractor help you identify when the caging and

A standing autoclave requires additional plumbing and electrical coordination. (Foto Imagery / Tim Murphy. Courtesy of VCA West Los Angeles Animal Hospital, Los Angeles, California [VCA, Inc.].)

equipment should arrive onsite so that you can work with your manufacturers to meet the deadline.

- Autoclaves: With a floor autoclave, considerations include the overall size of the unit, required floor clearances, and even the coordination of a floor sink and built-in hot and cold water plumbing for the unit. As one can imagine, these requirements will quickly begin to dictate the overall size of your pack/prep area. On a smaller scale, a general practice hospital will likely use a countertop autoclave, which might not seem like a big deal; however, most countertop autoclave models are actually deeper than a standard 24-inch counter. So building a deeper cabinet base might be imperative to the design. In addition, the manufacturers of these countertop models typically recommend the use of distilled water. Will you bring in outside bottles of distilled water? Or would you rather have a relatively inexpensive reverse osmosis system built in at your sink in pack/prep?

▼ ▼ ▼

VETERINARY HOSPITALS ARE equipment intensive. In order for the spaces to be efficient and highly functional, equipment coordination is an integral part of the design and construction process. Ultimately, the more equipment planning you can do up front, the better. Having an architect who knows the ins and outs of veterinary equipment and design can help immensely. The combination of your upfront planning and the architect's expertise will allow for the ultimate collaboration on your new hospital, a collaboration that will result in a smooth design process and a well-thought-out hospital that will work for you for many years to come.

SECTION FIVE

Construction and Occupancy

CHAPTER 54

REGULATORY REQUIREMENTS

Governmental regulations and requirements in the construction industry have increased dramatically in the past fifteen years. Where architects and engineers once spent a small amount of time on issues involving governmental regulations, they now spend as much as 20% of their time designing for or responding to these requirements. These evolving and growing requirements will also affect you as an owner of a veterinary hospital. They will affect your timeline for moving in, the fees that your design team charges, and the amount of money required to obtain permits.

If you live in an old city, a big city, or certain other jurisdictions in the United States or Canada, you will likely face even more hurdles. Some jurisdictions, such as Los Angeles, Miami, New York City, Washington, DC, and a few others, have such a reputation for difficulty that you will need a permit expeditor in addition to a skilled design team to get permits pushed through in a timely fashion. If you live in a large or established area, do your homework and talk with local commercial builders or developers to find out what you can do ahead of time to limit your exposure to permitting complications. If you want to hire a veterinary specialty architect, consider having the architect team up with local people who are more familiar with the area's regulatory processes.

PLANNING AND ZONING

Every significant town, county, or city in the US, with the exception of Houston, has planning or zoning laws and ordinances. These ordinances control the following:

- What a site can be used for.
- How far back from the property lines the building must sit.
- How many parking spaces are required.
- What the building must look like (in some instances).
- How much building can be located on the site.
- How tall a building may be.

Planning and zoning ordinances also dictate how a site is titled and platted. For this reason, it is critically important for you to know the planning and zoning requirements for a particular parcel before purchasing it. Although it may be possible to apply for and receive a variance from specific zoning requirements, the primary goal in acquiring a piece of ground is to buy a parcel where a veterinary hospital is a "use by right" and where your building will be able to conform to the setback, parking, height, and area requirements. In most municipalities, applying for a variance is a time-consuming and costly process, with no guarantees of success.

Furthermore, many urban areas have what the industry calls "overlay zones." As the name implies, these constitute another layer of zoning above and beyond the normal zoning issues that will also affect how a site can be developed and what can be built on it. Often overlay zoning deals with aesthetic or quality-of-life issues. These zones may include historic districts, view corridors, entrances to urban areas, urban redevelopment districts, and landscape districts.

The requirements of an overlay zone can be very stringent, and the review process can be both time consuming and very subjective in nature. Find out if the property that you are considering has any overlay districts and what the requirements may be.

DEALING WITH NEIGHBORS

When you submit for planning and zoning approval, it is a typical protocol for the planning agency to notify the neighbors within a certain radius of the project. Occasionally neighbors can bring up concerns in public meetings over anticipated issues that your project may create. For a veterinary hospital, oftentimes neighbors raise questions about three main areas:

- Noise from barking dogs.
- Odors.
- Traffic.

In facilitating discussions with neighbors, it is important to stay rational and calm and to have other rational and calm people advocating on your behalf. It helps to explain the nature of the project in ways that may mitigate people's concerns. For example, if neighbors are concerned about noise, you might explain that you are already planning to limit the hours that dogs will be kept in outside play areas or runs.

In some cases, neighbors can derail a project. If you think there is a danger of this in the neighborhood you are considering, work with your team to develop a bargaining chip, such as removing overnight boarding or creating one-way traffic flow. While you may use these only as a last resort, your project may ultimately move forward more quickly if the neighbors feel they are being heard.

LIFE SAFETY AND BUILDING CODES

Assuming your project has planning and zoning approvals, you can proceed with finishing the design and submitting for a building permit. In all but the most rural locations, you will be required to obtain a building permit for the construction of your facility.

When the building department reviews drawings for permitting, they are looking primarily at life safety and health issues, such as structural soundness, earthquake and hurricane resistance, emergency or fire exiting, containment of fire, elimination of hazardous conditions, necessary light provisions, and air supply and exhaust. They will also be concerned with infrastructure requirements, such as the details of site stormwater management, vehicular traffic circulation, installation of utilities, etc.

Be aware that the building permitting process may divide itself into several different departmental reviews that are developed to enforce codes. The departments involved may not coordinate or even talk much with each other. Sometimes it is up to the design team or an expeditor to herd the documents through the various departments.

Building permit timelines vary from two weeks, at minimum, to six months or more, depending on the jurisdiction. In a worst-case scenario, building permits can take a year or more to obtain. It is best to assume that even in the most accommodating cities your plans will require at least two rounds through the permitting office, which means that your permit process will likely be no shorter than six weeks and will be as long as three months on average.

Although most building permits are submitted to the local township, county, or city, some states also require state review of building plans. Check for your state's specific requirements early in the process.

SPECIAL STATE PERMITTING REQUIREMENTS

Some states have additional requirements for the construction of a project that will involve different reviews and permits. Here are a few examples:

- Florida wind zone requirements: Due to hurricanes in Florida, materials must be selected to comply with windborne debris testing. This is very relevant to you if you're renovating a building in Florida, as you may need to upgrade many materials that you would not otherwise consider upgrading in order to comply with today's hurricane codes. Miami Dade County has even more stringent requirements than most other locations.

- California Title 24: California has more stringent requirements than other states for seismic design and energy performance of buildings, along with the requirement for professionals to fill out the appropriate paperwork to prove compliance.

- Texas accessibility review: Texas has privatized handicap accessibility reviews, which has resulted in a more careful review and interpretation of accessibility law. Your design team will need a Registered Accessibility Specialist onboard to help ensure compliance.

AMERICANS WITH DISABILITIES ACT (ADA)

Originally passed by the US Congress in 1992 as a civil law, the ADA was two pronged, aiming to (1) ensure that the disabled public had reasonable and immediate access to and use of public buildings, and (2) protect disabled employees from being discriminated against because a facility might not be accessible to them. Most people are familiar with the public component of the act, but it is the employee component that often has the greater effect on business owners. It means that most buildings have to be accessible not only in the public areas but throughout the entire facility. Below are some typical results of accessibility law as applied to employee areas of buildings:

- "Common use facilities," such as restrooms, break rooms, conference rooms, shower and locker rooms, etc., must be accessible to all people, almost without exception.
- Exit paths throughout the building must be accessible.
- Door clearances and door hardware must be accessible.

Individual personal employee workspaces don't necessarily have to be handicap accessible initially, but employers are required to make "reasonable accommodations" for an employee with a disability.

Since the ADA's original passage, the essential requirements of the law have been adopted and/or incorporated by virtually every municipality in the country as part of the building code review and application process. Unfortunately, every municipality has a different interpretation of some of the smaller nuances of what constitutes "accessible" and "reasonable" accommodation for the disabled. If some minor thing is in question, your architect should work directly with the permitting authority to come to a resolution.

ENVIRONMENTAL, WETLANDS, AND STORM DRAINAGE REQUIREMENTS

One of the fastest-growing areas of governmental regulation is environmental protection. These regulations include the following:

- Protection of wetlands.
- Control of storm drainage runoff and protection of watersheds, waterways, and aquifers.
- Protection of historic or natural vegetation, including heritage trees.
- Protection of wildlife.
- Wildfire mitigation.
- Slope stabilization.
- Seashore protection.

While there are stringent federal regulations regarding the protection of wetlands and wildlife, the majority of these regulations are local. Therefore, they may vary by state and jurisdiction. The review and permitting process in locales where there are stringent regulations can add time and cost to a project and can limit or restrict some activities on building sites.

OCCUPATIONAL SAFETY AND HEALTH ADMINISTRATION (OSHA)

While horror stories abound of OSHA inspectors swooping in and closing a facility for even the most minor infraction, OSHA regulations are not a significant part of the design, application, or permitting process. OSHA regulations apply primarily to the operations of a facility, as there are no formal reviews by OSHA during the design process. However, some OSHA requirements do affect design. For example, you will need to be responsible for the following:

- Providing eyewash stations.
- Providing proper shielding for X-ray and other imaging equipment.
- Minimizing noise pollution.
- Controlling or eliminating hazardous air quality situations.
- Designating ventilation and handling standards for hazardous chemicals, such as the cytotoxic drugs used in chemotherapy, and complying with OSHA requirements for biological safety cabinets. See Chapter 34 for more information on the various requirements for handling chemotherapy drugs.
- Controlling access to hazardous materials and controlled drugs.

HAZARDOUS WASTES

The area of regulation with the greatest potential for liability and cost pertains to hazardous waste pollution and disposal. While most people are familiar with asbestos, there is also the potential for hydrocarbons, heavy metals, and industrial wastes to impact the buildability of selected sites. A high number of sites are contaminated by hazardous wastes in locations with a history of dense urban development and heavy industry. These issues are regulated primarily at the federal level, but states and local jurisdictions may have their own overlays.

In addition to the regulation and disposal of hazardous waste during a construction project, hazardous waste is also regulated within veterinary facilities. Most veterinary practices are designated as Small Quantity Generators of hazardous waste, meaning they generate between 100 and 1,000 kilograms of hazardous waste per month. A veterinary practice needs an EPA identification number for disposal of waste, and the practice should have a hazardous waste management plan, which will govern the disposal of the following materials:

- Sterilants and disinfectants.
- Radiological materials.

Regulated Medical Waste (RMW) is regulated at the state level. Veterinary practices must collect items designated by their state as RMW, such as sharps, and biohazardous wastes such as slides, blood products, etc., and send them to RMW brokers for disposal.

HEALTH DEPARTMENTS AND OTHER REGULATORY AGENCIES

It is relatively unusual, but sometimes specific state health departments are required to review and approve facilities that are built to hold animals, either for animal care or boarding. For the most part, these inspections are rather cursory and occur after the facility is built, but you should be aware that this can occur.

State or local health departments also often require that the installation of radiology equipment be inspected and that X-ray shielding be in place. Amazingly, this is one area where requirements are being relaxed, instead of increased, due to the improved safety and reduced scatter of modern X-ray machines.

▼ ▼ ▼

COMPLYING WITH CODES and regulations may not feel like a rewarding process, but it can be streamlined by teams that anticipate the requirements and work hard to manage them. Ultimately, governmental regulations may have a significant effect on project timelines and costs. The financial and time repercussions are great enough to justify hiring experts or expeditors in the toughest jurisdictions and in the toughest situations.

CHAPTER 55

PROJECT DELIVERY METHODS

A project delivery method, or procurement method, is the way in which a project is executed. It refers to the process by which the architect and contractor are hired to design and build your hospital. Often, an architect is hired first, and a contractor is hired once the design is in progress or completed. For smaller projects and leasehold buildouts, a common alternative is for owners to hire only a contractor and rely on the contractor's design team to produce the design documents.

There are variations on these methods, as explained below, each with its pros and cons. Understanding the options is the first step to making the best decision for your project.

WHY DOES THE DELIVERY METHOD MATTER?

The construction industry is affected more than nearly any other by fluctuations in the economy because so few construction projects can be funded when the economy is in turmoil. This also means business owners generally only have the ability and resources to build when the economy is strong. The downside is that prices are higher during a strong economy, and quality craftsmen are in high demand. As a result of these forces, construction prices in a newly recovered economy can skyrocket out of control, making construction more expensive than most owners anticipate.

Regardless of the status of the economy and the construction industry, every business owner wants to end up with a quality project for the lowest possible cost, and they want it within an efficient timeline. While this is an easier ideal to capture in a weak economy than it is in a strong one, choosing the proper delivery method and executing the contracts appropriately are the most important steps.

CHOOSING THE BEST METHOD

The following are typical goals for every project, though some weigh more heavily than others depending on the specific project needs:

- Time.
- Total cost.
- Quality of design and execution.
- Value.

While most clients want all four of these goals to be met, the reality is that strength in one category often leads to a weakness in another. For instance, does your hospital absolutely need to be open for business by a certain date? If so, are you willing to allow the quality of certain components, or of the design itself, to be modestly compromised to ensure you can reach this goal? Your own individual circumstances and desires make it critical to prioritize these goals before you make any procurement method decisions.

Once you know your priorities, you will want to decide whether to involve an expert in helping you make delivery-method decisions. If you know you want to avoid Design Build, you can hire an architect who should give you unbiased and impartial advice on hiring a contractor and who will author a very strong owner/contractor contract for you.

Many owners choose to hire a construction management consultant before hiring either the architect or contractor. This person can provide advice on delivery methods and contracts, which can be very advantageous, but going this route also carries a few risks. For one thing, construction management advisers tend to cost more (per hour) than architects, so small projects rarely benefit financially from their involvement unless their work is limited to certain tasks. Second, many construction management consultants either work for a company that is also a general contractor or have close ties to specific contractors, so there is no guarantee that their priority is first and foremost to protect your interests. Generally speaking, the larger the project, the more value a construction management consultant will provide. If you decide to use such a consultant, it is generally the first team member you will want to hire. Then he or she can help you procure the right design team.

PROJECT DELIVERY METHOD OPTIONS

Design Build

In a Design Build project, the owner hires the contractor first. The owner may seek proposals from a few different contractors before selecting one, or may simply negotiate an agreement with a contractor who seems capable and honest. In either scenario, the contractor most likely joins the project team right after the client obtains a schematic floor plan, or even before any design work is performed at all. Once the owner selects a Design Build contractor, the contractor will use his or her own architect and engineers to complete the design of the project and generate drawings for permitting and construction.

Design Build is typically the fastest way to complete a project, and it is often a desirable procurement method for smaller tenant buildout projects. The primary drawback for a veterinary hospital is that of the various delivery methods, it gives you the least control over project quality, because the contractor will only use products and methods that are comfortable, common, and affordable for him to use. The architects and engineers the contractor employs will most likely have no understanding of the special needs of an animal care facility. An additional drawback is lack of cost control, because the price will be determined and negotiated after the contractor has been hired, and this method therefore is a less competitive process than others. Here is the report card for this delivery method:

- Time: A. You only have to procure one entity, and there can be a degree of overlap between design and construction, since the fine detailing in the drawings is not critical to the beginning of construction.

- Total cost: B. You save yourself the cost of separately procuring an architect and engineers, and the cost of using the contractor's architect and engineers is generally lower than that of hiring an architecture firm. The difference in cost is partly because the level of required documentation and detailing is lower, and partly because the architect and engineers are designing to the contractor's common standards. However, you will probably have little control over the cost the contractor establishes for construction, other than to reduce the project scope.

- Quality of design and execution: D. Unless creative solutions are applied, Design Build projects deny you the opportunity to involve a specialist in animal care facilities in the design, detailing, and product recommendations for the hospital. Of the four methods, Design Build projects generally prioritize the specific needs of the owner the least. There is no expert third party (that is, a separate architect) to provide detailed requirements for the quality of the work that the contractor must meet.

- Value: C. While Design Build saves the cost of hiring a separate architect and engineers, there is indeed a reduced level of value in not having the participation of owner-centric specialists. Therefore, "what you get for what you pay" is less enticing than the upfront costs themselves.

Construction Manager/ General Contractor (at Risk)

The Construction Manager/General Contractor (CM/GC) method, also referred to as the Construction Manager at Risk (versus in an advisory-only role), is a method in which the contractor is procured before 100% completion of the architect's construction documents.

The CM/GC method typically provides for a preconstruction fee and a construction fee for the CM-contractor, and other terms are also applied (such as maximum markups). The CM/CG then provides advice to the architect during the design process about cost and feasibility and makes value recommendations. At a point decided by all parties, the CM/GC bids the project to subcontractors and establishes the Guaranteed Maximum Price (GMP) that the project will not exceed. The GMP includes the CM-contractor's fee, subcontractor costs, and general conditions costs as well as a contingency based upon the level of risk of the project as determined by the CM/GC. Only changes to the scope of the project or unanticipated existing conditions can result in the cost exceeding the GMP. Construction typically commences once a permit is obtained, even if this is prior to 100% completion of the construction documents.

The report card is as follows:

- Time: B. Because the GMP can be established prior to completion of the construction documents, construction can commence once the applicable permits have been obtained. This allows an overlap between the beginning of construction and final design detailing, and it also removes the bidding and contractor procurement period from the critical path of the project schedule.

- Total cost: C. In this method, there is no savings on design team fees, since they are hired as separate consultants. The cost control that you do have is limited to the contractor's fees and competitive subcontractor bidding, which is a decent portion of the work. Unfortunately, however, there is little control over general conditions costs and even less control over the project contingency.

- Quality of design and execution: B. Because the architect can hold the contractor accountable to standards of quality and craftsmanship, this delivery method is reasonable for overall project quality. An added benefit is the input the contractor provides during the preconstruction stages regarding the feasibility of the design and the availability of qualified subcontractors to execute it well. The only quality drawback of this method results from the level of control the contractor typically holds over the project relative to the control of the architect.

- Value: B. For the most part, this procurement method generates exceptional value. This value largely derives from the fact that you can obtain the early input of a contractor while still having the architect as a separate consultant with the authority to hold the contractor accountable. The primary cost drawback is the lack of control over the project contingency.

Design/Bid/Build (Competitive)

Design/Bid/Build is perhaps the most traditional project delivery method. In this method, the architect submits fully completed construction documents to contractors to bid competitively. Once you select the contractor and award the contract, assuming you already have the permit, construction can commence.

Many times, particularly on locally funded projects, the award is provided to the lowest bidder. In other cases, contractors submit technical qualifications and only the firms that the owner determines are prequalified are allowed to bid, in order to ensure that the low bidder is a firm capable of executing the project. Increasingly, a "best value" contractor is selected, based upon a combined scoring of the price proposal (bid) and the technical qualifications. Low-bid scenarios produce the highest risk for poor quality and schedule performance, while best-value scenarios typically result in solid quality and timeliness, but not necessarily the lowest possible price.

One major benefit of this procurement method is that the project is completely designed when contractors bid it. As a result, the prices are fully competitive, and the design is completely under the control of the architect and you, the owner. The only exception to the competitiveness of the pricing is when the market supply of labor cannot keep up with the demand of projects, in which case a different project delivery method might attract more interest from contractors. Here is the report card:

- Time: C. This method includes the most separation between the procurement steps of any method and allows for the least amount of overlap of activities. The design is fully completed before bidding takes place, and the bidding period can last six to eight weeks, depending on the size of the project and the speed with which the owner can compare bids and make a decision. Additionally, it takes a contractor two to four weeks to commence construction after receiving the award, because he must procure his subcontractors and obtain trade permits. The one positive effect this delivery method has on the project schedule, when the best-value selection path is pursued, is that the bidding contractors are also proposing construction schedules as part of the competitive process. They will be held contractually accountable to that schedule if awarded the job.

- Total cost: B. This delivery method will result in the lowest total project cost of any method, except for possibly Design Build. Bidding in this method is 100% competitive for both the contractor and the subcontractors, and no project contingency is added to the price. Therefore, the lowest market construction costs are realized, especially in the low-bid scenario.

- Quality of design and execution: B. Because the architect carries the most control in this method and can hold the contractor accountable to standards of quality and craftsmanship, high quality generally results. The only drawback is the absence of contractor feedback on constructability and feasibility during the design process.

- Value: A. Unless a tight overall project schedule is highly critical, the project contains unique requirements that will benefit significantly from a contractor's early input, or the availability of skilled labor cannot sustain the current demands of the industry, this project delivery method provides the best design and quality of execution for the price that is paid when compared to other methods.

Design/Bid/Build (Negotiated)

The only difference between this method and the one above is that the owner selects a preferred contractor once the design is complete and negotiates a construction price with that contractor in a noncompetitive manner. This is a risky method of delivery unless the contractor and owner have teamed up together before with positive results, in which case the outcome can be similar to its competitive counterpart, but with a slightly improved project schedule due to a simpler bidding process.

In other cases, the architect may recommend a negotiated bid to the owner with a specific contractor that the architect knows and trusts. You should never proceed with this method unless you are truly comfortable with the architect's recommendation and have sought feedback from other sources regarding the contractor's performance.

Always think twice before negotiating bids with contractors who are friends, friends of a friend, or family members. The outcome is rarely helpful to those relationships, the pricing is generally not as competitive as it should be, and the quality is not likely to meet the special needs of an animal hospital.

The best negotiated bids occur with contractors who have expertise with the project type and solid recommendations from similar past clients. In any negotiated bid scenario, you should obtain a detailed cost estimate from a qualified construction cost estimator and use it as leverage during the contract negotiation process.

CONTRACTS ARE KEY

A solid construction contract is key to holding a contractor accountable, regardless of the project delivery method. It is a good idea to develop an owner/contractor contract through your architect, a construction management consultant, or a construction attorney before beginning the procurement process. This allows you to establish the terms, rather than reacting to the terms the contractor includes with his or her pricing. Among the contracts you are likely to come across, American Institute of Architects contracts are typically the most legally defendable and the most owner friendly, although any contract should be refined to be specific to your project and to protect you in the fullest manner equitable. Regardless of who authors the contract, it should not be presented to the contractor or executed without the advice of a licensed construction attorney.

CHAPTER 56

ESTIMATING VERSUS BIDDING

Keeping a hospital construction project on budget is very important for the long-term success of any project. Projects that go over budget take time and resources to get back on track. It is also a well-known fact that it is more difficult to get the full monetary value of an added item back out of a project than it would have been not to add it in the first place. Therefore, a project should be developed with an integrated methodology for cost control.

The first step in managing costs is to develop a budget that is aligned with the scope of work from the outset. Prior chapters of this book describe the elements of a project budget as well as their relationship to the scope of the project. Once this budget is set, it is important that it is not exceeded along the way unless all parties agree that the budget should and can be increased. But most projects do not go over budget on purpose—they go over inadvertently. In order to prevent this problem, a mechanism for obtaining periodic cost estimates as the project develops should be part of your design process.

Veterinarians can consider these methods for developing periodic cost estimates:

- Hiring a contractor early during the design phase, with the idea that he or she will help manage the project costs and eventually build the project: This method is known as CM/GC, for construction manager and general contractor, and is described in more detail in the previous chapter. The most significant benefit of this method is transparency into project costs and a high degree of owner and design team input. The method is often sold as an "open book" approach that allows the participation of all parties. The CM-contractor develops periodic estimates as the project progresses, and the design is adjusted as needed to meet the budget requirements. This method works particularly well when the market is busy, because it helps a veterinarian secure a good contractor and develop a relationship with this person ahead of time. However, in a slow market, the CM/GC method can prevent an owner from obtaining the most competitive pricing for a project.

- Asking your architect to provide cost estimating: This method can allow for more freedom to make decisions about how to construct the project while still getting some information during the design phase about the project costs. Keep in mind that architects typically exclude this service; it would be provided as an addition to the normal scope of work. Some architects do well at estimating costs, however, others do not, so this approach can be risky. Ask your architect to provide you with examples of projects that have been successfully delivered utilizing their firm's preferred cost estimating method.

- Pursuing a Design Build method: In a Design Build approach, the design professionals work for the contractor. The contractor is thus responsible for managing the costs. This method can distance the owner from cost decisions, which has the potential to be positive or negative. Some contractors may make decisions to lower the quality of a system or material in order to keep a project on budget, and this can sometimes be detrimental. Nevertheless, Design Build can work for certain projects, particularly ones that have to prioritize cost control over all the other factors.

- Obtaining cost estimating through a third party: For example, you can hire a contractor to provide this service, or hire an independent and reputable project management company to help you estimate and otherwise manage the project. These methods can vary widely in terms of scope and approach, depending on the professional hired and the services provided. At their best, they keep the decision-making in your court.

Colleagues who have recently built hospitals will be good resources. Talk with them to find out how they managed project costs, and what pitfalls or benefits they discovered along the way. They will see things from your perspective as an owner and will have experiences to share that are both positive and negative. Your design professional can also be a great resource. He or she is likely to have had projects that have used all of the methods described in this chapter and may be able to guide you to good professionals in your area.

WHEN TO ESTIMATE, WHAT TO EXPECT

If you are considering including cost estimating services to keep your project on budget, successful estimating ideally occurs at the following design milestones:

- Schematic design: a general ballpark budget estimate.

- 50% permit drawings: first round of estimating.

- 75% permit drawings: second round of estimating.

- 90% permit drawings: third round of estimating.

A skilled cost estimator will carry a design contingency for unknowns and scope that is not yet identified by the design drawings. This contingency gets smaller as the project progresses and there are fewer unknowns. Using this methodology, the estimator helps to prevent surprises and budget overruns. If, however, the project does start to go over budget, you will become familiar with the term "value engineering." Value engineering is the art of redirecting some design ideas, materials used, system designs, and so on to bring a project in line and to provide the most value for an owner. In poorly managed projects, value engineering can be a euphemism for ruthless scope cuts. For example, a good value engineering decision might be changing from one type of brick to another on a building exterior. A more drastic decision might be to remove the brick entirely and use siding instead. If your estimates are rigorous and well done, you will likely avoid drastic value engineering, which is always the goal.

A good estimate is organized in the same way that architects organize their specifications. Modern specifications are organized into 50 categories knows as "divisions" (see Chapter 4). This organization makes it easier for your design and construction professionals to study unusual costs that the project is carrying. For example, site development costs average around 11% of a budget's total. If the costs in this division add up to a lot more than this, it could indicate that simplifying the site work may help to reduce the project budget.

THE BIDDING PROCESS

Once the design work is completed for your project, it will go out to bid. Bidding occurs even if you have already selected your general contractor, as he or she will need to bid out all of the subcontractor packages. To save time, bidding often occurs simultaneously with submission of the drawings to the building department for a permit. Bidding a project is the first step in actually securing a contract with the contractor to build the project. Assuming the project is still on budget, you would then proceed to contract negotiations and construction.

Your architect should play an active role during the bidding phase of the project. If you are "hard bidding" your project to several general contractors, then someone (your architect or project manager) needs to help you manage that process, review the bids, and evaluate all the information you will receive so you can make informed decisions. You are not obligated to take the lowest bid—unless you're representing a government agency—and this should be clear in the bid documents your architect releases. For example, if you receive a bid that is far lower than the others, it could have inherent problems, such as a major element missing from the scope of work.

Bids should be consolidated and submitted to you and your design professional using the same standardized format that was used in the estimating period. That way, major differences between your previous estimates and the final bids can be evaluated.

During the bidding process, your architect may issue one or more addenda. An addendum addresses questions that come up during the bid process, drawing clarifications that need to be issued or relaying comments from government agencies. The drawings and specifications, along with the bid addenda, become a portion of the contract. The contractor is obligated to build what is captured in these documents, which is why a formal paperwork process is required for any adjustments during the bid period.

As an owner, you have limited control over the selection of the subcontractors on a project. The contractor takes the risk for bidding the project and securing subcontractors for each trade. If you have a specific concern about a subcontractor for a major trade (for example, you happen to know that one of your friends had a very bad experience with a specific company), then relay that information to your general contractor. Most contractors will allow an owner to have some veto power for a situation like this, but otherwise the agreements between a contractor and his subcontractors are the general contractor's risk to manage.

▼ ▼ ▼

THE BEST WAY to ensure that your new hospital is built for a manageable cost is to carefully watch the budget throughout the design and construction process so you can control not only the costs but the design decisions affected by them.

CHAPTER 57

THE CONSTRUCTION PROCESS

If you have ever been involved in a building project, you may recall being confused by all the special terminology the design and construction professionals used. Veterinarians have jargon, too, but they intentionally try to simplify their words when talking with people outside their field. Part of the reason your architect and builders don't do this for you is that the process of building a hospital requires you to immerse yourself in their world. Ultimately, understanding the language of the construction process will help you to avoid misunderstandings and navigate smoothly through your project. The definitions in this chapter will get you off to a good start.

THE DRAWINGS SET THE STAGE

The drawings that your architect assembles for the contractor to use for construction are known as the construction documents (CDs). CDs include the detailed drawings and specifications required to obtain a building permit and construct the project. These include drawings pertaining to the engineering of the civil, landscape, mechanical, electrical, and plumbing systems as well as the structural and architectural design.

These drawings and specifications, along with the contract between the owner and contractor, are collectively known as the contract documents. In other words, the documents your architect creates (the construction documents) become part of the contract, and your contractor is legally obligated to provide what is in those documents. If the contractor needs to add, subtract, or change an item, he will submit a change proposal, which will eventually become a change order. A change order can be an addition or a deletion. For example, if you were to subtract a door from the project, you would receive a credit for this change.

CHOOSING THE RIGHT CONTRACTOR

We've discussed the different methods for delivering a project (Chapter 55). However, we haven't yet discussed some of the more nebulous considerations of contractor selection, which have a lot more to do with intuition than methodology.

Your contractor is at least as important as your architect in helping you realize your dream. You want the best team for your project.

Choose a contractor who has been recommended by others and who has experience with high-quality commercial construction projects. You can interview a few select contractors before making your choice. These are some qualifications you should look for:

- Experience in the project type.

- A good attitude.

- High level of interest in the project.

- Responsiveness to your inquiries.

- Positive references from others.

- The right-size company for the project. It's often not a good idea to choose a one-man band or a huge orchestra. You want the person who has a large enough firm to employ good subcontractors without it being so large that your project will get delegated to less-qualified staff.

- The right project manager and superintendent. Be sure you meet the team with whom you will be working.

CONSTRUCTION PHASE TERMS

Before work can begin, the contract with the contractor must be executed. The contractor should provide a comprehensive construction schedule with the contract.

Once construction commences, a whole series of processes begin. These processes may be new to you if this is your first commercial building project. Below is an overview of terminology and processes during the construction period of any project.

Builder's Risk Insurance

Builder's risk insurance is a special type of insurance that protects the owner against risk while the project is under construction. For example, if a building under construction catches on fire, this insurance would cover that sort of event, assuming the event was not caused by an Act of God (an actual legal term used in the industry). For instance, damage from an earthquake would not be covered. The policy also does not cover injuries on the jobsite. Coverage for such injuries is the responsibility of the general contractor.

A builder's risk policy may be held by the contractor or the owner. It is generally a better idea for the owner to hold the policy for a variety of reasons. Seek out more information from your lawyer and insurance company about this policy and be sure it is in place before construction commences.

Construction or Contract Administration (CA)

This is the term for the services that your architect provides during construction. During this phase, your architect will normally answer questions from the contractor, prepare architect's supplemental instructions, approve contractor applications for payment and change orders, and visit the project site at important milestones in the process.

Application for Payment (Pay App)

Under a normal industry process, a contractor cannot be paid until he or she has submitted an application for payment (pay app). This application will be reviewed, approved, and signed by the architect. Payment applications are generally submitted monthly, and they generally include a summary of work performed to date as well as materials purchased and stored onsite. Reviewing the progress of the work and comparing it to the pay app is part of the architect's service to ensure you don't pay way ahead of work completed on your project site, which could put you at risk.

Change Orders

Change orders are a normal part of the construction process. On a well-run project, they typically equate to 2%–3% of the construction contract. More changes can arise on a remodeling project, where unknown conditions are more likely. Change orders may arise for any of the following reasons:

- Something unexpected was discovered.
- You decided to change or add something.
- The contractor missed something in his bid.
- Your architect forgot something.
- A consultant to the architect forgot something.
- The team agreed that something should be changed or added.

On a normal project, you could expect change orders to occur for all of the reasons outlined above. In most of these cases, the item you are adding represents value to your project. For example, if your architect forgot to add the bathroom door to the door schedule, you would have had to purchase this door anyway, and therefore it is reasonable for you to pay for the value of this item.

If one team member is clearly messing up, the change requests will be numerous or large in scope, or you will hear complaints from others. In this case, you might have a larger problem that needs to be dealt with firmly. Your architect will help you review change orders, but be aware that if his or her documents are not well quality controlled, this may in itself result in a higher number of change orders.

Arm yourself with a project contingency to cover change orders so they do not drive you over budget or cause you tremendous financial stress. A 5% contingency should be carried for new projects and a 10% contingency for remodels.

Inspection Versus Observation

Various people will inspect your construction project while it is in progress. The building department will send inspectors at regular intervals, and products will need to be tested and inspected during the construction of the project. However, your architect does not inspect your project except at the end of the construction period. Instead, he or she will "observe" it in progress. This may seem like a silly distinction, but it is important because it keeps the responsibility for the construction of the project with the contractor.

STAYING SANE DURING CONSTRUCTION

If your deadline for finishing your project is not a true, hard deadline, then don't sweat it if delays occur. It can be frustrating not to be able to move in on time, but bad things can happen when contractors are forced to rush the completion of a project. In that situation, your general contractor will likely have way too many subcontractors on the jobsite when the most critical finishes and systems are being installed. This inevitably leads to important things going wrong, like flooring getting installed improperly. It is much better to accept some minor schedule hiccups and to allow the job to wrap up at a reasonable pace.

▼ ▼ ▼

AS THE OWNER of the practice, you will remember every little problem that occurred during construction. Naturally, it is easy to focus on the aspects of your project that you wish you could change, but chances are no one else notices these things. If you have planned your project well, have been involved from the beginning to the end, and have had a positive approach to your role during the construction process, small missteps should have little effect on your overall happiness or success in your new hospital.

CHAPTER 58

THE JOBSITE

When you build your hospital, you are the owner and the client. These are important roles on the construction site that can be both exciting and stressful in those moments when it becomes apparent that "we didn't think about that." In most cases, the project you build is also the project you own and manage after the construction is complete. Visiting your project site during the construction allows you to understand the spaces ahead of time, provide input to your design and construction team, and identify any concerns that you may have. In order to be most effective on your project site, it is imperative that you as the owner and client understand your role and responsibilities.

PERSONNEL ON THE SITE

Many different people in different kinds of leadership roles will be onsite. Below is a guide to the typical division of roles, starting with you, the owner.

The Owner
As the owner, you are responsible for paying for the project on a prescribed regular basis, for taking control of the project when it is finished, and for making decisions regarding changes and the use of funds as the project progresses.

One of your critical roles as the owner is to provide a clear line of communication between your design and construction teams. The best way to do this is to designate one person who will be your point of contact with the rest of the team and who will visit the project regularly (at least once per week, and ideally more often). This person could be you or a high-ranking staff member, such as your practice manager. Yes, it will put a strain on your hospital team, but it is very important to take the time to communicate regularly and thoroughly as the project progresses, as this prevents problems from developing.

If your project is large or complex, you may want to consider hiring an owner's representative to handle the day-to-day jobsite duties. The owner's representative records and reports work progress weekly to the owner and notes when payments need to be made. If you do hire an owner's representative, identify this cost ahead of time and choose one who has a great reputation with architects and contractors, as you will need this person to be effective in helping you solve any problems that may arise.

The Architect

Many people who are not familiar with construction may not understand that in a traditionally delivered project, the architect plays an important role as the client advocate. The architect must visit the project site on a regular basis to ensure that the project is being constructed per the drawings and specifications. The architect will prepare field reports to document his or her observations of the project site.

The Contractor

The contractor's team has multiple members. You must understand each person's role and the hierarchies on the project site in order to communicate your needs effectively. These team members include the following.

The Project Manager

The contractor's project manager is the person who is responsible for the paperwork side of the construction project. In most cases, he or she is the highest-ranking member of the active project team. The project manager must document the schedule and process the information that flows back and forth to the architect. Examples include:

- Requests for information (RFIs): These are requests for the architect to clarify items that may be unclear in the drawings.

- Architect's supplemental instructions (ASIs): These are instructions the architect issues to clarify information that does not generally affect the project cost or schedule. An example could be a missing dimension from the drawings.

- Proposal requests (PRs): These are documents, generally assembled by the contractor, that propose potential changes to the project cost or schedule. For example, if a door is added, the contractor may ask for a cost for this door from the door subcontractor and may bundle this price in a PR, which is then reviewed by the owner and architect. Multiple PRs may be bundled together into change orders.

- Submittals: Submittals are documents issued by the contractor for every significant item that is specified by the architect. For example, the contractor will submit the product information about the paint they intend to purchase. The architect then

REQUEST FOR INFORMATION (RFI) LOG

Project Name: Animal Hospital Project No: 01.000 Page_1_of_5_

RFI #	DESCRIPTION	DATE RECEIVED	STRUC	M/P	ELECT	SK	DATE RETURNED	CLOSED
1	Door Frames 1089 A & B	11/30/2017					12/03/2017 (web response)	12/09/2017
2	Full Height Wall Clarifications	11/30/2017	X				12/03/2017	12/09/2017
3	Wall Type IW-II	11/30/2017					12/03/2017 (web response)	12/09/2017
4	Roof Sheathing	12/04/2017	X				12/08/2017 (web response)	12/09/2017
5	Actual Wood Post Dimensions	12/29/2017	X				12/31/2017	01/05/2018
6	Clear Space in Mens R.R. 1098	12/29/2017					12/31/2017 (web response)	01/05/2018
7	Finish Sill	12/29/2017					01/20/2018	03/11/2018
8	CMU in Rm 1061	12/29/2017					01/07/2018	01/18/2018
9	Existing Storefront Door 1025A	12/29/2017					12/31/2017	05/06/2018
10	CT Foundation Dimensions	12/29/2017	X				01/05/2018	01/05/2018
11	Tackable Surface	12/29/2017					Email and PR	01/12/2018
12	Roof Screen	12/29/2017	X				01/04/2018 PR	01/11/2018
13	HIT-Z Anchor Rods	01/04/2018	X				01/05/2018 PR	01/05/2018
14	Blocking Size 4-S5.2	01/06/2018	X				01/11/2018 PR	01/25/2018
15	SDS Screws and No Lags	01/06/2018	X				01/07/2018	01/08/2018
16	Opening 1051A	01/06/2018					01/07/2018 PR	02/16/2018
17	Concrete Window Infill	01/08/2018	X				01/12/2018 PR	01/25/2018

An example of a request for information (RFI) log. This is a trackable way for the contractor to ask the design team questions.

reviews the submittal to confirm the paint meets the specifications.

- Shop drawings: These are items that require some design by the contractor's team members. Examples include structural steel, rebar, doors and frames, and fire sprinklers. The architect will also review these to be sure they conform to the drawings and specifications.

The Project Engineer

The project engineer assists the project manager with the project's paperwork. He or she generally works from the jobsite trailer and keeps all the paperwork straight on the jobsite. In many cases, the project engineer is a young person who will eventually become a project manager.

The Superintendent

The superintendent may be the most important person on your project site. He or she is the professional who is in charge of the entire project site, including foremen and subcontracting teams, project site safety, and workflow. The superintendent typically works hand in hand with the project manager. When navigating your project site, there are some very important things you must do that will be of concern to the superintendent:

- Check in with your superintendent when you arrive.

- Wear the proper safety gear before entering the jobsite. The superintendent is responsible for jobsite safety, including the safety of all visitors to the site. The contractor may require you to attend a safety training as well.

- Communicate only with the superintendent. Never talk with subcontractors regarding any jobsite business. The superintendent is in charge of all information that needs to be relayed back to the project manager or architect.

The Foreman

A foreman is a supervisor of work crews who reports to the superintendent and may occasionally be the highest-ranking person on the project site, if the superintendent is "out of the office." Large jobsites may have multiple foremen.

CONSTRUCTION MILESTONES REQUIRING OWNER PARTICIPATION

With an understanding of the responsibilities of your team members, you will know how to integrate into the flow of this exciting time when your dream gets built and becomes a reality.

The following are the critical moments during the construction of your project when it is especially important for you or your representative to be present and alert.

- Reviewing under-slab drainage before slabs are poured: Construction sites are boring, especially at the beginning, when it seems like the only thing happening is dirt being moved around for weeks on end! But it is critical to pay especially close attention to the installation of underground plumbing before the slab is poured. If a drain is missed, now is the time to catch it. Have your architect walk the site with you to review the plumbing work.

- Reviewing the under-slab vapor barrier: The under-slab vapor barrier must be installed correctly, with all seams taped, before the slab is poured. While it should be the responsibility of the architect to review the vapor barrier installation, it is important for you to pay attention to this review, as a good vapor barrier is critical to the installation of moisture-sensitive flooring such as epoxy or sheet vinyl.

- Reviewing concrete slabs after they are poured: Be sure that water will flow to the drains. You may ask your contractors to do a "flood test" to check for areas where water pools in rooms where it should flow to drains, such as in dog run rooms.

- Doing a box walk: This means walking around with your architect when the walls are framed but before they're closed in to make sure that all electrical outlets are in the right place. You and your architect should also review the location of in-wall blocking, which is the wood placed in the walls, to enable the hanging of heavy equipment, such as exam tables.

- Reviewing sound walls: If you have sound walls going into the structure around dog rooms, have your architect review them with you on the project site to be sure they are installed in the right places.

- Approving colors and materials: Your architect should coordinate these selections with you, but making timely decisions on final materials and colors is crucial to the construction schedule.

- Making flooring mockups: Insist on a mockup for any high-performance flooring, such as epoxy, and review it for texture and quality before the floor is installed.

- Reviewing mechanical, plumbing, and electrical rough-ins: You will likely not have the expertise to review these yourself, but because these infrastructure systems are so critical to the ultimate performance of the hospital, you should check to be sure that the engineer of record has reviewed these and made a list of any problems to correct before the ceilings go in. For example, a seemingly minor thing such as two pipes of dissimilar metals touching each other in a ceiling space could eventually cause a leak in your building.

- Installing owner equipment: If you have purchased some equipment that needs to be installed by the contractor, coordinate their installation at the appropriate time. (An example may be the surgery lights.) Discuss these items before the start of construction so that this installation can be included in the contractor's scope of work, and make sure the items arrive onsite on time. You may need to make minor decisions, such as the exact placement of a piece of equipment.

- Preparing a pre-punch list: A punch list is a document itemizing work that still needs to be completed toward the end of a project. Although it is prepared by the architect, this is a time when you can provide input about anything you've noticed that is left undone. A few weeks before the punch list walk through, walk the project site with your architect and the superintendent to discuss the level of quality and identify any major items that need to be corrected before it's too late.

- Preparing the punch list: You will need to be present and participating in the final punch list of the project. At this time, your architect will review the construction for any minor fixes that should be made before you move into the facility.

▼ ▼ ▼

IN NAVIGATING THE complex world of the jobsite, remember that most projects provide tremendous benefits to their owners in the end. This is an important reminder, because project sites can be stressful, and there will be good days and bad days. Start by hiring the most qualified, most experienced, and most highly recommended team members. Build on this by committing your time, your attention, and your communication skills to the project. Strike a balance of maintaining your sense of humor and being tough when it counts. Your team will respect you and do their best work.

CHAPTER 59

PROJECT CLOSEOUT

Many processes occur at the end of a construction project related to the legal and contractual requirements at the time of owner occupancy. Understanding these processes can help reduce the risk from improper project closeout.

HVAC TESTING, ADJUSTING, AND BALANCING (TAB)

HVAC systems are much more complex in veterinary hospitals than in typical office buildings, so it's even more important to verify that the HVAC systems are operating as designed. In a typical commercial building, all HVAC systems must be verified via a Testing, Adjusting, and Balancing (TAB) process. TAB is provided by a specific contractor who is certified to perform this work and who is provided for under the construction contract. This contractor will verify that the systems are operating according to the mechanical engineer's design airflow specs. Following the testing, the TAB contractor will submit a report, which should include the following:

- Verification that the air is flowing to each portion of the system as required by the mechanical engineering drawings.

- Verification of the amount of outside air, as required by the mechanical engineering drawings.

- Verification of building pressurization and pressure at each point in the system as designed. This is important because for veterinary hospitals the pressurization of different spaces is generally part of the overall odor control and biological risk management strategy.

Be sure that you receive this TAB report, as well as documentation showing that the equipment is operating according to the requirements described in the mechanical engineer's drawings and specifications.

Proper system start-up and TAB testing should catch the majority of the issues that may occur with mechanical unit installation. However, do contact your contractor during the warranty period if you feel that something may not be operating correctly. Mistakes do happen, and TAB does not cover all of the issues that may occur. TAB procedures follow the standards of the National Environmental Balancing Board (see *Procedural Standards*).

PUNCH LIST

Near the end of your project, the architect and engineers will review the work to ensure it is complete enough to release all payments other than the final retainage, which is the money that is retained until the project is fully complete.

During the inspection of the project, the architect will provide a "punch list," a list of items the contractor must fix or complete. Ideally, a punch list should include only minor items, such as adjusting door locks, touching up paint, etc. If the list includes items that would prevent the facility from being safely occupied, it is, by definition, not substantially complete.

For practical reasons, even though a project may be ready for occupancy, the contractor will generally prefer to finish correcting the punch list items before the owner takes occupancy to allow for these tasks to be completed efficiently.

Normally an architect will issue a "Certificate of Substantial Completion" along with the punch list. Legally, this means that the facility is safe and ready for occupancy. This certificate kicks off the one-year warranty for the project. If, for example, this certificate is issued in May, and you move into the building in June, your warranty lasts until May of the following year.

OPERATION AND MAINTENANCE MANUALS

The operation and maintenance (O&M) manuals are for items included in your project. Your contractor will bundle them and provide them to you before the project is turned over. These should be kept carefully, as you may need to refer to them when something breaks down or just to follow maintenance standards.

OWNER STOCK OF MATERIALS

Most architects include in their specifications a requirement for the contractor to provide a certain amount of "owner stock" of materials, such as carpet, paint, ceiling tiles, and the like. This is to help you make minor repairs or match the product in the future.

CONTRACT REQUIREMENTS

Before you take occupancy of the project, there are a number of other items that need to be completed:

- Lien releases: The contractor must demonstrate that all liens by subcontractors and others have been released prior to final completion.

- Insurance turnover: The owner's property insurance coverage must take over at the date of substantial completion. Gaps in insurance can put you and/or the property at risk.

- Utilities: The owner is responsible for heat and utilities at the date of substantial completion.

- Warranties: Copies of warranties for the work must be provided as required by the specifications.

CERTIFICATE OF FINAL COMPLETION

Once the punch list items are finished, the building department has issued a certificate of occupancy, and you take occupancy, the contractor will request final payment. At this time a Certificate of Final Completion is issued and the remaining money (the retainage) is released.

Retainage is carefully regulated, and regulations vary by state. California has particularly protective regulations for contractors and subcontractors as a result of payment issues that occurred during the 2008 recession. It is important that you be aware of your state's laws and the requirements of the contract in regard to final payment of the contractor.

For more information on the architect's role in contractual matters and other administrative tasks during the project and the closeout, see "Contract Administration" by Patrick Mays (listed in the Bibliography).

GRAND OPENINGS AND RIBBON CUTTINGS

The grand opening and ribbon cutting is a time to celebrate all you've accomplished, look forward with anticipation to the future, and communicate your vision and goals to community members as you welcome them into your brand-new building. It is best to schedule these for a date when you know you will have been in your new hospital for a couple of weeks to a month. Don't try to do a grand opening the day after you move in, or something will surely go awry! You'll be a lot better off with a quiet soft opening, which will allow you to get all your equipment moved in, operations ramped up, pictures on the wall, and so on before the big party.

CHAPTER 60

POST MOVE IN—
WARRANTIES AND MAINTENANCE

Moving into your new facility is a huge accomplishment! However, it can be easy to get so caught up in the excitement of the new space and all of the hustle and bustle of reorganizing your business that you forget about caring for the building itself, unless something is clearly not working. However, the first year is very important, particularly for warranty issues. Once you are settled in, you should start doing what it takes to protect your investment and keep your building working the way it was designed to work. Your building, like everything else in the universe, will trend toward greater disorder. Your responsibility as an owner is to hold it together as long as you can, and the key is to start off on the right foot.

The first step is to understand your building and its systems. You should be given a packet of information by your general contractor with warranty information and the operation and maintenance (O&M) manuals for all the components and equipment supplied by the contractor in the building. You should familiarize yourself with this information, as should key staff people. Keep the manuals safe and use them as the valuable resource they are, even if they do seem overly technical and boring.

WARRANTIES

In most cases, you will have a warranty of one year on the building and its systems, beginning from the date of substantial completion. This does not mean that during this year the contractor has to maintain your building. Rather, it means that if you maintain the building properly, and you use the building in a manner consistent with the way it was designed, then the contractor will warranty the building and its systems against failure above and beyond what would occur in normal use. If within the warranty period something is not working properly, you can submit a warranty claim to the contractor, and the contractor will send a person out to fix the issue. Typical examples may include glitches with the mechanical system balancing or controls, or minor failures, such as of caulk, hardware, etc.

Walk through the building once more with your architect and contractor before the end of the warranty period to catch anything that may have cropped up over the year, and submit claims before it is too late. This is known as a "one-year warranty walk."

MAINTENANCE

Along with generally familiarizing yourself with the systems and warranties for which you are responsible, it is also necessary to start immediately committing the necessary time and resources to building maintenance. For larger facilities, this will require a full-time maintenance person. Smaller facilities should retain a company to provide regular and routine maintenance. If you do not do this, systems will fail, fan belts will break, filters will clog up, and the building could be damaged. The first year is critical for this maintenance for two main reasons:

- You will be more likely to find and fix problems that fall within the warranty period if you are maintaining the systems.

- You will develop processes to protect the building systems over time.

The most important system to maintain is the HVAC system. Most practices contract this work out. Your contract should include the following:

- Regular filter changes. In veterinary hospitals, these need to be changed far more often than in most commercial buildings. Once per month is typical.

- Seasonal work, such as cleaning debris, winterizing, draining.

- Regular maintenance of belts, motors, fans, and other moving parts.

It is critical that you hire a responsible and high-quality maintenance company for this HVAC work. You will depend on these professionals to carefully maintain these systems so you can get the full lifespan out of the equipment.

In addition to maintaining the HVAC systems, you should strongly consider a maintenance contract for other critical systems and materials, including these:

- Medical gas systems.

- Central vacuum and cleaning systems.

- Flooring systems.

- Landscaping and irrigation.

Most of these items must be maintained if you expect to keep your warranties intact.

UTILITY COSTS

In many cases, veterinarians are moving into bigger and more modern facilities than they ever have before. Along with the bigger mortgage comes bigger utility bills. Some people are surprised by this, because they expect new HVAC systems to be more efficient. In truth, the systems are more efficient, but they are also typically doing much more than the old systems did. This often means utility bills are significantly higher. Compounding this situation, the first utility bills may also reflect installation or deposit costs that will occur one time only.

If after a few months your bills are still higher than you expected, do not hesitate to talk with your architect and contractor about these costs to ensure there is in fact nothing wrong. Oftentimes higher-than-normal utility bills are a function of the HVAC system not being balanced, operated, or maintained correctly.

PLUMBING

Some plumbing concerns may require the owner to have some basic understanding of the systems. To minimize potential damage when things go wrong, you should know where your main water shutoff is located. Likewise, it makes sense for you to know where the individual shutoff valves are located for each of the hose bibs and sinks. For example, if something freezes, it will be necessary to shut off water to these fixtures until the problem can be repaired.

Hair traps, if you have them, will need to be regularly maintained. This is a nasty job! A likely spot for a hair trap is underneath a grooming tub.

All plumbing systems may clog if faced with unusual challenges. Ask your staff and visitors to be careful with what they flush, and be particularly vigilant about keeping some items, such as dog toys and cat litter, from entering drains.

It is best to scoop feces before washing runs rather than forcing feces down drains, unless your drains are specifically designed to accept solid matter.

CONCRETE SLABS

All concrete cracks! Even in the best construction, concrete shrinks. It is normal to see some kind of superficial cracking in concrete floor slabs. This is also the case with tile or epoxy flooring. These materials are inflexible and bound to the concrete and will show minor cracking. While potentially annoying, these superficial cracks are part of the normal aging process of a building, and in most cases repair work is more unsightly than the original crack.

On rare occasions it is possible for floor and wall cracking to be more significant. If you have any significant cracks, larger than small, hairline cracks, discuss them immediately with your architect and contractor to determine whether an unusual condition is occurring.

FLOORING

Many flooring products require some maintenance. Follow these general rules:

- Use cleaners and disinfectants that are compatible with the flooring material in order to protect your investment.

- *Do not* use very hot water or steam on epoxy floors or they may fail, as epoxies do not have much tolerance for thermal shock.

- Regularly wax vinyl and other sheet floors, such as linoleum, on a schedule that prevents them from wearing. This may be more often than predicted by the flooring manufacturer because floors in veterinary settings get used hard.

- Reseal concrete and stained concrete as often as needed to prevent wear. For stained concrete floors, this may be every six months to a year. It is often possible to use a "sacrificial wax" on top that is applied more often but allows the sealer to wear longer.

- Tile and resinous floor products should not require any maintenance other than good cleaning and elbow grease.

CLEANING AND DISINFECTION

Improperly cleaning your facility can cause it to wear or age prematurely. The most common mistake is using disinfectants above the recommended dilution ratio. This practice is both expensive and potentially damaging to finishes.

Use the gentlest disinfectants that can be used to achieve the level of biological control required. For example, accelerated hydrogen peroxide, which is now the disinfectant of choice in human and animal hospitals, is gentler on surfaces than bleach, assuming it is diluted properly.

▼ ▼ ▼

THE VALUE IN a veterinary practice is primarily in the practice itself. Like most commercial buildings, the real estate investment is a fraction of the long-term costs of operating the practice, hiring personnel, and other expenses. This said, the initial investment of constructing a building comes all at once and takes decades, in some cases, to pay off. It is the single biggest one-time expense your business is likely to have.

Protect your building by paying attention to it, especially during the first year, to be sure it is working properly and as designed. Most importantly, be vigilant with maintenance so your building lasts for decades, does what it is supposed to do, and maintains its value over time.

CHAPTER 61

THE DOS AND DON'TS AND TALES FROM THE TRENCHES

When you build your hospital, you will likely enter into one of the most stressful times of your life. You'll be spending more money than ever before, you'll be adding a huge time commitment to your already full plate, and undoubtedly something else will be happening, like the arrival of a new baby or a personnel issue at the hospital, because that's how life works. The veterinarians who do the best with these projects, and who come back to build more, are the ones who see the big picture, who appreciate their many accomplishments—despite the probability of some minor failures—and who maintain their patience and sense of humor through it all.

In order to help prepare you for the wild ride called construction, below is a collection of a few war stories. These stories are pretty typical, and some repeat themselves regularly. It is a guarantee that nothing will go perfectly. But perhaps you'll get to avoid a few of your own battles by reading about some of them ahead of time, and maybe find a little humor along the way.

APPRAISAL WOES

A few years ago, one of our partners was getting an appraisal done on her house to get a construction loan. The appraiser arrived, all heels and high fashion. To everyone's mutual horror, within the first few strides into the yard, she stepped in dog poop, which enveloped itself around her high heel. While this embarrassing incident shouldn't have mattered to the appraised value of the property, somehow it did.

Sometimes it seems like veterinarians must be subject to the same sort of karmic intervention, because many of you are likely to struggle with your veterinary appraisal more than you should. The problem seems to be pulling the right comparable projects. Your hospital is not the same as a human dental clinic, for example. Veterinary hospitals are notoriously expensive buildings, and many local banks, and even some national ones, cannot seem to find appropriate comparable projects.

Assuming the architect has designed a building that meets the budget, as defined by a skilled veterinary financial adviser, and the project has been estimated accurately, then it is in your best interest to get the correct appraisal from the bank for the value of the project. The worst thing you can do is to go ahead anyway with a loan that is too low and hope for the best, as it is nearly impossible to bring a project in well under its initial estimated value.

Moral of the story—expect the financing of your project to take some time, and work with the group that is in alignment with your team. It often takes a bank experienced in financing veterinary projects to accomplish this.

GETTING ADVICE FROM UNCLE BOB

Everyone has an Uncle Bob. He's the guy who says, "Why are you paying so much for that project? I can do it for $150 per square foot!" Uncle Bob has probably been building other types of commercial or residential projects for decades. After hearing advice from Uncle Bob for months, you can really start to doubt yourself, your direction, and your team. After all, you don't want to pay too much for your project, and that's completely understandable.

Time and time again, veterinary projects prove themselves to be 25%–30% more expensive than would be anticipated by someone who has not built one before. These projects have more doors, walls, hardware, equipment, electrical outlets, cooling loads, ventilation requirements, plumbing fixtures, high-performance finishes, and specialty systems than any other commercial project except a human hospital.

Moral of the story—work with contractors who can accurately estimate your project. Give yourself a healthy contingency initially until you are certain your design meets your budget. Most importantly, understand that your Uncle Bob can be helpful, but he may not always be right.

HOW DO WE LOVE THEE, GOVERNMENT OFFICIALS? LET US COUNT THE WAYS

Every time you think you have seen it all, the Authorities Having Jurisdiction (an official term) dream up something else. There have been occasions when veterinary projects have been hung up for months, and even a year or more, navigating the various governmental approval requirements. While it would seem that veterinary projects shouldn't be any more difficult to permit than other commercial projects, they can be because they include unusual elements, such as medical gas systems, animal waste, etc. Here are some true and repetitive stories from the trenches:

- One practice discovered that their hospital was *not* an approved use in that zone after they'd finished all the design work and submitted for a permit. Never assume your project is zoned correctly, as it may not be in your design team's scope to verify. Find out for yourself, as the consequences can be severe.

- One jurisdiction decided that dog poop was equivalent to nuclear waste and would not permit the dogs to poop outside. Avoid drawing attention to dog poop in the first place, as whatever you do will likely be deemed a risk that needs to be dealt with. If it comes up, be prepared to quickly respond to demonstrate that your design protects health and the environment. Examples could include your protocol for scoop and disposal of solid matter, a separate yard for isolation animals, disinfectants—such as accelerated hydrogen peroxide—that are safe to use outside, etc. With the poop issue, wait until it comes up, and then be prepared with solutions. The answer, "What about wild animals? They poop outside all the time," may be true, but it is not a popular response.

- The neighbors around a practice were worried that the dogs would be loud and organized a group, armed with flaming pitchforks, to come to the next planning hearing meeting. As opposed to dog poop, which seems to be an issue that cannot be won, your best bet with neighbors is to talk to them proactively well ahead of time about noise concerns, actually listen, and show that you are addressing their concerns. Don't let this get out of control at official meetings, or your project could end up with serious limitations, such as not being able to keep hospitalized dogs overnight.

- In some cases, the authorities aren't exactly sure what it is that you do and have the practice make a huge list of hazardous materials you may have in the hospital. Expect this ahead of time. For most general practices, the only material that will be stored in enough quantities to be limited by the code is medical gas (specifically oxygen). Have this information handy. Hospitals providing specialty services, including radiation therapy and chemotherapy, will need to work harder to address applicable federal, state, and local requirements.

THE TOPPLING PORTA POTTY AND OTHER JOBSITE CHALLENGES

Jobsites can be rough and confusing places. Safety is always a concern, and your contractor is responsible for maintaining a safe jobsite. But concerns do arise, including personnel issues, thievery, vandalism, and graffiti.

Perhaps one of the most unique jobsite problems a veterinary practice has faced is the scourge of the late-night porta potty tippers. The potty tippers in this case hit the jobsite at least once a week for several weeks! No amount of basic security, such as bolting the potty, chaining the potty, and employing night watch security, could foil the potty-tipping enthusiasts, who clearly enjoyed the challenge. Eventually they tired of the game and moved on.

Moral of the story—although gross, the tipping porta potty was a fairly harmless problem compared to a whole host of more sinister and potentially dangerous activities a jobsite can face. Be absolutely sure that before your project begins, all the correct insurance is in place, including builder's risk insurance, which covers you, the owner, against damage or loss to the in-progress project during the construction period.

TILE OVER IT!

Existing buildings always have something special to share that will increase your construction budget. In one case, the veterinarians purchased an old church fellowship hall for conversion. When they pulled up the floor, the nightmare was exposed, which was the worst concrete slab, topped with an asbestos leveling product, ever known to construction.

Not only did the asbestos require remediation, but the slab was in such poor shape that it required a different approach to flooring material selection. In this case, they used a new patching and leveling product on top of the slab and then tiled the entire hospital, as tile covers irregularities better than other products.

The client has a highly functional and successful project now, but the flooring issues definitely added to everyone's stress levels.

Moral of the story—every construction project needs a contingency for unknowns. Remodeling projects need higher contingencies, in the 10%–15% range.

TRANSFORMER—MORE THAN MEETS THE EYE

This story is about the importance of visiting the project site, and having your professionals do the same. During the construction of this hospital, the owners and their families took a well-deserved vacation out of the country. While they were away, the contracting team decided to reroute the main electrical service to the building in a way that was more efficient. The result was that the main building transformer got placed directly in front of the entrance to the hospital.

When the owners returned, they were horrified. The work was too difficult to undo, so they live with it still. Fortunately, the practice is a huge success story, and the business has well exceeded its financial goals.

Moral of the story—some things are not worth the effort to undo. Visit your jobsite often, be available for questions, and leave competent decisionmakers in charge when you need to be away. This kind of diligence won't protect you from all surprises, but it will minimize them. In the end, small mistakes may not affect your long-term business success.

CEILING CATS, WALL CATS, SOFFIT CATS, GO! CATS GOING EVERYWHERE, NO, NO, NO!

Remodeling projects may be hard on people, but they're even harder on patients, and cats in particular. During one remodeling project, a scared cat escaped into the construction zone. He zoomed through ceilings and an open soffit until he fell down inside a finished tiled wall. Dismantling the finished wall was worth getting the cat out safely, but everyone was distraught.

Moral of the story—animals need to be kept very safe from construction zones in projects. They're more frightened and more agile, and the consequences for a loose animal are embarrassing at the least and possibly much worse.

PIGEONS AND RACCOONS, OH MY!

It seems that nothing good happens after closing time, and that's true of your project site as well. During more than one project, wild animals have entered and paraded through newly placed epoxy floors. The little footprints look pretty cute, but you probably didn't plan to pay $10 per square foot for raccoon prints.

Moral of the story—some minor problems are hard to predict, and may be harder to fix. Review all "fix" solutions with your contractor to be sure the patch isn't worse than the original problem. This doesn't mean that in general you should accept poor-quality work. Your architect can help you interpret whether an installation (raccoon feet aside) meets the requirements of the plans and specifications as well as required levels of quality. Work that does not meet these standards should be repaired or replaced.

HATERS GONNA HATE

Once you are finally ready to move in, all should be happy and bright, right? Not so for many veterinary practices. The first few months may be very challenging as you and your staff relearn every step that you take. Opening a new hospital can be very stressful.

Perhaps the most disturbing occurrence is the naysaying client who complains that his or her bill is too high because of the new fancy building. This person is out there, and you will meet him or her when you build.

The truth is, some people are just going to be unhappy no matter what. It is difficult to accept this, but we all know it in our hearts.

Moral of the story—new construction should help you provide the best service you can to your clients and their pets, which will make most people happy. Most of your clients want you to be successful and want to take their pets to a first-rate medical space. The few negative ones out there probably weren't your best clients anyway.

CONCLUSION: THE FUTURE OF VETERINARY CARE

As architects specializing in the design of veterinary hospitals, we may be uniquely positioned to understand the personal financial struggles, career goals, aspirations, and challenges facing veterinarians. As much as veterinarians themselves, we want to view the future of veterinary medicine with a positive lens, because this profession has so much to offer to individuals, communities, and the greater world. Fortunately, this positive lens is being sharpened on the future by the greater veterinary medical community, as a response to the repositioning of the profession after the events of the recession, when veterinarians suffered from radically increasing debt loads, low pay, and dwindling demand for services.

In a press release from the AVMA in April 2016 that summarized the results of a summit among experts to reexamine the debt-to-income ratio among recent graduates and to develop solutions, we noted that amongst these solutions was the idea "to inform pre-veterinary students about the current student debt issue and discuss what is being done to address it; and to change their mind-set from ownership to entrepreneurship, and work on developing a campaign where every veterinarian commits to being an entrepreneur" (AVMA).

We have always felt that ownership and better yet, entrepreneurship, form the backbone of financial success for veterinarians. Working for someone is a difficult way to make a path forward in life. But working for yourself, building your support, and becoming a leader can be some of the key ways to bring about financial success and to have enough of a support network to enjoy life.

New veterinarians with an entrepreneurial spirit may wonder how they can find the money to make money when student debt loads will still be a looming reality. The answer is not simple, and it varies for each person. We do know that for most, the days of building a dream hospital right out of school have passed. Today, the path to ownership may need to be followed collaboratively or incrementally. Anecdotally though, we have

When the dream becomes reality. (Foto Imagery / Tim Murphy. Courtesy of VCA PetCare Veterinary Hospital, Santa Rosa, California [VCA, Inc.].)

witnessed incremental approaches work remarkably well, often in a short period of time. Many entrepreneurial veterinarians ease themselves into the practice they can just barely responsibly afford, where they build equity and profit, and soon find themselves in a better place to do their next project.

Ultimately, veterinary hospitals will continue to be the most important physical asset for veterinary entrepreneurs. Hospitals need to be the best money-making spaces they can be. What this means changes as the years pass, but it is inspiring to us that the art of hospital design remains a vital part of supporting the veterinary profession itself.

Beyond the continuing need for veterinary entrepreneurship, we are curious about what the future holds for the veterinary profession. Perhaps the most interesting idea is the concept of One Health (humans, environment, and animals living together harmoniously). Leaders such as the University of Pennsylvania School of Veterinary Medicine have become active in supporting the One Health movement, which recognizes that veterinarians are uniquely trained and positioned to help the people of the world with the interrelationships between the wellbeing of humans, animals, and the environment. For example, veterinarians working together with public health professionals can help identify risks and find solutions to global zoonotic disease challenges. As Dean Joan C. Hendricks, VMD, PhD, of the University of Pennsylvania School of Veterinary Medicine states, "Veterinary medicine is the profession that stands between all of humanity and plague and famine" (Hendricks).

While it is a lofty and perhaps overwhelming goal to help the world via veterinary medical training, One Health is an example of veterinarians thinking beyond the basics of patient care and reaching out to embrace opportunities to help other fields. A closer-to-home example of this shift is the recently emerged specialty of shelter medicine. Shelter medicine specialists are trained to help animals in a shelter environment, which involves the professionalization of different concepts in companion animal medicine, such as herd health, biological risk management, animal behavior, and animal population control.

Our takeaway from all of these broad changes is that veterinarians are now being expected to think far beyond the four walls of their hospitals. Fear Free veterinary care is indicative of this greater thinking. We must fundamentally change the approach to practice in order to provide humane and compassionate care to each animal, to reinforce client loyalty, and to build healthy teams and practices.

Veterinarians who can think big will move beyond the transaction-based practice to whole-life care for pets. This has been the push for many years, but it is becoming ever more apparent that veterinary practices that bring humanity and individualized patient care to the forefront will be the next successful leaders.

We are constantly reminded of why we love this profession. Despite the complexities of the modern world we all face, veterinary medicine provides a positive contribution to the lives of individual animals, humans, healthcare in general, and our relationships with one another. We encourage each and every veterinarian to think, dream, and build, both for the present and for our future.

BIBLIOGRAPHY

AAHA Standards of Accreditation. AAHA. July 2015. Web.

"Acoustic Noise: What's All That Noise the Scanner Is Making?" Questions and Answers in MRI. N.d. Web.

"Bone Marrow Transplant." VCA West Los Angeles Animal Hospital. N.d. Web.

Choi, Joonho, and Liliana O. Beltran. "Study of the Relationship Between Patients' Recovery and Indoor Daylight Environment of Patient Rooms in Heathcare Facilities." *Proceedings of the 2004 ESES Asia-Pacific Conference*. October 17, 2004. Web.

"Feline Housing Considerations in a Shelter/Rescue, Veterinary Hospital or Boarding Facility." UC Davis Veterinary Medicine, Koret Shelter Medicine Program. June 2015. Web.

Fencl, Forrest. "Hospital Infection Control: Reducing Airborne Pathogens." *Heathcare Facilities Today*. June 2014. Web.

Fry, Richard. "Millennials Surpass Gen Xers as the Largest Generation in U.S. Labor Force." Pew Research Center. May 2015. Web.

Gilk, Tobias. "MRI Suites: Safety Outside the Bore." *Patient Safety and Quality Heathcare*. September/October 2006. Web.

Hendricks, Joan C. "What the World (Particularly Medical Doctors) Can Learn from Veterinarians." *Huffington Post*. March 2013. Web.

Heschong, Lisa. "Daylighting and Human Performance." *ASHRAE Journal*. June 2002. Web.

Mays, Patrick. "Contract Administration." Excerpt from *The Architect's Handbook of Professional Practice*, 13th ed. Washington, DC: American Institute of Architects. 2000. Web.

McConnell, Patricia. "What If You Were a Dog in a Noisy Kennel?" ASPCA. September 2013. Web.

"MRI Design Guide." Department of Veterans Affairs. April 2008. Web.

National Research Council (US) Committee on Recognition and Alleviation of Distress in Laboratory Animals. *Recognition and Alleviation of Distress in Laboratory Animals*. Washington, DC: National Academies Press (US). 2008. Part 2, "Stress and Distress: Definitions." Web.

Newberry, Sandra, Mary K. Blinn, and Philip A. Bushby, et al. "Guidelines for Standard of Care in Animal Shelters: Association of Shelter Veterinarians." Association of Shelter Veterinarians. 2010. Web.

"Participants from Across the Veterinary Profession Gather to Identify Ways to Alleviate Student Debt." American Veterinary Medical Foundation. April 2016. Web.

Petersen, Christine A., Glenda Dvorak, and Anna Rovid-Spickler. "Maddie's Infection Control Manual for Animal Shelters: For Veterinary Personnel." Iowa State University, Center for Food Security and Public Health. 2008. Print.

Procedural Standards for TAB Environmental Systems, 8th ed. National Environmental Balancing Bureau. 2015. Web.

"Sanitation in Animal Shelters." UC Davis Veterinary Medicine, Koret Shelter Medicine Program. June 2015. Web.

Snowden, Charles T., David Teie, and Megan Savage. "Cats Prefer Species-Appropriate Music." *Applied Animal Behaviour Science*. May 2015. Vol 166. Web.

"USP General Chapter <800> *Hazardous Drugs—Handling in Healthcare Setting*." Reprinted from USP 40—NF 35, Second Supplement (2017). United States Pharmacopeia. 2017. Web.

Weisse, Chick. "Interventional Radiology: A Trend in Veterinary Medicine." *Clinician's Brief*. October 2014. Web.

"Windows and Offices: A Study of Office Worker Performance and the Indoor Environment—CEC PIER 2003." Heschong Mahone Group. 2013. Web.

FURTHER READING

Animal Housing

National Research Council (US) Committee for the Update of the Guide for the Care and Use of Laboratory Animals. *Guide for the Care and Use of Laboratory Animals*, 8th ed. Washington, DC: National Academies Press (US). 2011. Web.

Biological Risk Management/HVAC Design

"ASHRAE Position Document on Airborne Infectious Diseases." American Society of Heating, Refrigerating, and Air-Conditioning Engineers. 2014. Web.

NAFA Guide to Air Filtration, 2nd ed. National Air Filtration Association. 1996. Print.

Emergency Eyewash Standards

"ANSI/ISEA Z358.1-2014: American National Standard for Emergency Eyewash and Shower Equipment." International Safety Equipment Association. 2014. Web.

Flooring

"302.2R-06: Guide for Concrete Slabs That Receive Moisture-Sensitive Flooring Materials." American Concrete Institute. 2006. Web or print.

Lighting

Energy Information Administration website, eia.gov.

Sustainable Design

"Checklist: LEED v4 for Building Design and Construction." United States Green Building Council. 2016. Web.

INDEX

A

AAHA accreditation standards, 68–73
    dental care areas, 166
    exam room design, 144
    exterior lighting, 22
    flooring in surgical areas, 202, 280–281
    isolation space, 223
    signage, 21
acoustical ceilings, 158, 202, 222, 262, 287–288
adaptive reuse projects, 27–30
architect's supplemental instructions (ASIs), 337, 340
additions to existing buildings, 38–42, 88–92
adoption centers: feline hospitals, 122
aerosol transmission of disease, 64–65, 72, 166, 199, 253
air conditioning. *See* HVAC systems
air exchanges. *See* HVAC systems
air pressurization. *See* HVAC systems
aluminum storefront doors, 292–293
Americans with Disabilities Act (ADA), 322
ancillary services, 226–231
    boarding, 226–229
    daycare, 228–229
    grooming, 229–231
    physical rehabilitation, 206–211
    zoning of the desired location, 21–22
    See also specialty equipment
anesthesia
    AAHA accreditation induction standards, 68–69
    equipment selection and purchase, 314
    medical gas design, 257–259
animal housing, 212–219, 215(figures), 216(figure), 217(figure), 218(figure)
    biological risk management, 62–67
    boarding facilities, 226–229
    cat boarding, 123
    equipment selection and purchase, 313–315
    furnishings, 302, 307
    housing for cats, 214–216
    housing for dogs, 216–218
    ICU housing, 163–164, 221
    isolation ward design, 225
    lighting design, 268–269
    noise control, 213–214
    plumbing design, 252
    treatment room housing, 159
    ventilated caging, 246–247, 247(figure), 248(figure), 249(figure)
    ward design, 220–222
antineoplastic drugs, 188–190
application for payment (pay app), 337
architects and architecture
    bidding process, 333–334
    construction administration (CA), 337
    construction drawings and documents, 44–45, 335–336
    construction milestones, 342–343
    contractor's application for payment, 337
    cost estimates, 332
    design milestones, 332–333
    green architecture, 93–98
    jobsite role, 340
    observation and inspection, 337–338
    predicting the size of the project, 12–13
    project delivery methods, 325–330
    schematic drawings, 44–45
artwork and photography, 307–308
autoclaves, 250, 314(figure), 315

B

bathrooms, public and staff, 96, 255
beaches, recovery, 159–160, 201, 202(figure), 220
bidding a project, 327–334
biological risk management, 62–67
    chemotherapy treatment, 188–190
    creating a healthy environment, 243–245
    Iodine-131 suites, 192–194
    separating the surgery suite from dirty areas, 199–200
    surgical pack/prep areas, 200–201
    See also cleaning and housekeeping, HVAC systems; sanitation; plumbing and plumbing design
biophilic design, 97–98
boarding services, 226–229
    feline hospitals, 121, 123
box walk, 342
branding, 74–79, 85–86, 137, 142
break rooms, 234–235, 306
    in floor planning, 103, 112

budget
  change orders, 337
  construction costs, 15–16
  defining the scope of a project, 13–14
  estimating versus bidding, 331–334
  equine and large animal hospitals, 126–127
  project budgeting, 15–18
  renovations, 39–40
  sustainable materials, 95
builder's risk insurance, 336
building codes and permits
  AAHA accreditation standards, 72–73
  environmental, wetlands, and storm drainage requirements, 322–323
  finding the right lease space, 29–30
  laboratory design, 151
  large animal hospitals, 126
  post-project verification, 352–353
  renovation versus building new, 39
  signage, 76
  state requirements, 321–322
  sustainable design, 93, 97–98
  timeline of a project, 45–46
  utilizing daylight, 273
  See also planning and zoning; regulatory requirements

C

cabinets
  biological safety cabinets, 323
  color palette selection, 299
  efficient and effective use of storage space, 233–234
  laboratory design, 150–151
  MRI room, 186
  surgery rooms, 69
  treatment room design, 157–159
  See also storage
caging and runs. See animal housing
C-arms (mobile fluoroscopy units), 173
carpet, 281, 283(figure)
cat-specific elements
  boarding facilities, 229
  Fear Free design, 52–54
  feline hospital design, 120–124
  housing for stress reduction, 213–216
  Iodine-131 for feline hyperthyroidism, 192–194
  ventilated enclosures, 246–247, 247(figure), 248(figure), 249(figure)
  waiting area furnishings, 304–305
  ward types and sizes, 221–222
ceiling construction, 285–290
change orders, 337

charting
  design and layout, 148–154, 153(figure)
  laboratory/pharmacy buffer area, 101
  multifunction areas, 156–158
  open core design, 117–118
  See also computer stations
chemotherapy, 188–190, 250, 323
circulation pathways. See traffic flow in a building
cleaning and housekeeping
  biological risk management design, 62–67
  cleaning runs, 252–254
  design for sanitation, 60–61
  door hardware, 295
  Fear Free design, 52
  flooring for heavily cleaned areas, 277–278
  flooring maintenance, 349–350
  isolation wards, 224–225
  siting janitorial closets, 236–237
  See also biological risk management; sanitation
client services. See reception area
color, interior and exterior
  color palettes, 296–301
  Fear Free design, 53–54
  flooring products, 284
  branding elements, 78, 142
  renovations, 41
  surgery rooms, 204–205
communication among staff and clients
  AAHA accreditation standards for surgical area design, 72
  fish bowl workstations, 153
  transparency in the hospital and practice, 80–83
compounding room for antineoplastic drugs, 188–190
computed radiography (CR), 167, 171–172
computer stations
  cardiology and ultrasound, 175
  chairs and stools for, 305
  dental stations, 169
  diagnostic imaging and radiation safety, 71, 172
  laboratory areas, 150
  oncology treatment areas, 190, 192
  physical rehabilitation, 207, 210
  reception areas, 141
  treatment areas, 158
  See also charting
concierge services, 86–87, 87(figure), 141
concrete flooring, 202, 277, 281, 282(figure), 283(figure), 349–350
concrete block/masonry units (CMUs), 192, 286
  equine and large animal hospitals, 130
  sound isolation, 262, 263

concrete slabs, 349
    construction milestones, 342
    CT rooms, 180
    existing conditions, 23
    floor design and installation, 276–277, 284
    MRI rooms, 184, 185
    noise control, 263–264
    plumbing, 65, 251
conference rooms, 235–236, 306
construction documents and drawings (CDs). *See* architects and architecture
Construction Manager at Risk delivery method, 327–328
Construction Manager/General Contractor (CM/GC delivery method), 327–332
construction or contract administration (CA), 337
construction phase, 45–46, 46(figure), 333–338
    construction costs, 15–18
    construction terms, 336–338
    delivery methods, 325–330
    equipment planning, 312–315
    jobsite elements, 339–343
consultation rooms, 146
contract negotiations, 46(figure), 47, 329–330
contractors
    cost estimates, 352
    jobsite roles, 340–341
    managing project costs, 331–332
    observation and inspection, 337–338
    project delivery methods, 325–330
    selection of, 336
    timeline of a project, 45–47
cooling. *See* HVAC systems
cost estimators, 332–333
costs
    boarding spaces, 227–228
    defining the scope of a project, 11–14
    estimating versus bidding for the project, 331–334
    loans, 9–10
    See also budget
coved floors, 66, 202, 278, 280(figure), 281, 281
critical care unit (CCU). *See* ICU wards
computed tomography (CT), 176–178, 177(figure), 177(figure), 180–182, 181(figure)
curb appeal, 74–79

D

dental stations, 156, 166–170
    chairs and stools, 305
    flex exam rooms, 106
    HVAC design, 245
dermatology, 197–198
Design Build delivery method, 326–327, 332
Design/Bid/Build delivery methods, 327–330
digital radiography (DR), 167, 171–172
disease transmission
    AAHA accreditation standards for isolation, 69
    biological risk management design, 62–67
    isolation ward design, 223–225
disinfection, 64, 253–254, 323
    See also biological risk management; cleaning and housekeeping; sanitation
doctors' stations. *See* charting; computer stations
doggy daycare, 228–229
dog-specific elements
    biological risk management, 64–65
    Fear Free design, 52–53
    housing areas, 216–218
    noise control in animal housing, 214
    ward types and sizes, 221
door hardware, 295
doors and windows, 291–295
drains. *See* water and drainage
dry rehabilitation areas, 207

E

electrical requirements
    CT suites, 180–182
    finding the right lease space, 24–25
    ICU, 164
    laboratory design, 70–71, 151
    LINAC equipment, 191
    MRI rooms and mobile units, 184, 186–187
    radiology and fluoroscopy, 172–173
    underwater treadmills and swimming pools, 207–208
elimination areas, 79
    animal housing, 213
    housing areas for dogs, 216–218
    ventilated caging, 246–247, 247(figure), 248(figure), 249(figure)
emergency generators, 114, 190
emergency hospitals, 115–119
    exam room layout, 146–147
    ICU design, 161–162
emotional wellbeing of veterinary patients. *See* stress reduction
endoscopy services, 195–196
energy strategies
    emergency generators, 114
    HVAC design, 247, 250
    sustainable design, 93–97
environment, animal
    choosing a color palette, 296–301
    creating a healthy environment, 243–245
    See also animal housing

environmental quality
　assessments, 36
　requirements, 322–323
　sustainable design, 97
equine and large animal medicine, 125–131
equipment, specialty. *See* specialty equipment
equipment coordination, 310–315
ergonomics, 59–60, 103, 174, 305
euthanasia
　comfort rooms, 122
　consultation rooms, 146
　emergency hospitals, 116–117
evaporative cooling systems, 96
exam rooms, 143–147
　AAHA accreditation standards, 68–69
　chairs and stools, 305
　emergency hospitals, 116
　equine and large animal hospitals, 128, 128(figure)
　Fear Free design for cats, 53–54
　feline hospitals, 122
　flexible rooms, 106, 114, 116–117
　floor plans to maximize capacity, 102–103
　maximizing capacity in large hospitals, 105–106
　one-door exam rooms, 102–103, 144, 203
　open exam room design, 144–145
　planning for future expansion, 90–91
　the transparent approach, 81–82
　treatment room layout and, 156
　two-door exam rooms, 102–103, 144, 203
existing conditions of a desired location, 22–26
expansion of the practice, 88–92
　boarding areas, 226–227
　designing for increased traffic flow, 138–139
　mixed animal hospitals, 133–134
　planning a large animal hospital for expansion, 127
　specialty/referral hospitals, 112–114
exterior design
　curb appeal, 76–79
　doors, 291–293
　equine and large animal hospitals, 126–127
　existing conditions, 22–23
　outdoor furnishings, 306
　outdoor waiting areas, 139–140
　sustainability and, 94–95
eyewash station, 151, 190, 255, 323

F

Fear Free initiative, 10, 51–55
fecal/oral transmission of disease, 63–64
feline hospitals, 120–124
final completion, certificate, 346
financing, 15–18, 17(figure)

fire safety, 23–24, 73, 126, 257–258, 314
fish bowl workstations, 153
5-gauss line, 178, 186–187
floor designs and flooring materials, 275–284, 278(figure), 279(figure), 280(figure), 282(figure); 283(figure)
　color palette selection, 299–300
　construction milestones, 343
　equine and large animal, 130
　for noise control, 262–264
　neurology rooms, 198
　physical rehabilitation spaces, 210–211
　post move-in examination, 349–350
　surgery rooms, 202
floor plans and floor planning
　CT suite, 178–182
　dermatology suite, 197(figure)
　endoscopy rooms, 195–196
　equine and large animal hospitals, 127–130, 128(figure)
　exam room layouts, 144–146
　heating and cooling zones, 244(figure)
　laboratory, pharmacy, and charting stations, 149(figure)
　large hospitals, 104–108
　LINAC vault, 192(figure)
　mixed animal hospitals, 134, 134(figure)
　MRI room, 178–186
　renovation versus building new, 39
　small hospitals, 99–103
　specialty/referral hospitals, 109–114, 112(figure)
　surgery rooms, 202–2042
　transparent design approach, 83(figure)
　X-ray shielding, 172
fluoroscopy, 172–173, 201
fomite transmission of disease, 62–63
food preparation areas, 234, 243, 256
foreman of the project, 342
freestanding buildings, 31–37
　planning for growth and expansion, 89–92
　timeline of a project, 45–46, 46(figure)
furnishings, 302–309

G

gas scavenging, 258–259, 314
geothermal systems, 97, 242
greeter's station, 81, 141
grooming services, 229–231

H

handwashing sinks, 158, 174, 200, 224, 254
hard costs, 15–18, 17(figure)
handicap accessibility, 22, 66, 256, 322

hazardous materials
    hazardous drugs, 188–189
    hazardous waste, 36, 323
    OSHA regulations, 323
health departments, 324
heating systems. See HVAC systems
hemodialysis, 196–197
HEPA (high-efficiency particulate air) filtration, 72, 189–190, 203, 247
historic sites, 36–37, 320, 322
hollow metal doors, 292, 293
horses, 5–6, 81, 125–131
hose systems and bibs. See plumbing and plumbing design
HVAC systems, 241–250
    air exchanges, 203, 246–247
    air pressurization, 189–190, 199, 203, 225, 245, 250, 345
    animal housing, 212–213, 215–216, 246–247, 247(figure), 248(figure), 249(figure)
    biological risk management, 64–65
    boarding spaces, 227
    grooming facilities, 230–231
    isolation wards, 223–225
    maintenance, 348
    MRI and CT suites, 178, 182, 184–185
    noise control and, 265–266
    physical rehabilitation spaces, 210–211
    reducing energy consumption, 96–97
    surgery rooms, 72, 203
    sustainable design, 96–97
    sterile compounding room, 189
    testing, adjusting, and balancing, 344–345
    utility requirements, 26
hydrotherapy, 207–209

I
ICU wards
    animal housing, 221
    design and layout, 161–170
    hemodialysis units, 196–197
    oxygen systems, 258
    step-down wards, 118–119
illuminance levels, 267–269
imaging services, 167, 171–175
    AAHA accreditation standards, 70–71
    CT, 176–178, 177(figure), 180–182, 181(figure)
    equipment selection and purchase, 312–313
    MRI, 114, 176–177, 179(figure), 182–186
    ultrasound, 106, 110, 173–175
    See also radiology areas and technology; shielding
insurance, builder's risk, 336, 346
inventory control systems, 152(figure), 153

Iodine-131 (I-131), 123, 192–194
isolation rooms, 223–225
    AAHA accreditation standards, 68–69, 70(figure)
    biological risk management, 63
    HVAC requirement, 243, 245, 246, 250

J
janitors' closets, 254–255

K
knock down (KD) steel doors, 293–294

L
laboratory spaces
    AAHA accreditation standards, 70–71
    as a buffer, 101–102
    design and layout, 148–154, 149(figure)
    mixed animal hospitals, 133
    plumbing design, 255
landscaping, 32–33, 76–77, 94–96
large animal practices, 125–134
Leadership in Energy and Environmental Design (LEED), 93, 95
lead-lined doors, 294
leasehold practices, 19–26, 46(figure), 88–89
lien releases, 346
lighting, 267–274, 268(figure), 269(figure)
    color temperature, 271–272
    connecting treatment rooms to the outside, 156–158
    CT suites, 180–182
    daylighting in animal housing, 213
    dermatology rooms, 197–198
    exterior lighting at an emergency hospital, 115
    Fear Free design, 54–55
    ICU layout, 162–163
    LED fixtures, 97, 203, 270–272, 271(figures)
    MRI rooms, 184
    reception area design, 141; 271(figure)
    rehabilitation areas, 208
    renovations, 41
    solar orientation, 94
    surgery rooms, 203–204
    sustainable design, 97
    ultrasound rooms, 175
LINAC (linear accelerator), 190–192, 192(figure), 193(figure)
linoleum, 279–281, 283(figure)
loans for constructing a practice, 9–10
lobby. See reception area; vestibules; waiting areas
location
    adaptive reuse projects, 27–30
    choosing the right space, 19–26

location, *continued*
   designing for context, 56–58
   environmental protection regulations, 322–323
   existing conditions, 22–26
   for a large animal hospital, 125–126
   market viability of a location, 19–21, 27
   renovation versus building new, 39
   siting a freestanding building, 31–32
   state permitting requirements, 321–322
   sustainable design, 93–95
   zoning and neighbors, 21–22, 320–321
logos, 74, 78, 79(figure)
luxury vinyl tile (LVT), 282–283, 283(figure)

M

materials
   animal housing, 215–216, 222
   biological risk management design, 63
   doors and door hardware, 291–293, 292(figure), 293(figure), 295
   equine and large animal hospitals, 130
   Fear Free design, 53
   fine-tuning reception area design, 141–142
   interior branding elements, 78
   isolation wards, 225
   laboratory design, 151
   for noise control, 260, 262–264, 263(figure)
   surgery room ceilings, floors, and walls, 202–203
   sustainable design, 94–95
   walls and ceilings, 285–290
   See also floor design; flooring materials
mechanical requirements. *See* HVAC systems
medical areas
   AAHA accreditation standards, 69–72
   air filtration, 247
   avoiding compartmentalizing in emergency hospitals, 117–118
   designing functional spaces, 59–61
   floor plans for large hospitals, 104–108
   floor plans for small hospitals, 99–101, 103
   flooring materials, 279–281
   mixed animal hospitals, 133–134
   the transparent approach, 81
   See also treatment areas
medical gas design, 182, 257–259, 314. *See also* anesthesia
mixed animal hospitals, 132–134
mobile units (MRI), 186–187
monitoring systems
   isolation wards, 224
   MRI rooms, 183–184
   placement of wards for monitoring, 220–221
mop closets, 254–255

MRI (magnetic resonance imaging), 114, 176–177, 179(figure),182–186, 201
multipurpose rooms, 87, 116–117, 146, 235–236
multistory hospitals, 108, 110–111

N

nephrology, 196–197
neurology, 146, 198
nitrogen gas systems, 259
noise control, 61, 260–266
   acoustic ceilings, 287–288
   animal housing areas, 213–214
   door hardware, 295
   Fear Free design, 54–55
   HVAC design and, 265–266
   ICU layout, 162–164
   LED lighting, 270
   MRI rooms, 186
   open ceilings, 288, 290
   sound lids, 264
   Sound Transmission Class (STC), 262–263
   specialty doors and windows, 294
   treatment room design, 158–159
Noise Reduction Coefficient (NRC), 222, 262, 288

O

Occupational Safety and Health Administration (OSHA) standards, 190, 323
office areas, 236
   furnishings, 305–306
   the transparent design approach, 82
oncology, 188–194
One Health concept, 357–358
one-year warranty walk, 348
open ceilings, 288–290
open core design, 117–119
operation and maintenance manuals (O&M), 345, 347
outdoor furnishings, 306
outpatient services
   designing specialty and referral hospitals, 110
   exam room layout, 144
   minor procedures treatment areas, 160
   specialty/referral hospitals, 112(figure)
owner's role in the project, 339–340, 342–343
oxygen cages, 164
oxygen systems, 257–259
   in treatment, 158, 160
   equipment coordination, 314

P

pack/prep areas, 200–201, 314(figure)
   biological risk management, 63, 66
   combining with treatment areas, 156

equipment selection and purchase, 314–315
    plumbing design, 255–256
    surgical zone, 103, 123, 199–201, 203
parking
    curb appeal and flow, 76
    MRI mobile units, 186–187
    planning and zoning, 35
    siting a freestanding building, 33
patient status boards, 164(figure), 165
permits. *See* building codes and permits
pharmacy
    design and layout, 148–154
    floor planning, 101–102
    mixed animal hospitals, 133
    open core design in emergency hospitals, 118
phone rooms, 87(figure), 108
photography and artwork, 307–308
physical rehabilitation, 110, 206–211, 208(figure)
planning and zoning
    adaptive reuse projects, 28–29
    approval requirements, 352–353
    finding the right lease space, 21–22
    renovation versus building new, 39
    site capacity for freestanding buildings, 32–33
    siting a freestanding building, 34–36
plumbing and plumbing design, 251–256
    construction milestones, 342, 343
    dental areas, 168
    finding the right lease space, 24
    hose systems and bibs, 65, 66, 222, 254, 255 (figure)
    planning for future expansion, 90
    post move-in, 349
    trench drains, 65–66, 252, 256
    See also water and drainage
pod layouts
    exam room layout, 144
    maximizing exam room capacity in large hospitals, 106
    specialty/referral hospitals, 112, 112(figure)
power. *See* electrical requirements
predesign phase, 43–44, 46(figure)
pre-punch list, 343
pressurization, air. *See* HVAC systems
pro forma, 16–18, 17(figure)
procedural spaces, design considerations for, 59–60
project closeout, 344–346
project delivery method, 325–330
project engineer, 341
project manager, 340–341
project timeline, 43–47, 46(figure)
punch list, 343, 345
PVC wall covering, 286

Q
quench (MRI coolant boil), 183–184

R
radiation safety
    AAHA accreditation standards, 71
    dental areas, 168–169
    hazardous waste, 323
    Iodine-131, 192–194
    LINAC, 191–192, 192(figure)
    CT suites, 176–178, 182
    OSHA regulations, 323
    radiology suite, 172, 201
    surgical areas, 173, 201
    See also shielding
radiology areas and technology
    AAHA accreditation standards, 71
    dental care, 167–168
    design and layout, 171–173
    designing a specialty hospital, 110
    equipment selection and purchase, 313
    health department requirements, 324
    ICU layout, 162–163
    LINAC, 191–192, 192(figure), 193(figure)
    open core design in emergency hospitals, 118
    surgical area, 201
    See also radiation safety; shielding
reception areas, 137–142
    emergency hospitals, 115–117
    large hospital layouts, 106–108
    the transparent approach, 81
recovery areas, 69, 159–160, 201, 202(figure), 220
referral hospitals. *See* specialty/referral hospitals
Regulated Medical Waste (RMW), 323
regulatory requirements, 319–324
    chemotherapy drugs, 188–189, 250, 323
    health departments, 324
    medical gas systems, 259
    OSHA, 323
    unusual constraints on a building location, 36–37
    See also planning and zoning; hazardous materials
remodels, 38–42, 88–92, 354–355
renovation of existing buildings
    adaptive reuse spaces, 27–30
    leasehold spaces, 19–26, 88–89
    remodels and additions, 38–43, 89–92, 91(figure), 354–355
rent-to-income ratio, 16–17
requests for information (RFIs), 340, 341(figure)
resident cats, 123–124
residential-style windows, 294
resinous floors, 277–278, 283 (figure)
RSMeans, 15

rubber flooring, 281–282, 283(figure)
run to back room, 147
runs. *See* animal housing

S

safety standards
    AAHA accreditation standards, 73
    emergency hospital design, 118
    life safety and building codes, 321
    MRI and CT equipment and areas, 176–178, 185
    See also biological risk management; radiation safety

sanitation
    AAHA accreditation standards, 69
    biological risk management, 62–67
    designing functional procedural spaces, 59–60
    HVAC systems, 244–245
    isolation ward design, 224–225
    See also biological risk management; cleaning and housekeeping; plumbing and plumbing design; water and drainage

schematic drawings, 44–45, 332
scope of the project, 11–14, 39–40, 44
security, 118
    pharmacy design, 152–153, 152(figure)
"shelling" a building, 90
shielding
    MRI and CT suites, 176–178, 182, 185
    See also radiation safety
shop drawings, 341
signage
    building, 21
    curb appeal, 76
    emergency hospitals, 115
    MRI and CT suites, 178, 182, 185, 186
    radiology and fluoroscopy, 172, 173
sinks
    biological risk management design, 62–63, 66
    handwashing sinks, 254
    isolation rooms, 224–225
    laboratory design, 151
    plumbing design, 254–256
    siting a freestanding building, 32–34
    treatment room design, 157–158
skylights, 41, 159(figure), 163(figure), 273
soft costs, 12, 15–16, 17(figure), 127
soils, 33–34, 44
    LINAC design, 190–191
solar orientation, 94, 94(figure)
solar tubes, 273
solid waste management, 63, 66, 252. *See also* elimination areas; plumbing requirements
sound. *See* noise control

Sound Transmission Class (STC) rating, 262–263
specialty equipment
    CT, 176–178, 177(figure), 181(figure), 180–182
    dental care areas, 167–169
    designing specialty/referral hospitals, 109–110
    equipment coordination, 310–315
    feline hospitals, 121
    ICU layout, 164–165
    imaging systems, 71, 82, 113, 176–187
    laboratory design, 151
    LINAC selection, 191
    MRI, 114, 176–177, 179(figure), 182–186, 201radiography equipment, 171–173
    treatment room design, 156–158
    ultrasound and cardiology equipment, 173–175
    treadmills and swimming pools, 207–209, 209(figure), 210
specialty/referral hospitals, 109–114, 146, 150
specialty services
    dermatology, 197–198
    endoscopy, 195–196
    nephrology, 196–197
    neurology, 198
    oncology, 188–194
staff areas
    break rooms, 234–235, 306
    chairs and stools for employees, 305
    charting, 153, 156, 236
    creating a pleasant surgery room, 204
    fish bowl workstations, 153
    furnishings, 302
    support space design, 234–236
    the transparent design approach, 83(figure)
    See also cabinets; storage
state permitting requirements, 321–322
step-down wards, 118–119, 221
sterile compounding room, 189–190
stocks for large animal hospitals, 127–129
storage
    AAHA accreditation standards, 69
    design elements, 232–234
    designing functional procedural spaces, 59–60
    endoscopy rooms, 196
    Iodine-131, 192
    oxygen storage, 257–258, 314
    physical rehabilitation, 210
    surgery rooms, 69
    ultrasound areas, 174
    See also cabinets
stress reduction
    animal housing 212–219, 216(figure), 229
    biological risk management design, 65
    designing for noise mitigation, 61, 260–266

emergency hospitals, 116, 118
equine facilities, 130–131
Fear Free design, 10, 51–55
feline hospital design, 122, 123
housing environments, 212–215, 217–218
ICU layout, 163
reception area design, 139–140, 139(figure)
superintendent of the project, 341–342
surgery zone, 199–205
    AAHA accreditation standards, 69–72
    avoiding compartmentalizing in emergency hospitals, 117–118
    bone marrow transplants, 194
    designing functional spaces, 59–61
    equine and large animal hospitals, 128–130
    feline hospitals, 123
    floor plans for small hospitals, 103
    flooring materials, 279–281
    pack/prep areas, 200–201
    postsurgical housing, 218
    radiology and fluoroscopy, 172–173
    surgery prep, 200
    surgery room, 201–202
sustainable design, 93–98
swimming pools, 207–209, 209(figure), 210
system furnishings, 305–306

T

tables, treatment
    built-in, 158
    dental care, 167
    dermatology suites, 197–198
    endoscopy rooms, 195–196
    ICU, 165
    layouts, 156, 157(figure)
    radiography equipment, 171–172
    treatment rooms, 255
    ultrasound, 174
test fit, 14
Testing, Adjusting, and Balancing (TAB), 344–345
Texas accessibility requirement, 322
tile flooring, 278–279, 282
topography and soils: siting a freestanding building, 33–34
traffic doors, 295
traffic flow in a building
    gaining capacity in older buildings, 89–90
    equine hospitals and large animal hospitals, 127
    laboratory, pharmacy, and charting layout, 148–154
    large hospitals, 104–108
    planning for future expansion, 89–91
    racetrack pattern, 112–1113, 113(figure)
    radiology areas, 172–173

reception space design, 138
remodels and additions, 38
separating the surgery suite, 199
shared and separate spaces in mixed animal hospitals, 132–134
specialty/referral hospitals, 109–110, 112
traditional and triangulated floor plans, 99–101
treatment room layout, 156
trailers (MRI units), 186–187
transparency, 80–83
    creating a pleasant surgery room, 204
    in emergency hospitals, 117–118
    system furnishings, 305–306
    vestibule design, 138
    visibility of wards, 220–221
trauma exam rooms, 146
treatment areas, 155–160
    designing functional procedural spaces, 59–60
    Fear Free design, 52
    feline hospitals, 122
    plumbing design, 255
    separate spaces in mixed animal hospitals, 133
treadmills, 207–209
trench drains, 65–66, 252, 256
triage areas, 112, 116–119, 117(figure), 160, 161, 163
triangulated floor plan, 100–101, 101(figure)

U

ultrasound rooms, 106, 110, 173–175
underwater treadmills, 207–209
USP <800 standards>, 188–190
utility requirements, 24
    AAHA accreditation standards, 70–71
    adaptive reuse projects, 29
    dental care areas, 169
    designing functional procedural spaces, 59–60
    encumbrances and easements on property, 36
    equipment coordination, 312–313
    for a large animal hospital, 126
    planning for future expansion, 90
    renovation versus building new, 39
    sustainable design, 93–98
UVGI (ultraviolet germicidal irradiation), 245

V

vacuum systems, 71, 158, 200, 253
vapor barriers, 210, 276–277, 342
vapor drives, 276
variance, zoning, 320
ventilation. *See* HVAC systems
vestibules, 118, 118(figure)
    feline hospitals, 121,
    Iodine-131 suites, 192

vestibules, *continued*
   isolation ward design, 224–225
   reception area design, 137–138
vinyl flooring, 280–283, 283(figure)
vinyl wall protection, 286

W

waiting areas
   branding, 78
   designing functional spaces, 60–61
   emergency hospitals, 116–117
   Fear Free design, 52–53
   feline hospitals, 121–122
   furnishings, 302–305
   results waiting rooms, 119
   separate spaces in mixed animal hospitals, 133
   the transparent approach, 81
wall construction, 285–290
   color palette selection, 53–54, 54(figure), 296–301
ward spaces, 220–222
   biological risk management design, 63–64
   configuring, 221–222
   Fear Free design, 53–54
   isolation wards, 223–225
   large hospital design, 107
warranties, 346–348
waste anesthetic gas disposal (WAGD), 259

water and drainage
   biological risk management, 64–66
   curb appeal and flow, 76
   equine facilities, 131
   environmental regulations, 322–323
   isolation wards, 225
   reduction strategies, 95–96
   siting a freestanding building, 33
   ward design, 222
   See also plumbing and plumbing design
wellness procedures and spaces
   exam room design, 143–144
   the wellness room, 87
wetlands, 36–37, 322
whole-life care, 357–358
windows
   building orientation in sustainable design, 94–95
   connecting treatment rooms to the outside, 156–158
   exam room layout, 145(figure)
   integrating daylight into the design, 272–273
   shielding MRI and CT rooms, 182
   specialty windows, 294–295
   sustainable design, 94–96

Z

zoning. *See* planning and zoning

ABOUT THE AUTHORS

VICKI J. POLLARD has had a passion for caring for animals since she volunteered at a raptor center while a college student at the Pennsylvania State University in State College, where she received her Bachelor of Architecture degree in 1998. After graduation, she spent weekends volunteering at a zoo in Norristown, Pennsylvania.

Vicki's passion then led her to Colorado to earn her Associate of Applied Science degree in veterinary technology at the Bel-Rea Institute of Animal Technology. She has been a Licensed Veterinary Technician since 2003. While acting as the owner's representative for the renovation of the Alameda East Veterinary Hospital campus in Denver, Colorado, she was drawn back into architecture.

In 2006, Vicki joined Animal Arts in Boulder, Colorado, where she has used her unique combined experience in architecture and veterinary technology to manage the design of a variety of general veterinary and veterinary specialty hospital projects. She has been a principal with the firm since 2008 and is currently licensed to practice architecture in 19 states.

Vicki is a blessed wife and mother to three amazing children, twins and a singleton.

ASHLEY M. SHOULTS is an architect and one of the principals at Animal Arts in Boulder. She knew as a teenager that she wanted to pursue a career in architecture and went straight for that goal as she entered college. She studied for two years at the University of Michigan before transferring to the University of Colorado in pursuit of mountains and sunshine as she finished her degree. Ashley joined Animal Arts in 2006 and became a partner in 2012.

Ashley has a varied architecture portfolio, managing both veterinary/boarding and animal shelter projects for the firm. She also plays a large role in overseeing the office, including software and IT systems as well as day-to-day financial and business management.

When she's not busy wearing her many hats in the office, Ashley enjoys spending time with her husband, Chadwick; her two young sons, Braxton and Harrison; her Maltese, Jack; and her two cats, Casper and Nala. Her hobbies include playing soccer, skiing, camping, traveling, and enjoying the beauty of her home state of Colorado.